The Chinese Short Story

Harvard–Yenching Institute Monograph Series

Volume 21

Patrick Hanan

The Chinese Short Story

Studies in Dating, Authorship, and Composition

Harvard University Press   Cambridge, Massachusetts

1973

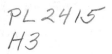

© Copyright 1973 by the Harvard-Yenching Institute
All rights reserved
Library of Congress Catalog Card Number 72-87776
SBN 674-12525-8
Printed in the United States of America

Any work which claims to be authentic must have had witnesses, and competent witnesses; this is external evidence. Or it may be its own competent witness; this is called internal evidence.
—Samuel Taylor Coleridge, "Intercepted Correspondence,"
  Morning Post (London), February 3, 1800

Preface

A disclaimer must be entered about the purpose of this book, in case the reader opens it seeking to sharpen his taste for Chinese fiction. It is not a critical study—in any sense of that phrase. It is a sustained attempt to break through an impasse in literary scholarship, an impasse which has long barred the way to most varieties of critical approach. I began the study with the critic's interests in mind, feeling that if only the impasse could be breached, even slightly breached, a new criticism might well result. But the study itself merely clears the way for that criticism.

The same purpose governs the book's arrangement, which is *antichrono-logical*, moving backwards in time from what is known—editions and catalogues—to what can only be conjectured. Thus Chapter III divides the surviving stories on either side of an imaginary line drawn in the sixteenth century; Chapter V proceeds to divide the *earlier* stories about an imaginary line in the fifteenth century; and Chapter VII, very tentatively, subdivides the earlier group of *those* stories. The accompanying analysis, mostly in terms of authorship, composition, and theme, concerns the stories left behind at each stage of our progress into the past; the "late" story is analyzed in Chapter IV, the "middle" story in Chapter VI, and the various categories of "early" story in Chapter VIII. To compensate for this arrangement, the last chapter, IX, offers a summary of general conclusions in their chronological order. There is also an index to the results obtained for each story.

Several points need to be made about the book's main method—the use of stylistic criteria for dating. First, to choose criteria arbitrarily was out of the question; the danger of unconsciously gerrymandering the evidence is simply too great. At the outset of each major division, therefore, I have tried to examine the whole of some definable category, in order to see whether the groups under discussion are distinguishable in principle by stylistic means. When they prove to be distinguishable, I have then chosen additional criteria which set off the distinction as starkly as possible. This is not an ideal method—all criteria should result from the examination of whole categories—but it will serve, particularly if the additional criteria are checked with the original. Secondly, the method is exploratory. One can observe the stylistic differences between texts in the same genre without knowing what the causes are: personal styles, or the styles characteristic of some coterie or class or region or period. It requires a further step to find the meaning of one's results. Thirdly, in an age of computer analysis, this must be considered a do-it-yourself or "backyard" method; the numbers are small, hardly susceptible to statistical handling, and the features counted are simple and easily recognizable. The method reflects the way in which the study developed; it began with the realization that a number of obvious, quantifiable features distinguished the short story in one period from the short story in another. Finally, this is a pragmatic study, which seeks to get results for the short story only, and in a particular age. It is not primarily methodological, and its methods are certainly not designed for export.

Like all stylistic studies, however, it is more than a little fallible. If Frederick Mosteller and David L. Wallace, assessing their statistical analysis of *The Federalist Papers*, feel compelled to describe their method as "subjectivity tempered with empiricism,"* what claim can this study make? Furthermore, the interpretation of stylistic analysis is even more hazardous than the analysis itself. I have had to resort frequently to speculation, particularly in Chapter VII, although I have tried always to label it as such. I hope the qualifications will be taken at their face value, not discounted as mere scholarly defensiveness.

Any piece of textual scholarship has to set its own degree of fineness or delicacy. Given the scope of this study, the degree was bound to be fairly crude. For example, it can be demonstrated that *Hsing-shih heng-yen* 31 is an early story of which the last three or four pages have been written or rewritten by a late editor. It would have taken a much more elaborate study than this to find out whether, and to what extent, this editor touched up the rest of the story.

All translations unless otherwise noted are my own.

---

* *Inference and Disputed Authorship: The Federalist* (Reading, Mass.: Addison-Wesley Publishing Co., 1964), p. 226. The Coleridge quotation on my title page comes from David V. Erdman's essay "The Signature of Style" in Erdman and E. G. Fogel, *Evidence for Authorship* (Ithaca, N.Y.: Cornell University Press, 1966).

The debts incurred in the course of writing this book are far too many for me to list—to teachers, colleagues, students, and libraries. However, I cannot fail to mention two of my colleagues at Harvard University, James R. Hightower and John L. Bishop, who kindly read and commented upon the manuscript. I am also grateful to Harvard's East Asian Research Center for summer research grants in 1968 and 1969.

Cambridge, Massachusetts   P.D.H.
August 30, 1971

Contents

Tables

The Chinese Short Story

I Introduction

Chinese vernacular fiction is a half-buried literature, like the literature of Anglo-Saxon England. Popular in its time and lightly regarded by the very nature of that popularity, it was never adequately preserved or even documented. Until the second decade of this century its merits were recognized by only a small number of critics. Then a flood of interest arose, some of it with extraliterary motives. But it was already far too late. Many of the essential facts about the early literature had been lost.

Had it not been for the enduring appeal of the early vernacular fiction, it would probably have been lost too, along with the facts surrounding its history. The sixteenth and seventeenth century collections, on which its survival depended, were frankly commercial ventures, intended to sell rather than to preserve.

The problem of how to date this mass of literature has been wrestled with by more than one generation of scholars. It is not just an intellectual puzzle. Some of the works *seem* to belong to the Sung dynasty, say the thirteenth century, although the earliest records of them date from some four hundred years later. The gap in time during which they may have been written is too large for any scholar's peace of mind. Without a solution to the problem of dating, he cannot see the genre historically, nor deduce the lines of its development, and he finds it harder to see with what social strata it is connected, or with what patterns of idea and belief. Further, the vernacular story's relationships to the oral story on the one hand, and to the Classical tale on the other, the poles between which it moves, are virtually impossible to determine. These matters are important to the critic as well, and, until they are settled, no satisfactory critical account, let alone literary history, can be written.

This study is a first attempt to disinter the history of the early vernacular fiction, particularly the history of the short story.[1] Chiefly, this means working out a reliable system of dating, but it also means trying to find out where in China the stories were written, who wrote them, and how they were written. Some of the questions cannot be answered, some can be answered only vaguely or tentatively, but a surprising number can be settled, enough anyway to give a general idea of the short story's history. No doubt the use of other methods, or a more refined use of these methods, will improve upon these results in the future. Meanwhile, this study is intended as a first set of rough answers.

I mentioned that the dating problem, to say nothing of the others, had been wrestled with by generations of scholars. Their labors have not given us satisfactory answers. The problems are obdurate, and the means used to solve them have been simplistic; one can hardly be surprised at the jumble of often inconsistent results. I have offered a general critique of this scholarship elsewhere, and will not repeat the arguments here. The conclusion of that critique was that "the claims of scholarship to have provided a firm later limit [that is, for the dating of Sung and Yüan vernacular fiction] are thus invalid except in the case of a handful of works. [None of these are short stories.] For the rest, the later limit for the time being will have to be the editions and bibliographical references of the sixteenth century, chiefly the editions of Hung P'ien 洪楩, the Pao-wen-t'ang 寶文堂 catalogue, and the Hua-ts'ao ts'ui-pien 花草粹編. This is not a satisfactory conclusion. A gap of several hundred years between the earlier and later limits of a work is in itself intolerable. What is more, it conflicts with one's strong subjective impression, based no doubt on a host of minute particulars, that a good number of other works antedate the Ming dynasty."[2] These editions and bibliographical references, and others like them, are the only reliable evidence we possess. They are described briefly below.

---

1 "Short story" means the vernacular short story, a genre which flourished until about the end of the seventeenth century. There are very few significant collections after that date. It has been traditional to date the composition of some extant stories as early as the Sung dynasty, although the grounds for such a dating are negligible. See Patrick Hanan, "Sung and Yüan Vernacular Fiction: A Critique of Modern Methods of Dating," *Harvard Journal of Asiatic Studies* 30 (1970), 159–184. The definition of short story is here the usual one, not the restrictive definition applied in Hanan, "The Early Chinese Short Story: A Critical Theory in Outline," *Harvard Journal of Asiatic Studies* 27 (1967), 183–189, where the term was confined to stories with unitary plots.

2 See Hanan, "Sung and Yüan Vernacular Fiction," pp. 183–184.

Editions. One short story survives in a 1498 edition, reprinted along with a famous play. This is the *Ch'ien-t'ang meng* 錢塘夢.[3]

Twenty-nine stories, rediscovered in this century, have been shown to come from a collection originally published by Hung P'ien 洪楩 of Hang-chow about the middle of the sixteenth century.[4] Some of the stories—they were discovered in three separate groups—appear to be in a later reprint than Hung P'ien's. The original title of the collection was apparently *Liu-shih chia hsiao-shuo* 六十家小說 "Sixty Stories," and so the surviving stories, some of which are fragmentary, represent only half of the collection. The original title was not known at the time the first groups of stories were discovered and described, and so the title *Ch'ing-p'ing-shan-t'ang hua-pen* 清平山堂話本 was concocted for them, after Hung P'ien's studio name. They will be referred to here as the "Hung stories," and will be numbered (Hung 1, Hung 2, and so forth) in the order in which they appear in modern editions.[5]

Two of the Hung stories, one of them much adapted, also appear in the [*Ch'üan-pu*] *Pao Lung-t'u p'an pai-chia kung-an* 全補包龍圖判百家公案, which survives in an edition of 1594.[6] This is the earliest version of the work which is widely known as the *Lung-t'u kung-an* or *Pao kung-an*, "Cases of Judge Pao." The other accessible versions do not contain the Hung stories.[7]

Despite the rather specialized nature of its contents, and despite the fact

3 It is printed with the *Hsi-hsiang chi* 西廂記 in an edition of 1498. There is a facsimile reprint in the *Ku-pen hsi-ch'ü ts'ung-k'an* 古本戲曲叢刊, First Series, Peking, 1954.

4 A facsimile edition of twenty-seven stories, under the title of *Ch'ing-p'ing-shan-t'ang hua-pen*, was published in Peking in 1934. A revised edition appeared in 1955. A modern punctuated edition, with textual notes, edited by T'an Cheng-pi 譚正璧, was published in Shanghai in 1957. Page references are to the latter. The other two stories are described by A Ying 阿英, who discovered them, in a brief article "Chi Chia-ching pen *Fei-ts'ui hsüan chi Mei Hsing cheng ch'un*" 記嘉靖本翡翠軒及梅杏爭春, which was published in A Ying's *Hsiao-shuo hsien-t'an* 小說閒談 (Shanghai, 1936), pp. 41–46, and reprinted in T'an's edition, pp. 188–192. A Ying gives the fragmentary text of the *Mei Hsing cheng ch'un* but not of the other story, which he refers to as a Classical tale. For a study of these editions, see André Lévy, "Etudes sur trois recueils anciens de contes chinois," *T'oung Pao* 52.1–3 (1965), 97–110. Lévy notes how slight the published evidence is for associating the last two stories with Hung P'ien.

5 The order is that of T'an's edition, from 1 through 27. *Mei Hsing cheng ch'un* is Hung 28, and *Fei-ts'ui hsüan* is Hung 29.

6 It is preserved in the Hōsa Bunko 蓬左文庫 in Nagoya. For a description, see Li Tien-yi 李田意, "Jih-pen so-chien Chung-kuo tuan-p'ien hsiao-shuo lüeh-chi" 日本所見中國短篇小說略記, *Ch'ing-hua hsüeh-pao* 清華學報 NS 1.2 (1957), 79–80.

7 See Sun K'ai-ti 孫楷第, *Chung-kuo t'ung-su hsiao-shuo shu-mu* 中國通俗小說書目, rev. ed. (Peking, 1957) p. 111, for the most important of these editions. The *Pao Hsiao-su kung pai-chia kung-an yen-i* 包孝肅公百家公案演義 which, according to Sun (pp. 110–111), was formerly preserved in Korea, has not been available. To judge from its title, the edition, which probably dates from 1597, may have been close to the *Ch'üan-pu Pao Lung-t'u p'an pai-chia kung-an*.

that its language tends toward Classical Chinese, the *Pai-chia kung-an* can be regarded as on the borderline of the vernacular short-story genre. The same cannot be said of the many collections of *kung-an* or courtcase stories which appeared in the decade following its publication.[8] They have few, if any, of the short story's formal features, and their language is a simple form of Classical Chinese.

One Hung story also appears, in an abridged form, in the novel *Chin P'ing Mei tz'u-hua* 金瓶梅詞話, written probably at some time between 1582 and 1596.[9] The story is represented as a piece of oral fiction told by one of the novel's characters.

Four stories, including one of the Hung stories, exist in editions published by Hsiung Lung-feng 熊龍峯 about 1590.[10] They are referred to here as the "Hsiung stories," and given a letter (Hsiung A, Hsiung B, and so on) in the order in which they are reprinted in the modern edition.[11]

Four more stories, under the collective title of *Hsiao-shuo ch'uan-ch'i* 小說傳奇, exist in an edition evidently published in the Wan-li 萬曆 period (1573–1620). Rediscovered in China in the 1950's, they have not yet been republished.[12]

A number of stories exist here and there among the late-Ming miscellanies such as the *Yen-chü pi-chi* 燕居筆記 (there are several more or less divergent works of this title), the *Kuo-se t'ien-hsiang* 國色天香, the *Wan-chin ch'ing-lin* 萬錦情林, and so on.[13] (The miscellany is a potpourri of diverting and useful matter, and might be called a magazine if the term did not denote serial publication.) Altogether, they contain ten different vernacular stories —the same story often occurs in several miscellanies—including the *Ch'ien-t'ang meng* and three Hung stories. The stories will be referred to here by their titles or by an abridgement of their titles.

8 See Sun K'ai-ti, *Chung-kuo t'ung-su hsiao-shuo shu-mu*, pp. 112–113, for the extant works of this kind. Two others should be added: the *Lü-t'iao kung-an* 律條公案 preserved in the Naikaku Bunko in Tokyo and the *Hsin-min kung-an* 新民公案 preserved in the National Taiwan University.

9 See P. D. Hanan, "The Text of the *Chin P'ing Mei*," *Asia Major* NS 9.1 (1962), 39–43. For the story's use in *Chin P'ing Mei*, see Hanan, "Sources of the *Chin P'ing Mei*," *Asia Major* NS 10.1 (1963), 37.

10 There is an edition of *Hsi-hsiang chi* (in the Naikaku Bunko) published by Hsiung Lung-feng in 1592. See Ma Yau-woon 馬幼垣, "Hsiung Lung-feng so-k'an tuan-p'ien hsiao-shuo ssu-chung k'ao-shih" 熊龍峯所刊短篇小說四種考釋, *Ch'ing-hua hsüeh-pao* NS 7.1 (1968), 259.

11 *Hsiung Lung-feng ssu-chung hsiao-shuo* 熊龍峯四種小說, ed. Wang Ku-lu 王古魯 (Shanghai, 1958).

12 See Lu Kung 路工, ed., *Ming-Ch'ing p'ing-hua hsiao-shuo hsüan* 明清平話小說選, *Ti-i chi* 第一集 (Shanghai, 1958), preface, pp. 4–5.

13 For a detailed description of these works, see Chapter III.

The main repositories of the short story are the three great collections edited by the playwright Feng Meng-lung 馮夢龍 and his associates and published between 1620 and 1627. These are the *Ku-chin hsiao-shuo* 古今小說 (also published under the title of *Yü-shih ming-yen* 喻世明言), the *Ching-shih t'ung-yen* 警世通言, and the *Hsing-shih heng-yen* 醒世恆言, each of which contains forty stories.[14] They are known collectively as the *San yen* 三言, the "Three *yen*," after the last element in their titles. They contain fifteen stories that also appear in one or more of the above collections, alongside a number of other stories which are definitely late, some of them quite possibly written by Feng Meng-lung himself. The editors make no attempt to distinguish the late stories from the rest, and the resulting mélange is a baffling problem for the modern scholar. The stories are referred to here by an abbreviation for the collection (KC for *Ku-chin*, TY for *t'ung-yen*, HY for *heng-yen*) and the position in which they appear in modern editions (KC 1, KC 2, and so on).[15]

Collections later than the *San yen* appear to be the work of individual authors, although this is assumption rather than established fact. Under the influence of the *San yen*, the short story became extremely popular, and there are numerous collections in the late Ming and early Ch'ing. The largest and most famous of these were the two forty-piece collections by the late-Ming playwright Ling Meng-ch'u 凌濛初: the *P'ai-an ching-ch'i* 拍案驚奇, and its sequel, the *Erh-k'e P'ai-an ching-ch'i* 二刻拍案驚奇.[16] Another well-known collection, one to which Feng himself wrote the preface, was the anonymous *Shih tien t'ou* 石點頭, containing fourteen stories.

Bibliographical references. One story is referred to in what is probably a post-1345 revision of the *Lu kuei pu* 錄鬼簿, the famous account of Yüan dynasty

14 The *Ku-chin hsiao-shuo* was published between 1620 and 1624, the *Ching-shih t'ung-yen* in 1624, and the *Hsing-shih heng-yen* in 1627.

15 The best editions available are those edited in facsimile reprint by Tien-yi Li and published by the Shih-chieh shu-chü in Taipei in 1958 and 1959. However, they are awkward for reference, because the original page numbers are not always clearly printed, and there is no superimposed pagination. With some misgivings, I am using the modern editions for reference, that is, the *Ku-chin hsiao-shuo* published in Peking in 1958 by the Jen-min wen-hsüeh ch'u-pan-she 人民文學出版社; the *Ching-shih t'ung-yen* published in Peking in 1957 by the Tso-chia ch'u-pan-she 作家出版社; and the *Hsing-shih heng-yen* also published in Peking in 1956 by the same house. At the time of writing, all are available in Hong Kong reprints, the first of them under the title of *Yü-shih ming-yen*. Note that the order of the stories within a collection sometimes varies in the early editions. The chief drawback about the modern editions is that they occasionally omit erotic passages without informing the reader. The celebrated erotic story, no. 23, is omitted entire from the modern edition of the *Hsing-shih heng-yen*. In this case, I use the Shih-chieh shu-chü edition.

16 The first collection was published in 1628, the second in 1632.

dramatists and their work. It was on the same subject as an extant story, the main story of KC 36. If the identification of this story with the *Lu kuei pu* reference were correct, it would mean that we possess a story written about 1300. But there is no way of being certain that it is correct, and it is best to accept it as a possible or even probable identification and await further evidence.[17]

The earliest reliable references are found in the library catalogue *Pao-wen-t'ang shu-mu*. The library was built up by Ch'ao Li 晁瑮 and by his son Tung-wu 東吳, who died in 1554.[18] The catalogue itself can be traced only as far back as the end of the Ming dynasty, so that there is an element of uncertainty in claiming that it represents the state of the library around the time of Tung-wu's death. Both library and catalogue could conceivably have been increased after that date. We can gain a general impression of the catalogue's effective date by noting the other works which it includes, but that is negative evidence at best. Clearly, if the catalogue is to be used as an indicator of pre-1560 publication, it will have to be used with caution. Its value for us is that it deigns to list a great deal of vernacular literature, virtually the only library catalogue of the Ming dynasty to do so. References to over forty extant short stories have been remarked—the exact number is in dispute—as well as to several novels.

The *Hua-ts'ao ts'ui-pien* 花草粹編, an anthology of early (T'ang through Yüan) *tz'u* 詞 poems which was published in 1583, is important because it contains several *tz'u* from vernacular fiction, including at least three short stories.[19] There is a distinct possiblility that the anthology was originally the work of Wu Ch'eng-en 吳承恩, putative author of the great novel *Hsi-yu chi* 西遊記 (*Monkey* in Arthur Waley's translation). If so, the actual date of compilation was about 1559. Whoever the compiler was, Wu Ch'eng-en or the former patron who apparently appropriated his work, he *thought* the stories from which he selected *tz'u* came from the Yüan dynasty or before, but of course we cannot accept that view without other evidence. The year 1583, or perhaps 1559, becomes the later limit for the three short stories.

Beyond this date there is no need to go, because other bibliographical references are actually later than the surviving editions. A few references, however, are of interest. On four occasions, the editorial notes in the *San*

17 See Hanan, "Sung and Yüan Vernacular Fiction," pp. 164–165.

18 The father died in 1560. For these dates, see *Ming-jen chuan-chi tzu-liao so-yin* 明人傳記資料索引 (Taipei, 1965), I, 446–447.

19 See Hanan, "Sung and Yüan Vernacular Fiction," p. 183, n. 121. There is a 1933 facsimile reprint of this work.

yen identify a story as early, or by a Sung author, or existing in a Sung edition. Similarly, the library catalogues of the bibliophile Ch'ien Tseng 錢曾 (1629–1701) name seventeen stories, some of which do not survive, as "stories by Sung authors."[20] Obviously, these comments cannot be taken at face value. We shall see later how far they are confirmed by our results.

On surveying these dates, one is struck by the fact that there are two important later limits for the short story. One of these is the period circa 1550, and the other the period of the 1620's. The former is the later limit for the Hung stories and, with some reservations, for the Pao-wen-t'ang and even the *Hua-ts'ao ts'ui-pien* references; the latter is the later limit for the rest of the *San yen* stories. Only one story can be firmly dated before the 1550's, and only a handful have a later limit between the two periods. The recognition of these two key dates thus seems a natural place for research to begin.

Before proceeding to speak of methods, I should point out that several works of vernacular fiction, mainly historical narratives, survive in Yüan dynasty editions.[21] One work even survives from the Sung dynasty. None of these, however, makes great or sustained use of the vernacular language. The novels which do so survive only in much later editions, of the middle and late sixteenth century.

A List of Extant Short Stories

This is a list of editions of short stories up to and including the *Hsing-shih heng-yen*, published in 1627. The *Pai-chia kung-an* stories, which are on the borderline of the short-story genre, are not included; they are discussed separately in Chapter III. Stories are arranged below under the collections in which they appear, but note that those that survive in the miscellanies are treated as a single group, because of the duplication among them. On the left of the story's title is the abbreviation, indicating its position in the collection, by which it will be identified. On the right is a cross-reference to any other editions in which it appears prior to 1628. Note that the equals symbol does not mean that the texts concerned are identical, merely that they are recognizably the same work despite any textual differences. If the story is referred to in the Pao-wen-t'ang catalogue, the fact is also noted.

20 "Sung and Yüan Vernacular Fiction," pp. 173–174. I have omitted reference here to the *Tsui-weng t'an-lu* 醉翁談錄 of Lo Yeh 羅燁, which survives in what appears to be a Yüan edition. It is a work of capital importance for our knowledge of oral narrative. There are no grounds for taking it necessarily as a catalogue of written stories. See pp. 164–173.
21 "Sung and Yüan Vernacular Fiction," pp. 162–164.

The identification of titles with Pao-wen-t'ang entries is discussed below, in Chapter II, note 26. Abbreviations used are as follows:

Hung   The Hung P'ien collections originally known as *Liu-shih chia hsiao-shuo*, but commonly called *Ch'ing-p'ing-shan-t'ang hua-pen*

Hsiung   The stories published by Hsiung Lung-feng

KC   *Ku-chin hsiao-shuo*

TY   *Ching-shih t'ung-yen*

HY   *Hsing-shih heng-yen*

PWT   The catalogue of the Pao-wen-t'ang library.

Bibliographical details of the miscellanies are given in Chapter II. A dagger denotes a fragmentary version. The editions are:

Ch'ien-t'ang meng   =miscellanies
(Reprinted with 1498 edition of *Hsi-hsiang chi*)

THE HUNG COLLECTIONS

Hung 1   *Liu Ch'i-ch'ing shih chiu Wan-chiang Lou chi* 柳耆卿詩酒翫江樓記   =miscellanies, PWT

Hung 2   *Chien-t'ieh ho-shang* 簡貼和尚   =KC 35, PWT

Hung 3   *Hsi-hu san t'a chi* 西湖三塔記   PWT

Hung 4   *Ho-t'ung wen-tzu chi* 合同文字記   =*Pai-chia kung-an* 27, PWT

Hung 5   *Feng-yüeh Jui-hsien T'ing* 風月瑞仙亭   =prologue of TY 6, PWT

Hung 6   *Lan-ch'iao chi* 藍橋記   PWT

Hung 7   *K'uai-tsui Li Ts'ui-lien chi* 快嘴李翠蓮記   PWT

Hung 8   *Lo-yang san kuai chi* 洛陽三怪記   =*Pai-chia kung-an* 29, PWT

Hung 9   *Feng-yüeh hsiang-ssu* 風月相思   =Hsiung C, miscellanies, PWT

Hung 10   *Chang Tzu-fang mu Tao chi* 張子房慕道記   PWT

Hung 11   *Yin-chih chi shan* 陰騭積善   PWT

Hung 12   *Ch'en Hsün-chien Mei-ling shih ch'i chi* 陳巡檢梅嶺失妻記   =KC 20, PWT

Hung 13   *Wu-chieh Ch'an-shih ssu Hung-lien chi* 五戒禪師私紅蓮記   =*Chin P'ing Mei tz'u-hua* chap. 73, KC 30, miscellanies, PWT

Hung 14	*Wen ching yüan-yang hui* 刎頸鴛鴦會	=TY 38, PWT
Hung 15	*Yang Wen "Lan-lu Hu" chuan* 楊溫攔路虎傳	PWT
Hung 16	*Hua-teng chiao Lien-nü ch'eng Fo chi* 花燈轎蓮女成佛記	
Hung 17	*Ts'ao Po-ming ts'o k'an tsang chi* 曹伯明錯勘贓記	
Hung 18	*Ts'o jen shih* 錯認屍	=TY 33
Hung 19	*Tung Yung yü hsien chuan* 董永遇仙傳	
Hung 20	*Chieh-chih-erh chi*† 戒指兒記	=KC 4
Hung 21	*Yang Chiao-ai ssu chan Ching K'o*† 羊角哀死戰荊軻	=KC 7, PWT
Hung 22	*Ssu sheng chiao Fan Chang chi shu*† 死生交范張鷄黍	=KC 16, PWT
Hung 23	*Lao Feng T'ang chih chien Han Wen-ti*† 老馮唐直諫漢文帝	PWT
Hung 24	*Han Li Kuang shih hao Fei Chiang-chün* 漢李廣世號飛將軍	PWT
Hung 25	*K'uei-kuan Yao Pien tiao Chu-ko* 夔關姚卞弔諸葛	PWT
Hung 26	*Cha-ch'uan Hsiao Ch'en pien Pa-wang*[22] 霅川蕭琛貶霸王	PWT
Hung 27	*Li Yüan Wu-chiang chiu chu-she*† 李元吳江救朱蛇	=KC 34, PWT
Hung 28	*Mei Hsing cheng ch'un*† 梅杏爭春	PWT
Hung 29	*Fei-ts'ui Hsüan*† 翡翠軒	PWT

THE STORIES PUBLISHED BY HSIUNG LUNG-FENG

Hsiung A	*Chang Sheng ts'ai-luan teng chuan* 張生彩鸞燈傳	=KC 23, PWT
Hsiung B	*Su Ch'ang-kung Chang-t'ai Liu chuan* 蘇長公章臺柳傳	PWT
Hsiung C	*Feng Po-yü feng-yüeh hsiang-ssu hsiao-shuo* 馮伯玉風月相思小說	=Hung 9, miscellanies, PWT
Hsiung D	*K'ung Shu-fang shuang-yü shan-chui chuan* 孔淑芳雙魚扇墜傳	PWT

22 Sun K'ai-ti, *Chung-kuo t'ung-su hsiao-shuo shu-mu*, p. 80, reports a comment by Ma Lien 馬廉 that Hung 26 is also found in Chang Ch'ou's 張丑 *Ming shan tsang* 名山藏, a work which Sun had not seen. Chang Ch'ou was a writer and editor who lived from 1577 to 1643, but I have not been able to find any record of his compiling such a work. There is, of course, a well-known *Ming shan tsang*, compiled by Ho Ch'iao-yüan 何喬遠, of which a 1640 edition exists.

THE HSIAO-SHUO CH'UAN-CH'I

1. *Wang K'uei* 王魁
2. *Li Ya-hsien chi* 李亞仙記   possibly PWT
3. *Kuei chien chiao ch'ing* 貴賤交情   =TY 1
4. *Nü Han-lin* 女翰林   =HY 11

THE STORIES PRESERVED IN THE MISCELLANIES
(Note that the title given here is that of the first work referred to)

Chang Yü-hu su nü chen kuan 張于湖宿女眞觀   PWT
   (Ho 9, Lin 6, Yü 7, *Wan-chin* 1, *Kuo-se* 10)
Cheng Yüan-ho p'iao-yü Li Ya-hsien chi 鄭元和   possibly PWT.
嫖遇李亞仙記   Note that this is a
   (Yü 7, Lin 5 †)   different work
                                                 from entry 2 above
Ch'ien-t'ang meng 錢塘夢   =1498 edition, see
   (Lin 4)   above
Hsiang-ssu chi 相思記   =Hung 9, Hsiung
   (*Kuo-se* 8)   C, PWT
Hung-lien nü yin Yü-t'ung Ch'an-shih 紅蓮女   =KC 29,
淫玉通禪師   possibly PWT
   (Ho 9, Yü 8, *Hsiu-ku* 8)
Liu Ch'i-ch'ing Wan-chiang Lou chi 柳耆卿翫   =Hung 1, PWT
江樓記
   (Ho 10†, Lin 6, Yü 7, *Wan-chin* 1, *Hsiu-ku* 4)
Lü-chu chui lou chi 綠珠墜樓記   =prologue story
   (Ho 10, Lin 8, Yü 8)   of KC 36, PWT
P'ei Hsiu-niang yeh yu Hsi-hu 裴秀娘夜遊西湖
   (Lin 5 †, *Wan-chin* 2)
Tu Li-niang mu se huan hun 杜麗娘慕色還魂   PWT
   (Ho 9, Yü 8)
Tung-p'o Fo-yin erh shih hsiang hui 東坡佛印   =Hung 13, *Chin
二世相會   P'ing Mei tz'u-hua*
   (*Hsiu-ku* 12 †, Yü 9)   chap. 73, KC 30,
                                                 PWT

KU-CHIN HSIAO-SHUO

KC 1   *Chiang Hsing-ko ch'ung hui chen-chu
        shan* 蔣興哥重會珍珠衫
KC 2   *Ch'en Yü-shih ch'iao k'an chin ch'ai
        tien* 陳御史巧勘金釵鈿
KC 3   *Hsin-ch'iao Shih Han Wu mai ch'un-*   PWT
        ch'ing 新橋市韓五賣春情

23 The title in the table of contents differs from the title in the text. This is the title in the text of the first edition. Similar discrepancies exist in the cases of TY 16, TY 26, TY 35, TY 36, HY 9, HY 22, and HY 29.

KC 24	*Yang Ssu-wen Yen-shan feng ku-jen* 楊思溫燕山逢故人	PWT (two titles)
KC 25	*Yen P'ing-chung erh t'ao sha san shih* 晏平仲二桃殺三士	PWT
KC 26	*Shen Hsiao-kuan i niao hai ch'i ming* 沈小官一鳥害七命	PWT
KC 27	*Chin Yü-nu pang ta po-ch'ing lang* 金玉奴棒打薄情郎	
KC 28	*Li Hsiu-ch'ing i chieh Huang chen-nü* 李秀卿義結黃貞女	
KC 29	*Yüeh-ming Ho-shang tu Liu Ts'ui* 月明和尚度柳翠	=miscellanies, possibly PWT
KC 30	*Ming-wu Ch'an-shih kan Wu-chieh* 明悟禪師趕五戒	=Hung 13, *Chin P'ing Mei tz'u-hua* chap. 73, miscellanies, PWT
KC 31	*Nao yin-ssu Ssu-ma Mao tuan yü* 鬧陰司司馬貌斷獄	
KC 32	*Yu Feng-tu Hu-mu Ti yin shih* 遊酆都胡母迪吟詩	
KC 33	*Chang Ku-lao chung kua ch'ü Wen-nü* 張古老種瓜娶文女	PWT
KC 34	*Li Kung-tzu chiu she huo Ch'eng-hsin* 李公子救蛇獲稱心	=Hung 27, PWT
KC 35	*Chien-t'ieh seng ch'iao p'ien Huang-fu ch'i* 簡帖僧巧騙皇甫妻	=Hung 2, PWT
KC 36	*Sung Ssu-kung ta nao "Chin-hun" Chang* 宋四公大鬧禁魂張	PWT (The prologue is found independently in miscellanies, PWT)
KC 37	*Liang Wu-ti lei hsiu kuei Chi-lo* 梁武帝累修歸極樂	
KC 38	*Jen Hsiao-tzu lieh hsing wei shen* 任孝子烈性爲神	PWT
KC 39	*Wang Hsin-chih i ssu chiu ch'üan chia* 汪信之一死救全家	
KC 40	*Shen Hsiao-hsia hsiang hui Ch'u-shih piao* 沈小霞相會出師表	

CHING-SHIH T'UNG-YEN

TY 1	*Yü Po-ya shuai ch'in hsieh chih-yin* 俞伯牙摔琴謝知音	=Hsiao-shuo ch'uan-ch'i 3

TY 24   *Yü-t'ang-ch'un lo nan feng fu*   玉堂春
落難逢夫

TY 25   *Kuei Yüan-wai t'u ch'iung ch'an hui*
桂員外途窮懺悔

TY 26   *T'ang Chieh-yüan i hsiao yin-yüan*   唐
解元一笑姻緣

TY 27   *Chia shen-hsien ta nao Hua-kuang Miao*
假神仙大鬧華光廟

TY 28   *Pai Niang-tzu yung chen Lei-feng T'a*
白娘子永鎮雷峯塔

TY 29   *Su-hsiang T'ing Chang Hao yü Ying-*   PWT
ying 宿香亭張浩遇鶯鶯

TY 30   *Chin-ming Ch'ih Wu Ch'ing feng Ai-ai*
金明池吳淸逢愛愛

TY 31   *Chao Chun-erh ch'ung wang Ts'ao-chia*
Chuang   趙春兒重旺曹家莊

TY 32   *Tu Shih-niang nu ch'en pai-pao hsiang*
杜十娘怒沉百寶箱

TY 33   *Ch'iao Yen-chieh i ch'ieh p'o chia*   喬彥   =Hung 18
傑一妾破家

TY 34   *Wang Chiao-luan pai nien ch'ang hen*
王嬌鸞百年長恨

TY 35   *K'uang T'ai-shou tuan ssu hai-erh*   況
太守斷死孩兒

TY 36   *Tsao-chiao-lin Ta Wang chia hsing*   皂
角林大王假形

TY 37   *Wan Hsiu-niang ch'ou pao shan-t'ing-*   PWT
erh 萬秀娘仇報山亭兒

TY 38   *Chiang Shu-chen wen ching yüan-yang*   =Hung 14
hui 蔣淑眞刎頸鴛鴦會

TY 39   *Fu-lu-shou san hsing tu shih*   福祿壽三
星度世

TY 40   *Ching-yang Kung t'ieh-shu chen yao*   = *T'ieh-shu chi* 鐵
旌陽宮鐵樹鎭妖   樹記 by Teng Chih-
mo 鄧志謨. Also
contained in *San-
chiao ou-nien* 三教偶
拈, ed. Feng Meng-
lung.

HSING-SHIH HENG-YEN

HY 1   *Liang hsien-ling ching i hun ku-nü*
兩縣令競義婚孤女

HY 2   *San hsiao-lien jang ch'an li kao-ming*
三孝廉讓產立高名

HY 3   *Mai-yu lang tu chan Hua-k'uei*   賣油
郎獨占花魁

HY 4   *Kuan-yüan sou wan feng hsien-nü*
灌園叟晚逢仙女

HY 5   *Ta-shu P'o i-hu sung ch'in*   大樹坡義虎
送親

HY 6   *Hsiao-shui Wan t'ien-hu i shu*   小水灣
天狐詒書

HY 7   *Ch'ien Hsiu-ts'ai ts'o chan feng-huang
ch'ou*   錢秀才錯占鳳凰儔

HY 8   *Ch'iao T'ai-shou luan tien yüan-yang
p'u*   喬太守亂點鴛鴦譜

HY 9   *Ch'en To-shou sheng ssu fu ch'i*   陳多
壽生死夫妻

HY 10   *Liu Hsiao-kuan tz'u hsiung hsiung ti*
劉小官雌雄兄弟

HY 11   *Su Hsiao-mei san nan hsin-lang*   蘇小   = *Hsiao-shuo*
妹三難新郎   *ch'uan-ch'i* 4

HY 12   *Fo-yin Shih ssu t'iao Ch'in-niang*   佛
印師四調琴娘

HY 13   *K'an p'i-hsüeh tan cheng Erh-lang Shen*   PWT
勘皮靴單證二郎神

HY 14   *Nao Fan-lou to ch'ing Chou Sheng-
hsien*   鬧樊樓多情周勝仙

HY 15   *Ho Ta-ch'ing i hen yüan-yang t'ao*   赫
大卿遺恨鴛鴦絛

HY 16   *Lu Wu-han ying liu ho-se hsieh*   陸五   Claimed to be
漢硬留合色鞋   PWT

HY 17   *Chang Hsiao-chi Ch'en-liu jen chiu*
張孝基陳留認舅

HY 18   *Shih Jun-tse T'an-ch'üeh yü yu*   施潤
澤灘闕遇友

HY 19   *Pai Yü-niang jen k'u ch'eng fu*   白玉孃
忍苦成夫

HY 20   *Chang T'ing-hsiu t'ao sheng chiu fu*   張
廷秀逃生救父

HY 21   *Lü Tung-pin fei chien chan Huang-lung*
呂洞賓飛劍斬黃龍

HY 22   *Chang Shu-erh ch'iao chih t'o Yang
Sheng*   張淑兒巧智脫楊生

HY 23   *Chin Hai-ling tsung yü wang shen*   金
海陵縱欲亡身

HY 24   *Sui Yang-ti i yu chao ch'ien*   隋煬帝逸
遊召譴

HY 25   *Tu-ku Sheng kuei t'u nao meng*   獨孤
生歸途鬧夢

HY 26   *Hsüeh Lu-shih yü-fu cheng hsien*   薛錄
事魚服證仙

HY 27   *Li Yü-ying yü-chung sung yüan*   李玉
英獄中訟冤

HY 28   *Wu Ya-nei lin-chou fu yüeh*   吳衙內鄰
舟赴約

HY 29   *Lu T'ai-hsüeh shih chiu ao kung hou*
盧太學詩酒傲公侯

HY 30   *Li Ch'ien-kung ch'iung ti yü hsia-k'o*
李汧公窮邸遇俠客

HY 31   *Cheng Chieh-shih li kung shen-pi kung*   PWT
鄭節使立功神臂弓

HY 32   *Huang Hsiu-ts'ai yao ling yü-ma chui*
黃秀才徼靈玉馬墜

HY 33   *Shih-wu kuan hsi yen ch'eng ch'iao-huo*   PWT
十五貫戲言成巧禍

HY 34   *I wen ch'ien hsiao hsi tsao ch'i-yüan*   一
文錢小隙造奇冤

HY 35   *Hsü Lao-p'u i fen ch'eng chia*   徐老僕義
憤成家

HY 36   *Ts'ai Jui-hung jen ju pao ch'ou*   蔡瑞虹
忍辱報仇

HY 37   *Tu Tzu-ch'un san ju Ch'ang-an*   杜子
春三入長安

HY 38   *Li Tao-jen tu pu Yün-men*   李道人獨
步雲門

HY 39   *Wang Ta-yin huo fen Pao-lien Ssu*   汪
大尹火焚寶蓮寺

HY 40   *Ma-tang shen feng sung T'eng Wang Ko*
馬當神風送滕王閣

Note that the stories here represented as HY 21 and HY 22 appear in the reverse order in the first edition of *Hsing-shih heng-yen*. This is the order favored by modern editors.

In all, we have one hundred and forty-nine or fifty separate works, depending on whether or not the prologue story to KC 36 is regarded as a story in its own right. (It appears elsewhere as an independent story.) Twenty-five works exist in two or more pre-1628 editions.

A couple of stories were adapted or rewritten in later collections. Hung 11, for example, was adapted as the prologue to story 21 in the *Ch'u-k'e P'ai-an ching-ch'i*, and TY 28 was rewritten as story 15 of the *Hsi-hu chia-hua* 西湖佳話, an early-Ch'ing collection.[24] The *San yen* collections were published and republished, and some of the stories were selected for other anthologies, one of which, the late-Ming *Chin-ku ch'i-kuan* 今古奇觀, eventually eclipsed the *San yen* themselves. But this belongs only to the history of publishing, and we do not need to bother with it.

24 See the Shanghai, 1956 edition.

II Style as a Criterion of Date

I propose to use style as the means of finding the approximate dates of these undated works. The approach is experimental in two respects. Literary historians have tried to distinguish one man's style from another's, but they have rarely tried, in contrast to art historians, to distinguish the style of one period from that of another. And even when one man's work has been distinguished from another's, the criterion used has really been language rather than style. No doubt a stylistic judgement has often been implied, particularly when it has not been so necessary to analyze style; the *Junius Letters* and the *Federalist Papers*, on which so much work has been done, are pure exposition and persuasion, stylistically simple by the standards of other genres. But in general, it is true that linguistic items have been selected for comparison without consideration of style.[1]

1 This applies particularly to the quantitative methods, of which the pioneer work is G. Udny Yule's *The Statistical Study of Literary Vocabulary*, Cambridge, 1944. The most detailed studies of the *Junius Letters* and the *Federalist Papers* are, respectively, A. Ellegård, *A Statistical Method for Determining Authorship: The Junius Letters*, Gothenburg, 1962, and Frederick Mosteller and D. L. Wallace, *Inference and Disputed Authorship: The Federalist*, Reading, Mass., 1964. Nonstatistical approaches are exemplified and assessed in *Evidence for Authorship*, edited by D. V. Erdman and E. G. Fogel, Ithaca, N.Y., 1966. Virtually the only work to apply quantitative methods to Chinese fiction is Bernhard Karlgren's "New Excursions in Chinese Grammar," *Bulletin of the Museum of Far Eastern Antiquities* 24 (1952), 51–80.

These studies are concerned with authorship, of course, not with date of composition. (Karlgren chooses linguistic criteria some of which are temporally distinctive, but for the purpose of determining authorship.) Most of them deal with works of a relatively uniform style, or else they ignore the different major styles found in the same work. The statisticians, with computers to aid them, look for criteria of very high frequency, whether it be sentence-length, or proportion of nouns to adjectives, or the use of function words. "Context," writes one of them, "is a source of risk. We need variables which depend on the author and nothing else. Some function words come close to this ideal, but others do not." (Mosteller, p. 265.) This seems to deny the importance of stylistic analysis, except in an extreme interpretation of *Le style, c'est l'homme même*, but actually it does not. The most successful determinants of Hamilton's or Madison's authorship ("while" or "whilst," "upon," etc.) can be defined as stylistically comparable. In the *Federalist Papers*, it may be that stylistic analysis is either unnecessary (because of the relatively uniform nature of the papers) or else performed automatically (by the choice of certain criteria). In other kinds of literature, however, it will be necessary to analyze style explicitly.

So simple an approach will not work with a genre which, like fiction, is stylistically complex. To take an obvious example, it makes no sense to compare the frequency of words for the first-person pronoun in a narrative genre which has varying amounts of dialogue. Even if the scholar confines himself to dialogue, he will still need to distinguish one speaker's language from another's, for they may speak different regional or class dialects. Furthermore, each speaker has not one style but a whole range of them ("registers," as they are sometimes called) which are suitable for different occasions. He may very well refer to himself differently according to whether he is addressing an inferior or a superior, or whether he is angry or penitent. Since each work contains its own selection, in its own proportion, from a very large number of styles, it is inviting disaster to compare linguistic items regardless of style.

The analytic description of style is a field in which the literary critic and the linguist both work but never actually meet. The methods of even the best literary critics are likely to contain an arbitrary element—at least, the first step in the critical process is usually intuitive—and are hence unsuitable for the purposes of historical scholarship. Certainly, the impressionistic judgement of style ("early style," "Sung style," and so forth) has been tried on the short story and found wanting.[2] The linguists, on the other hand, presumably from a desire not to go beyond what is demonstrable by formal means, have mostly confined themselves to the smaller units of speech and the simplest written texts, and the results of linguistic scholarship are not of much value for the study of literary works.

The approach that comes closest to our requirements is the "contextual" method of analysis, particularly as described in an essay by Nils Erik Enkvist.[3] Mr. Enkvist's aim was to provide teachers of foreign literatures with a method of stylistic analysis. His approach has the great advantage of providing relatively precise categories and quantifiable data while remaining broad enough to cope with literary works. In Enkvist's definition, "style is concerned with frequencies of linguistic items in a given context, and thus with *contextual* probabilities. To measure the style of a passage, the frequencies of its linguistic items of different levels must be compared with the corresponding features in another text or corpus which is regarded as a norm and which has a definite contextual relationship with this passage."[4] He gives a tentative list of categories of context. The two main divisions are textual and extratextual. The former is subdivided into

2 See Hanan, "Sung and Yüan Vernacular Fiction," p. 178.

3 Nils Erik Enkvist, John Spencer, and Michael J. Gregory, *Linguistics and Style*, Oxford: Oxford University Press, 1964. Enkvist's essay is "On defining style," pp. 1–56. My account does not do justice to his argument, simplifying it considerably.

4 *Linguistics and Style*, p. 29.

"linguistic frame," including, for example, phonetic, syntactic, and lexical contexts; and "compositional frame," including, for example, the relationship of the text to surrounding textual portions, metre, and literary form. Extratextual contexts include period, type of speech, genre, relationship between writer and reader, context of situation, dialect, and language, among others.[5]

Each work or each passage, of course, participates in a number of different categories of context. Style is measured by comparing the frequencies of linguistic items in texts which have a significant number of contexts in common. For example, texts might be compared which have all other relevant contexts in common except that of author, in which case we would be attempting to define a personal style, or all relevant contexts in common except period (and naturally author), in which case we would be working toward a definition of a period style.

This kind of analysis depends heavily on the definition of contexts. It must be admitted that the scholar's judgement plays a part in choosing and defining some of the appropriate contexts for a given work. He must decide, for example, to what genre a work belongs, sometimes an impossible thing to determine. But contextual analysis does eliminate the more subjective procedures. As Enkvist says, "an appeal to context here obviates the need for references to extra-linguistic meaning; the context of a given text is presumably better accessible to objective, linguistic and sociolinguistic classification."[6]

In practice, context-bound linguistic items, that is, those restricted to a certain group of contexts, help to indicate style. "Style markers occurring in the same text form a stylistic set for that text. A stylistic set shared by a large number of contextually related texts forms a major stylistic set occurring within a major contextual range. Texts sharing the same major stylistic set are in the same major style."[7] A single literary text may contain more than one style. A play contains many styles, including the various styles which may be used by a single character. The same is true of most narrative. Markers are normally used to indicate the shift from one style to another.

Let us now apply these notions to the Chinese short story. The major stylistic categories which make up the work should first be distinguished. Obviously, dialogue is a whole separate category, consisting of a large number of different styles. The descriptive set piece, usually in unrhymed parallel prose and more or less Classical in language, has its own major

5 *Ibid.*, pp. 30–31.
6 *Linguistics and Style*, p. 29.
7 *Ibid.*, p. 55.

style. Occasional verse, and the unrhymed couplet, have other major styles. After excluding these categories and styles, only the plain narrative is left.

If this plain narrative is considered with reference to the whole corpus of vernacular fiction, it will be found to share the same major stylistic set. At this high level of generalization, it can be said that the plain narrative portions of the vernacular fiction share the same major style, which will be called the "vernacular fiction style." This common style is, of course, the main reason for the impression that the traditional novel and story remained remarkably static during their long history.

The contexts which the vernacular fiction has in common are significant. Apart from language, which I shall deal with below, and genre, the important contexts are those of the narrator and reader and the situation in which the fiction is communicated from one to the other. All of the vernacular fiction is represented as being told by a generalized narrator to a generalized audience. Since neither narrator nor audience has individual features, both seem, in broad terms, *constant* throughout the whole history of vernacular fiction. And the context of situation in which they metaphorically meet is, in broad terms, constant too; it represents, at one remove or another, the situation of oral storytelling.

Of course, this context of situation is itself a metaphor for the real communication that is being practiced. The constant, standardized narrator is no more the author than we readers are the constant, standardized audience. The storytelling situation is a metaphor, a working model of another kind of communication, a pretence in which both sides, writer and reader, acquiesce in order to provide the context necessary for successful communication.[8] As a model or metaphor, it has been quite successful, if we are to judge from its extraordinary durability in Chinese fiction.

There are two important contexts which appear to vary from work to work: dialect and language. (By language, I mean the position on the spectrum from Classical Chinese to colloquial.) But the main stylistic markers of the vernacular fiction style seem to function more or less independently of language and dialect differences. A glance at the few extant novels that are written in an obviously divergent dialect will confirm this. Language presents a more difficult problem. I have been using the word "vernacular" to cover a lexical and syntactical range from somewhere close to Classical Chinese all the way to the spoken language. Moreover, even within the same text, the language of the vernacular fiction style is not

---

8 There is a possibility for irony in manipulating the author's relationship to the narrator, ours to the audience. To some extent, the story of the late period begins to exploit the possibility.

constant; in the functions of summary and comment,[9] for example, it some-times approaches closer to the Classical. However, although the style markers vary somewhat according to language differences, they do not vary in proportion to those differences. Thus a work close to Classical will usually mark the shift from the vernacular fiction style to a dialogue style with the word *yüeh* 曰 rather than *tao* 道, but despite this it will still share a number of style markers with more vernacular texts. In broad terms, these style markers still form the same major stylistic set.

The markers of this style will be its most context-bound expressions. For example, the *hua shuo* 話說 at the beginning of the story proper is enough on its own to signify the use of the vernacular fiction style; it practically never occurs in other styles in this syntactical context, that is, at the head of a sentence.[10] In general, we would expect the style markers to be related not to the variable subject matter of fiction but to those basic operations of narrative which will be common to all fiction. Since the essence of narrative is the description of events in their causal and chronological relationships, we would expect expressions indicating these relationships to function as style markers. It scarcely needs saying that an expression meaning "after some time" is more likely to be a style marker than, say, "army officer." Other basic operations include the shifting of styles, for example, from the vernacular fiction style to a dialogue style; the beginning, sectionalizing, and closing of a text; and the introducing of the narrator's explanations and evaluations.

The first step in the use of stylistic criteria for dating is to find out whether we can really speak of period styles in the short-story genre. It will be necessary to select two groups of stories which differ, so far as can be dis-covered, only with regard to period, and then to see whether they differ regularly and systematically in terms of style. The style to examine will be the vernacular fiction style, that is, the plain narrative, and the point of comparison will be the style markers. Clearly, even if there prove to be regular and systematic differences among the style markers, it still cannot be concluded that the existence of period styles has been demonstrated. We can never be certain that the stories are typical of the stories of their periods. There may be hidden contexts of which we are unaware, and the differences in style may be due to them rather than to period. To take the obvious instance, all the stories of one period might have been written by one man and all the stories of the other period by a second man; in that case, our

9 See Hanan, "The Early Chinese Short Story," p. 174, for a discussion of these terms.
10 *Hua shuo* is also used in some other vernacular narrative genres, as well as in oral literature.

differences might merely indicate a difference in personal style. Or the stories might differ regionally, in which case the differences might indicate regional styles rather than period styles. Tests will have to be devised to eliminate these and other possibilities.

The Trial Groups and Their Stylistic Differences

The only periods that can be easily examined are those determined by the two significant dates which were noted in Chapter I: circa 1550 and the 1620's. The former is the later limit for the Hung stories, and the probable later limit for the stories referred to in the Pao-wen-t'ang catalogue; the latter is the later limit for most of the *San yen* stories. Thus 1550 is the approximate time barrier which will divide the two periods.

The membership of the older group is simply decided: the twenty-nine Hung stories. The Pao-wen-t'ang catalogue will not be used, since there is some uncertainty about its date as well as about the identification of some of its references. The newer group will consist of all those *San yen* stories which can be shown, by internal or other evidence, to have been written after about 1550. The kinds of evidence admitted are these: time setting of Chia-ching (1522–66) or later; clear attribution to a late-Ming author; internal evidence that points clearly to a late-Ming date. Only the last kind needs explanation. It is used in the case of one story which contains songs to a tune which came into popular favor only in the late sixteenth century; this is much the strongest kind of internal evidence available, apart from that of time setting. Arguments drawn from the date of written sources have been rejected here, although I have used them myself elsewhere;[11] the evidence is stronger for some stories than for others, and it is hard to find a simple and objective principle of selection. The following nine stories form the newer group:

KC 40 *Shen Hsiao-hsia hsiang hui Ch'u-shih piao* 沈小霞相會出師表. Explicitly concerned with historical events of the Chia-ching period.

TY 18 *Lao men-sheng san shih pao en* 老門生三世報恩. Feng Meng-lung tells us in the preface to a play that he was the author of this story.[12]

TY 32 *Tu Shih-niang nu ch'en pai-pao hsiang* 杜十娘怒沉百寶箱. The story is set in the years after 1592, and since the opening of the story mentions the length of the Wan-li emperor's reign, it must have been written after 1619.

11 See Patrick Hanan, "The Authorship of Some *Ku-chin hsiao-shuo* Stories," *Harvard Journal of Asiatic Studies* 29 (1969), 190–200.
12 The play is the *San pao en* 三報恩 by Pi Wei 畢魏, of which there is a facsimile edition in the *Ku-pen hsi-ch'ü ts'ung-k'an*, Second Series, Peking, 1955. Feng's preface is dated 1642.

TY 40 *Ching-yang Kung t'ieh-shu chen yao* 旌陽宮鐵樹鎮妖. This story exists in editions prior to TY.[13] They attribute the novel, in fifteen chapters, to the Ming writer Teng Chih-mo 鄧志謨. The earliest extant edition has a preface by him dated 1603. The attribution seems to be correct; the work is of a similar type to others that are attributed to him. It contains the date of 1518 in a context that makes it clear that the book was composed much later than that.[14]

HY 3 *Mai-yu lang tu chan Hua-k'uei* 賣油郎獨占花魁. The story contains some songs to the *kua-chih-erh* 掛枝兒 tune which became popular only in the latter part of the sixteenth century.[15]

HY 18 *Shih Jun-tse T'an-ch'üeh yü yu* 施潤澤灘闕遇友. Set in the Chia-ching period.

HY 20 *Chang T'ing-hsiu t'ao sheng chiu fu* 張廷秀逃生救父. Set in the Wan-li period.

HY 29 *Lu T'ai-hsüeh shih chiu ao kung hou* 盧太學詩酒傲公侯. Set in the Chia-ching period.

HY 35 *Hsü Lao-p'u i fen ch'eng chia* 徐老僕義憤成家. Set in the Chia-ching period.

Four of the nine stories have prologues, consisting of a short introductory essay or of another story, set before the story proper.[16] Since there is a chance that prologue and main story might have had separate origins, I am excluding the prologues from consideration at this stage.

It has been mentioned that the plain narrative portions of the text are the best passages to examine and that within the plain narrative the style markers make the best points of comparison. Since our aim is to see if the markers which have precisely the same set of contexts (syntactic, compositional, and so on) differ systematically in the two groups of stories, it is vital that the sets of contexts chosen should be both easily identifiable and of frequent occurrence.

The sets that seem to meet these requirements best are the following: first, the words immediately before a shift from the vernacular fiction style

13 See Sun K'ai-ti, *Chung-kuo t'ung-su hsiao-shuo shu-mu*, p. 169. One is preserved in the Naikaku Bunko.

14 TY 40, p. 645.

15 The authority for the date is Shen Te-fu's 沈德符 "Shih-shang hsiao-ling" 時尚小令 in his *Wan-li yeh-huo pien* 萬曆野獲編 (Peking, 1959 ed.), *chüan* 25, p. 647. Another is Hsüeh Ch'ao's 薛朝 *T'ien-hsiang lou wai-shih chih-i* 天香樓外史誌異 (lithographic ed., 1900), *chüan* 5. 13a. "At the end of the Cheng-te period and the beginning of the Chia-ching, they mostly sang the *Shan-p'o-yang* tune in the streets and lanes. At the close of Lung-ch'ing and the beginning of Wan-li, it was the *T'ung-ch'eng-ke* 桐城歌 . . . Nowadays they sing the so-called *Kua-chih-erh*." The author's preface is dated 1603.

16 The four with prologues are TY 18, HY 3, HY 18, and HY 35.

to dialogue or thought, or those immediately after a shift back from dialogue or thought to vernacular fiction; and, second, the words immediately before or after style shifts between the vernacular fiction style on the one hand, and the set piece, regular verse, *tz'u* and the (unrhymed) couplet on the other. Within these definitions, I shall further confine myself to the words just before a style shift from vernacular fiction to dialogue or thought, or just before a shift from vernacular fiction to the couplet or the four-lined verse.

There is no practical difficulty in identifying the shift; the few cases in which I punctuate differently from modern editors are indicated in the notes.[17]   What has to be defined is the extent to which the words before the shift to dialogue or thought should be examined. To keep the numbers of possible combinations low, I shall limit the survey to the three positions just before the shift: (1) the connective or monosyllabic adverb or place-word (for example, *hsin-li* 心裏 "in one's heart," *k'ou-chung* 口中 "in one's mouth"); (2) the verb or verb-object construction; (3) *tao, yüeh*, and so on. In a particular case, any of these three positions may be unfilled, although it is unlikely that the second and the third would be unfilled at the same time. If an item from some other category intrudes between any two of these three, only the words after it will be counted. For example, if a coverb plus object comes between the first and the second, only the second and third positions will be considered.

It remains only to set standards of dispersion and of aggregate frequency. Let us set as a minimum six occurrences in four stories. (The stories of the later group, though fewer in number, are generally longer, and it seems reasonable that the same standards should apply.) All of the criteria must be mutually exclusive items.

I will spare the reader the details of the laborious process of cancelling out markers which both groups of texts have in common. So far as I am able to determine, these are the criteria peculiar to the older group which emerge from the survey.

   1. *ssu-liang tao* 思量道 "thought, as follows." Or *ssu-liang* without *tao*,
      but prefaced by *hsin-li* or *tu-li* 肚裏.

        Twenty-one instances in ten stories. (Hung 2, two instances;
        Hung 5; Hung 11; Hung 13; Hung 14, two instances; Hung 15,

17 Sometimes there is room for doubt as to whether speech or thought is "direct" or "indirect," since Chinese does not have clear syntactical signals to distinguish *oratio recta* from *obliqua*. I have included all cases where the possibility exists of direct speech or thought. Instances in which I differ from the modern punctuation are marked by an asterisk in this chapter and the next.

five instances; Hung 16, two instances; Hung 18; Hung 19; Hung 20, five instances.)

2. *tzu-ssu* 自思 or *tzu-ssu tao* 自思道 "thought, as follows."[18]

Twelve instances in six stories. (Hung 4, two instances; Hung 5, three; Hung 7, two; Hung 12, three; Hung 14; Hung 17.)

3. *nai yen* 乃言 "and then said, as follows."

Twelve instances in four stories. (Hung 4, two; Hung 12, two; Hung 18, four; Hung 19, four.)

4. *shuo yü* X (*tao*) 說與 X (道) "said to X, as follows." This is not the last part of a construction like *pa* Y *shuo yü* X 把Y說與X "tell X about Y";[19] there is no object of *shuo* expressed or understood. *Yü* serves normally as a coverb, and this use, as a kind of postverbal complement, is exceptional, and is included here for that reason.[20]

Thirteen instances in five stories. (Hung 12, six; Hung 13; Hung 15; Hung 17; Hung 18, four.)

5. *ch'ang je tao* 唱喏道 "made obeisance, saying."[21] *Sheng* 聲, and *ying* 應, with slightly different meanings, can substitute for *ch'ang*, and *yüeh* or *yün* for *tao*. *Tao* may also be omitted.

Seven instances in five stories. (Hung 2; Hung 3; Hung 12; Hung 15, three; Hung 25.)

6. *cheng so-wei* 正所謂 "it was truly a case of," before an unrhymed couplet or a four-lined poem.[22] (Poems represented as spoken by characters are naturally excluded.) *Cheng* may be omitted, and *shih* 是 may be added after *so-wei*.

Seven instances in five stories. (Hung 5; Hung 13; Hung 14; Hung 15, three; Hung 20.)

The following criteria are peculiar to the newer group:

(a) *hsiang tao* 想道 "thought, as follows," provided there is no *hsin-li*, and so on, close before it.

---

18 *Tzu-ssu* is a common feature of Classical and raises problems when one is dealing with Classically oriented stories.

19 Compare HY 9, p. 189, *chiang . . . shuo yü . . . tao.*

20 *Shuo yü* is here regarded as a single verbal unit, and hence capable of occupying position 2. *Yü* as a complement to other verbs than *shuo* does not distinguish the older group of stories from the newer.

21 Criteria 1 and 5 are also found among the T'ang dynasty *pien-wen* 變文. See Wang Chung-min 王重民 et al., ed., *Tun-huang pien-wen chi* 敦煌變文集 (Peking, 1957), passim.

22 Two other possible preverse and precouplet formulae were rejected. One was the phrase *ju-hua* 入話 preceding the opening poems in most of the Hung stories; it was altogether in too vulnerable a position. The other was the word *ssu* 似, in the forms *hao-ssu* 好似, *i-ssu* 一似, etc., introducing a couplet. It is used in Chapter III, where the sample is larger.

Thirty-one instances in eight stories. (KC 40, two; TY 18, three; TY 32, two; HY 3, four; HY 18, five; HY 20, seven; HY 29, five; HY 35, three.)

(b) *yu hsiang* 又想 or *yu hsiang tao* 又想道 "thought again, as follows."
This feature is not included in the figures given under *a*.
Eighteen instances in six stories. (TY 18, two; HY 3; HY 18, two; HY 20, three; HY 29, six; HY 35, four.)

(c) *ssu-hsiang* 思想 or *ssu-hsiang tao* 思想道 "thought, as follows."
Six instances in four stories. (KC 40; HY 3, two; HY 29, two;[23] HY 35.)

(d) *nai tao* 乃道 "and then said, as follows."
Twenty-nine instances in four stories. (HY 18, ten; HY 20, ten; HY 29, five; HY 35, four.)

This restricted survey has shown that it is possible to find style markers of high frequency in one group of stories which do not occur at all in the other. Can one say that the style markers of the two groups differ significantly? Mere frequency means little unless it is shown in proportion to the total incidence. If we choose as a sample set of contexts the words introducing direct thought and proceed to count all the relevant markers in both groups whether they happen to coincide or not, we should get a meaningful result. The total number of instances in the older group is forty-nine, and in the newer group ninety-one. Of the forty-nine, thirty-three have already been shown to belong to types peculiar to the older group, a proportion of about 67 percent. Of the ninety-one, fifty-five have similarly been shown to belong to types peculiar to the newer group, a proportion of about 60 percent. Of course, the total incidence of markers exclusive to one group or the other is really much higher than this; all of the markers which occur below a certain level of frequency have been excluded. There can be no doubt that, so far as this set of contexts is concerned, the styles of the two groups do differ significantly. And it may be inferred that they will also differ in other sets.

Of course, the difference in style cannot simply be explained as difference of period. As mentioned above, hidden factors other than period may be responsible. Clearly, there is no positive way of showing that each group represents a fair sampling of the fiction of its period. All that can be hoped for is to show that the difference of style applies *generally* in other works of the two periods. If it can be shown to apply generally, we shall be entitled to use it as a criterion of date.

23 This figure includes a possible instance, on p. 606.

Testing the Criteria

The following four tests have been devised to show how far the criteria work in distinguishing the relevant literature of the two periods. The groups are described as "older" and "newer," instead of as "earlier" and "later," in order to avoid possible confusion with the tripartite division made in Chapter V into early, middle, and late. (The present "newer" stories will then be described as "late"; the present "older" stories will be divided into "early" and "middle.") For convenience I shall use the terms "older criterion" and "newer criterion" to refer to the criteria of the two groups. Of course, the criteria have not yet been established as indicators of date.

The obvious first recourse is to the text of the *San yen* anthologies themselves. They contain the text of ten short stories which are duplicated among the Hung collections.[24] In some cases, the *San yen* text differs a good deal from the Hung text, and the usual assumption is that the *San yen* editors, or other editors before them, adapted the stories. Accepting this assumption, we can consider the adaptation, for comparative purposes, under three headings: changed passages, in which the basis of the Hung text is preserved, and the changes are minor; added passages, the text of which is entirely new; and omitted passages. If our criteria apply in terms of date, we should expect to find that no older criteria have been introduced into the changed passages and to find no older criteria at all in the added passages. We might also find, in the changed and added passages, that some older criteria have been changed to neutral forms, and that some newer criteria have been introduced.

Comparison of the text bears out these expectations. In the changed passages, no additional older criteria have been introduced, but in four instances older criteria have been turned into neutral forms: a 2 in Hung 5, adapted as the prologue story of TY 6; a 6 in Hung 14, adapted as TY 38; and two instances of 3 in Hung 18, adapted as TY 33. The added passages contain no older criteria at all, but they do contain three instances of the newer criteria, an *a* and a *c*★ in KC 30, adapted from Hung 13, and another *a* in KC 4, adapted from Hung 20.

A second test is provided by the Pao-wen-t'ang catalogue. Despite the reservations about its date which I have mentioned above, it is still likely that the catalogue's apparent references are to stories which existed before

---

24 The ten stories are KC 4 (Hung 20); KC 7 (Hung 21); KC 16 (Hung 22); KC 20 (Hung 12); KC 30 (Hung 13); KC 34 (Hung 27); KC 35 (Hung 2); TY 6P (Hung 5); TY 33 (Hung 18); TY 38 (Hung 14).

1560. Where these references can be plausibly identified with the titles of existing *San yen* stories, we should expect to find that the stories show the same features as the adapted Hung stories, that is to say, that they contain older criteria with perhaps a sprinkling of newer criteria added by the *San yen* editors.[25]

There are nineteen *San yen* stories which, in the general scholarly opinion, are the subject of Pao-wen-t'ang references.[26] As the following list shows, they have a preponderance of older criteria:[27]

KC 3 has three older criteria (2, 4, 6).[28]

KC 11 has one older criterion (6).

KC 15M (M stands for main story only, excluding the prologue) has two older criteria (1, three instances, 5).

KC 23 is largely the same as Hsiung A(M). In the KC version, there is one older criterion (2, three instances). The Hsiung story has two older criteria (2, three instances, 6).

KC 24 has one older criterion (5).

KC 25 has no criteria.

KC 26 has one older criterion (1) and one newer (a).

KC 33 has one older criterion (1, two instances).

KC 36P (P stands for prologue only) has one older criterion (2, two instances).

25 The reference is to the *San yen* stories not in the Hung collections.

26 T'an Cheng-pi, "*Pao-wen-t'ang shu-mu so lu Sung Yüan Ming jen hua-pen k'ao*" 寶文堂書目所錄宋元明人話本考, *Hua-pen yü ku-chü* 話本與古劇 (Shanghai, 1956), pp. 38–60, gives the most detailed list of these identifications. Some of them are open to criticism. See Hanan, "The Early Chinese Short Story," p. 181, n. 28. T'an identifies fifty-three references to extant vernacular stories, twenty-three of them to Hung stories. (The reference to Hung 29 is omitted.) Of the remaining thirty, nine are to stories outside the *San yen*; they are not suitable material for this test, since their editions are neither uniform nor easily dated. Two others, the references to *Feng Yü-mei chi* 馮玉梅記 and *Hsiao chin ch'ien chi* 小金錢記, cannot be identified in the way T'an claims. The former identification depends on the belief that the *Ching-pen t'ung-su hsiao-shuo* 京本通俗小說 collection is a pre-*San yen* work; this has been shown to be false. It is hard to see how the latter title can stand for TY 16, unless it has been garbled; we must leave it on one side for the present. One of T'an's suggestions, in regard to the title *San meng seng chi* 三夢僧記, seems less likely than Wu Hsiao-ling's 吳曉鈴 claim that it refers to KC 3. See Wu's review of a *Ku-chin hsiao-shuo* edition in *Han-hiue* 2.4(1949), 445. Wu's identification is accepted here provisionally. I have suggested that the title *Hung-lien chi* 紅蓮記 may stand for KC 29, but since the point is debatable, do not include it here. See "The Authorship of Some *Ku-chin hsiao-shuo* Stories," p. 195, n. 24.

27 Only that part of each story which the catalogue title explicitly refers to is the subject of the test. This means that only the main stories are considered, except for the prologue to KC 36.

28 Criteria are arranged in the order of their first appearance in the story. An asterisk denotes that the instance or instances of this criterion are not punctuated by modern editors as introducing direct speech or thought.

KC 36M has two older criteria (1, five instances, 5, two instances).

KC 38 has two older criteria (1, two instances, 6).

TY 8 has two older criteria (5, 4).

TY 20 has two older criteria (1, 5).

TY 29 has one older criterion (2*, two instances).

TY 37 has four older criteria (5, 4, two instances, 1, 6).

HY 13 has no older criteria, but has one newer criterion (a).

HY 16 has no older criteria, but has three newer criteria (a, b, c).

HY 31 has three older criteria (5, two instances, 1, two instances, 2) and two newer (a, b*).

HY 33M has no criteria.

In the case of most stories, these results confirm our expectation. Only two stories, HY 13 and HY 16, show a preponderance of newer criteria, and it would therefore be dangerous to assume that they are indeed the stories referred to in the catalogue. If we exclude these two stories for the time being, we find that the remaining seventeen stories show a total of twenty-seven older criteria as against only three newer criteria. If we count instances rather than criteria, these figures become forty-three and three, respectively. The average number of older criteria per story is about 1.6, and the average number of instances 2.5. The best comparison is with the *San yen* stories adapted from the Hung collections; in their *San yen* versions, they average 1.7 criteria and 3.3 instances, a fairly close parallel. It is worth noting that two of the instances of newer criteria are of criterion *a*, which was also found twice amongst the added passages in the ten adapted stories.

A suitable third test is with some late-Ming collections of short stories. The earliest datable collections after the publication of the *San yen* are the two *P'ai-an ching-ch'i* and the *Shih tien t'ou*. If our criteria have any general validity as indicators of date, these stories should show a preponderance of newer features.

The first ten stories of *P'ai-an ching-ch'i* have seventeen instances of newer criteria (thirteen *a*, two *b*, two *c*) and only one older criterion, an instance of 1. The first five stories of the *Shih tien t'ou* have twenty instances of newer criteria (eight *a*, five *b*, two *c*, five *d*) and no older criteria.

For the final test, we will consider vernacular fiction outside of the short story. Unfortunately, the two vernacular novels which are listed in the Pao-wen-t'ang catalogue survive only in late editions. The twenty-chapter *P'ing-yao chuan* 平妖傳 exists in a Wan-li edition,[29] as does the earliest

---

29 See Sun K'ai-ti, *Chung-kuo t'ung-su hsiao-shuo shu-mu*, pp. 163–164.

surviving edition of the *Shui-hu chuan* 水滸傳.[30] It would be naïve to expect late-sixteenth century editions to remain faithful to their earlier form. Nonetheless, these editions should still show a considerable number of the older criteria.

The *P'ing-yao chuan* is of particular interest, because it was Feng Meng-lung, editor of the *San yen* collections, who later rewrote and extended it into a forty-chapter version. The first fifteen chapters in the latter are entirely new, and, from chapter 16 on, Feng has both rewritten the old text and inserted new material. One can quite easily confirm that the forty-chapter version is an expansion of the original twenty-chapter version; whereas the language of the twenty-chapter version is more or less consistent within itself, the language of the other version differs radically between the material that is peculiar to it and the material that it shares.

In the twenty-chapter edition, there are twenty-nine instances of older criteria (twenty-one 1, two 2, five 5, one 6) against two instances of newer criteria (both *a* and both in chapter 7). In the first fifteen chapters of the forty-chapter version, all of which were written by Feng Meng-lung, we find an entirely different pattern. There are twenty-four instances of newer criteria (twenty *a*, two *b*, two *c*) and only one instance of an older criterion (6). In the rewritten chapters, where we would expect to find Feng Meng-lung most influenced by the original work, there are frequent newer criteria. For example, in the text of chapter 16, which is based on chapter 1 of the twenty-chapter novel, there is one newer criterion (*c*) and no additional older criteria. In chapter 17, which has been added, there are three instances of *a*, one of *b*, and no older criteria. In chapter 19, which has been rewritten, there is one instance of *c*, one of *d*, and no additional older criteria. So accurate do these criteria prove to be that, if we did not possess the twenty-chapter novel, we could reconstruct it in very broad outline from Feng Meng-lung's reworked version.

The *Shui-hu chuan* was supplemented also, probably during the Wan-li period. In the 120-chapter edition, we should expect to find a clear contrast between the inserted chapters (91–110) and the rest of the novel.

The twenty inserted chapters do indeed show a marked preponderance of newer criteria—fourteen instances (four *a*, ten *c*) against one instance of an older criterion (2).[31] The rest of the novel, however, gives a much less clear result. In the first ten chapters, there are only six instances of older

---

30 The edition used was the variorum edition of the "full" texts of the novel, the *Shui-hu ch'üan chuan* 水滸全傳, Peking, 1954.
31 A possible instance on p. 1547.

criteria (one 2, three 5, two 3) against one instance of a newer criterion (*a*). Moreover, the instances of criterion 3 should perhaps not be counted, since they are restricted to special contexts.[32] Nor is the instance of *a* a rare occurrence; it is scattered throughout the novel. Our results would be consistent with the belief that the *Shui-hu chuan* was revised in the sixteenth century, but obviously they do not *prove* that belief to be true.

These four tests seem the most appropriate. We cannot try the criteria on other kinds of vernacular literature, for example on the dialogue portions of the drama, for the criteria are genre characteristics which occur almost exclusively in narrative fiction. Imperfect though they are in many ways, the tests do show that our criteria function, in effect, as broad indicators of date.

We cannot hope to guess at, let alone uncover, all the hidden contexts which might account for the incidence of the criteria. In some cases, the criteria may indicate a personal style. Feng Meng-lung rewrote the *P'ing-yao chuan* and at least one of the newer stories. Quite conceivably, too, it was Feng who adapted the Hung stories in the *San yen*. Furthermore, it will be shown in Chapter IV that the anonymous author of the *Shih tien t'ou* was also probably the author of some of the newer stories. But these facts and possibilities do not account for all of the differences we have noted. It still seems reasonable to conclude that these stylistic features, characteristic of a few writers' personal styles though they may be, were also in some measure shared by the fiction writers of the day. They can be seen as part of the minutiae of the writer's craft, acquired, probably unconsciously, in the practice of the profession in a given period.

It must not be imagined that these minutiae remain stable after circa 1550. What validity the newer criteria have is in respect of the late Ming, not the Ch'ing. By the Ch'ing dynasty, some of the newer criteria have dropped away, and some older criteria have been restored to favor.[33]

---

32 It is often used to introduce the speech of distinctive types such as soothsayers.

33 E. g., a special form of criterion 1 is found in the *Shih-erh lou* 十二樓 collection of the seventeenth century writer Li Yü 李漁.

III Identifying the Newer Stories

It would be possible to use our present criteria to classify the rest of the stories, grouping them with either the older or the newer stories, and deducing their dates of composition. However, in most stories the incidence of these criteria is low, and the possibility of a mistaken conclusion correspondingly high. At this stage, therefore, we can classify only stories that show a striking incidence of either exclusively older or exclusively newer criteria. If we accept three separate criteria as the minimum for the older stories, and a total of three instances of any two criteria as the minimum for the newer stories, we will be able to enlarge the pilot groups considerably.[1]

These stories can be added to the older group:[2]

TY 7, with three older criteria (4, 2, 3).

TY 14, with three older criteria (1, two instances, 4 and 5).

HY 21, with three older criteria (5, two instances, 1, three instances, 2, two instances).

These stories can be added to the newer group:[3]

---

1 The different standards are due to the different quantities of older and newer criteria: six older, four newer.

2 For this purpose we are considering prologues and main stories as separate units. There is always the possibility that a prologue and its main story may have different origins and dates of composition. What constitutes a prologue? I have attempted in this chapter to distinguish *prologues*, which are, potentially at least, distinct stories, from *introductions*, often amounting only to a poem and a few general remarks, that are tied specifically to the main story. In practice, there is not likely to be much ambiguity. Note that reference to a story in this list means the main story (plus introduction) only.

3 HY 16, with three later criteria (*b*, two instances, *a*, *c*) and no earlier, qualifies as a member of this group. It is not accepted here as a member of the pilot group because of the Pao-wen-t'ang catalogue's apparent reference to it. See below, where it proves indeed to be a later story.

KC 2, with two newer criteria (*a*, four instances, *b*).

KC 10, with two newer criteria (*b*, two instances, *a*).

TY 1, with three newer criteria (*a*, three instances, *b*, *c*).

TY 5, with two newer criteria (*a*, four instances, *c*).

TY 15, with three newer criteria (*c*★, *a*, *b*, four instances).

TY 21, with two newer criteria (*a*, five instances, *c*).

TY 31, with three newer criteria (*b*, *a*, three instances, *c*).

TY 35, with three newer criteria (*a*, *c*, *b*).

HY 4, with two newer criteria (*d*, four instances, *b*, two instances).

HY 6, with two newer criteria (*d*, eight instances, *b*).

HY 7, with two newer criteria (*a*, five instances, *b*, two instances).

HY 8, with three newer criteria (*a*, four instances, *b*, two instances, *d*, five instances).

HY 11, with two newer criteria (*b*, *a*, two instances).

HY 15, with four newer criteria (*a*, five instances, *d*, four instances, *b*, *c*).

HY 17, with three newer criteria (*a*, four instances, *b*, two instances, *d*, four instances).

HY 19, with three newer criteria (*a*, four instances, *b*, *c*, three instances).

HY 25, with two newer criteria (*a*, five instances, *b*, six instances).

HY 26, with three newer criteria (*a*, six instances, *b*, three instances, *d*, two instances).

HY 27, with four newer criteria (*a*, eight instances, *d*, three instances, *b*, six instances, *c*).

HY 28, with three newer criteria (*a*, three instances, *b*, five instances, *d*, three instances).

HY 30, with four newer criteria (*c*, two instances, *d*, nine instances, *a*, six instances, *b*, five instances).

HY 34, with three newer criteria (*a*, three instances, *b*, four instances, *d*, three instances).

HY 36, with four newer criteria (*d*, *a*, two instances, *b*, five instances, *c*★).

HY 37, with four newer criteria (*b*, six instances, *a*, three instances, *d*, two instances, *c*).

HY 38, with two newer criteria (*a*, nine instances, *b*).

HY 39P, with three newer criteria (*b*, two instances, *a*★, *d*).

There are obvious advantages to having the pilot groups as large as possible. But there is also a danger that the newer group may become less representative of the *San yen* collections by the addition of these twenty-six stories. Eighteen of the twenty-six are from HY, and there is evidence emerging that certain criteria, *d*, for example, are in fact peculiar to that collection. We shall therefore keep the proportion of HY stories in the newer group about the same as before, by admitting just the first eight HY stories. Thus the older pilot group will be increased by three (TY 7, TY 14, and HY 21) and the newer pilot group by sixteen (KC 2, KC 10, TY 1, TY 5, TY 15, TY 21, TY 31, TY 35, HY 4, HY 6, HY 7, HY 8, HY 11, HY 15, HY 17, and HY 19).

Further, we can add to the older pilot group most of the stories apparently referred to in the Pao-wen-t'ang catalogue. As we have seen, not all of the identifications normally made by scholars can be accepted. But there is a strong presumption that most of the stories apparently referred to will be older, and we may so consider any story that has a majority of older criteria over newer. This means adding fourteen stories, including one prologue,[4] to our pilot group out of the nineteen *San yen* stories in question; the five stories excluded are KC 25, KC 26, HY 13, HY 16, and HY 33. The catalogue seems to refer to only a few extant stories outside of the Hung collections and the *San yen*, and only one of them, Hsiung A, can qualify at this stage as an older story.[5]

Thus the older pilot group now contains forty-six stories, consisting of the *Ch'ien-t'ang meng*, the twenty-eight accessible Hung stories, the three added *San yen* stories, and fourteen stories apparently referred to in the Pao-wen-t'ang catalogue. The newer pilot group now contains twenty-five stories, the original nine plus sixteen added stories. Note that with all of these stories except the *Ch'ien-t'ang meng* and the Hung stories, it is the main story only, not the prologue, if one exists, that is included in the pilot groups.[6]

The Criteria

Some increase in our criteria will be needed in order to classify the remainder of the stories. But to find the additional criteria, it will not be

---

4 The prologue to KC 36 is the story *Lü-chu chi* 綠珠記 which is listed in the Pao-wen-t'ang catalogue and is found as a separate story in several late-Ming miscellanies.

5 Two stories, the *Tu Li-niang chi* and the story of Chang Yü-hu, exist in a pair of distinct though textually related versions. Although one version of the former and both of the latter would qualify as earlier stories here, I am postponing consideration of them until later.

6 Unless the prologue story has itself qualified.

necessary to repeat the laborious procedure of Chapter II and explore the whole of some objectively definable context. Having shown by that method that the two groups were distinguishable by stylistic criteria and that this difference is related to date of composition, we can now assume that other stylistic criteria which also distinguish the two groups will work to the same end, as rough indicators of date of composition.

Criteria will come from among the style markers of the "vernacular fiction" style. That is to say, they will be verbal formulae that are concerned with some of the basic operations of narrative. Each criterion should occur in five or more stories of one group only. If the incidence of an older criterion is well above the minimum, one occurrence will be tolerated in a newer story; this allows for the possibility of an occasional archaic usage. If the incidence of a newer criterion is well above the minimum, one occurrence will be tolerated in a *San yen* older story (not in a Hung story) because of the possibility of editorial change. These rules are somewhat relaxed in comparison with those of Chapter II above, where the aim was to see if the two groups could be distinguished stylistically.[7]

There are eleven additional criteria for the older group. They are here numbered to follow the six criteria established in Chapter II.

Prespeech, prethought position:

> 7. *tzu tao* 自道 "said to himself, thought to himself, as follows."
> Seven instances in six stories. (Hung 2; Hung 8; KC 11; KC 33★; KC 38; TY 37, two.)

Precouplet position:

> 8. *ch'üeh-ssu* 却似 or *ch'ia-ssu* 恰似 or *hao-ssu* 好似 or *i-ssu* 一似. Because *ssu* can be pronounced *shih*, *ch'üeh-shih* 却是 is also accepted.[8]
> Fifteen instances in thirteen stories. One instance in the newer group (*ch'üeh-ssu* in HY 7). *Ch'üeh-ssu* is found in Hung 5, 18, TY 8, 14, HY 21, two. *Ch'üeh-shih* is found in Hung 13, *ch'ia-ssu* in Hung 15, *hao-ssu* in Hung 14, KC 15, HY 21, and *i-ssu* in Hung 8, KC 33, TY 37, HY 31, two.

The passing of time, the setting of time, and so on:

> 9. two four-character phrases, the second of which is *jih yüeh ju so* 日月如梭 "the days and months were as (swift as) a shuttle." The definition is framed in this way so as to accommodate a number of

---

7 For an assessment of how these criteria fare in comparison with those of the trial groups, see below.

8 These expressions are considered only when they introduce a couplet, never when they occur in the middle of a sentence, even when what follows can be regarded as two short balanced phrases.

slightly divergent forms of the first phrase. The whole expression is used by the narrator to skip over a period of time.

Eight instances in seven stories. (Hung 4; Hung 13; Hung 16, two; Hung 18; Hung 20; TY 8; HY 31.)

10. *nien-chih* 撚指 "in a snap of the fingers." The expression, which is used as above, often appears in a string of similar phrases.

Six instances in five stories. (Hung 14; Hung 19, two; KC 33; KC 38; TY 14.)

11. *chi ts'an k'e yin, yeh chu hsiao hsing* 饑餐渴飲, 夜住曉行 "when hungry he ate, when thirsty he drank, at night he stopped, in the morning he travelled." This expression is used by the narrator to gloss over the details of an uneventful journey.

Eleven instances in ten stories. One instance in the newer group (TY 15). (*Ch'ien-t'ang meng;* Hung 11; Hung 12; Hung 15; Hung 19; KC 11, two; KC 15; KC 36; TY 8; HY 31.)

12. *i-li* 迤邐 "travel, wend one's way." This word is generally used in contexts like the above.

Thirty-five instances in nineteen stories. (Hung 1; Hung 5; Hung 8, two; Hung 11, three; Hung 12, four; Hung 15; Hung 16; Hung 19, two; Hung 20, three; Hung 27; KC 3; KC 15, two; KC 33, three; TY 8; TY 14; TY 20, three; TY 37, two; HY 31, two; Hsiung A.)

13. *shih yü* 時遇 "it chanced to be the time of."

Nine instances in nine stories. One instance in the newer group (TY 21). (Hung 8; Hung 13; Hung 20; Hung 26; KC 15; TY 7; TY 8; TY 14; TY 20.)

Narrator's comment on action:

14. *wan-shih chieh hsiu* 萬事皆休 "nothing (untoward) would have happened." The expression occurs in such contexts as "if he had not heard that remark, nothing untoward would ever have happened, but he did hear it and. . ." *Chü* 俱, *ch'üan* 全, and *tu* 都 may substitute for *chieh.*

Seven instances in six stories. (Hung 3; Hung 4; KC 15; TY 20; HY 21, two; Hsiung A.)

15. *li-pu-te* 離不得 "inevitably," that is, "of course, needless to say."

Thirteen instances in nine stories. (Hung 11; KC 15; KC 36; TY 7; TY 8; TY 14; TY 20, three; TY 37, two; HY 31, two.)

Other expressions:

16. *feng kuo ch'u* 風過處 "when the (divine) wind had passed by."

Twelve instances in six stories. (Hung 3; Hung 8, three; Hung 12, two; KC 24; TY 14, two; HY 21, three.)

17. *t'ien-ti* 田地 "distance," after a measure-word of distance. The expression is generally used in the context of journeys the details of which are glossed over.

Ten instances in five stories. (Hung 2P; Hung 8; Hung 15, three; KC 33, two; TY 37, three.)

There are fourteen additional criteria for the later group. They follow on from the four criteria established in Chapter II.

Formula introducing poem:

(*e*) attribution of a poem in the text of the story to *hou-jen* 後人 "a later writer." There is a variety of formulae which introduce the poem. The formula *hou-jen p'ing ti hao* 後人評得好 "a later writer made this apt assessment" is excluded, as it occurs in two older stories, TY 8 and TY 37.[9]

Fifteen instances in ten stories. One instance in older group (KC 38). (KC 2; TY 1; TY 15; TY 18; TY 21; TY 31; TY 40, six; HY 8; HY 19; HY 29.)

Prespeech, prethought position:

(*f*) *an-hsiang (tao)* 暗想(道) "secretly thought, as follows." *Hsin-li an-hsiang* is not accepted. Note that hitherto *an-hsiang tao* has been considered a variant of *hsiang tao*.[10]

Twelve instances in eight stories. (TY 1; TY 15, two; TY 31, four; HY 8; HY 19; HY 20; HY 29; HY 35.)

(*g*) *hsiang-che (hsiang-chao)* 想着, with or without a following *tao*, "thought, as follows."

Eight instances in seven stories. (KC 2; KC 10; TY 1; TY 5, two★; TY 35; HY 3; HY 20★.)

The passing of time, the setting of time, and so on:

(*h*) *pu i shih* 不一時 "before long."

Eleven instances in seven stories. (TY 31; HY 4; HY 7; HY 17, two; HY 18, three; HY 20, two; HY 35.)

(*i*) *cheng tsai* 正在, followed directly by a predicate and then by a second

---

9 Such phrases do occur in the historical novels of the older period, in particular the *San-kuo yen-i*. Note that there is a real possibility that the phrase has been inserted in KC 38 by a KC editor. This is one of the noticeable additions made to Hung stories reprinted in the *San yen*; it is inserted in KC 7 (adapted from Hung 21) and in TY 33 (adapted from Hung 18). The expression in TY 8 is actually *hou-jen p'ing-lun ti hao*.

10 Thus some of the instances formerly classified as *a* are now to be reclassified as *f*.

clause, "just as (one thing was happening, something else happened)." Expressions like *cheng tsai . . . chih chi* 之際, and those in which an object, even *na-li* 那裏, follows *tsai*, are therefore excluded.

Eleven instances in seven stories. (KC 2, two; TY 5; TY 31; TY 35; HY 4, two; HY 29, three; HY 35.)

(*j*) *tao-(le) wan-shang* 到(了)晚上 or *chih wan-shang* 至晚上 "when evening came."

Seven instances in six stories. (HY 4; HY 8; HY 15; HY 17; HY 18 (*chih*); HY 20, two.)

Narrator's comment on action:

(*k*) *tzu ku tao* 自古道 "from olden times it has been said," introducing a proverb.

Fifteen instances in eleven stories. (KC 10; KC 40; TY 15; TY 31; HY 3, two; HY 8; HY 11; HY 17; HY 19; HY 20, three; HY 29, two.)

(*l*) *tzu pu pi shuo* 自不必說 "it goes without saying," "naturally we don't need to tell how . . ."

Twenty instances in eleven stories. (KC 2, two; KC 40, four; TY 5; TY 18; TY 21; HY 6; HY 15; HY 17, two; HY 19; HY 20, four; HY 35, two.) One instance in the older group (HY 31.)

(*m*) *hsien-hua hsiu-t'i* 閒話休題 "let us cease this idle talk (and get back to the story)." This expression is usually found after a comment by the narrator. *Hsü* 敘 can substitute for *t'i*.

Eight instances in eight stories. (KC 2; KC 10; KC 40; TY 18; . TY 31; HY 4; HY 8; HY 29.) One instance in the older group (HY 31.)

(*n*) *yeh-shih* 也是, followed by a number of similar phrases meaning "it was fated that" or "it was his fate to be . . ."

Thirteen instances in eleven stories. (KC 10, two; KC 40, two; TY 18; TY 35; HY 3; HY 8; HY 15; HY 17; HY 20; HY 29; HY 35.)

(*o*) *tan piao* 單表 "our story is solely concerned with . . ." This formula is often used when the narrator is singling out one person for his tale. It is to be distinguished from *tan piao* after a poem, meaning "this poem is solely concerned with;" the latter *is* found among the earlier stories.

Seven instances in six stories. (TY 32; HY 3; HY 7; HY 11; HY 19; HY 20, two.)

(*p*) reference to the story being told, or about to be told, as (*che*) *chuang ku-shih* (這)椿故事 "this tale."

Five instances in five stories. (KC 2; TY 1; HY 8; HY 18; HY 35.)
Other expressions:

(*q*) *hsin sheng i chi* 心生一計 "thought of a plan."

Thirteen instances in eight stories. (KC 2; KC 10; TY 21, three; TY 35; HY 3, four; HY 7; HY 19; HY 35.)

(*r*) *li-chung* 里中 "in the neighborhood." The word is used normally in connection with a character's reputation.

Eight instances in five stories. (KC 10; TY 18; HY 17, three; HY 18, two; HY 35.)

Tables 1 and 2 show the incidence of separate criteria occurring in the older and newer stories, respectively. The number of instances of a particular criterion in a particular story is not given.

TABLE 1.   Incidence of Separate Criteria in the Pilot Group of Older Stories.

Story	Older criteria	Newer criteria	Total Older to newer	
Ch'ien-t'ang meng	11		1	0
Hung 1	12		1	0
Hung 2P [a]	17		1	0
Hung 2M [b]	5, 7, 1		3	0
Hung 3	16, 5, 14		3	0
Hung 4	9, 14, 2, 3		4	0
Hung 5	1, 2, 8, 6, 12		5	0
Hung 6			0	0
Hung 7	2		1	0
Hung 8	13, 12, 8, 7, 17, 16		6	0
Hung 9			0	0
Hung 10			0	0
Hung 11	15, 12, 11, 1		4	0
Hung 12	4, 12, 11, 16, 2, 3, 5		7	0
Hung 13	1, 6, 9, 13, 8, 4		6	0
Hung 14	1, 2, 8, 10, 6		5	0
Hung 15	11, 12, 1, 5, 8, 4, 17, 6		8	0
Hung 16	1, 9, 12		3	0
Hung 17	4, 2		2	0
Hung 18	3, 4, 9, 8, 1		5	0

TABLE 1—*Continued*

Story	Older criteria	Newer criteria	Total Older to newer	
Hung 19	3, 12, 10, 11, 1		5	0
Hung 20	9, 13, 1, 12, 6		5	0
Hung 21			0	0
Hung 22			0	0
Hung 23			0	0
Hung 24			0	0
Hung 25	5		1	0
Hung 26	13		1	0
Hung 27	12		1	0
Hung 28 c			0	0

(The following are stories apparently referred to in the Pao-wen-t'ang catalogue which have a majority of older criteria.)

Story	Older criteria	Newer criteria	Total Older to newer	
KC 3M	2, 12, 6, 4		4	0
KC 11	11, 7, 6		3	0
KC 15M	13, 5, 1, 15, 11, 14, 8, 12		8	0
KC 24	5, 16		2	0
KC 33M	12, 17, 10, 8, 7, 1		6	0
KC 36P	2		1	0
KC 36M	1, 15, 11, 5		4	0
KC 38	1, 10, 6, 7	e	4	1
TY 8M	13, 15, 11, 12, 9, 8, 4, 5		8	0
TY 20	12, 15, 13, 14, 1, 5		6	0
TY 29	2		1	0
TY 37	17, 7, 5, 15, 4, 12, 1, 6, 8		9	0
HY 31	1, 12, 11, 8, 5, 15, 9, 2	a, m, b, l	8	4
Hsiung A(M)	14, 12, 2, 6		4	0

(The following are the three added stories.)

Story	Older criteria	Newer criteria	Total Older to newer	
TY 7	13, 4, 15, 2, 3		5	0
TY 14M	10, 15, 13, 1, 12, 8, 4, 16, 5		9	0
HY 21	16, 5, 1, 14, 8, 2		6	0

a P = prologue.

b M = main story.

c The text of Hung 29 is not accessible. For a general description, see A Ying, *Hsiao-shuo hsien-hua*, p. 42.

TABLE 2.   Incidence of Separate Criteria in the Pilot Group of Newer Stories.

Story	Older criteria	Newer criteria	Total Older to newer	
KC 40		*a, l, k, n, c, m*	0	6
TY 18M		*m, n, r, b, a, l, e*	0	7
TY 32		*o, a*	0	2
TY 40		*e*	0	1
HY 3M		*o, k, q, c, g, a, b, n*	0	8
HY 18M		*p, a, r, b, d, h, j*	0	7
HY 20		*o, j, k, l, f, h, d, b, a, n, g*	0	11
HY 29		*a, b, f, d, k, i, c★, m, n, e*	0	10
HY 35M		*p, d, i, l, c, a, q, n, b, f, h, r*	0	12

(The following are the sixteen added stories.)

Story	Older criteria	Newer criteria	Total Older to newer	
KC 2M		*p, q, a, b, g, l, m, i, e*	0	9
KC 10M		*n, k, b, g, q, a, m, r*	0	8
TY 1		*p, a, b, g★, c★, f, e*	0	7
TY 5M		*a, c, l, g★*	0	4
TY 15M	13	*f, c★, a, b, k, e*	1	6
TY 21M	11	*a, q, c, l, e*	1	5
TY 31		*k, m, f, b, h, c★, i, a, e*	0	9
TY 35		*a, g, n, i, q, c, b*	0	7
HY 4M		*j, d, h, i, b, m*	0	6
HY 6M		*d, b, l*	0	3
HY 7	8	*o, a, q, b, i, h*	1	6
HY 8		*p, m, k, a, b, d, f, j, n, e*	0	10
HY 11M		*o, k, b, a*	0	4
HY 15M		*a, j, d, b, c, n, l*	0	7
HY 17		*k, a, b, n, r, j, d, h, l*	0	9
HY 19		*o, a, k, c, b, f, q, l, e*	0	9

Application of the Criteria

In classifying the rest of the stories, it seems reasonable to set the following conditions: For a story to be classified as older, it must contain instances of at least three separate older criteria and no instances of a newer criterion;

if it does contain newer criteria, they must be outnumbered by older criteria in the ratio of at least four to one. For a story to be considered newer, the conditions will be exactly reversed. Note that in Table 3 prologues and main stories are still regarded as separate items.

The two versions of the *Chang Yü-hu* story have considerable textual differences, but both qualify as older. The version appearing in the respective *Yen-chü pi-chi* edited by Ho, Lin, and Yü and in the *Wan-chin ch'ing-lin* has five older criteria (10, 11, 5, 14, 2) and no newer criteria, while the *Kuo-se t'ien-hsiang* has three older criteria only (11, 5, 2). For further discussion of this story, see below, on the stories referred to in the Pao-wen-t'ang catalogue.

The number of stories classified as older is eleven, as shown in Table 3.

TABLE 3.   Stories Classified as Older.

Story	Older criteria	Newer criteria	Total Older to newer	
			Older	to newer
KC 29[a]	11, 2*, 3		3	0
TY 13	4, 10, 1		3	0
TY 16	1, 9, 10, 13, 12, 2		6	0
TY 19	13, 1, 9, 10, 5, 14, 16		7	0
TY 28	12, 1, 14, 9, 8, 11, 5, 16	c, n	8	2
TY 36M[b]	12, 1, 13, 17, 10		5	0
TY 39	1, 12, 4, 16, 14	i	5	1
HY 14	1, 14, 15, 2*, 12, 5, 8	b	7	1
Hsiung D	12, 11, 9		3	0
P'ei Hsiu-niang yeh yu Hsi-hu chi[c]	12, 2, 3		3	0

[a] There are other versions of this story. See below.

[b] *Ssu-hsiang* on page 551 may mean "thought about" or "wanted to," not "thought, as follows."

[c] It is preserved in two of the miscellanies. For details, see below.

The number classified as newer is forty-five, including three prologues, as shown in Table 4.[11]

TABLE 4.   Stories Classified as Newer.

Story	Older criteria	Newer criteria	Total Older to newer	
			Older to newer	
KC 1	6	$o, m, l, n, c\star, i, g\star,$ a, b	1	9
KC 5	12	$o, k, g\star, c\star, i, r, e$	1	7
KC 6M		$l, o, k, a, g\star, e$	0	6
KC 8		e, a, g, l, c, r	0	6
KC 12M	12	$p, q, k, g\star, e$	1	5
KC 13		a, p, m, e	0	4
KC 17	2★	p, i, l, e	1	4
KC 18M a		m, l, a, n	0	4
KC 21	1	$e, n, r, q, g\star, k, a, l, i$	1	9
KC 22M	2★	n, c, i, a, q, h, l, m	1	8
KC 27M		m, r, a, q	0	4
KC 28M	2★	c, g, k, m	1	4
KC 31		a, q, e	0	3

11 We have not looked into the short-story collections by individual authors to see whether they may have included the occasional earlier story. Sun K'ai-ti, in his *Chung-kuo t'ung-su hsiao-shuo shu-mu*, and T'an Cheng-pi, in his *Hua-pen yü ku-chü*, claim that several stories in the *Shih tien t'ou*, the *P'ai-an ching-ch'i* collections, and the *Hsi-hu erh-chi* 西湖二集, are not by the authors of those collections and that some of the stories belong to the older period. (The *Hsi-hu erh-chi* is a collection of stories by the late-Ming author Chou Chi 周楫. See the Shanghai, 1936 edition.) The grounds for the belief are either apparent reference in the Pao-wen-t'ang catalogue or in Lo Yeh's *Tsui-weng t'an-lu* (the pitfalls of which have been pointed out by Hanan in "Sung and Yüan Vernacular Fiction") or statements by the stories themselves that they derive from storytellers' tales. In fact, all of these claims can be disproved. The two stories T'an and Sun claim are referred to by the Pao-wen-t'ang catalogue will be dealt with below. Sun also claims that two stories in the *P'ai-an ching-ch'i* collections are not by Ling Meng-ch'u. He considers *Ch'u-k'e* 28 may be the story, apparently on the same subject, which is referred to in the *Tsui-weng t'an-lu*. (See *Chung-kuo t'ung-su hsiao-shuo shu-mu*, p. 14.) The story's prologue, of course, cannot be early; it mentions the "Wan-li period of our dynasty." In terms of our criteria, the main story has one older (10) and two newer criteria (*m, g★*). It also refers to the *San-yüan chi* 三元記, which is presumably the early-Ming play by Shen Shou-hsien 沈受先 rather than one of the other two known plays of that title. Since the *Tsui-weng t'an-lu*'s edition appears to be pre-Ming, its reference cannot be to this story. Because the main story of *Erh-k'e* 29 claims to be storytellers' material and includes a title different from the title given it by the collection, Sun thinks it may not be by Ling Meng-ch'u. (See p. 88.) There is little question about its being a later story; it contains three later criteria (*f, q, l*) to one borderline instance of 6. But even a superficial examination shows that it is likely to be by Ling. For example, it contains several instances of *erh-chin* 而今 "now," a feature of his writing.

TABLE 4—*Continued*

Story	Older criteria	Newer criteria	Older to newer	
			Total	
TY 3M		*b, l, f, e*	0	4
TY 11P		*a, c, f*	0	3
TY 11M[b]	6	*p, n, a, i, g★, q, l, k,* *b, h, e*	1	11
TY 12M		*k, n, l*	0	3
TY 17M		*r, a, i, e*	0	4
TY 22		*l, i, a, k, r, f, q, n, e*	0	9
TY 23M		*a, f, l*	0	3
TY 24	2	*f, b, q, n, a, l, i*	1	7
TY 25		*r, e, n, b★*	0	4
TY 26		*k, l, a*	0	3
TY 34M		*i, l, q, m, b*	0	5
HY 1M		*p, o, m, c, h, a, l, e*	0	8
HY 2M		*c, r, e*	0	3
HY 5P		*q, a, e*	0	3
HY 5M	6	*k, a, q, g★*	1	4
HY 9M		*l, k, r, m, n, g*	0	6
HY 10M	11	*l, a, h, d*	1	4
HY 16M		*h, b, j, a, c*	0	5
HY 22		*n, b★, a, i*	0	4
HY 23		*a, n, i, q, e*	0	5
HY 25M	12	*l, k, a, j, b*	1	5
HY 26		*a, b, i, h, d*	0	5
HY 27M	17	*a, d, f, m, b, q, i, c,* *n, l, e*	1	11
HY 28M		*q, h, f, b, d, a, g★, i*	0	8
HY 30	13	*c, d, a, b, i, h, l, k, q*	1	9
HY 32		*a, h, q, k, n, i*	0	6
HY 34M	14	*o, k, a, b, h, d, l, i,* *m, q, n*	1	11
HY 36		*d, a, b, i, f, c★, h, l*	0	8
HY 37c		*b, a, i, d, c, f*	0	6
HY 38		*h, a, b*	0	3
HY 39P		*b, a, d*	0	3
HY 39M		*n, h, a, q*	0	4

a The example of *hao-ssu* on page 260 of KC 18 is not included, since it comes right in the middle of a sentence.

b The word *i-wen* 異聞 appears here in place of the *ku-shih* of criterion *p*.

c Here and elsewhere, *an-an hsiang-tao* is counted as *f*.

Reassessment of the Criteria

It is important to check the effectiveness of our criteria before we consider the stories which we have not so far been able to classify.

In Table 5, which compares the effectiveness of the older criteria, column 1 lists the criteria; column 2 gives the number of stories in which the criterion appears from among the twenty-eight Hung stories and the *Ch'ien-t'ang meng;* column 3 gives the number of stories from among the fourteen apparently referred to in the Pao-wen-t'ang catalogue; column 4 gives the number of stories from among the three added ones; column 5 gives the number from among the stories just classified as older; column 6 gives the total number of older stories in which the criterion appears, that is, the sum

TABLE 5.   Comparative Effectiveness of the Older Criteria.

	Incidence in older stories						Total	
Criterion	Original group	Pao-wen-t'ang	Added group	Just classi-fied	Total older	Incidence in newer stories	Older to newer	
1	10	7	2	7	26	KC 21	26	1
2	6	5	2	5	18	KC 22, KC 28, TY 24	18	3
3	4	0	1	2	7		7	0
4	5	3	2	2	12		12	0
5	5	7	2	4	18		18	0
6	5	5	0	0	10	KC 1, TY 11, HY 5	10	3
7	2	4	0	0	6		6	0
8	6	5	2	2	15	HY 7	15	1
9	5	2	0	4	11		11	0
10	2	2	1	5	10		10	0
11	5	5	0	4	14	TY 21, HY 10	14	2
12	10	8	1	7	26	KC 5, KC 12, HY 25	26	3
13	4	3	2	3	12	TY 15, HY 30	12	2
14	2	3	1	5	11	HY 34	11	1
15	1	6	2	1	10		10	0
16	3	1	2	3	9	HY 4	9	1
17	3	2	0	1	6	HY 27	6	1
Size of groups	29	14	3	11	57			

of the previous four columns; column 7 lists the newer stories in which the criterion appears; and columns 8 and 9 juxtapose the totals of older and newer stories, respectively.

Among the ten stories just classified as older, it is the *Yen-chü pi-chi* version of the Chang Yü-hu story that is used, not the *Kuo-se t'ien-hsiang* version.

The table shows that the least effective criteria are, in order, nos. 6, 2, 13, 17, and 11. The classification of three stories, KC 29, Hsiung D, and *P'ei Hsiu-niang yeh yu Hsi-hu chi*, depends largely on these less effective criteria, and the case for considering them older is consequently weakened. Later sections discuss these stories further.

In Table 6, comparing the effectiveness of the newer criteria, column 1 gives the criterion; column 2 gives the number of stories in which it occurs

TABLE 6.   Comparative Effectiveness of the Newer Criteria.

Criterion	Incidence in newer stories				Incidence in older stories	Total	
	Original group	Added group	Recently classified	Total newer		Newer to older	
a	8	14	35	57	HY 31	57	1
b	6	14	18	38	HY 14, HY 31	38	2
c	4	8	13	25	TY 28	25	1
d	4	5	9	18		18	0
e	3	7	18	28	KC 38	28	1
f	3	5	9	17		17	0
g	2	5	11	18		18	0
h	3	4	13	20		20	0
i	2	5	20	27	TY 39	27	1
j	2	4	2	8		8	0
k	4	7	15	26		26	0
l	4	7	23	34	HY 31	34	1
m	3	5	11	19	HY 31	19	1
n	6	5	16	27	TY 28	27	1
o	3	3	5	11		11	0
p	2	3	5	10		10	0
q	2	6	18	26		26	0
r	3	2	9	14		14	0
Size of groups	9	16	45[a]	70			

[a] This figure includes three prologues.

from among the original group of nine; column 3 gives the number from among the added group of sixteen; column 4 gives the number from among the recently classified stories and prologues; column 5 gives the total number of newer stories in which the criterion appears, the sum of the preceding three columns; column 6 lists the older stories in which it appears; and columns 7 and 8 juxtapose the totals of newer and older stories, respectively.

The table shows that all of the criteria are effective, remarkably so, since, as will be shown later, some of the instances in older stories are the result of late editorial emendation.

It is a useful precaution to see how our additional criteria work in the tests used in Chapter II on the original criteria.

In the first test, we find that they work about as well as the original criteria. In the changed passages, one older criterion has disappeared, an instance of 9 in KC 4.[12] (adapted from Hung 20). In the added passages, four instances of newer criteria are found, an l in KC 4,[13] a g in KC 30[14] (adapted from Hung 13), an e in KC 7 (adapted from Hung 21) and another e in TY 33 (adapted from Hung 18). No older criteria have been added to the *San yen* versions.[15]

The second test is not applicable, since the additional criteria are, in part, based on the stories referred to in the Pao-wen-t'ang catalogue.

The third test concerned two collections of stories by individual late-Ming authors. The first ten stories of the *P'ai-an ching-ch'i* contain twenty-two instances of newer criteria (e; two f; g; seven i; four l; m; five n; r) and five instances of older criteria (four 7, 9). It appears that 7 is a characteristic feature of this writer's style. In total, the stories show thirty-eight instances of newer criteria to six older.[16]

The first five stories of the other collection, the *Shih tien t'ou*, show twenty-four instances of newer criteria (four e; seven f; two g; h; k; l; m; three n; p; three q) to three older (three 7).[17] In total, these stories contain forty instances of newer criteria to three older. In terms of our criteria, all five would easily qualify as newer stories.

---

12 It is changed to a neutral form. See p. 81.

13 KC 4, p. 88.

14 KC 30, p. 456.

15 Note that in the KC 4 adaptation of Hung 20 an instance of criterion 6 has been shifted, when the poem it prefixed was deleted, to another neighboring poem that lacked a prefixed introduction. See Hung 20, p. 256. Furthermore, the Hung version of the story is incomplete; the last pages have been lost. Evidently the KC editor had a complete text, for two earlier criteria (14, 6) are found in the corresponding part of KC 4.

16 Note that a few of the instances previously classified as a have been reclassified as f; hence the total falls a little short of the sum of the instances of the original and additional criteria.

17 Two instances of criterion 11 with *su* 宿 in place of *chu* are not counted.

In the twenty-chapter "early" *P'ing-yao chuan*, we find thirteen instances of the additional older criteria (three 7; two 9; 12; two 13; 14; four 16) and two of the additional newer criteria (*k, q*).[18] In total, this text has forty-two instances of older criteria to four newer. On the other hand, the first fifteen chapters of the forty-chapter *P'ing-yao chuan*, chapters which are presumed to be by Feng Meng-lung, contain forty-four instances of newer criteria (four *e;* nine *f;* five *g;* three *h;* eight *i; k;* four *l;* three *m; n;* two *o; p;* three *q*) and only four older (11, 12, two 16).[19] In sum, the instances of newer and older criteria are sixty-one and five, respectively.

The first ten chapters of the *Shui-hu chuan* provide a result as indecisive as before. There are ten instances of additional older criteria (7; three 11; 12; three 13; 16; 17) and four newer (*k; l;* two *n*), all of the latter occurring in chapter 2.[20] The twenty added chapters, 91 through 110, again show a preponderance of newer criteria; there are thirty-three instances of the additional newer criteria (*e; f;* two *g;* twenty-six *i;* three *n*) to six older (three 10; 12; 13; 14).[21] In sum, there are now forty-seven instances of newer criteria to seven older in these chapters.

Thus, although the additional criteria are not quite as effective as the original criteria, they work reasonably well. (The exception is criterion 7, but it should be noted that so far no story has been classified with the aid of this criterion.) Of the newer stories considered, none would have been classified as older according to our criteria, while most would have been classified as newer. None of them has a majority of older criteria over newer.

The Prologues

For the purposes of classification, we have considered the prologues separately. This was necessary as a precaution against the possibility that prologue and main story might have been written by different authors at different times. (Two prologues also survive as independent stories.) Nevertheless, there is a strong likelihood that, in most cases, prologue and main story will have originated together, and we shall assume that where the

---

18 One instance of criterion *k* with *le* 了 is not counted.

19 All of the older features occur in the last three chapters before Feng begins copying the old *P'ing-yao chuan*. Three of the older features (6, 11, 12) are among those we have recognized as the least effective.

20 Three of the instances occur within a page of each other.

21 There are four instances of *shih pu pi shuo* 是不必說, which may stand to criterion *l* as *wu-shih* 兀是, the common form in these chapters, stands to the normal *wu-tzu* 兀自. Note that criterion 14 is among the formulae that close the chapter.

criteria of the prologue do not actually contradict those of the stories already classified, prologue and main story are of the same period and, by a further assumption, *probably by the same author.* That is to say, if a prologue has no criteria of either variety, or if the majority of its criteria accord with those of its main story, it will be taken as belonging with its main story.

Because the text of the Hung stories is older, any prologues they contain have already been taken as such. The prologues attached to the rest of the older pilot group all qualify as older:

No criteria: prologues to KC 3, KC 33, TY 8, TY 14.

Older criteria only: prologues to KC 15 (criterion 13), Hsiung A (criterion 12). The prologue to KC 36 was included in the older pilot group in its own right, as a story referred to in the Pao-wen-t'ang catalogue.

All of the prologues attached to the newer pilot group also qualify as newer:

No criteria: prologues to TY 18, HY 3, HY 35, KC 10, TY 21, HY 15.

Newer criteria only: prologues to KC 2(a), TY 5(a, i), TY 15 (o, l, a), HY 4 (h, d), HY 6 (d, i), HY 18(a, b, h), HY 11(o).

Among the stories classified as older, only TY 36 has a prologue. It has no criteria.

Among the stories classified as newer, all but one of the prologues also qualify as newer.

No criteria: prologues to KC 18, KC 27, TY 3, TY 17, TY 34, HY 2, HY 9, HY 10, HY 28.

Newer criteria only: prologues to KC 6(a), KC 12(e), KC 22(n), KC 28(e), TY 12(i), HY 1(a), HY 16(r), HY 25(l), HY 27(l), HY 34(g, i).

Three prologues, those to TY 11, HY 5, and HY 39, have already qualified as newer with the requisite number of criteria.

The sole exception so far to the matching of prologue with main story is provided by TY 23. The main story was classified as newer, with three newer criteria to no older. The prologue, however, has two older criteria (13, 3) and no newer. This problem will be taken up in a later section.

Stories Referred to in the Pao-wen-t'ang Catalogue

There is also a strong presumption as to date of composition in the case of another group of stories: those referred to, or apparently referred to, in the Pao-wen-t'ang catalogue. We are now in a position to confirm or reject the identifications made by earlier scholars, especially those of T'an Cheng-pi[22] and Sun K'ai-ti,[23] and to make new identifications of our own.

No confirmation is needed, of course, by the twenty-four Hung stories listed in the catalogue. In addition, we can accept all of the references to stories in the older pilot group: KC 3, KC 11, KC 15, KC 24, KC 33, KC 36, KC 38, TY 8, TY 20, TY 29, TY 37, HY 31, and Hsiung A. The entry San meng seng chi 三夢僧記 in the catalogue was identified by Wu Hsiao-ling 吳曉鈴 as KC 3,[24] whereas T'an Cheng-pi thought that it might be HY 25;[25] it could not have been the latter, since HY 25 proves to be a newer story, and Wu's guess is corroborated. Such prologues as exist do not conflict with the dating of the main stories, and we may assume that the catalogue reference is to both prologue and main story together.

The reference to the Lü-chu chi 綠珠記 can also be accepted. Evidently it existed as a separate story in the Pao-wen-t'ang library, just as it still exists separately in a number of miscellanies, as well as in the form of the prologue to KC 36. Although the story had an independent existence in the Pao-wen-t'ang library, we cannot necessarily conclude that it was combined with the main story of KC 36 at a late date.

The reference to the Chang Yü-hu wu su nü-kuan chi 張于湖誤宿女觀記 can also be accepted. This story exists in two somewhat different versions, one in the Kuo-se t'ien-hsiang, and the other in the Yen-chü pi-chi and Wan-chin ch'ing-lin miscellanies. Since the latter version has five older criteria, two of which are omitted in the former, we can conclude that the Yen-chü pi-chi version is closer to the original and that the other is an abridgement of it.

The entry Hsiao chin-ch'ien chi 小金錢記 has been thought by some scholars to refer to TY 16,[26] the title of which is Hsiao fu-jen chin-ch'ien tseng nien-shao 小夫人金錢贈年少. I have resisted this identification so far, because it is hard to see how the former could be a meaningful abridgement of the latter. However, the story has qualified as older, with six older criteria to one newer criterion, and one is tempted to accept this identification, despite the obscurity of the reference.

Six stories not accepted in Chapter II as older because they did not have a preponderance of the original older criteria now need to be reassessed.

22 Hua-pen yü ku-chü, pp. 38–60.
23 Chung-kuo t'ung-su hsiao-shuo shu-mu, pp. 79–83.
24 See Han-hiue 2.4 (1949), p. 445. This speculation is also noted by Sun K'ai-ti, Chung-kuo t'ung-su hsiao-shuo shu-mu, p. 82.
25 Hua-pen yü ku-chü, p. 53.
26 T'an Cheng-pi, Hua-pen yü ku-chü, p. 41.

They are: KC 25, KC 26, HY 13, HY 33, Hsiung B, Hsiung D. In terms of our criteria, they come out as follows:

KC 25, no criteria.

KC 26, four older criteria (8, 9, 11, 1), and two newer (*n*, *a*).

HY 13, one older criterion (14), and one newer (*a*).

HY 33P, no criteria.

HY 33M, one older criterion (17), and two newer (*m*, *q*).

Hsiung B, one older criterion (13), and no newer.

Hsiung D, three older criteria (12, 11, 9), and no newer.

Hsiung D qualifies as an older story, and the reference can be accepted. If we apply to these stories the same standards as to the prologues in the last section, we can accept KC 25, KC 26, and Hsiung B as the older stories referred to in the catalogue. No such conclusion can be reached about HY 13 and HY 33. It will be argued in the next section that both are older stories which have been considerably adapted by a late editor. The Pao-wen-t'ang reference is therefore, presumably, to the earlier form of these stories prior to their adaptation.

This is a convenient place to note how the additional criteria provide a striking confirmation of the verdict of the original criteria. In the second test of Chapter II, the following stories were the only ones among those apparently referred to in the catalogue which had any of the original newer criteria (that is, *a* through *d*), or which lacked older criteria entirely:

KC 25 none.

KC 26 one newer.

HY 13 one newer.

HY 16 three newer.

HY 31 two newer.

HY 33 none.

Now if we look at the stories referred to in the catalogue in the light of the additional criteria, we find that the only stories which have any of the additional newer criteria are:

KC 15 one additional newer.

KC 26 one additional newer.

KC 38 one additional newer.

HY 16 two additional newer, qualifying as a newer story.

HY 31 two additional newer.

HY 33 two additional newer.

That is to say, there is an extraordinary correlation between the incidence of the original newer criteria and that of the additional newer criteria.

One other existing identification can be accepted, though not in quite the form in which it is presented. The reference to the *Tu Li-niang chi* 杜麗娘記 is held to be to a story in Classical Chinese which exists in two of the works that are entitled *Yen-chü pi-chi*.[27] Sun K'ai-ti, on whose description of these texts scholars rely, has not noticed that one of the versions is in the form of a vernacular short story and has labelled it a Classical Chinese tale like the other. Although the two are textually related, the language of the one is closer to the vernacular, while the other is closer to Classical. The problem is to decide which is the earlier form of the story; was it a Classical tale rewritten as a vernacular short story, or a short story rewritten as a tale? For a number of reasons, I believe that the latter is the case and that the vernacular version is closer to the original form of the story. First, the tale contains more of the formulae of the short story than one would expect to find; this is consistent with the explanation that the tale is the adapted form and that the adaptation of the language is not complete. Second, the short story has the only instances of any of our criteria, and both of them are older, an instance of 2 and a rather questionable instance of 9. Third, and most important, if we compare the text of the four other stories that the Ho and Yü miscellanies hold in common, we find that, in two cases, the version in the miscellany edited by Ho Ta-lun is more vernacular and closer to what appears to be the original form of the story; in the case of the remainder, there is no distinction to be made. Ho Ta-lun is the editor of the *Yen-chü pi-chi* in which the short-story version of the *Tu Li-niang chi* appears; the changes made in it would be entirely consistent with those made in the other two stories. We may therefore tentatively accept the short-story version of it as the one referred to in the Pao-wen-t'ang catalogue and add it to our list of older stories.

One new identification can be made. The entry *Hung-lien chi* 紅蓮記 may be taken to refer to KC 29, a story which has qualified as older. In both Hung 13 (adapted as KC 30) and KC 29 the heroine is named Hung-lien, but the Hung 13 story has already been referred to independently and unambiguously in the catalogue as *Wu-chieh Ch'an-shih ssu Hung-lien* 五戒禪師私紅蓮, and this reference is therefore probably to the other story. It is worth noting that in the *Yen-chü pi-chi* versions of this story, the short title, found in the margins, is *Hung-lien*.

Certain common identifications can be *rejected*.

The supposed reference to HY 16 must be rejected. According to our

27 It appears in *chüan* 9 of the *Yen-chü pi-chi* edited by Ho Ta-lun and in *chüan* 8 of the *Yen-chü pi-chi* edited by Yü Kung-jen.

criteria, HY 16 qualifies as a newer story. As we shall see in Chapter IV, there is good reason to consider it a very late story.

The identification of the entry *Feng Yü-mei chi* 馮玉梅記 with TY 12 depended on the assumption that the *Ching-pen t'ung-su hsiao-shuo* story of that title had been severely adapted, including the name of the heroine, by the TY editor. Since the *Ching-pen* is in fact based on the *San yen*, there is no need to take the identification seriously. It is interesting, nonetheless, to note that this story actually qualifies as a newer story, with three newer criteria and no older.

The identification of the title *Yü-hsiao-nü liang-shih yin-yüan* 玉簫女兩世 姻緣 with the ninth story of the *Shih tien t'ou* 石點頭 collection can also be rejected.[28] That story has eight newer criteria (*b, a, g, d, f, h, c★, l*) to one older criterion (7★).

Similarly, the identification of the title *Hsing Feng Tz'u-chün T'ang yü-hsien chuan* 邢鳳此君堂遇仙傳 with the fourteenth story of the *Hsi-hu erh-chi* 西湖二集 collection cannot be upheld.[29] That story has none of our criteria, older or newer, but there are indications that it is a newer story.[30]

The entry *Li Ya-hsien chi* 李亞仙記 may not refer to the story *Cheng Yüan-ho p'iao-yü Li Ya-hsien chi* 鄭元和嫖遇李亞仙記 which appears in two versions of the *Yen-chü pi-chi*.[31] There is another story on this theme, in the inaccessible *Hsiao-shuo ch'uan-ch'i* collection, which has an equal right to be the object of the Pao-wen-t'ang reference.[32]

The entry *Kuo Han yü hsien* 郭翰遇仙 may well refer to the story in the Yü Kung-jen version of the *Yen-chü pi-chi*.[33] But that story is entirely in simple Classical Chinese, and does not qualify as a short story.

A Note on the Priority of Texts

As listed in Chapter I, there are twenty-five stories which exist in two

---

28 T'an Cheng-pi, *Hua-pen yü ku-chü*, p. 51, and Sun K'ai-ti, *Chung-kuo t'ung-su hsiao-shuo shu-mu*, p. 83, both make this identification.

29 See *Hua-pen yü ku-chü*, p. 52, and *Chung-kuo t'ung-su hsiao-shuo shu-mu*, p. 83. This is a famous story, for which there are half a dozen possible sources in Classical fiction.

30 It contains a secondary criterion, *tsai-hsia*, for which see below.

31 See *Hua-pen yü ku-chü*, p. 52, and *Chung-kuo t'ung-su hsiao-shuo shu-mu*, p. 9. The same version also appears, incomplete owing to faulty printing, in *chüan* 5 of the *Yen-chü pi-chi* edited by Lin Chin-yang. The question of the story's date is considered below.

32 See Lu Kung, *Ming-Ch'ing p'ing-hua hsiao-shuo hsüan*, preface, p. 5. Lu Kung claims that it differs from the other story and that it is a "*hua-pen* from Sung or Yüan time." The claim about date was presumably based on the kind of prima facie considerations discussed and rejected in Hanan, "Sung and Yüan Vernacular Fiction."

33 See *Hua-pen yü ku-chü*, p. 53. *Chung-kuo t'ung-su hsiao-shuo shu-mu*, p. 86, lists this among the titles of vernacular stories no longer extant.

or more pre-1628 editions.[34] Although it is far beyond the scope of this study to produce a critical text of these stories, it seems worthwhile to indicate, where possible, which is the "best text" of a story, that is, the text that represents its earliest form. And for scholarly work, it may also be important to know which text is the second best. These questions can be decided in general terms, without going into the matter of precise textual derivation.

The alternative texts of two stories, TY 1 and HY 11, are inaccessible. A third, the *T'ieh-shu chi*, is available in an edition with the original author's preface, and is obviously a better text than TY 40. The alternative texts of the remaining twenty stories are found principally in the following works:

The Hung collections (approximately 1550).

The Hsiung Lung-feng stories (probably about 1590).[35]

Ch'üan-pu Pao Lung-t'u p'an pai-chia kung-an, 1594.

Ku-chin hsiao-shuo, between 1620 and 1624.

Ching-shih t'ung-yen, 1624.

Kuo-se t'ien-hsiang. There is a 1587 edition.[36] (*Kuo-se.*)

Wan-chin ch'ing-lin 萬錦情林. There is a 1598 edition.[37] (*Wan-chin.*)

Hsiu-ku ch'un-jung 繡谷春容, also known as *Chüeh-she t'an-yüan* 嚼麝譚苑. There is a Wan-li edition.[38] (*Hsiu-ku.*)

Yen-chü pi-chi, edited by Lin Chin-yang 林近陽. There is a Ming edition.[39]

Yen-chü pi-chi, edited by Ho Ta-lun 何大掄. There is a very early Ch'ing edition.[40]

Yen-chü pi-chi, edited by Yü Kung-jen 余公仁. There is an early Ch'ing edition.[41]

Where the Hung collections and the *San yen* have stories in common, we have assumed that the Hung version is the better one, and the assump-

---

34 I am assuming that versions after the time of the *San yen* will depart further from the original than the *San yen* versions. One example must suffice. *Hsi-hu chia-hua* 西湖佳話 15 has a version of TY 28, but, though textually related to TY 28, it is obviously a late adaptation. It has three newer criteria (*i, f, q*) to only one older (8), as well as other indications of late composition. By contrast, TY 28 itself has eight older criteria, including (8), to two newer criteria.

35 See Chapter I, n. 10.

36 Preserved in the Naikaku Bunko. It has a preface dated 1587.

37 Preserved in the Chinese Literature Department, Tokyo University.

38 Preserved in the Sōkōdō 雙紅堂, formerly Nagasawa Kikuya's private collection, in the Tōyō Bunka Kenkyūjo, Tokyo University. The Library of Congress also has a copy.

39 Preserved in the Naikaku Bunko.

40 Preserved in the Naikaku Bunko. The Harvard-Yenching Library also has a copy.

41 Preserved in the Zushoryō of the Kunaishō in Tokyo.

tion has been borne out by our results so far. This accounts for nine of the twenty-two stories (Hung 2, 5, 12, 14, 18, 20, 21, 22, 27).

Hung 9 appears as Hsiung C, and also appears in the *Kuo-se t'ien-hsiang*.[42] Hung 9 and Hsiung C differ somewhat, but the *Kuo-se* text is clearly derived from the former. The largest difference between the Hung and Hsiung versions consists of a piece of text amounting to exactly two double pages which is missing in Hung 9.[43] Obviously the Hsiung text is the better text in general, though in places other than this lacuna there may be little to choose between them.

Hsiung A appears as KC 23. The Hsiung version has an instance of an older criterion, 6, which is changed to a neutral form in KC 23, indicating that, as might be expected, Hsiung A is the better text.

Where the Hung collections and the *Pai-chia kung-an* have stories in common, the Hung version is the better. The *Pai-chia kung-an*'s version of Hung 4, number 27, *Cheng p'an ming ho-t'ung wen-tzu* 拯判明合同文字, introduces no newer criteria but changes two instances of 3 to neutral forms. Its version of Hung 8, number 29, *P'an Liu hua-yüan ch'u san kuai* 判劉花園除三怪, changes one neutral form to an older criterion (2), which proved one of the weakest of the older criteria, and reduces another older criterion (16) to a neutral form. Three other older criteria (7, 8, 12) are lost when their contexts are omitted.

Hung 1 appears also in the *Hsiu-ku ch'un-jung*, in the Ho, Lin, and Yü versions of the *Yen-chü pi-chi*, and in the *Wan-chin ch'ing-lin*.[44] The differences are fairly small. The texts in the miscellanies are closer to each other than they are to Hung 1. Of the four, the Ho *Yen-chü pi-chi* is the closest to Hung 1; for example, it labels its introductory poem *ju-hua* in the manner of the Hung stories. With little evidence to go on, we must take Hung as the best text and Ho as the next best.

Hung 13 appears as KC 30, with an added prologue and an enlarged ending. The changes have been made by a late editor, most likely Feng Meng-lung. The story appears also in the *Hsiu-ku ch'un-jung* and in the Yü version of the *Yen-chü pi-chi*.[45] The Yü and *Hsiu-ku* texts share some features, but the *Hsiu-ku* is closer to Hung 13 and, in some trivial respects, is an even fuller text than Hung 13. The KC 30 text, if one ignores its prologue and ending,[46] is the closest to Hung 13 and may well be based upon it.

---

42 *Chüan* 8.
43 See Lévy, "Etudes," pp. 107–110.
44 See *Hsiu-ku, chüan* 4; Ho, *chüan* 10; Lin, *chüan* 6; Yü, *chüan* 7; *Wan-chin, chüan* 1. The Ho version lacks the last page or so.
45 See *Hsiu-ku, chüan* 12, in which the story is left incomplete, and Yü, *chüan* 9.
46 See Hanan, "Authorship," p. 195.

We must take Hung as the best text and the relevant part of KC 30 as the second best.

KC 29 also appears in the *Hsiu-ku ch'un-jung* and in the Ho and Yü versions of the *Yen-chü pi-chi*.[47] The last three lack the final pages of KC 29 and seem to end rather abruptly, with a shameless suggestion to the reader: "Reader, if you wish to know all the details, please read the *Yüeh-ming Ho-shang tu Liu Ts'ui* 月明和尚度柳翠." One would naturally expect the three short versions to be abridgements of an original text like that of KC 29, but the relationship proves to be more complicated. The extra sections of KC 29 appear to have been based on two adjacent passages in the *Hsi-hu yu-lan chih* 西湖遊覽志, the same source which supplied the prologue of KC 30, and the most likely explanation is that Feng Meng-lung took the hint contained in the suggestion given above and proceeded to supplement the story with the aid of a written source.[48] Thus, there may have been an original long version, which was curtailed in a second version. This second version would have been the common ancestor of the three versions found in the miscellanies. By this explanation, Feng Meng-lung took the second version and expanded it.[49]

If we exclude the final added sections of KC 29, and compare the rest of its text with that of the other three versions, we find it to be fuller than any of them. Ho is the closest to it, preserving the short-story opening with its *hua shuo*, and so on, as it preserved the *ju-hua* in the other case. Of this story, then, KC 29, if shorn of its added passages, provides the best text, and Ho the next best.

The *Tu Li-niang chi* appears in the Ho and Yü versions of *Yen-chü pi-chi*.[50] The Ho version is in the form of a vernacular short story, while the Yü version, though it makes some concession to short-story formulae, is really a Classical tale. I have already argued above that the Ho version represents the earlier form of the story.

The *Chang Yü-hu* story appears in *Kuo-se t'ien-hsiang*, *Wan-chin ch'ing-lin*, and in the Lin, Ho, and Yü versions of *Yen-chü pi-chi*.[51] As explained above, there is a clear distinction between the *Kuo-se t'ien-hsiang* version on the one hand, and the *Yen-chü pi-chi* and *Wan-chin ch'ing-lin* versions on the other, and we have shown that the former is probably an abridgement of the latter. The Lin, Ho, and Yü versions differ only slightly

---

47 See *Hsiu-ku*, *chüan* 8; Ho, *chüan* 9; Yü, *chüan* 8.
48 See "Authorship," pp. 196–197.
49 KC 29 has an extra instance of an older criterion, a 3 on p. 430.
50 Ho, *chüan* 9; Yü, *chüan* 8.
51 *Kuo-se*, *chüan* 10; Lin, *chüan* 6; Ho, *chüan* 9; Yü, *chüan* 7; *Wan-chin*, *chüan* 1.

amongst each other, but for reasons given above, the Lin or Ho versions should probably be preferred to the Yü version.

KC 36P also appears in the Lin, Ho, and Yü versions of *Yen-chü pi-chi*.[52] Among the four versions, there are minor differences only. Judging from our experience with other stories, we should probably take KC 36P as the best text (ignoring perhaps the passage which links it to the main story) and the Ho and Lin versions as the next best.

The *P'ei Hsiu-niang* story appears in both the *Wan-chin ch'ing-lin* and the Lin version of *Yen-chü pi-chi*.[53] The latter is incomplete, lacking most of the text in the last third of the story owing to faulty printing.[54] But the text it does have is fuller than that of the *Wan-chin*, and it clearly represents the better version.

The *Ch'ien-t'ang meng* also appears in the Lin version of *Yen-chü pi-chi*.[55] Although there are minor differences only, the 1498 edition, because it is so much older, should be preferred.

The *Cheng Yüan-ho* story appears in both the Lin and Yü versions of the *Yen-chü pi-chi*. The differences are slight, but the Lin text is probably the better.

In general, this hasty survey confirms the expectation that the best text is Hung or Hsiung, followed by the *San yen*, and then by the miscellanies, among which Ho and Lin provide the better versions.[56]

Mismatched and Adapted Stories

Among the Hung stories copied into the *San yen*, we have noticed instances of a prologue being added, of endings changed and enlarged, and of piecemeal rewriting throughout the length of the story. These kinds of adaptation showed up quite clearly in the distribution of criteria. It is possible, therefore, that from the distribution of their criteria we can infer a similar process of adaptation in the case of other stories for which no older version exists. We shall not be able to identify piecemeal adaptation throughout the length of the story, because our criteria are simply not effective enough. In other words, we cannot with our present methods distinguish such adaptation from a genuine mixture of criteria in the original version. If, however, we find that older and newer criteria are concen-

---

52 Lin, *chüan* 8; Ho, *chüan* 10; Yü, *chüan* 8.
53 *Wan-chin, chüan* 2; Lin, *chüan* 5.
54 Two double pages are blank.
55 Lin, *chüan* 4.
56 Note that Hung 11 is adapted as the prologue to *Ch'u-k'e P'ai-an ching-ch'i* 21.

trated in different places within the same text, we may be able to infer that large-scale adaptation has taken place.

There are at least two texts in which the prologue or introduction seems not to match the main story in terms of our criteria. In one of them, TY 23, the prologue has two older criteria (13, 3) and no newer, while the main story has three newer criteria (*a, f, l*), qualifying as a newer story. There are other indications also of the date of the main story.[57] Although it is not decisive evidence, it may be worth noting that the dialogue-introducing word in the main story is *tao*, in the prologue *yüeh*. It seems possible that the prologue, a legend about the founder of Hangchow, is an older story attached to a newer main story.

Precisely the opposite seems to have happened in HY 12. Here there are four criteria in all, two older and two newer, the newer criteria occurring in the introduction and the older in the main story. The newer criteria are *l* and *h*, the latter of which has been found so far exclusively in the newer stories; the older criteria are 1, two instances, and 8. It is possible to sense the difference in style between the introduction on pages 232–234 and the main story. It is significant, perhaps, that this is another story about the poet Su Shih and his friend and verbal sparring partner, the priest Fo-yin, like the Hung story which was adapted as KC 30. One discerns a tendency in the *San yen* to rewrite stories about poets, sometimes in order to reha-bilitate men whose characters have suffered in scurrilous legends. The most drastically altered Hung stories in the *San yen* are Hung 1 and Hung 13, both stories about famous poets. (Hung 1 is completely rewritten as KC 12.) In any case, HY 12 appears to be an older story with an introduction added by a late editor.

There are several other stories in which severe local adaptation seems to have occurred. The clearest example is HY 31, a story referred to in the Pao-wen-t'ang catalogue, and a member of the pilot group of older stories. It has twelve criteria in all, eight older and four newer. In terms of their distribution in the story, they are entirely separate, all of the newer criteria occurring at the end of the story, on pages 670–672. (There is at least one other indication of late composition on page 671.)[58] Clearly, the end of the

---

57 The term *kang-kang ti* 剛剛的, p. 332. *Kang-kang* or *kang-kang ti* "only, just (time or number), no sooner" occur in the text of thirty-five of our stories, dialogue included. Thirty-two have been shown to be newer stories: KC 1, 2, 8, 10, 13, 27, TY 1, 11, 15, 17, 18, 22, HY 3, 4, 5, 7, 15, 16, 20, 25, 26, 27, 28, 29, 30, 32, 34, 35, 36, 37, 38, 39. One, KC 19, is as yet undetermined. The other, HY 14, is an older story, but I argue below that it has been adapted by a late editor.

58 The term *yü-so* 寓所 "lodging-place." It occurs in seventeen of our stories altogether; fifteen have been shown to be newer stories (KC 1, 5, 22, 40, TY 17, 18, 24, 25, 32, HY 6, 11, 17, 19, 20, 36) and one is as yet undetermined (HY 33P).

story has been added or rewritten by a late editor, though it is not easy to guess why. Pages 670–672 are a new section of the story—they tell of the delivery of the hero's children to Mr. Chang and of his meeting with the hero—and they could represent a changed or extended ending. But equally possibly, they may have been written to round out a fragmentary text, for since stories were sometimes circulated singly, the first and last pages must have been highly vulnerable.[59]

The ending of HY 14 may also have been written by a late writer. There are eight criteria in all, seven older and one newer, but the newer criterion occurs last, at the very end of the story. In addition to the newer criterion, an instance of *b*, there is also another indication of late composition in these same pages, 275–276.[60] There is no doubt that, in the main, this is an older story, but it seems possible that the last couple of pages have been rewritten or supplied. There is some reason, admittedly rather slight, to believe that it may have been rewritten. I have pointed out elsewhere a tendency on the part of the *San yen* editors to soften the harsh verdict of the older stories, especially if they touch on love.[61] This is a love story that turns into a horror story—the dead girl is restored to life, then killed by her lover in the belief that she is a malignant ghost—and it is only at the end, when the girl's ghost rejoins her lover in his prison cell, that the horror is mitigated. If this passage, which is precisely where the newer criteria occur, has been added by a late editor, it would parallel those textual changes apparently made in Hung 20.

HY 13, apparently referred to in the Pao-wen-t'ang catalogue, has only two criteria, 14, two instances, and *a*. There is little doubt that it is, in the main, an older story, for a number of probable older criteria can be adduced.[62] However, there may have been some rewriting, especially in the passage on page 247 in which Lady Han rethinks her disordered thoughts, a piece of self-communion that is rare in older fiction.[63] Indeed, some of

---

59 Note that the stories listed in the Pao-wen-t'ang catalogue are mostly single publications. The fragmentary stories in the Hung collections lack openings or endings or both. The four stories published by Hsiung Lung-feng and the four stories that make up the *Hsiao-shuo ch'uan-ch'i* are essentially sets of individually published items in a common format, rather than "collections."

60 An instance of *kang-kang* on p. 276. Criterion *b* occurs on p. 275, but after the two instances of criterion 12 on that page.

61 See Hanan, "Early Chinese Short Story," p. 197.

62 For example, *wang chih so ts'o* 罔知所措 "was at a loss as to what to do," p. 250, is found frequently in the older stories, rarely in the newer.

63 The expression *yu hsiang i hui tao* 又想一回道 "thought again for a moment, as follows" occurs several times on p. 247. It has not been included under criterion *b*, though it works to distinguish newer stories from older.

the difficulties which the modern critic finds in this story may be owing to late rewriting.[64] The problem lies in the sympathy the reader inevitably feels for the deluded Lady Han, and although the flaw must have been present in the plot from the beginning, it may have been aggravated by the later tendency to make all lovers sympathetic.

HY 33, also apparently referred to in the Pao-wen-t'ang catalogue, has three criteria in the main story, one older (17) and two newer (m, q). Other probable older criteria can be adduced in the first part of the main story.[65] The significant point is that the newer criteria both occur toward the end of the text, from page 702 on. In fact, they begin with the disquisition on justice on page 702, a passage which is itself unlike anything we have noticed among older stories so far.[66] The first part of the main story, which is almost certainly older, is the perfectly symmetrical tale of the crime and the unjust punishment. The last part of the story, in which the newer criteria occur, is the distinctly inferior account of the murderer's apprehension and execution. It is difficult to believe that the original text ended without this meting out of justice; although one older story of the same type allows the villain to get away with his crime,[67] this is altogether a more blatant and outrageous case, and a gross miscarriage of justice has occurred. Perhaps the original story ended perfunctorily, and was extended; or perhaps the original ending was lost.

Not much can be said about the prologue. On the strength of the term *te-sheng t'ou-hui* 德勝頭廻, it has been thought very early indeed, but the term occurs in at least one newer story,[68] and in no older story, to the best of my knowledge. The prologue has one probable newer criterion, but its evidence is, of course, not conclusive.

It is remarkable how many of the rewritten stories are in HY. It will be argued in Chapter V below that this is due to a different editorial practice and, perhaps, to a different editor, although the possibility must be borne

---

64 See C. T. Hsia, *The Classic Chinese Novel* (New York, 1968), appendix, pp. 299–303.

65 E.g., the expression *ch'a shou pu li fang-ts'un* 叉手不離方寸 "crossed his hands over his heart" is peculiar to the older stories, occurring in Hung 1, KC 36M, TY 37, etc. The expression *tao-te* 到得 followed immediately by a timeword is also characteristic of the older stories. It is found in three Hung stories, as well as in KC 36M, TY 20, and HY 31.

66 Note also an instance of *pu shang* 不上 followed by a time expression on p. 704. It functions well as a newer criterion, occurring in eighteen newer stories and only one older (TY 13).

67 Hung 18, adapted as TY 33.

68 HY 6, p. 113. The subject matter of the HY 33 prologue resembles that of Hung 2P, but no conclusions can be drawn from that. The probable criterion is *yü-so*. For the term *te-sheng t'ou-hui*, see the *Ch'i-hsiu lei-kao*, vol. I, p. 330.

in mind that the stories available to the HY editor were mostly incomplete.

The one other story which arouses our suspicions is TY 30, whose main story has five criteria, three older (12, 5, 8) and two newer (*n*, *l*). Both of the newer criteria occur at the end, on page 469, after the older criteria. In the main, this is clearly an older story—other probable older criteria could be adduced—but it seems possible that the ending has been rewritten or supplied.[69]

Classifying the Remainder of the Stories

If we accept the tentative judgements of the last section, only fourteen stories remain unclassified. In the following list, prologues are included with the story except where specified: KC 9, KC 14, KC 19, KC 32, KC 37, KC 39; TY 2, TY 4, TY 6M, TY 9, TY 10, TY 27; HY 24, HY 40.

I have argued elsewhere that certain stories in the *Ku-chin hsiao-shuo* were probably written by Feng Meng-lung, on the grounds of their source material.[70] KC 9, KC 32, and KC 39P were included in this group and can be accepted as newer stories. In any case, two of them have a strong preponderance of newer criteria.[71] KC 9 has three newer (*k*, *n*, *b*) to one older (2), and KC 39M has six newer (*c*, *q*, *o*, *m*, *l*, *e*) to two older (2, 1); these are significant proportions when it is considered that criterion 2 is the weakest of the older criteria. The evidence for Feng's authorship of KC 32 was particularly strong.

In an investigation of authorship in Chapter IV, it will be shown that several other stories are by late authors, and there is no point in discussing their dating here with inadequate evidence. KC 14 and TY 4 are by a late author, probably Feng himself; KC 19 and KC 37 are both by a single, presumably late, author; TY 27 may well be by the same man; HY 24 may be by a third, late author.[72]

The remaining five stories may be tentatively classified by stylistic or typological means. TY 2M has two newer criteria (*a*, *k*) and no older.[73]

---

69 In fact, Chapters V and VII below do not uncover any evidence that substantial adaptation has taken place.

70 Hanan, "Authorship."

71 The other, KC 32, has one newer criterion, *e*.

72 All of these stories have a preponderance of newer criteria. KC 14 has one criterion, *c*. KC 19 has an instance of *kang-kang*, and also another probable criterion, *chiu-shih* 就是 as a mild exhortation at the end of a spoken sentence. It occurs in seventeen stories in all; fourteen have been shown to be newer (KC 5, 21, 28, TY 5, 11, 15, 25, 34, HY 5, 6, 10, 28, 34, 35) and only one has been classified as older, KC 38. KC 37 has two newer criteria (*b*, *a*) and one older (10). TY 4 has one criterion, *a*, three instances. TY 27 has one criterion, *r*. HY 24 has one criterion, *e*.

73 It also has an instance of *chiu-shih*.

TY 6M, a virtuoso story of a kind not found among the newer stories,[74] has three older criteria (1, 5, 12) and two newer (q, a). Its prologue story, Hung 5, has been severely adapted in its TY version, its older criteria cut from five to three. TY 6M is probably an older story, and it may have suffered the same fate. TY 9, a story about Li Po, resembles one of those late *San yen* stories which tend to glorify poets.[75] TY 10 is close to Classical in its language and exhibits few of the features which distinguish older stories from newer, but it neatly fits the older category of virtuoso; it was a common theme in Yüan oral literature, and its habit of inaccurately quoting famous poems is characteristic of the early story.[76] The opening of HY 40 has a number of probable newer criteria. It is either a newer story, or an older story much rewritten.[77] Very tentatively, we can take TY 6M and TY 10 as older, TY 2, TY 9, and HY 40 as newer. There is little point in trying to reinforce this tentative judgement now with ad hoc criteria; a couple of the stories we can never be quite certain about, while others will be dated incidentally in later chapters.

The Pai-chia kung-an Stories

With one partial exception, the various collections of *kung-an* or court-case stories which flourished in the late Ming fall outside the scope of the vernacular short story; they make practically no use of the characteristic markers of the vernacular fiction style, and they are generally written in a simple form of the Classical language. It is a sign of their divergence from the short story that the *San yen* authors were obliged to rewrite them entirely, rather than merely adapt them, in order to use their stuff-material.

The partial exception, of course, are the cases of Judge Pao. It is significant that they are the earliest *kung-an* collection, for among the various differing versions of the Judge Pao collection,[78] it is again the earliest—as judged by the date of its edition—which is closest to the short-story genre. This is the *Pai-chia kung-an*, which survives in an edition of 1594. Its adaptations of

74 Cf. KC 11.

75 Cf. KC 12, about Liu Yung as paragon.

76 See Chapters V and VII for a discussion of this story.

77 It has one newer criterion (p) and one older (2). It also has two probable newer criteria. The narrator refers to himself by the humble term *tsai-hsia* 在下, which occurs in ten stories, the other nine of them newer (KC 10, TY 1, 17, HY 2, 6, 8, 27, 28, 34). The term *ch'u tsai* 出在, denoting that the story "originates in" some place or period, occurs in twelve stories, the other eleven of them newer (TY 34, HY 1, 2, 4, 8, 10, 27, 28, 34, 35, 39).

78 For other forms of the Judge Pao collection, see Sun K'ai-ti, *Chung-kuo t'ung-su hsiao-shuo shu-mu*, pp. 110–112. The 1597 edition mentioned by Sun has not been accessible to me.

Hung 4 and Hung 8 are not found in the other accessible versions of the Judge Pao collection.[79] Moreover, the stories which it does have in common with the other versions contain much more verse in the *Pai-chia kung-an* than elsewhere. By contrast, the other versions frequently give the text of accusations and verdicts in full; they seem a step away from the short story in the direction of a more restricted genre. Here I shall confine myself to the *Pai-chia kung-an*. Little is known about its authorship or date.[80] The 1594 edition was not the earliest; its title is *ch'üan-pu* "expanded throughout," and it designates the first thirty-four stories as "added." The incidence of our criteria is too low to give much indication of its date of composition. If we omit the two adapted Hung stories, the total of separate criteria in the remainder is thirty-two older and twenty-five newer.[81] However, the criteria are restricted to a surprising degree—for instance, twenty-one of the twenty-five consist of just two criteria, d and q[82]—and hence it seems likely that only a small number of writers was responsible for the bulk of the stories. It is clear that the collection was composed well on in the Ming dynasty, for Ming place-names and institutional terms abound. The Pao-wen-t'ang catalogue does not mention a Judge Pao collection, and we may therefore guess that the date of composition was between about 1540 and 1590.

Can we distinguish other older short stories which the collection has adapted? Despite severe condensation, its versions of Hung 4 and Hung 8 are still recognizable as older stories, retaining three and four older criteria, respectively. By such standards, however, only two other stories would qualify as older, numbers 21 and 28, each with three criteria.[83] Of the two, number 28 has the stronger claim, both because it is sandwiched between the two adapted Hung stories, numbers 27 and 29, and also because it contains one of the few set pieces in the entire collection. Entitled *P'an Li Chung-li mou fu chan ch'i* 判李中立謀夫占妻, it is the story of Chiang Yü-mei 江玉梅, who foils her would-be seducer and sees him brought to justice. (It

---

79 Note that no. 41, *Yao seng kan she Shan Wang ch'ien* 妖僧感攝善王錢, is a condensation of chaps. 11 and 12 of the twenty-chapter *P'ing-yao chuan*, in which Judge Pao appears. In addition, there are other items which have a nontextual, presumably indirect, connection with older short stories. Nos. 20 and 56 are analogues of Hung 2M, and no. 51 deals with the stuff-material of Hung 12.

80 The 1594 edition attributes the compilation to An Yü-shih 安遇時 of Hangchow. He is otherwise unknown.

81 Each unit signifies one or more instances of a single criterion in a single story.

82 Criterion d is found in nos. 41–47, 51, 52, 64, 68, q in 17, 19, 26, 34, 48, 53, 55, 57, 61, 62. The incidence of older criteria is almost as restricted; there are eleven 2, nine 9, and six 12.

83 No. 21 has 12, 2, and 5; no. 28 has 2, 9, and 13. Note that 2, 9, and 12 are found commonly elsewhere in the collection and may not be significant.

appears under the title of *Ti-chiao* 地窖, "The Cellar," in other versions of the Judge Pao collections.)[84] But the Pao-wen-t'ang catalogue does not refer to it, and our judgement can only be tentative.[85]

The Terms "Older," "Newer," and "Late"

What we have done so far is to choose a pilot group of stories written before circa 1550 and another written between circa 1550 and the 1620's. We have found stylistic criteria which distinguish the two groups and, having shown that these criteria are helpful in distinguishing date of composition in the short story, have applied them to the rest of the short stories. There are plenty of other criteria, linguistic as well as stylistic, which will confirm this broad division, but it hardly seems necessary to apply them.[86] Some, in any case, will be used in Chapter IV in the investigation of authorship.

What is the time division that the enlarged groups of older and newer stories reflect? It need not be simply 1550. If all the older stories proved to have been written in the Yüan while all the newer stories had been written in the 1560's, that would make nonsense of the 1550 boundary. In fact, as will appear from Chapter V, the older stories are spread over a wide time range, from before the Ming dynasty up to the middle of the sixteenth century. As will be shown in Chapter IV, the newer stories are almost entirely by authors writing in the 1620's. Therefore, the boundary ought, if anything, to be later than 1550. Perhaps, to anticipate matters, we should say that the older stories were written before circa 1575 and the newer stories after circa 1550.

Working backwards like this in time, sifting out the later stories as we go, we find nomenclature an increasing problem. Let us now use the word "late" for the period after circa 1550, for the stories written in that period and for the authors who wrote them, and retire the word "newer." "Older" we shall keep for the time being, to refer to the period, stories, and authors before circa 1575, but in later chapters we shall have occasion to divide "older" into "middle" and "early."

84 See *Lung-t'u kung-an* 龍圖公案, Kuei-wen t'ang 貴文堂 ed., *chüan* 7.
85 However, no. 28 is certainly a Ming story. It contains a place-name, Ju-ning fu 汝寧府, instituted in the late Yüan.
86 Note how these results accord with the original ten criteria of Chapter II. None of the stories now classified as older, and only one of the stories now classified as newer, has a majority of the "wrong" kind of original criteria. KC 17 has only one of the original criteria, an instance of 2, which we saw to be among the least effective.

IV The Late Stories: Individual Style and Authorship, Origins, and Composition

Our intention has been merely to date the stories as best we can, not to group them as the work of this or that author. However, some of the late (newer) criteria we have used, or a combination of late criteria, may be peculiar to the style of an individual writer. Some of the evidence does indeed point in this direction, and it would be foolish to ignore it. At the same time, I shall not go much beyond the data already given in dealing with the question of authorship; a more detailed study will need to be made at a later date.

There is a clear difference in kind between using stylistic or lexical criteria to show that two parts of a single work cannot be by the same author and using the same kinds of criteria to show that two separate works are by the same person. In the former case, we can generally assume that the work itself will provide us with the standards of consistency against which any part of it is to be measured. In the case of two separate works, we do not know what degree of "tolerance," to use a machineshop metaphor, may exist between what a man writes at two different times, even when he is writing in the same mode and for apparently similar purposes. Presumably, the degree of tolerance will vary with the writer. In a literature about which we know little, and about which no stylistic studies have been made, the most we can do is to point to patterns which convincingly unite the works under discussion and set them off from other contemporary writing.

The X Stories

It is best to begin by studying whether any restrictive patterns can be seen in the incidence of the late criteria. Since the criteria were set up for another purpose, we are able, by using them, to avoid some of the dangers of subjective judgement.

Criterion *d* is the clearest example. Its incidence is entirely restricted to late stories in HY:

HY 4	6 instances	HY 27	3 instances
HY 6	8 ,,	HY 28	3 ,,
HY 8	5 ,,	HY 29	5 ,,
HY 10	1 instance	HY 30	9 ,,
HY 15	4 instances	HY 34	3 ,,
HY 17	4 ,,	HY 35	4 ,,
HY 18	10 ,,	HY 36	1 instance
HY 20	10 ,,	HY 37	2 instances
HY 26	2 ,,	HY 39	1 instance

Totals   18 stories   81 instances

These eighteen stories, which contain all the instances of criterion *d* to be found in the *San yen*, comprise about one-fourth of the total of late stories. Since the incidence of *d* is not only concentrated within a fraction of the late stories but is also restricted to one of the collections that make up the *San yen*, we are led to wonder whether these eighteen stories may not be of separate authorship.

Evidence to support this view is fairly easy to find. Criterion *j*, though less common than *d*, is also restricted to late stories occurring in HY, many of them the same stories that contained *d*.

HY 4	1 instance	HY 17	1 instance
HY 8	1 ,,	HY 18	1 ,,
HY 15	1 ,,	HY 20	2 instances
HY 16	1 ,,	HY 25	1 instance

Totals   8 stories   9 instances

Six of the eight stories, all but HY 16 and HY 25, correspond with the first list.

An elaboration of criterion *b* helps to confirm this general grouping. Whereas *yu hsiang tao* is found widely among late stories, the form *ch'üeh yu hsiang (tao)* 却又想(道) "but then he thought again, as follows" is confined to HY.[1]

HY 20	1 instance	HY 30	3 instances
HY 25	5 instances	HY 35	2 ,,
HY 26	1 instance	HY 36	1 instance
HY 27	4 instances	HY 37	3 instances
HY 29	1 instance	HY 38	1 instance

Totals   10 stories   22 instances

---

1 There is one instance of an analogous form, *ch'üeh yu ssu-hsiang tao*, in HY 19, p. 389.

Eight of the ten stories belong to the original eighteen, while two of them correspond with the list showing incidence of *j*.

A probable criterion, *jen-yang* 恁樣, helps to strengthen this grouping:[2]

HY 4	2 instances	HY 29	2 instances
HY 6	1 instance	HY 30	8 ,,
HY 8	5 instances	HY 35	3 ,,
HY 10	2 ,,	HY 36	1 instance
HY 15	2 ,,	HY 37	4 instances
HY 16	1 instance	HY 38	2 ,,
HY 17	2 instances	HY 39	1 instance
HY 18	3 ,,	KC 29	1 ,,
HY 20	8 ,,	KC 31	1 ,,
HY 25	2 ,,	TY 11	1 ,,
HY 27	3 ,,		

Totals   21 stories   55 instances

Although the distribution is not as clear-cut as that of *d*, it is significant that fifty-two of the fifty-five instances occur in HY. Moreover, all fifty-two instances occur within stories that have appeared on our previous lists.

Before combining these results, let us introduce one new criterion in the prethought position, *an-tao* 暗道 "secretly thought, as follows," the incidence of which in the *San yen* is confined to late stories in HY.[3]

HY 20	3 instances	HY 30	1 instance
HY 22	5 ,,	HY 35	1 ,,
HY 25	1 instance	HY 36	1 ,,
HY 27	1 ,,	HY 38	1 ,,
HY 28	4 instances	HY 39	2 instances

Totals   10 stories   20 instances

Nine of these stories have appeared in one or more of the previous lists.

If we now combine these five criteria, we can delineate a group of stories with a fair amount of precision. In Table 7, *ch'üeh* stands for *ch'üeh yu hsiang tao*.

It is apparent that stylistically these twenty-two stories form a distinct group, set off from the other *San yen* stories.[4] It is unlikely that any subdi-

---

2 Instances are counted wherever they occur, even in dialogue. Though it was not used in Chapter III, *jen-yang* functions perfectly as a late criterion. The only older story in which it appears is KC 29, but the instance in KC 29 is on p. 439, in the last section of the story which I have argued is by Feng Meng-lung. See "Authorship," pp. 196–197.

3 The form *an-an tao* is included.

4 There seems to have been a spasmodic effort to group or alternate the stories within HY. Here are the stories outside the group as constituted so far: HY 1, 2, 3, 5, 7, 9, 11, 12, 13, 14, 19, 21, 23, 24, 31, 32, 33, 40. In the first edition of HY, HY 21 and HY 22 were in reverse order.

TABLE 7.   Incidence of Five Restrictive Criteria in HY.

Story	Criteria	Total number of instances
HY 4	*d, j, jen-yang*	9
HY 6	*d, jen-yang*	9
HY 8	*d, j, jen-yang*	11
HY 10	*d, jen-yang*	3
HY 15	*d, j, jen-yang*	7
HY 16	*j, jen-yang*	2
HY 17	*d, j, jen-yang*	7
HY 18	*d, j, jen-yang*	14
HY 20	*d, j, ch'üeh, jen-yang, an-tao*	24
HY 22	*an-tao*	5
HY 25	*j, ch'üeh, jen-yang, an-tao*	9
HY 26	*d, ch'üeh*	3
HY 27	*d, ch'üeh, jen-yang, an-tao*	11
HY 28	*d, an-tao*	7
HY 29	*d, ch'üeh, jen-yang*	8
HY 30	*d, ch'üeh, jen-yang, an-tao*	21
HY 34	*d*	3
HY 35	*d, ch'üeh, jen-yang, an-tao*	10
HY 36	*d, ch'üeh, jen-yang, an-tao*	4
HY 37	*d, ch'üeh, jen-yang*	9
HY 38	*ch'üeh, jen-yang, an-tao*	4
HY 39	*d, jen-yang, an-tao*	4
Totals 22 stories		184 instances

vision can be made among the twenty-two, because the criteria overlap to a considerable degree. (The fact that *an-tao*, for example, is restricted to a part of HY must be attributed to that tolerance to be found in any writer's style.) It would not be difficult to find further striking cases of ad hoc criteria to reinforce the grouping, but it is scarcely necessary. (Some of them will be introduced below for a different purpose.) Our inference from these criteria must be that the stories form a distinct group because they were written by a single author. Let us call the anonymous author X, and his stories the "X stories."

Are there other stories within the *San yen* which X may have written? There is little, if any, evidence. Since the X stories have so far been found exclusively within HY, it would seem most likely that, if there are other X stories, they would be found there. It is possible that there are others; for example, the probable criterion *ch'u tsai* 出在 is restricted to eight X stories,

HY 4, 8, 10, 27, 28, 29, 35, 39, and to HY 1, 2, 40 and TY 34,[5] but we cannot say for certain.

The X Author, the Question of His Identity, and the Shih tien t'ou Stories

The first possibility that comes to mind is that Feng Meng-lung, supposedly the editor of the *San yen* collections, may have been the author of the X stories. This can be quickly disposed of. There is a good deal of fiction which can justifiably be attributed to Feng, and it does not exhibit the distinctive characteristics of the X stories.[6]

On the other hand, one is struck by the similarities between the X stories and the *Shih tien t'ou* 石點頭, the late-Ming collection of fourteen stories. If we examine the *Shih tien t'ou* according to the criteria used above, we have the following results:

Story 1.	No criteria.
Story 2.	*d*, three instances.
Story 3.	*d*, two instances, *jen-yang* two instances, *an-tao*, two instances.
Story 4.	No criteria.
Story 5.	*Jen-yang, an-tao*, four instances.
Story 6.	No criteria.
Story 7.	No criteria.
Story 8.	*d*.
Story 9.	*d*, two instances, *ch'üeh*.
Story 10.	*d*, four instances, *jen-yang, an-tao*, three instances.
Story 11.	*An-tao*, three instances.
Story 12.	*d, an-tao*, two instances.
Story 13.	*d, ch'üeh, an-tao*.
Story 14.	*Jen-yang*.

Although, with the exception of *an-tao*, there is a clear difference in frequency of occurrence, the resemblance is still significant, as Table 8 shows; most of the criteria occur only rarely outside of these two collections.[7]

Further objective evidence of identical authorship could be obtained by examining comprehensively some stylistic (or grammatical, or even lexical)

---

5 See TY 34, p. 518. For this criterion, see Chapter III, n. 77.
6 In the first fifteen chaps. of the forty-chapter *P'ing-yao chuan*, there are two instances of *jen-yang*, none of the other criteria.
7 Some of the criteria, e. g., *an-tao*, are found in other late-Ming vernacular fiction, but this combination of criteria is not found elsewhere, to the best of my knowledge.

category. But since we began with a consideration of criteria established for another purpose, and since there is other evidence of a nonstylistic kind to adduce, it is scarcely necessary. However, it is interesting to note how easy it is, using an arbitrary procedure, to pick out elements common to both the X stories and the *Shih tien t'ou* stories which distinguish them from the other late stories in the *San yen* collections.

For example, the word *tsung-jan* 總然 "even if" occurs twelve times among late stories in the *San yen*, in each case in an X story. (HY 6, 17, 18, 20, three instances, 25, 27, 29, 35, 36, 38, ten stories in all.)[8] In the *Shih tien t'ou* it occurs fourteen times, in eight stories (2, 4, 5, four instances, 6, two instances, 8, two instances, 10, 11, 12, two instances). In the form 縱然, it occurs in five *Shih tien t'ou* stories (3, 4, 7, 10, 14, two instances), in some X stories, as well as in HY 7.[9]

Shih-lai 適來 "just now" is a feature of certain older stories.[10] Among late stories in the *San yen*, it is confined to eight of the X stories (HY 8, three instances, 17, two instances, 18, 20, four instances, 25, 30, three instances, 36, four instances, 39, two instances), as well as to one instance in TY 26.[11] Eight *Shih tien t'ou* stories contain it (3, 7, 8, 9, 11, 12, 13, 14).

Finally, the stylistic marker *an-hsia* 按下 "let us put aside (this part of the

TABLE 8.   Incidence of the Five Restrictive Criteria in the X Stories and the *Shih tien t'ou*.

Criterion	Number of instances in the 22 X stories	Number of instances in the 10 *Shih tien t'ou* stories which show the criteria
d	81	14
jen-yang	52	5
ch'üeh	22	2 [a]
an-tao	20	15
j	9	0

[a] There are three extra analogous forms in the *Shih tien t'ou*, one in story 6, two in story 13.

8 All instances are counted, including instances in dialogue. There are two instances in older stories, in Hung 18 and TY 30.

9 All instances are counted. Among late stories, HY 20 and HY 25 have both forms, and there is an instance in TY 24, p. 351.

10 All instances are counted.

11 It appears three times in HY 40, which has proven impossible to date. The language is close to Classical, and the story is certainly taken from a Classical source. On the other hand, the introductory section is late and is consistent with X's practice.

story or this character)" is confined to the X stories in the *San yen* (HY 4, two instances, 20, 27, 35). It appears three times in *Shih tien t'ou* (3, two instances, 14).

The incidence of merely these three criteria covers fourteen of the twenty-two X stories and serves to prove again that those stories comprise a single group by a single author. The same criteria cover thirteen of the fourteen *Shih tien t'ou* stories, all but story 1,[12] extending to three of the four stories that the original five criteria did not reach.

We could give further instances of similarities between the X stories and the *Shih tien t'ou*, as well as divergences—the latter contains a number of instances of dialectal *fu* 弗 for the negative *pu* 不 [13]—but there is other evidence of a stronger kind. The principal evidence is the close connection between the *Hsing-shih heng-yen*, in particular, and the *Shih tien t'ou*. The preface to the first edition of the *Shih tien t'ou* was written by Lung Tzu-yu 龍子猶 of Ku-wu 古吳 (Soochow), a well-established pseudonym of Feng Meng-lung. In the preface, he refers in familiar fashion to the author of the collection, and, under the pseudonym of Mo-han chu-jen 墨憨主人, Feng is credited with the annotation (*p'ing* 評) of the text. Furthermore, the publisher of the first edition of the *Shih tien t'ou*, Yeh Ching-ch'ih 葉敬池 of Chin-ch'ang 金閶,[14] is known as the publisher of just three works of fiction, the *Shih tien t'ou*, the first edition of the *Hsing-shih heng-yen*, and the first edition of the *Hsin Lieh-kuo chih* 新列國志, also by Feng Meng-lung.[15] The connection between the anonymous author of the *Shih tien t'ou* and Feng Meng-lung, between his collection and the *Hsing-shih heng-yen*, could hardly be closer.

12 This is not the only respect in which *Shih tien t'ou* 1 differs from the other thirteen stories. It contains as many as fifteen instances of the connective *yin* 因 in the short phrase or clause introducing direct speech or thought. A quick check shows no other instances in *Shih tien t'ou*. I doubt that *yin* could be a misreading of *nai*, although in some hands they could look similar. *Yin shuo-tao* occurs four times in *Shih* 1, and there is no *nai shuo-tao* in X's work as we know it. There are other minor differences between *Shih* 1 and the other *Shih* stories; it has no couplets, and it does not use the same introductory formulae for four-line verse.

13 This negative is found frequently in the Soochow songs collected by Feng Meng-lung. See *Huang-shan mi* 黃山謎, Shanghai, 1935. Note that there are Wu dialect expressions in the X stories as well as in the *Shih tien t'ou*. Chao Ching-shen 趙景深 notes a number of Wu expressions in HY 34. They do not, however, distinguish the X stories from other late stories in the *San yen*. See "*Hsing-shih heng-yen* ti lai-yüan ho ying-hsiang" 醒世恆言的來源和影響, *Hsiao-shuo hsi-ch'ü hsin-k'ao* 小說戲曲新考 (Shanghai, 1939), p. 27.

14 Part of Soochow.

15 See Nagasawa Kikuya, "Genson Mindai shōsetsusho kankōsha-hyō shokō" 現存明代小說書刊行者表初稿, *Shoshigaku* 書誌學 3.4 (1934), 3. The *Hsin Lieh-kuo chih* refers to HY on its title page. Note that our author is known by the pseudonyms T'ien-jan ch'ih sou 天然癡叟 and Lang hsien 浪仙. The *Shih tien t'ou*'s author is given as the former; Feng Meng-lung refers to him in his preface as the latter.

Secondly, there are internal respects in which the two collections seem similar. As compared with the rest of the late stories, the X group is remarkable for the number of well-known T'ang dynasty *ch'uan-ch'i* tales that have been turned into vernacular fiction.[16] This is also a feature of the *Shih tien t'ou*.[17] Again, the *Hsing-shih heng-yen* as a whole, not just the X stories, is distinguished by the number of erotic or risqué stories it contains,[18] paralleling the *Shih tien t'ou* in this respect; modern editions of the former exclude HY 23, and a modern edition of the latter excludes stories 11 and 14.[19] Both the X stories and the *Shih tien t'ou* are noteworthy for the amount of attention given to such details as the life of the peasantry and the tribulations of the corvée.[20] (In general, the older stories often dealt with the life of the artisan class, rarely with peasants; the late stories in the *San yen* are concerned largely with the class of officials and their families.) And there are even some faint similarities between the stories of the two collections.[21]

There are also distinct differences. The *Shih tien t'ou* stories are overtly didactic in a way more characteristic of the *P'ai-an ching-ch'i* than of the X group. Though they widen the short story's sociological range in one or two respects, they lack some of the common themes of the X group: the spiritual quest, for example, or the nightmare. And they show a falling off in quality.

Though positive proof eludes us, most of the *Shih tien t'ou* stories come within the "canon" of the X author as we have roughly established it. We can concede a strong probability, if nothing more, that the anonymous author of the *Shih tien t'ou* was also the author of the X stories in the *Hsing-shih heng-yen*. Furthermore, since X was a contemporary of Feng Meng-lung, it is likely that the X stories were not culled from some earlier publication, but were written expressly for HY and published there for the first time. We have thus not merely identified twenty-two late stories as by one author, albeit anonymous, we have also indicated that they were written shortly before the publication of the collection in 1627.

16 The following are based on well-known T'ang supernatural tales: HY 4P, 6, 25, 26, 37.

17 *Shih* 9 and 13 are based on well-known T'ang tales.

18 E. g., HY 10, 15, 39.

19 E. g., the Tso-chia edition of HY, Peking, 1956, and the Ku-tien wen-hsüeh ch'u-pan-she edition of *Shih tien t'ou*, Shanghai, 1957.

20 See *Shih* 3, 6. (Also *Shih* 1, but it seems not to be by X.) Compare HY 18, 20, 34, 35, etc. There are no X stories which deal with important historical events from a public point of view, whereas there are many such among the other *San yen* late stories.

21 Story 10, with its magical fish and its stress on the fish-eating taboo, could be an echo of HY 26, itself derived from a T'ang tale. Story 5, with the abductor's shoe left behind at the scene of the abduction, seems an echo of HY 13. Story 13 refers to Lady Han, whose tale is represented as told by a storyteller in HY 13.

Indeed, we can go further and suggest the likelihood that the author of the X stories may have been involved in the editing of HY. If he was so close an associate of Feng Meng-lung as to write the majority of the stories for HY, is it not likely that he helped in the editing? A more ruthless attitude toward the rewriting of older stories is apparent in HY,[22] and although it is not possible to find in any of the rewritten or added passages the special characteristics of the X author, it seems probable that there has been a change of editor since the publication of the TY collection.

The argument of this section would support the following reconstruction of events. After the publication of TY in 1624, an associate of Feng Meng-lung wrote twenty-two or more stories for the next volume, HY, published in 1627. He may have helped to edit the volume, in which case he was presumably responsible for rewriting several of the early stories it contained. After 1627, another thirteen of his stories (*Shih tien t'ou* 1 has distinctive characteristics of style), some of them showing the influence of HY stories, were published by the same house, with a preface by Feng Meng-lung. If the argument is correct, this anonymous associate of Feng Meng-lung was one of the most prolific, as well as one of the best, writers of the Chinese short story.

Nine Stories by Various Authors, Known and Unknown

We might expect, since at least twenty-two stories are by a single author, to be able to find other groups of stories by different authors. In fact, with a few exceptions only, this is difficult to do. Most of the other late stories are written in a fairly concise, economical style which relies on a relatively small number of common stylistic devices. These stories do not, in the main, share the colloquial exuberance of the X stories. Although their late criteria are enough to set them off from the X stories, or from other collections such as the *P'ai-an ching-ch'i*, this does not necessarily mean that they form a group composed by a single author. We shall return to this question below. Here we shall deal only with the handful of stories of which the authorship is known, or suspected, or which stand out from the others so conspicuously that they must be by different authors.

There are two stories of which the authorship is well established. TY 18, as mentioned above, was probably written by Feng Meng-lung himself. TY 40 was written by Teng Chih-mo 鄧志謨, a prolific author and compiler; there is an edition of the story which has a 1603 preface by him. Feng

---

22 Of the six older stories in HY, only HY 21 appears to have escaped adaptation.

Meng-lung used this story twice, once in TY, and once in his collection of three long stories entitled *San-chiao ou-nien* 三教偶拈.[23]

Two other stories, TY 1 and HY 11, exist in Wan-li editions in the inaccessible *Hsiao-shuo ch'uan-ch'i*. They have evidently been substantially adapted by the *San yen* editors.[24] In any case, they are no longer readily distinguishable by stylistic means.

Besides these external means of establishing authorship, it is also possible to find internal means. The soundest procedure would be to check the whole of some objectively defined category in the text of the late stories. Here we shall do this only in a perfunctory fashion. If we consider again the positions immediately before the style shift to speech, we shall find formulae which help to isolate a small number of stories. For example, while the choice of *yüeh* or *tao* before the style shift is not of much significance, the choice of *tao* or *shuo* 說 does differentiate stories. Whereas many stories have a few instances of *shuo*, in others it is the regular way of marking the style shift.[25] Again, the coverb used with *shuo* or *tao* in late stories is almost always *tui* 對 or *hsiang* 向, hardly ever *yü* 與; yet in some stories *yü* is common.[26] Finally, when the subject immediately precedes the "verb of saying," the compound form *shuo-tao* is rarely used; it is reserved for more complex groupings, including, for example, the coverb and its object. Yet there is a small number of stories which normally use *shuo-tao* immediately after its own subject.[27]

The works defined by these criteria are the late story TY 24 and the undetermined stories KC 19, KC 37, and TY 27. It seems unlikely that TY 24 can be ascribed to the same author as any of the other stories, for it has several distinctive features, including a formula for a time expression that is not found elsewhere in the *San yen*.[28] At least two of the other stories, however, appear to be by a single author; KC 19 and KC 37, both on supernatural themes, share the same stylistic mannerisms to an extraordinary degree.[29]

23 The work is preserved in the Tōyō Bunka kenkyūjo. For a description, see Li Tien-yi, "Jih-pen so-chien Chung-kuo tuan-p'ien hsiao-shuo lüeh-chi," pp. 70–71.

24 See Lu Kung ed., *Ming-Ch'ing p'ing-hua*, preface, p. 5.

25 KC 19 has eleven; KC 37 ten; TY 27 fifteen; and TY 24 innumerable.

26 *Yü . . . shuo* is distributed in these stories as follows: KC 19 two; KC 37 three; TY 27 three; TY 24 two.

27 Subject plus *shuo-tao* is distributed in these stories as follows: KC 19 sixteen; KC 37 nine; TY 27 three; TY 24 two.

28 It consists of *cheng* 正 followed by a verb followed by *chung-chien* 中間, the whole meaning "while just in the act of . . ." By contrast, verb or verb-object plus *chung-chien* is quite common. So is *cheng* plus verb or verb-object plus *chien* or *chih chien* 之間.

29 E. g., they are the only stories in the *San yen* that use the term *i hui-chien* 一回間 "a short space of time." They also frequently begin a new section with *shuo che* 說這, which is found once in KC 1, but nowhere else in KC.

The one other story which stands out clearly from the rest of the late stories is the well-known erotic story, HY 23. Here I shall not attempt to explore a stylistic category but will merely give a striking, though arbitrary, instance of lexical peculiarity. The words *jen* 恁 and *jen-me* 恁麼 appear in this text where other late stories have *shen* 甚 and *shen-me* 甚麼, "what." This is evidently a phonetic, rather than merely a graphic difference, although a graphic difference would be almost as significant for our purpose. It occurs at least seventeen times, all in conversation, as against two instances of *shen-me*. It appears only once in the other late stories.[30]

This example confirms our general impression of the story, that it is different from any other story in the *San yen* collections. It is shapeless, retaining evidently the form of a chronicle based ultimately upon unofficial history.[31] There is little of the narrator's rhetoric, and little evidence of the narrator's instinct for introducing people, disposing of people, and explaining things.

Stories Attributable to Feng Meng-lung

If we exclude the stories dealt with in the last two sections, we are left with forty-eight late stories in the *San yen*. Thirty-nine of these are definitely late, while nine are putatively late.[32] With these stories, our present methods are ineffective. It would take an elaborate stylistic analysis to establish their authorship. Instead, I shall use whatever indications can be gained from an examination of the most obvious stylistic markers and combine these indications with various kinds of nonstylistic evidence, in an attempt to arrive at a preliminary estimate of the stories' authorship. It must be stressed that to do this is to traffic not in scholarly certainties but in different degrees of probability. To add to the hazards, there is the possibility that some of these stories may have had two authors, an original author and a reviser or adapter. Noticing a feature or two of the adapter's characteristic style, we are only too likely to attribute the story to him in toto.[33]

With these reservations, it can be stated that the principal author of the

---

30 TY 31, p. 479.

31 It is based on a sequence of tales in the *Yen-i pien*. See the Shanghai, 1936, edition, *chüan* 14, pp. 188–195. The tales are obviously based on historical sources.

32 I.e., KC 9, 14, 32, 39; TY 2, 4, 9; HY 24, 40. KC 19, KC 37, and TY 27 were discussed in the last section.

33 We can guard against this error by requiring some other criterion which has nothing to do with style, e. g., patterns in the use of sources or thematic material.

remaining stories, in fact the principal author of the *San yen*, is its editor, Feng Meng-lung.

In a recent article,[34] I showed that Feng was the probable author of over a dozen of the KC stories. Here is the gist of the argument of that article. The criterion used had nothing to do with style but was concerned with the nature of the stories' source-material. The two companion works of the sixteenth century writer T'ien Ju-ch'eng 田汝成, the *Hsi-hu yu-lan chih* 西湖遊覽志 and the *Hsi-hu yu-lan chih-yü* 西湖遊覽志餘, were shown to contain the sources of five late KC stories, KC 21, 22, 27, 32P, and 39P, and to provide the source-material for the reworking of two older stories, KC 29 and KC 30. It is already significant that the stories were all found in the latter part of KC, and the grouping becomes all the more marked if one counts only the late stories in that part of the collection. Since KC 23, 24, 25, 26, 29, 30, 33, 34, 35, 36, and 38 are all older stories, our group comprises as many as five of the nine late stories in the latter half of the KC collection. (The exceptions are KC 28, 31, 37, and 40.) I argued that this rough grouping of stories from a common source indicated a common authorship. The stories could hardly have been from an independent collection, since two editorial notes betray a knowledge of the source such as only an author is likely to possess. (There is also the fact that two stories in the middle of the group, KC 29 and KC 30, have been adapted with the aid of one of the sourcebooks.) The conclusion is that the stories must have been written by the editor of KC.

I then argued that another grouping of stories from a common source, this time in the first part of KC, also indicated a common authorship. KC 5, 6, 8, 9, and 13 all have sources which appear in the *T'ai-p'ing kuang-chi* 太平廣記.[35] Of course, the *Kuang-chi* does not contain the *ultimate* source of any of these stories, but it is the immediate, not the ultimate, source that we are concerned with. Among the stories mixed in with the above are two older stories (KC 7 and KC 11) and another, KC 12, that is widely

---

34 "Authorship." Note that the *Hsi-hu yu-lan chih* and the *Hsi-hu yu-lan chih-yü* were first published, in a combined edition, in 1541. See *T'ien Shu-ho wen-chi* 田叔禾文集 by T'ien Ju-ch'eng, ed. T'ien I-heng 田藝衡 (1563), "List of Miscellaneous Collections Already Published."

35 The source of KC 8, under the title of *Ch'i nan-tzu chuan* 奇男子傳 and collated by Feng Meng-lung, is found in the *Ho-k'e san-chih* 合刻三志, compiled by Ping-hua chü-shih (pseud.) 冰華居士, of which a late-Ming edition exists. It is minimally different from the *T'ai-p'ing kuang-chi* version, its title and attribution differ, but it does suggest that Feng did not use the *Kuang-chi* for this story, as I thought. ("Authorship," p. 197.) Versions of the sources of KC 5, 6, and 9 appear in another compilation of Feng's, the *Ch'ing shih lei-lüeh*, and the introductory poem of KC 13 appears in Feng's *Ku-chin t'an-kai, chüan* 25.3b. For these works, see below.

believed to be the work of Feng Meng-lung. (KC 12 is a reworking of the theme of Hung 1, and Hung 1 is criticized in an editorial note to KC 12 as well as in the preface to the KC collection.) I also showed that KC 2 and KC 10 are based on sources that are found in a single work, the court-case collection *Huang-Ming chu-ssu lien-ming ch'i-p'an kung-an chuan* 皇明諸司廉明奇判公案傳; they are the only two stories in KC or TY to be derived from it. Since both KC 3 and KC 4 are older, the fact that KC 2 and KC 10 have a common source is significant; it seems that a solid block of late stories, extending from KC 2 through KC 13, may be by a single author. If we put this tentative conclusion together with our earlier one, we can say that Feng Meng-lung was probably responsible for at least thirteen stories, KC 2, 5, 6, 8, 9, 10, 12, 13, 21, 22, 27, 32P, and 39P, in the KC collection, exclusive of adaptations.

There is an obvious need to bolster any argument from sources with other kinds of evidence. Although our late criteria do not give clear evidence of common authorship, it is not difficult to find other criteria of a similar kind which will help to confirm our conclusions.

One distinguishing feature is the narrator's discourse at the point at which he is ushering in the main theme. At this point, the styles of different stories are directly comparable; in our terms, that is, the contexts are virtually identical.

At such a point in the story, after a brief prologue, KC 9 has

Tse-chin t'ing wo shuo . . . che-chieh ku-shih 則今聽我說...這節故事
"Now hear me tell this story . . . "
At the corresponding point, KC 6 has

K'an-kuan, wo tsai shuo i-ko yü ni t'ing . . . 看官，我再說一個與你聽
"Audience, I shall tell you another . . . "
In such expressions, simple as they are, there are several distinctive elements: *tse-chin* "now," *wo* (the narrator's reference to himself), *k'an-kuan* (the narrator's term of address for the audience), and, though this is less distinctive, the reference to the story as *che-chieh ku-shih* "this story" or *i-chieh ku-shih* "a story." Each of these elements serves, to some degree, as a criterion.

The combination *tse-chin*, for example, is found, in this position in the story, only in the following stories of the *San yen*: KC 1 (*tse chin-jih* 則今日), KC 4 (also *tse chin-jih*), KC 9, KC 14, KC 18, and KC 21. The only older story among these six is KC 4; it is an adaptation of Hung 20. The formula in Hung 20 is *tzu-chia chin-jih* 自家今日 "I (shall) today . . . " *Tzu-chia* "(my)self" is the narrator's reference to himself; as such, it is confined almost exclusively to older stories.[36] Since other instances of *tzu-chia* in older stories have been allowed to remain in the *San yen* versions, it is likely that this change made in Hung 20 was a mere slip, caused by a slight visual and phonetic similarity, rather than a deliberate imitation of KC 1.

Oddly enough, the narrator's reference to himself as *wo*, the usual word for "I, me," is very rare in older fiction. Among the older stories, it occurs only twice, in KC 36 and TY 14.[37] Where a pronoun is used at all in older stories, *tzu-chia* is the word. In late stories, the humble terms *tsai-hsia* 在下 and *hsiao-tzu* 小子 are favored.[38] Among all of the late stories in the *San yen*, *wo* is used for the narrator only in KC 1, KC 2, KC 6, KC 8, KC 9, KC 10P, KC 12, and KC 13, a total of eight stories. Thus it is used in all of the late stories up to this point, with the single exception of KC 5.

K'an-kuan, immediately before a phrase such as "now I shall tell," is confined to the following stories: KC 1, KC 2, KC 6, KC 13, HY 2.

The reference to the story as *che-chieh* (or *i-chieh*) *ku-shih* is less restricted. It occurs in KC 9, KC 10M, KC 18, TY 21, and HY 2.

Use of the first three elements is thus confined to a small number of stories most of which are contiguous, as the following list makes clear:

KC 1	*tse chin-jih, wo, k'an-kuan*	KC 12	*wo*
KC 2	*wo, k'an-kuan*	KC 13	*wo, k'an-kuan*
KC 4	*tse chin-jih*	KC 14	*tse-chin*
KC 6	*wo, k'an-kuan*	KC 18	*tse-chin, k'an-kuan*
KC 8	*wo*	KC 21	*tse-chin*
KC 9	*tse-chin, wo*	KC 36	*wo*
KC 10P	*wo*	HY 2	*k'an-kuan*

If we exclude KC 4 (for reasons given above), KC 36 because it is an older story, and HY 2 because it is not contiguous, we can see a prima facie case for believing that the rest of the stories may be of common authorship.

The correlation between this group and the second group of stories mentioned above (KC 2, 5, 6, 8, 9, 10, 12, and 13) is obvious. There is only one story of the second group, KC 5, which is not listed above. As many as eight of the thirteen stories which we have attributed to Feng Meng-lung are in this list. Two separate kinds of criteria have been found in these eight, common sourcebooks and common stylistic markers. Since they have common source-material, it is scarcely conceivable that any of the stories can be independent stories merely adapted by the common author of the other

---

36 E. g., KC 3, 15, 29; TY 14.
37 See KC 36, p. 528; TY 14, p. 188. Neither use is in precisely the above context.
38 Note that the blind storyteller in HY 38, p. 823, refers to himself as *tsai-hsia*.

stories. Again, it is virtually inconceivable that any two men would work together so closely as both to choose the same sourcebooks and to use the same stylistic markers. Thus these eight stories must be by a single author.

But if the eight stories are by a single author, what of the stories originally grouped with them? If KC 21 is by this author, must not KC 22 and the rest of them be attributed to him also? Thus, rather less definitely, we must attribute the other five stories to him too. And, tentatively, because we have nothing but stylistic similarity to go on, we can also attribute to him KC 14 and KC 18.

It is natural to ask why, if the same author was responsible for all of these stories, the stylistic markers die out after KC 21. The stylistic markers occur in *all* of the late stories in KC up through KC 21, except for KC 5, 17, and 19. (KC 19 is, as we have shown above, by a different author.) The only possible answer is the guess that the stories were written over a period of time, and that the author's style, as measured by such trivia as the stylistic markers we have mentioned, was gradually changing. Indeed, the change is so regular as to be almost suspicious. Another reason for the change may have been the new kind of source-material, generally unofficial history of the Sung period, on which the author embarked in the second half of the KC collection.

Feng Meng-lung's other fiction helps to corroborate this guess. TY 18, a story which Feng himself claimed as his work, has none of the style markers. But his adaptation of the *P'ing-yao chuan* does have them. The parts of the novel added by Feng contain instances of *tse-chin, wo,* and *k'an-kuan. Tse-chin* is found once in the early part of the work, in a position that roughly corresponds to that of the short stories, in the sentence *tse-chin hsien-hua hsiu t'i* 則今閒話休題 "now let us stop this idle talk."[39] It also appears once in the (vernacular) introduction.[40] *Wo* appears twice, and *k'an-kuan* once, as in the following:

K'an-kuan, ch'ieh t'ing wo chieh shuo . . . 看官, 且聽我解說 "Audience, let me just explain . . ."[41] Not only does this help to confirm that Feng was the author of the stories, it also fits in with our notion of the ways in which his narrative style changed. The adaptation of the *P'ing-yao chuan* was done before the *Ku-chin hsiao-shuo* was written and compiled. The former was published in 1620, and the latter at some time between then and

39 Chap. 2, p. 10. *Tse-chin* also occurs in chapter 7, p. 33.

40 The introduction (*yin-shou* 引首) is not reprinted in modern editions. See Sun K'ai-ti, *Jih-pen Tung-ching so-chien Chung-kuo hsiao-shuo shu-mu* 日本東京所見中國小說書目 (Shanghai, 1953 ed.), pp. 125–127, for a text of it.

41 Chap. 3, p. 11. *Wo* also occurs in chapter 2, p. 10.

1624, the date of publication of TY. It is therefore not implausible to suggest that, in some respects, the *P'ing-yao chuan* should be closer in style to the first half of the *Ku-chin hsiao-shuo* than to the last half.

So far, we have dealt with KC stories, and we have used only two kinds of criteria: uniformity of source-material and uniformity of stylistic markers. To these, in our study of the rest of the stories, we shall need to add a third, uniformity of thematic material, even though its use is bound to be somewhat arbitrary.

Source study produced useful results in KC, but it fails to do so in TY, perhaps because some of the sources are not discoverable. There are stories in both KC and TY which are based on sources drawn from the same works, but the incidence is not impressive. For example, the sources of both KC 18 and TY 22 come from the *Hsin-k'e Erh-t'an* 新刻耳譚,[42] a work much quoted in another compilation of Feng Meng-lung, the *Ch'ing shih*, while the sources of two famous stories, KC 1 and TY 32, are by a single writer.[43] This evidence is too weak to permit one to make any claims about authorship.

Even a superficial study of stylistic features yields more. If we examine again the prologues or introductions of the stories, we shall find some similarities in the form of the narrator's exposition. (This is not the narrative proper, but the narrator's discourse or argument, his dialogue with the audience.) He often poses a condition, or asks a question in a conditional form. The prologue to KC 1 asks, at the end of a few introductory remarks, "If you had a beautiful wife or a cherished concubine and someone seduced her, how would *you* feel?" Here the word for "if" is *chia-ju* 假如, common in Modern Chinese, but not in regular use in these stories. KC 9P asks a similar question, also using *chia-ju,* "If the highest and most honored minister were to do some shameful thing . . ." KC 10P has two examples, each with *chia-ju,* one of which runs "If you had been born into a poor family . . ." KC 14P has a similar example, as do KC 18P and KC 31P. All have *chia-ju,* but not all are actually questions. The example in KC 18 is followed by the formula *so-i shuo* 所以說 "hence one says . . ." KC 27P has *chia-ju,* but in its meaning of "for example," a less distinctive use. KC 13 and KC

---

42 *Chüan* 6 and 1, respectively. No other edition is known of the former. The latter is also found in the *Hung shu* 鴻書 of Liu Chung-ta 劉仲達, of which there is a 1611 edition. See Sun K'ai-ti, introduction to Ya-tung edition of *Chin-ku ch'i-kuan* (Shanghai, 1933), pp. 27–28.

43 The *Chiu-yüeh chi* 九籥集 of Sung Mao-ch'eng 宋楙澄. Its preface is dated 1612. See Index to the Extant Stories for details. It is clear from his comments that Sung wrote the source story of TY 32 in 1607.

22 have similar constructions in the course of the narrator's exposition, though not at the opening of the story.[44]

Both TY 3 and TY 4 have identical uses of this formula. Each includes a question, with a condition, introduced by *chia-ju*, of the same kind as Pascal's speculation about Cleopatra's nose. The one in TY 3P runs "If Chieh and Chou had been ordinary humble folk, how much potential for evil do you think they would have had?" It is followed by *so-i shuo,* as in KC 18P. The example in TY 4P runs "If Wang Mang had died eighteen years before he did . . ." and is followed by *so-i ku-jen shuo* 所以古人說 "and so the ancients said . . ." TY 4 has a second example near the beginning of the main story, "If (*chia-jo* 假若) at the height of his fame he had simply passed away in his sleep . . ." TY 17 has a hypothetical question with *chia-ju*. So has TY 18P, written by Feng Meng-lung, "If Kan Lo 甘羅, becoming Minister at the age of twelve, had died at the age of thirteen . . ." In dialogue at the beginning of the main story, there is another example, "If Confucius had taken the examinations and failed . . ."

There are no other late stories with this formula. Only two other stories have *chia-ju* in their prologues, both in the "for example" meaning.[45] On the other hand, there are two instances of this formula in Feng Meng-lung's adaptation of the *P'ing-yao chuan*.[46] The incidence of the formula does give further evidence for the linking of KC 1, 9, 14, and 18, and it provides first evidence for the linking with these stories of KC 31, TY 3, TY 4, TY 18, and possibly TY 17. Strictly speaking, however, our evidence applies mainly to the introductions, the most vulnerable part of the story to the renovating editor.

At this point, I shall make the hypothesis that most of the late stories in TY are by a single author and then proceed to give evidence of stylistic and thematic similarities. The hypothesis cannot be *proven* in this way, because our choice of similarities is arbitrary, but it will at least indicate that the hypothesis is probably correct. There seems to be a group of stories with marked similarities: TY 11, 15, 17, 22, 25, and 31. And there is another group of stories which share some of those similarities: TY 3, 4, 5, 12, 23M, 26, and 32.

For example, several of these stories inform the reader about some local custom by saying *Yüan-lai* . . . *yu* (*che-*) *ko feng-su* (or *kuei-chü*) 原來 . . . 有(這)個風俗(規矩) "Now it so happened that in . . . there was (this) custom

44 KC 13, pp. 198–199; KC 22, p. 340.
45 HY 3, HY 15.
46 Chaps. 2, p. 9, and 3, p. 11.

. . ." In the *San yen,* this is confined to KC 17, TY 11M, 15, 23M, 25, and 31. TY 22 has a slightly different version. Four of these stories, TY 15, 22, 25, and 26 are set in Soochow prefecture (Feng's native place), and two of them, TY 15 and TY 22, are set in K'un-shan county of that prefecture. TY 11M and TY 15 (twice), along with KC 5, contrast the customs of the North with those of the "South" (the Yangtse estuary).

One form of criterion *f* is confined to stories in TY, namely TY 3, 11, 22, 23M, 24, and 31.[47] TY 24 is, of course, by a different writer, and if its three instances are not to be dismissed as coincidence, they may indicate some degree of rewriting by the editor of TY. All occur near the beginning of the story.[48]

A number of minor similarities may be summarized. The features listed below are peculiar to the stories mentioned, among all of the late stories in the *San yen*: TY 11 and TY 17 both describe the story they tell as *che-tuan p'ing-hua* 這段評話; TY 11, 17, KC 12, 17, and HY 5 describe the story as *chia-hua* 佳話 "an edifying tale"; use of the formula *hou-jen lun* 後人論 or *hou-jen p'ing* 後人評[49] is confined, among late stories in the *San yen,* to KC 13, TY 3, 4, 12, 22, 25, 32, and HY 5; one formula introducing a piece of verse is confined to TY 15, 22, and 25;[50] another is confined to KC 8, 32, TY 11 and 33 (the adapted form of Hung 18), but is found in the novels adapted by Feng Meng-lung;[51] TY 17 and TY 22 have remarkably similar incidents and an identical image;[52] and there is a similar parallel of text and image between KC 27P and TY 18.[53]

In more general terms, it is possible to see broad thematic similarities among stories in the same parts of the collections. The story of public morality, involving well-known historical figures, is concentrated in KC and the early part of TY—KC 5, 6, 8, 9, 21, 22, perhaps 31, 32, 39, 40, TY

47 Plain *an-hsiang,* without *tao.*

48 Pp. 339, 343, 344.

49 "Someone of a later day in discussing (or criticizing) . . ." It occurs in two older stories, TY 8 and TY 37, where it introduces a poem.

50 *Hou-jen yu shih t'an* (or *tsan*) *Y chih Z* 後人有詩嘆 (贊) Y之Z, where Y is a person's name and Z is a virtue, "someone of a later day wrote a poem grieving for (or celebrating) Y's Z." It is also found in the *P'ing-yao chuan* in the added sections (see chap. 18, p. 120) and in the *Hsin Lieh-kuo chih.*

51 *Hou-jen yu shih yün* 後人有詩云 "someone of a later day wrote a poem as follows." Compare *P'ing-yao chuan,* chaps. 9, p. 53, and 15, p. 103, and the *Hsin Lieh-kuo chih.*

52 The incident in which a child dies of smallpox is told in some of the same words in TY 17, p. 240, and TY 22, p. 316. The image of Wu Tzu-hsü is also similar in TY 17, p. 239, and TY 22, p. 313.

53 KC 27, p. 405; TY 18, p. 248, in the passages about Kan Lo and Chiang T'ai-kung 姜太公.

3 and 4.[54] Most of these stories have already been shown to be by Feng Meng-lung. Even the early stories reprinted in KC reflect the same interest; KC 7 (Hung 21), KC 16 (Hung 22), KC 25, and KC 34 (Hung 27) are the only members of the group of historical tales in simple Classical Chinese,[55] a definable class, to be included in the *San yen*. In the middle and latter part of TY, there is a different emphasis, less easy to characterize. Many of the stories deal with minor officials below the level of magistrate—there is some interest in relationships among members of the magistrate's staff—or with scholars who have not passed the examinations and must make do with teaching or minor office jobs. Examples are TY 11, 15, 17, 18, 26, 31, and 34. A number of these stories are set in the Ming period.

Again, in very general terms, some similarity can perhaps be seen in the use made of source-material. Many of these stories in KC and TY have substantial known written sources. Most of them are reasonably faithful to their sources, adding and changing incident, but preserving a good deal of text minimally altered, and generally preserving names.[56] This description would cover the following stories: KC 1, 2, 5, 6, 8, 9, 10, 13, 14, 17, 18, 21, 22, 27, 28, 32, 39, TY 4, 12 (P and M), 22, 25, 26, 32, 34P, and 35. None of the stories, so far as is known, is made from a combination of independent sources the way some stories in HY are. (Of course, the above description would also fit a number of other stories in HY.)

We can now sum up the heterogeneous evidence for Feng Meng-lung's authorship of KC and TY stories.

The following sixteen stories and four additional prologues or introductions can be attributed to Feng Meng-lung *beyond reasonable doubt*:

Feng's own statement: TY 18.

Uniformity of sourcebook plus stylistic evidence: KC 2, 6, 8, 9, 10, 13, 21, 27.

Uniformity of sourcebook with the above: KC 5, 22, 32P, 39P.

Prologues by Feng (see above), general uniformity of thematic material: KC 32M, 39M. (KC 32M also has an editorial note indicating that the editor and author are one and the same.)

---

54 KC 12 and TY 9, both of which show their poets in a public role, might also be included.

55 See Chapter V.

56 The process does not amount to translation in any accepted sense of the word. The genre of the vernacular story demands more detail, multiplication of incident, chronological arrangement, the narrator's "rhetoric." Nonetheless, sections of the short story often amount to a rough equivalent of the Classical source. Surprisingly, the direct speech of the Classical is often mirrored, in a closely related vernacular, in the text of the short story.

Editorial note tending to equate editor and author plus stylistic evidence: KC 12.

Stylistic evidence of introduction plus general uniformity of thematic material: TY 3, 4.

Stylistic evidence (introductions only): KC 1P, 14P, 18P, 31P.

The following five stories can be described as *probably* by Feng:

Stories of which the introductions have been shown to be by Feng: KC 1M, 14M, 18M, 31M.

Stylistic evidence: KC 17.

The following stories may be described as *possibly* by Feng:

The homogeneous group of stories in TY: TY 5, 11, 12, 15, 17, 22, 23M, 25, 26, 31, and 32. (Of these, TY 11, 15, 22, 25, and 31 are the most cohesive and, even if not by Feng, must be by a single author.) As TY 23 is given an alternative title in the text, it may well have been merely adapted by Feng.

Uniformity of general theme: KC 40.

Six stories remain unaccounted for in the KC and TY collections: KC 28, TY 2, TY 9, TY 21, TY 34, and TY 35. There are some slight reasons for linking several of these stories to Feng Meng-lung, but they are not sufficient for even a tentative attribution.[57] However, it seems likely that most of them were either by Feng or his associates.

To return to HY. After we attributed twenty-two stories to X, and HY 11 and HY 23 to unknown authors, there were ten late stories left unaccounted for. There was some faint evidence that HY 7 might be by X. There was much more evidence that HY 24 might be by X, considering that it uses the method of combining various source materials to make a story that X practiced in HY 16 and HY 25 but which is not found elsewhere in the *San yen*, except in HY 23.

---

57 So far, these stories have not even provided a basis for speculation. KC 28 mentions a *chantefable* on its topic, and, in view of its clumsy technique at one point, it is argued below that it may derive from a vernacular work partly assimilated. TY 2P deals with the *san chiao* or "Three Doctrines." Feng was evidently fond of these ecumenical discourses, as witness the prologues to KC 10 and KC 13 and the compilation *San-chiao ou-nien*. But it is a trite subject for a prologue and cannot be said to mark this story as Feng's. The note of bitterness about contemporary mores which appears in the same prologue is certainly characteristic of Feng; see KC 8P, 10P, 14P, TY 3P, etc., as well as the editorial notes to KC 8, KC 21, KC 39, etc. There is also a passage of similar import in KC 13, p. 198. A note to TY 9 says the story corrects a discreditable rumor about Li Po's birth; this suggests the work of rehabilitation performed in KC 12, and perhaps the story is by Feng or one of his associates. The text of TY 21 contains a title different from its TY title; the story may come from some prior collection. The source of TY 34P is the *I-chien chih*, the same sourcebook used by TY 12P, a possible Feng story. They are the only two late stories in the *San yen* to make use of the *I-chien chih*. The source of TY 35 is taken from a *kung-an* collection, as were the sources of KC 2M and KC 10M, two Feng stories, as well as (possibly) TY 24 and HY 39.

The remaining eight stories are: HY 1, 2, 3, 5, 9, 19, 32, and 40. There has been some evidence to link HY 2 and HY 5 to the stories written by Feng, but it is not convincing on its own. Feng *might* have written a number of these stories, but he is hardly likely to have written HY 3, which is in a freer and more exuberant vernacular than his, or HY 40, which is largely in Classical Chinese. There is little else that can be said about their authorship. The sources used by the authors of HY 5, HY 19, and HY 32 are reprinted in the *Ch'ing shih lei-lüeh*.[58] The stories follow their sources faithfully, in the main, and preserve a good deal of the original text: it seems likely that these stories too, were written by Feng or his associates.[59]

The San yen and Feng's Collections of Classical Tales

Feng Meng-lung made collections of Classical tales as well as of vernacular stories, and the relationship between the two kinds is a vital subject for both scholar and critic. It is, of course, part of the larger subject of the use of written sources in the composition of the vernacular story, a matter with which I shall deal in the next section. Here I shall merely try to unravel something of their tangled relationship.

There are three collections of Classical tales: the *Ch'ing shih lei-lüeh* 情史 類略;[60] the *Chih-nang* 智囊 and its supplemented form, the *Chih-nang pu* 智囊補; and the *Ku-chin t'an-kai* 古今譚概.[61] None of them is dated, although

---

58 The sources of both HY 5P and HY 5M are printed in the *Ch'ing shih*. See Index to the Extant Stories for details of sources mentioned in this chapter.

59 There is a marked stylistic resemblance between HY 1 and HY 2.

60 Twenty-four *chüan*. The earliest extant editions, published in the early Ch'ing, have a preface by Feng and describe themselves as "annotated and compiled" by a pseudonymous Chan-chan wai-shih 詹詹外史, whom Feng mentions in his preface. According to the table of contents, a few of the chapters should have supplementary items; but most editions do not contain them.

61 It was published by Yeh K'un-ch'ih 葉昆池 of Soochow, perhaps a brother of the Yeh Ching-ch'ih who published HY in 1627, as well as the *Shih tien t'ou* and the *Hsin Lieh-kuo chih*. Feng also edited the *Ch'i nan-tzu chuan* for the *Ho-k'e san-chih*. (See n. 35 above.) In addition to these three collections, Feng also made a selection from the *T'ai-p'ing kuang-chi* called the *T'ai-p'ing kuang-chi ch'ao* 太平廣記鈔, of which the sole surviving edition is preserved in the Jigendō 慈眼堂 at Nikko. In 80 *chüan*, it has a preface by Feng dated 1626. See Nagasawa Kikuya, *Nikkōzan Jigendō shoko genson kanseki bunrui mokuroku* 日光山慈眼堂 書庫現存漢籍分類目錄, Nikko, 1961. The *T'ai-p'ing kuang-chi ch'ao* has been inaccessible to me. Note that the only two of Feng's compilations of Classical fiction that can be dated, the *Chih-nang* and this, were both published in 1626. Two editions of the massive *Wu-ch'ao hsiao-shuo* 五朝小說 (one entitled *Wu-ch'ao chi-shih* 五朝紀事) in the Hōsa Bunko at Nagoya claim Feng Meng-lung as their compiler, but on their title pages only. The claim need not be taken seriously on such evidence. The *Ku-chin Lieh-nü chuan yen-i* 古今列女傳 演義, extant in a late-Ming edition, also claims Feng as its compiler. It is a simple vernacular translation, not a "genre translation," of the Classical work. For several reasons, the claim must be considered bogus; the simple, awkward language is not Feng's, the themes of some of the stories would surely have been repugnant to him, and the mode of reference to Feng is not characteristic.

the preface to the *Chih-nang pu* mentions that the *Chih-nang* was completed in 1626. The only cross-reference among them is to the *T'an-kai;* the *Ch'ing shih* refers to it on several occasions.[62] As their names imply, the collections are anthologies devoted to different general subjects: the *Ch'ing shih* to *ch'ing* "feelings," but here generally to romantic feeling; the *Chih-nang* to wisdom; and the *T'an-kai* to the satirical and the merely amusing. The *Ch'ing shih*'s subject is the most unusual. Its range of themes exceeds that of those mid-Ming and late-Ming collections of love stories and female biographies, and it is far more explicit about the place of *ch'ing* in life. In fact, it helps to explain Feng Meng-lung's purpose and preoccupation in writing and compiling the *San yen*.

As one might expect, it is the *Ch'ing shih* which has the greatest degree of connection with the *San yen*. Among late stories, there are at least thirty main stories and two prologue stories of which the *Ch'ing shih* contains Classical versions.[63] Among older stories, there are at least five.[64] In comparison, the *Chih-nang* has versions of six late stories and no older,[65] and three of these are found also in the *Ch'ing shih*.[66] Certain whole sections of the *Ch'ing shih* are closely connected to the *San yen*. *Chüan* 2, for instance, has four subsections, and in two of these, "surprise matches" and "husband and wife reunited," we recognize the familiar stuff of vernacular fiction. Of the sixteen tales in the former, four have vernacular versions in the *San yen*.[67] Of the thirteen tales in the latter, six have vernacular versions.[68]

The relationship between the Classical and vernacular members of each pair varies. If we look only at their observable features and do not bother with the causal connections between them, we can distinguish, somewhat arbitrarily, three different degrees of relationship.[69] First, there is the connection that is so close that it encourages us to believe that one member of the pair must be derived directly from the other. Even here we cannot speak of "translation," at least as the term is commonly used, but need to coin the phrase "genre translation" instead. The first loyalty of each is to the laws and conventions of its genre. (Hence the differences of "rhetoric,"

---

62 See *chüan* 17, 22.

63 KC 1, 5, 6, 9, 12, 17, 18, 27, 28, 40; TY 12P, 12M, 22, 23M, 24, 26, 31, 32, 34M; HY 3, 5P, 5M, 7, 8, 9, 10, 15, 16 (this story combines two sources, one of which is in the *Chih-nang*), 19, 23, 28, 32. For details of sources, see Index to the Extant Stories.

64 KC 4 (adapted from Hung 20), KC 35 (adapted from Hung 2), TY 30M, HY 14. A Classical item related to KC 23P (adapted from Hsiung A[P]) is found among the supplementary items of *chüan* 3. See the Li-pen-t'ang 立本堂 edition.

65 KC 28, KC 40; TY 31; HY 2, HY 16, HY 39.

66 KC 28; TY 31; and KC 40. The versions differ in the case of KC 28.

67 KC 5, KC 28; HY 7, HY 8.

68 KC 17, KC 18, KC 27; TY 12P, TY 24; HY 19.

69 Analogues, i.e., similar stories that need not be related in terms of derivation, are ignored completely.

modes or styles, specificity of setting, and so on, to say nothing of language.)[70] Nevertheless, there are in these pairs many incidents that are precisely the same save for language, there are patches of dialogue in which each utterance is in the same context and of the same import and, most important of all, there is some verbal correspondence. Thus, *in parts*, one member of a pair can sometimes read like a very rough translation of the other. Secondly, there are pairs which have a "distant" connection. They have a good deal of incident in common, certainly enough to identify them as versions of the same story, but they have no verbal correspondence, or at least none that would signify that one author had worked directly from the *text* of the other at the time he was writing his story. Finally, there are some Classical items so short that they amount merely to the gist of the vernacular story.

In general, within each pair, the Classical version is primary. Many of the *Ch'ing shih* versions also exist in other works that certainly antedate the *San yen*.[71] Since many of these correspond to late stories, including some of those written by Feng Meng-lung and by X for the *San yen*, there can be no doubt that, in the great majority of cases at least, it is the *San yen* story which has been derived from the Classical, and not vice versa.

This does not mean, however, as some scholars have concluded, that the *Ch'ing shih as a collection* was the immediate sourcebook for these *San yen* stories.[72] While the *Ch'ing shih* is sometimes a direct reprint of the earlier version, and more often a slight abridgement of it, occasionally it makes substantial changes. In these cases, it is the earlier version, not the altered *Ch'ing shih* version, on which the *San yen* stories have relied.[73] We must conclude that Feng Meng-lung and his associates first wrote and compiled the vernacular collections, relying on Classical versions for the most part, and that they then gathered up these sources, rewrote some of them, and published them in the *Ch'ing shih* along with many other Classical tales.

70 See Hanan, "The Early Chinese Short Story."

71 There are works which the *Ch'ing shih* names as sources, but which are no longer extant, e. g., the sixteenth century *Ching-lin tsa-chi* 涇林雜記, from which the *Ch'ing shih* versions of TY 26 and HY 15 have been taken.

72 See Chao Ching-shen, "*Hsing-shih heng-yen* ti lai-yüan ho ying-hsiang." Because the *Ch'ing shih* version of HY 5M is followed by an editorial comment which seems to reflect the changes actually made by HY 5M, Chao concludes that the vernacular story is by Feng, and that the comment in the *Ch'ing shih* is a blueprint for it.

73 See the Classical versions of KC 1, KC 5, KC 27, and HY 10M. For precise references, see Index to the Extant Stories. The one apparent exception concerns HY 5P. The Classical version in *Ch'ing shih* 23 is closer to HY 5P in one important respect than is the original. But of course it is still possible that the *Ch'ing shih* adaptation of the original took place in the light of HY 5P.

That the *Ch'ing shih's* compilation is later than that of the *San yen* is confirmed by the editorial comments in the *Ch'ing shih*, some of which must have been written after the compilation of HY. The comments on Classical versions of the HY 7 and HY 8 stories,[74] for example, refer to vernacular stories on the same theme in such detail, giving the names of the characters and even quoting parts of the text,[75] that there can be no doubt that HY 7 and HY 8 are being referred to. Since HY 8 is an X story, presumably written for HY in the first instance, this must mean that the comments were written after the completion of HY. Furthermore, the comment on the version of HY 7 mentions that the dramatist Shen Tzu-chin 沈自晉[76] made the vernacular story (HY 7) into a play. This is the *Wang-hu T'ing* 望湖亭, an extant play which follows HY 7 fairly closely. While not precisely datable, its writing is probably later than the publication of HY.[77] It is still possible, of course, that the *Ch'ing shih* was accumulated in stages and that these comments may not have belonged to its earliest form. But if we treat it as a single act of compilation, apart from the few stories labelled supplementary, we must place it after the *San yen*.

At first sight, the comments seem to be a unique source of information on the vernacular stories. However, the *Ch'ing shih* is a haphazard collection which has borrowed heavily, although rarely acknowledging the fact, from a number of mid-Ming and late-Ming collections.[78] Some comments, which may seem to be by Feng, are in fact by some earlier author or editor and have been reprinted along with the story.[79] Many of the persons whose opinions are quoted are not, as one might imagine, from Feng's circle of friends and associates, but are the editors of the books from which both

---

74 *Chüan* 2.

75 In each case, the judge's findings are given verbatim.

76 A nephew of the famous dramatist Shen Ching 沈璟 and a close friend of Feng Meng-lung, one of whose plays he edited.

77 The first scene of the play lists the great playwrights of Shen Ching's school, including the author's friends Yüan Yü-ling 袁于令 and Fan Wen-jo 范文若. It is unlikely that they would have appeared in the list if the play had been written before 1627 when HY appeared. All of Fan's extant plays exist in editions published after the beginning of Ch'ung-chen (1628). In fact, his career as a playwright seems to have consisted largely in turning *San yen* stories into plays—he wrote plays based on HY 9, 10, 13, and 14 in HY alone.

78 For example, *Yen-i pien*, *Erh-t'an*, *Ch'i nü-tzu chuan* 奇女子傳, and *Ch'ing ni lien-hua chi* 青泥蓮花記.

79 The comment on the Classical version of TY 24, which mentions a play on the same subject, is found together with the version itself in *Pai-shih hui-pien* 稗史彙編, comp. Wang Ch'i 王圻 (1608), *chüan* 49. It must have appeared in the lost *Ching-lin tsa-chi*, the professed source of the *Ch'ing shih* version (*chüan* 2). The comment on the *Ch'ing shih* version of HY 5P is actually the comment written by Chu Yün-ming 祝允明 to accompany his original story. The comment on the *Ch'ing shih* version of TY 32 is actually that of the author of the Classical tale, Sung Mao-ch'eng.

tale and comment have been taken.[80] And when the comment is anonymous it is often impossible to guess whether it is by an old editor or a new.

Nevertheless, some of the comments are so important that they cannot '
be ignored. At the very least, it is necessary to clear up the confusion that
surrounds them. The Classical version of KC 1, after giving the comment
by its author, Sung Mao-ch'eng 宋楙澄, then refers to a vernacular story
on the same theme. This remark has generally been taken by scholars to
mean that the vernacular story existed before KC was compiled. Because
KC 1 refers to itself as a *tz'u-hua* 詞話, it has even been supposed that it is
derived directly from an oral story. But the term *tz'u-hua* has no meaning
as precise as this in late-Ming times, and we have seen that the style of the
introduction to KC 1 fits the style of stories by Feng Meng-lung and that
KC 1 itself has a close connection with, and appears to have been directly
derived from, Sung Mao-ch'eng's story. It is natural, therefore, to suppose
that the reference in the *Ch'ing shih* is a reference to KC 1, and nothing
more. The same may be true of TY 23M; the comment to the Classical
version says the story "appears in vernacular fiction."[81] The case of HY 28,
the only other *San yen* story that may be the object of a direct *Ch'ing shih*
reference, is more complex. The comment to the Classical version that
corresponds to HY 28—it is a matter of a "distant" connection—begins with
the words "the story is entitled *Ts'ai chou chi* 彩舟記."[82] The word for story
is *hsiao-shuo* which, in the usage of the *Ch'ing shih*, generally means vernacular fiction. Here, however, it may be intended differently. *Ts'ai chou
chi* is the title of a Classical tale in the *Hsü Yen-i pien* 續艷異編,[83] *chüan* 4,
the last item. Although the *Hsü Yen-i pien* survives only in a late-Ming
edition which cannot be dated precisely, the *Ts'ai chou chi* is closely related,
possibly as source, to the play of the same name by Wang T'ing-na 汪廷訥
which certainly antedated the compilation of the *San yen*.[84] It appears
likely that the *Ch'ing shih* has here reprinted, under a different title, an
existing Classical tale, the *Ts'ai chou chi*. Even if this inference is not correct,
the word *hsiao-shuo* in the *Ch'ing shih* can hardly refer to HY 28, which
differs widely from both *Ts'ai chou chi* tale and play.

80 E. g., Wu Chen-yüan 吳震元, style Ch'ang-ch'ing 長卿, compiler of the *Ch'i nü-tzu chuan*.
81 TY 23, like HY 5, has an alternative title below its main title. I do not know what significance this has, but it might indicate publication in some form prior to the *San yen*.
82 In some editions of the *Ch'ing shih*, *ts'ai* has been miswritten *lü* 綠.
83 Nineteen *chüan*. Printed together with the *Yen-i pien* in forty *chüan*. There is a late-Ming edition in the National Central Library, Taipei.
84 A facsimile of the Wan-li edition of the play is included in the *Ku-pen hsi-ch'ü ts'ung-k'an*, Second Series.

There is one curious complication. In the editorial comments attached to the *Ch'ing shih* items which correspond to TY 23M and HY 28, and there alone, we find opinions that are verbatim the same as the upper-margin comments in the first editions of the vernacular stories. No such comments are found attached to the *Ts'ai chou chi* tale in the *Hsü Yen-i pien*. The simplest explanation parallels the cases of HY 7 and HY 8. There, parts of the text of the vernacular stories were quoted in the comment on the *Ch'ing shih* version; here one or two of the upper-margin notes are quoted.

The *Ch'ing shih* comment which appears to refer to HY 3 is a different matter. No Classical version is given of HY 3, but in the editorial comment on another item we are told that there is a parallel story "in vernacular fiction." A very short summary of the plot of HY 3 then follows. The comment thus implies that there was no Classical version available. It also indicates that, in general, the *Ch'ing shih* editors did not turn vernacular stories into Classical tales, and it suggests that HY 3 was either written by someone unconnected with Feng and his associates or that it was not developed from a Classical source. Similarly, a comment at the end of the Classical version of HY 15 is also perhaps a reference to that story. Without referring specifically to vernacular fiction, the comment gives the gist of "another story." HY 15, though textually related to the Classical tale in the *Ch'ing shih*, differs from it in just the way the comment indicates. It seems likely, therefore, that the comment is a description of HY 15 itself.[85]

To return to the question of sources. We mentioned that most of the apparent *Ch'ing shih* versions of *San yen* stories have been copied from other works. Its versions of the following stories have not so far been found in works antedating the *Ch'ing shih*: KC 4, KC 40, TY 23M, TY 31, TY 34M, HY 7, and HY 8. But the *Ch'ing shih* version of KC 4 appears in the *Hsü Yen-i pien*, and although the latter is not precisely datable, we may guess that it is probably the *Ch'ing shih* version which is the copy. And the long poem in both TY 34M and its *Ch'ing shih* counterpart is found in a pre-TY collection of poetry in a form closer to the TY 34M version;[86] it seems that both TY 34M and the *Ch'ing shih* are derived separately from some lost, Classical tale. The Classical versions of KC 40, TY 31, HY 7,

---

85 Cf. n. 72 above. The comment attached to the *Ch'ing shih* version of HY 5M seems to reflect a knowledge of the vernacular story. TY 34M may be a similar case. The comment attached to the *Ch'ing shih* version of it may reflect a knowledge of TY 34P.

86 The poem is found in the *Ku-chin ming-yüan shih-kuei* 古今名媛詩歸, compiled by Chung Hsing 鍾惺 (1574–1624), *chüan* 27. 13a–17b. It is preceded by a summary of the story which is identical with the plot of TY 34M. See Index to the Extant Stories.

and HY 8 differ widely from the vernacular stories and could hardly have been based upon them. TY 23M is the only case remaining about which we have no evidence.

Although the *Ch'ing shih* version of the KC 4 story (itself an adaptation of Hung 20) is probably just a copy of the Classical tale that appears in the *Hsü Yen-i pien*, it poses an interesting problem. It does not have a close connection with either Hung 20 or KC 4. Its personal names are the same, much of its incident is the same, it never strays far from the story as we have it in Hung 20 and KC 4, but it has hardly any significant verbal correspondence, and its dialogue is seldom of the same import or in the same context as in the vernacular versions. Although its derivation remains obscure, it does exemplify the tendency which lies behind the adaptation of Hung 20 into KC 4. The changes made in Hung 20, presumably by Feng Meng-lung, eliminated some of the story's earthiness along with its harsh judgements and softened it into an edifying tale. The Classical tale in the *Ch'ing shih* seems to go further in the same direction. It is not only an elaborate story, with greater attention given to description and motivation, it also includes the text of a handful of poems composed by the heroine as messages or as an outlet for her feelings. It is almost a virtuoso tale.

The relationship of the *Chih-nang* to the *San yen* is slight compared to that of the *Ch'ing shih*, but one of its items is the apparent source of an X story, HY 16, and, since the *Chih-nang* was completed in 1626, it is conceivable that X used it in writing his story. The *Ku-chin t'an-kai's* connection with the *San yen* is even slighter; it merely reprints one or two possible subsidiary sources of *San yen* stories.[87]

In passing, we have noted that X's HY stories have been almost as much involved with the *Ch'ing shih* as have Feng Meng-lung's, although X was freer with his sources. It is significant that the *Shih tien t'ou's* connection with the *Ch'ing shih* is even closer. Fully half of its main stories have *Ch'ing shih* versions.[88]

The Late Stories and Their Composition

In general, the late story takes its sources from Classical narrative and its form from the older vernacular story. This is a truism; only the qualifications to it are interesting. What follows is a brief discussion of certain points regarding source study, literary form, and history that the last two chapters

---

87 It contains a reprint of the evident source of KC 2P and a probable secondary source of KC 12. It is chiefly important to us, however, as an indication of Feng's reading and opinions.

88 See Harada Suekiyo 原田季清, "*Jōshi* ni tsuite 情史に就て," *Taidai bungaku* 臺大文學 2.1 (1937), 53–60. The stories are nos. 2, 5, 9, 10, 11, 13, 14.

have uncovered. It is not a survey of the late story, because for such a survey we would need to compare the late story with the older story. This we cannot do while working, as we are, against the historical clock.

There is no evidence that any oral sources have been used in the late stories. (By their nature, oral sources are the least likely to be detected.) This is true of the oral narrative of the professional storyteller, the oral literature that scholars are most often concerned with. But it is also true of that other kind of oral narrative, quantitatively much more important, which is the main vehicle for transmitting stories, in China as elsewhere: the casual storytelling that takes place in company. This latter storytelling evidently provided material for the Classical tale as well as for professional storytelling; there are T'ang stories that say a story was first heard in so-and-so's house, and there are even collections, like the *I-chien chih* of the Sung and the *Hsin-k'e Erh-t'an* of the late Ming, that give the informant's name and native place. It is possible, even probable, that this casual storytelling provided sources for some of the late stories, though we have no evidence of it.[89]

Vernacular narrative also provided few sources. Older short stories, and some late stories by other authors, were adapted rather than rewritten. One exception is Hung 1, rewritten as KC 12, which we have discussed above. Two other possible exceptions are KC 28 and TY 11, both of which mention *chantefable* versions of their themes.[90] There is some reason for believing that KC 28, in particular, may have followed a vernacular source at one point. Near the end of the story, the narrator asks a question, and answers himself with the words "please look at the next installment and you'll learn the explanation." There is then a discursive piece on the three classes of graduates, priests, and matchmakers, followed by a rhyming description of the last of them. At this stage of the story, this is clumsy technique; it could be due to the influence of the *chantefable*, partly assimilated. But the most interesting case is that of HY 38. It is not derived from the celebrated

89 Of course, there are plenty of examples of casual storytelling which has been turned into a Classical tale and *then* into a vernacular story. The most interesting is that of the famous story of Tu Shih-niang, TY 32, translated as the title story of the collection *The Courtesan's Jewel Box*. Sung Mao-ch'eng tells us how he heard the story told among his friends and hesitated for years about writing it up. He finally did so in 1607, despite the threats made to him by the girl's ghost. This story was then turned into a vernacular story, possibly by Feng. The author must have composed it not long before the publication of the TY collection in 1624, because in his introductory remarks he refers to the closing of the Wan-li period, which terminated in 1619. The author of the vernacular story clearly based himself not only on the text of the Classical tale but also on Sung's other remarks elsewhere in his collected works.

90 The statements made in other stories, e. g., KC 2P, that they derive from oral tradition, cannot be taken at their face value. Such statements were clearly a mere rhetorical device.

T'ang tale, as generally supposed, but from a Ming *chantefable*, of which the printed text survives in the former Rare Book Collection of the Peking National Library. This *chantefable*, entitled *Yün-men chuan* 雲門傳, is itself derived from the T'ang tale, and it has bequeathed enough of the tale's text to HY 38 to give rise to the erroneous assumption.[91] The amount of text it shares with HY 38 makes it clear that the latter is based on the written version of the *chantefable*, not on some auditory memory. Quite possibly, there are other *San yen* stories, including some which we confidently believe to be derived from Classical tales, which are in fact based on some vernacular intermediary.

Several stories are drawn from the *kung-an* or courtcase collections of the late Ming: KC 2, KC 10, TY 35,[92] and possibly TY 24 and HY 39.[93] These

91 For the details of the *Yün-men chuan* and the T'ang tale, see Index to the Extant Stories. There is some formal evidence for the assumption that HY 38 is derived from the *Yün-men chuan*, rather than vice versa. Although the prose sections of the *Yün-men chuan* are so close to HY 38 that it is impossible to determine which derives from the T'ang tale, the verse sections contain scraps of material from the source which are shared with neither the prose sections nor with HY 38. Thus, if a simple relationship is assumed, the story could have been based on the *chantefable*, whereas the *chantefable* could not have been based on the story. This conclusion is borne out by the stylistic evidence. The features of X's style are found in HY 38, but not in the *Yün-men chuan*, and some of the *Yün-men chuan*'s features are found in HY 38, but not in the other X stories. The two instances of *jen-yang* (pp. 812, 834), the instance of *ch'üeh yu hsiang tao* (p. 819), and the instance of *tsung-jan* (p. 823) all occur in passages peculiar to HY 38. (Note, however, that the *Yün-men chuan* does have an instance of *jen-yang*, in one of the verse sections.) HY 38's instance of *an-tao* (p. 820) corresponds to a neutral form in the *Yün-men chuan*. By contrast, in the style of the latter, *tao-te* 到得 followed directly by a timeword is quite common, even in verse. On two occasions, HY 38 has a corresponding neutral form, but in one place, p. 836, it also has *tao-te*.

92 For details of all the sources given in this chapter, see the Index to the Extant Stories. The similarity between TY 35 and TY 33 (adapted from Hung 18), which was noted in "The Early Chinese Short Story," p. 201, n. 68, is explicable with reference to one of these *kung-an* collections, the *Hai Kang-feng hsien-sheng chü kuan kung-an* 海剛峯先生居官公案傳 by Li Ch'un-fang 李春芳, of which there is a 1606 edition. TY 35 is derived directly from the last item in the collection, *P'an mou hsien kua-fu* 判謀陷寡婦. The author of the vernacular story has changed the source minimally and kept all the names except that of the judge. For its part, the *kung-an* collection has derived the story, directly or indirectly, from Hung 18. The relationship between TY 33 and TY 35 is then of the following kind:

```
Hung 18----------------(influenced) ------------ Hai Kang-feng story
     |                                                  |
  (adapted)                                          (adapted)
     |                                                  |
   TY 33                                              TY 35
```

Although it must have been of this kind, the relationship may have been much more complex. Note that the *Hai Kang-feng* version, or some direct antecedent of it, was borrowed by another *kung-an* collection, the *Huang-Ming chu-ssu kung-an chuan*, the sequel to the work of similar name we have noted. See the item *Yen yin p'an mou hsien kua-fu* 顏尹判謀陷寡婦 in *chüan* 2. There has been no change of text except for names.

93 The precise source of HY 39M has not been discovered, but it must be the common antecedent of the two known Classical versions. However, the vernacular story is closer to its counterpart in the *Huang-Ming chu-ssu lien-ming ch'i-p'an kung-an chuan*, and the text of the verdict is identical. One can only assume that its source was a *kung-an* collection.

collections are popular fiction; they have nothing to do with fact, although they sometimes bear a slight resemblance to model casebooks of criminal law. They are generally closer to the Classical tale than to the vernacular story. Their language is simple Classical or limited vernacular, and they have little or none of the narrator's explicit rhetoric. As a result, Feng Meng-lung and X have been obliged to rewrite them rather than merely adapt them as they did the older stories.

Drama provides few, if any, direct sources. There are plays which ante-date the corresponding late stories, but where there is also a Classical version it generally proves to be the Classical version which is the source of the short story.[94] In cases where there is no Classical version, or where the Classical version we have is not the immediate source, it would be dangerous to claim that the play is necessarily the source. The kind of plot beloved of the Ming *ch'uan-ch'i* dramatists, symmetrical, with intricate workings and a happy dénouement,[95] was also favored on occasion by Feng Meng-lung and by X. The plots of X's stories, in particular, fall easily into two groups, the one rounded like the *ch'uan-ch'i*, the other linear like ordinary narrative. Some of the former are the subject of plays that antedate the *San yen*.[96] It is interesting to note that neither X nor Feng Meng-lung hesitated to use plots that must have been familiar to contemporary audiences.

Most late stories, as many as forty-six main stories out of the seventy-eight, have been derived from Classical narrative. With few exceptions, notably the KC stories based on the *Hsi-hu yu-lan chih-yü*, the late stories have not quarried their sources out of larger works but have used ready-made tales. By far the most common source of the vernacular story is thus the Classical tale.

This is not quite the kind of "genre translation" with which we are nowadays familiar. The process of turning a novel into a play or a film is something different; dramatic presentation itself forces certain kinds of practical change.[97] In translation between two narrative genres, there is none of this; the changes are conventional, not practical. It is the remark-

94 E. g., KC 17 is based on the Classical narrative source despite the fact that there are two plays on the subject which antedate KC, the *Shuang-yü chi* 雙魚記 by Shen Ching and the *Ch'ang ming lü* 長命縷 by Mei Ting-tso. Mei, who evidently based his play on the Classical narrative also, reprints the source in his *Ch'ing ni lien-hua chi, chüan 7*. HY 19 is another good example; it is based on the narrative source rather than on any of the three Ming plays, all of which antedate the *San yen*. See Index to the Extant Stories.

95 It is an indication of this quality that the word *shuang* "pair, double" is probably the commonest element in the titles of *ch'uan-ch'i* plays.

96 E. g., HY 8, 20, 28.

97 A closer parallel might be the translation of the French romances into English. It does not seem that the European literatures clung as tenaciously to the conventions of their genres as did the Chinese.

able feature of Chinese narrative that it clings stubbornly to the characteristics of its own genre, purely conventional though they may be.

The imperatives of the short story form, as distinct from the form of
the Classical tale, have been described elsewhere: the explicit rhetoric, the
modes of commentary and description, the formal realism, and so on.[98]
Most of these need no further comment here. One tendency, related to
formal realism, accounts for many of the changes made in the Classical
source: the vernacular story's passion for completeness. Completeness of
detail—the word has to be taken relatively—of person, time, and place is
part of what is meant by formal realism. An extension of this is causal completeness and chronological completeness. The vernacular story is anxious
to provide causes, even to the extent of finding supernatural cause in pre-
destination. And it is anxious to give the whole of an action, beginning with
the ultimate beginning (as conventionally conceived) and ending with the
ultimate end. It cannot begin, like the Classical tale, *in medias res*, nor end
at a sudden point. Thus Classical stories like the sources of KC 6, KC 9,
TY 12M, or HY 26 which relate the past in a conversation are entirely
reordered by Feng Meng-lung and by X.[99] The vernacular story, which
must deal with events of some fame or notoriety, local or national—unlike
the Classical tale which *can* deal with private events or even mental events—
seems to have little freedom to set the limits of an action and only a restricted freedom to focus on part of that action. The Classical tale, with its
relative freedom to define and to focus, is the closer to our modern short
story. The vernacular short story is more like the European short story,
such as it was, before Chekhov, a "novel in miniature" as it has been
described.[100]

Other major causes of change are the complication of plot—one incident in the Classical is often expanded to two similar incidents in the vernacular, and two incidents to three[101]—and the use of the narrator's commentary, part of what is meant by "explicit rhetoric." The narrator of the
late stories is as much teacher as entertainer, alternately cajoling and patron-
izing, but explaining, endlessly explaining.[102] The relatively simple facts

98 "The Early Chinese Short Story."

99 See Index to the Extant Stories.

100 See V. S. Pritchett, "The Anti-Soporific Art," *New Statesman and Nation*, December
6, 1968, p. 793.

101 KC 1 is a good example of this common trait. The vernacular story also empha-
sizes badinage, persuasion, and debate, as can easily be seen by comparing KC 1 with its
source.

102 See, e.g., KC 27 on the unionization of beggars, or TY 32 on the purchase of admis-
sion to the National University.

and allusions which are explained remind us of the wide reading public for which the short story was intended.

The vernacular story's frequent dependence on ready-made Classical tales should not be taken as a reason for depreciating it. The story is a different work in a different narrative genre, and it deserves to be judged as such. Indeed, if the notion of formal realism is fully accepted, the short story's very specificity of detail is itself a qualitative difference. In addition, the writers have made the stories their own in many ways, large and small. On the other hand, it is wrong to treat the sources, except the most rudimentary of them, merely as so much material for the short-story writer. Many of them are good stories in their own right, and some few are first-rate, such as the sources for KC 1 and TY 32. Naturally, the umbilical relationship between two first-rate stories in different narrative genres is a subject of vital interest to the critic.

The sources include tales from the T'ang to the Ming periods. T'ang sources are used particularly among Feng's stories in the first part of KC (KC 5, 6, 8, 9, 13) and among X's stories in HY (HY 4P, 6, 25, 26, 37). X's sources are the better-known tales, and always involve the supernatural; Feng's are mainly historical biography, though with a fictional tinge.

Sung tales are used in KC 17, 39, TY 12P, 12M, 34P, HY 1 (possibly), 5M, 17, 19. Ming sources include tales from some of the best collections of the Ming period. As we observed, the *Hsi-hu yu-lan chih-yü* provides sources for a number of stories in the latter half of KC (KC 21, 22, 27, 32P, 39P). The sources of KC 1 and TY 32 are drawn from Sung Mao-ch'eng's *Chiu-yüeh chi* 九籥集, the sources of KC 18 and TY 22 from the *Erh-t'an*, and those of TY 4 and TY 25 from the *Hsiao-p'in chi* 效顰集 and the *Mi teng yin-hua* 覓燈因話, respectively. A tale by the celebrated Chu Yün-ming 祝允明 was the original basis for HY 5P, and a famous tale by T'ien Ju-ch'eng, author of the *Hsi-hu yu-lan chih-yü*, was the source of HY 35. Other stories with Ming sources include KC 32M, TY 26, HY 15, 23, 27, and 32, in addition to several others.[103] Even some of the stories for which no immediate source has been discovered deal with familiar material.[104]

103 As argued above, the *Ch'ing shih* versions of TY 23M and TY 34M may be reprints of the sources of those stories. Although the immediate sources of KC 32M, TY 24, and HY 10M have not been identified, it seems certain, from their similarity to existing Classical versions, that they must have been at least partly based on Classical sources. The same may be true of HY 40, a story of undetermined date.

104 E.g., KC 31; TY 2, 3, 9, 11, 21; HY 11. Only a dozen or so stories for which no source has been discovered or presumed deal with relatively unfamiliar material: KC 19, 37; TY 1, 5, 15, 17, 18, 27; HY 3, 4, 7, 18, 22, 34. Of these, TY 1 is from a pre-*San yen* collection, and KC 19 and KC 37 are by a single author.

In form, the late story is remarkably true to the example of the older story. It is hard to find technical features of the latter which are not duplicated somewhere within the late stories. Inevitably there are differences of use, but the main differences between the stories of the two periods lie outside our present scope—typology, concept of character, complexity of morality. Among the minor differences that showed up in our older and newer criteria, a few are of interest. The poem or opinion introduced by *hou-jen*, "a later writer," adds a new dimension of comment to the short story, freeing the reader from his complete dependence on the narrator.[105] The upper-margin notes in the *San yen* have a similar effect, as well as adding a measure of respectability. The inner debate in a character which is signalized by *yu hsiang tao* "and then he thought again" is something new to the short story.[106] Although set pieces are still used in the late story, they are no longer the only way, or the most important way, of describing; ordinary prose is now used. Finally, the limited and stereotyped ways by which the earlier story managed time or signalized a change of mode are altered and increased in the late story.[107]

The upper-margin notes have one specific comment about the form of the older story. The chains of poems which serve as prologue for some older stories are twice pointed out as a feature of the old story.[108] Needless to say, the poem-chain prologue is not imitated by the late story.

If we examine Feng's and X's contributions to the *San yen*, we can infer that the late story as we know it was the creation of Feng Meng-lung. Not only did he collect late stories along with older, and write more like them, he was responsible for developing the short story and enlarging its range. The handful of late stories which we know to have been in existence before the *Ku-chin hsiao-shuo* are either not true short stories—TY 40 existed as a fifteen-chapter novel— or else they belonged to types common among the older stories. For example, both TY 1 and HY 11 can be classified as virtuoso stories, especially the latter. TY 24, which may have existed before KC, is quite obviously of the same type as the Li Wa 李娃 story, of which there is an older specimen. Furthermore, Feng's influence on the other two important Ming writers, X and Ling Meng-ch'u, was clearly crucial. X was Feng's associate in HY, and Ling frankly acknowledges the influence of Feng's work.[109] Thus Feng is revealed not merely as the writer of short

---

105 This formula is found in Ming historical fiction prior to the *San yen*. Note that it has been inserted into the *San yen* versions of two Hung stories, KC 7 and TY 33.

106 Thought is included in some late stories, such as HY 34, without any formal marker.

107 Note also that the narrator's dire warnings and forebodings that characterize the "folly and consequences" story are omitted or decreased in the *San yen* versions, e.g., KC 4 and TY 33.

108 See the original editorial notes to TY 8.2a and KC 33.2b.

109 See his preface to *P'ai-an ching-ch'i*. He makes it clear that the *San yen* were both relatively respectable and commercially successful.

stories—as distinct from the editor and adapter he is generally said to be—but as the creator of the late story in all its diversity, and as the main influence on the other two principal Ming writers.

One aspect of Feng's achievement was to make the short story comparatively respectable. Not only did he enlarge its range, he also introduced a new concern for private and public integrity, he made characterization more subtle and morality more complex. His collections reflect the fact that he is seeking to raise the level of readership to a different educational, hence social, level; they are published in good editions, with interesting notes and fine illustrations. Feng could be critical of the vernacular literature; the preface to his *Hsin Lieh-kuo chih* rejects all other historical novels except the *San-kuo*, and the preface to KC harshly criticizes two early stories. His *San yen* were evidently designed both to improve the short story and to raise its position with the reading public.

The impact of the *San yen* is seen clearly in late Ming drama. A score or more stories were put into dramatic form, some of them several times, in the decade or two before the Ming dynasty ended. In fact, the only occasion on which Feng admitted writing a short story himself was in the preface to a play based upon it.[110] However, among the dramatists there does seem to be an undue preponderance of men linked in some way to Feng Meng-lung. For example, Yüan Yü-ling 袁于令, whose comments appear in the *Ku-chin t'an-kai* and who edited one of Feng's plays, wrote plays based on KC 1 and KC 7. Shen Tzu-chin, who also edited a play of Feng's, wrote a play based on HY 7. Li Yü 李玉, some of whose work Feng edited, wrote plays based on KC 10, KC 33, TY 21, HY 3, and HY 11. Fan Wen-jo 范文若,[111] a close friend of Shen Tzu-chin, who is counted among the school of Shen Ching 沈璟 (along with Feng, Yüan, Shen Tzu-chin, and others), wrote plays based on KC 27, TY 30, HY 9, 10, 13, and 14. Yeh Hsien-tsu 葉憲祖, a somewhat older dramatist who was also considered to belong to the Shen Ching school, wrote several *tsa-chü* plays on *San yen* themes. Wang Yüan-shou 王元壽, whose *Li-hua chi* 梨花記 is one of only two late-Ming plays named in the *Ch'ing shih*,[112] wrote plays based on HY 10, 32, 37, and possibly on HY 7. Clearly, writing plays on *San yen* themes was at least partly the work of the loose coterie to which Feng Meng-lung belonged.

110 The *San pao en* by Pi Wei. Feng's preface, dated 1642, indicates that Pi is a literary protégé; he is praised as a young man "of great promise." The play is based on Feng's TY 18. Pi also wrote a play based on Feng's *P'ing-yao chuan*. See *Ch'ü-hai tsung-mu t'i-yao* 曲海總目提要 (Peking, 1957), *chüan* 21, p. 991.

111 Fan died in 1634. He must have written his HY plays within a few years of the collection's publication in 1627; the preface to one of them is dated 1632. Six of the sixteen known plays of Fan's are based on *San yen* stories.

112 See *chüan* 12, item Chao Ju-chou 趙汝舟. The reference to the other play, attached to the *Ch'ing shih*'s version of the TY 24 story, was not added by the *Ch'ing shih* editors but was borrowed with the version itself from another work. See Index to the Extant Stories.

Something must be said about Feng Meng-lung and X as writers. As we have mentioned, Feng is concerned with history, especially with the question of public morality, in KC and at the beginning of TY. But his is not a simple view, and he is able to see even the arch-villains of Chinese history, men like Chia Ssu-tao 賈似道, as explicable beings. His story on Wang An-shih 王安石, though condemnatory in the manner of the source story, is still an effort to understand him as he was—remarkable in the context of the short story—and an occasion for reflecting on the vagaries of fame. In these and other stories, as shown by his notes, he is much preoccupied with the nature of heroic behavior, and much given to railing against contemporary mores. It is tempting to see in them something of the character of Feng Meng-lung the Ming loyalist, chronicler of defeat in the last days of the dynasty.

In TY, among the stories tentatively attributed to Feng, there is a group which deals with the educated man at the bottom of, or below the level of, the official class. The main characters are minor functionaries in some magistrate's yamen or perennial failures in the examinations, forced to take up tutoring for a living. It is perhaps too fanciful to see in these stories a little of Feng's own experience, but they do indicate a sympathy for the unsuccessful literatus.[113]

Stories filled with poems are also common among Feng's works but not found in X's; KC 21, 22, 32, TY 3 and 4 are examples. These are, of course, quite different from the virtuoso type of the older story.

X's stories are of several kinds. The most notable is the story of fantasy, for example HY 4, the story of the old man and the flowers, or HY 6, the man who is haunted by foxes, or HY 26, the man who turns into a fish. He is interested in the boundaries between reality and illusion. He excels at invoking an atmosphere of vague menace as in the flower story, or of nightmare as in the fox and fish stories. Indeed, dreams and nightmares appear frequently in his stories. But X was also capable of the best example of naturalism in late-Ming fiction, HY 34,[114] and a story almost as good,

---

113 Feng never passed the *chin-shih* examinations and did not hold office until late in his life.

114 It is possible that HY 34, a work of brutal naturalism, has been patterned on KC 26, an older story of the "folly and consequences" type. The plot is the same concatenation of murders caused by base motives, and it springs from a similarly trivial cause—in this case, a quarrel over a single copper cash. One incident is strikingly similar. In HY 34, the landowner and his son cold-bloodedly murder an elderly relative who is sick with an incurable disease and unable to work, in order to incriminate a rival and save their own skins. This echoes the murder by the two sons in KC 26; they kill their father, nearly blind and unable to work, in order to claim a reward. It is significant that HY 34 is the only late story to contain an instance of criterion 14, a favorite device of the "folly and consequences" story.

HY 16. He has several stories about peasant life and conditions. And he has a number of stories of the well-made variety, full of twists and symmetries like the *ch'uan-ch'i* drama.

A simple indication of the differences between Feng and X as writers is their attitude to women. Here Feng is the new author, X the old. X's heroines tend to be paragons of filial piety, the matriarchal ideal, dominating their menfolk by sheer force of goodness, but they are not realized as people. None of the stories which treat women as individuals with potentialities of their own are by X, stories such as KC 1, 2, TY 32, 34, and 35.[115] The adulterous heroine of KC 1 is forgiven her sin by the narrator, and the widow of KC 2 is allowed to remarry with his blessing. TY 35 describes with sympathy the cruel predicament of the widow who is trying to live up to the social ideal of chastity. TY 32 and 34 both describe women abandoned by their lovers.

These are random remarks which do not amount to a considered critical view. I include them here to show that Feng and X are two distinct writers and that, although in the kind of story they wrote a close adherence to a source was commonplace, their stories are still the work of individual writers.

115 Notice the spasmodic grouping of stories by theme in the *San yen*. KC 1 and KC 2 both show leniency toward women; TY 32, 33, 34, and 35 are all tragedies, of women and love. There are several other examples, some of which have been pointed out. Such thematic grouping is more than merely superficial and needs to be taken into account by the critic.

V Identifying the Stories of the Middle Period

In Chapters II and III, over sixty stories (known as older stories) were shown to have been written before circa 1575. Can these now be divided into stories of a middle period and stories of an early period? In short, can the general method which served to separate the late stories from these sixty-odd now be used over again?

Obviously, the method cannot be applied unless there are pilot groups of stories which can be dated within reasonable limits. But granting this, we still cannot assume that it will work under any and all circumstances. The factors that created the multitude of tiny stylistic differences (amounting to a major stylistic change) between the late stories and the stories written before circa 1575 may not have operated at an earlier stage. The short story may not have been in constant change throughout its history; the changes found in the style of the late stories may have been the result of a special development, for example, the use of a new kind of composition or the rise of a new class of author. It will have to be established all over again that broad, natural distinctions do exist between the two pilot groups.

Even when this is done, the precise significance of such distinctions cannot be known at once. We would expect them to have some bearing on date of composition, but we will still not know whether we are dealing with a representative selection of writers, or with the writers of a particular region, or with a particular coterie, or with a few individuals. For example, in Chapters II, III, and IV, we began by separating the late stories from the rest and ended by showing that most of the late stories are the work of just two authors, Feng Meng-lung and X. Use of the method is therefore exploratory, and the meaning of the results can only be assessed at a later stage.

The later of the two pilot groups will, as before, be established by internal evidence: time-setting, place-names, institutional terms,[1] and so forth. Since only two stories are actually set in the Ming, and since place-names change as a rule only with a new dynasty, the dividing line between the two groups will have to be the beginning of the Ming dynasty. Thus the pilot group of middle-period stories will be those that can be shown by internal evidence to belong to the Ming.

The Pilot Group of Middle Stories

Even among the stories with distinctively Ming place-names, it is necessary to exercise judgement. It would have been an easy matter for an editor to make some minor change in a place-name, for example, by adding a *fu* 府 to it, and thereby change it into something distinctively Ming. In at least one story there is evidence that this has happened, and in several others the place-name appears in two forms, one distinctively Ming and the other not distinctive at all.[2] I list below the twelve stories for which there is relatively strong evidence of Ming composition and will discuss later all of the stories which, despite some evidence, have not been admitted to the pilot group.

KC 3M. There are two Ming place-names and a third which is probably Ming.

> Wu-lin men 武林門, page 71, the Wu-lin Gate of Hangchow, a Ming creation.
>
> Hu shu 湖墅, page 63, also referred to as Hu shih 湖市 on page 73. Evidently a corruption of the Hu-chou shih 湖州市 of the Sung local histories.[3]
>
> Hsin-ch'iao shih 新橋市, page 63, refers to the Pei hsin-ch'iao shih 北新橋市, which is mentioned for the first time, among extant local histories, in the Wan-li *Hang-chou fu chih* 杭州府志, *chüan* 34. 16a.[4]

---

1 In practice, only the *li-chia* 里甲 system of Ming local administration is used as a criterion. Place-names are generally less ambiguous than institutional terms.

2 This is the *Chang Yü-hu*; for details, see below. A name is distinctively Ming when it has not been used before the Ming dynasty for the place in question. Note that stories sometimes use out-of-date (but well-known) geographical names and that the use of a name that, say, dropped out of official nomenclature between the T'ang and the Ming is no guarantee of Ming composition.

3 The *Hang-chou fu chih* 杭州府志, comp. Shao Chin-han 邵晉涵 et al. (1784), *chüan* 6.3b–4a, contradicts the etymological explanation of the name *Hu chou shu* 湖洲墅, a variant of *Hu-chou shu* 湖州墅. It notes that in Sung and Yüan geographical works the name is always in the form Hu-chou shih and that the *chou shu* forms do not occur in records before the Ming.

4 Comp. Ch'en Shan 陳善 et al., 1579. The 1784 *Hang-chou fu chih, chüan* 6.7b describes it as ten *li* outside the Wu-lin Gate, about the same description as in KC 3.

KC 26. Wu-lin men, page 391. See KC 3.

Hu shu, page 399, also called Hu-chou shu 湖州墅 on page 393. See KC 3.

Ou-hua chü 藕花居, page 396, was built in the Hung-wu period (1368–1398).[5]

Li-chia 里甲, to which there are two references on page 394, is the Ming system of local government instituted in 1381.[6]

KC 29. For a discussion of this story, see under TY 7.

KC 38. Yen Kung miao 晏公廟, page 580. Completed in 1390.[7]

TY 7 and KC 29. (The latter part of KC 29 is not included, since, as was shown in Chapter IV, it was probably added by Feng Meng-lung.)[8] Both stories refer to Wen-chou fu 溫州府, a Ming creation, in prominent positions in the text, but neither can be convincingly taken as a Ming story on this ground alone. TY 7 apparently refers to a Ming institution, but the reference is not precise.[9] The reason for taking the stories as Ming is that they are evidently related to each other and to a Ming play. Since this is part of a larger argument that involves several other stories, I shall give only the gist of it here. Briefly, there is a *tsa-chü* play, *Hsiao Shu-lan ch'ing chi p'u-sa-man* 蕭淑蘭情寄菩薩蠻,[10] by the Yüan and Ming playwright Chia Chung-ming 賈仲明 which is on a subject clearly related to that of TY 7. Story and play are certainly connected, directly or indirectly. Since the play also has the hero come from Wen-chou fu, and since it must have been written in the very early Ming, its use of the place-name can hardly have been derived from the story. Presumably, the story derived the place-name, along with some of its plot, from the play. (The actual derivation could be along these lines and yet be far more complicated.) Thus the Ming place-name is unlikely to have been the result of casual alteration on the part of some Ming editor. As for KC 29, it will be argued below, in Chapter VI, that it is derived from TY 7, as well as from other stories. The name Wen-chou fu

---

5 See *Hsi-hu yu-lan chih, chüan* 3.34.

6 See *Hsü Wen-hsien t'ung-k'ao* 續文獻通考, *chüan* 13. The passage is translated and discussed by Ping-ti Ho, *Studies on the Population of China, 1368–1953* (Cambridge, Mass., 1959), pp. 7ff. The term *li-i* 里役 in KC 3, p. 64, apparently refers to the corvée under this system.

7 See *Hsi-hu yu-lan chih, chüan* 23.280–281. The 1579 *Hang-chou fu chih, chüan* 12.9a, gives the date as 1390.

8 See Hanan, "Authorship," pp. 195–197. Feng's additions begin on p. 435, and from p. 436 the text is entirely his.

9 See the note on *Seng lu ssu* 僧錄司, *Ching-shih t'ung-yen* (Peking, 1957), p. 88, n. 7.

10 It is contained in the *Yüan-ch'ü hsüan*.

is then part of its legacy from TY 7, and is not an editor's casual alteration.

Hung 9. The story is set at the beginning of the Ming.

Hung 14. (Main story only.)

Hang-chou fu 杭州府, a Ming creation.

Wu-lin men, see KC 3 and KC 26.

Hung 17. The story is set in the "Chih-cheng 至正 period of the Great Yüan." This was the last reign-period of the Yüan, and the story can therefore be regarded as of Ming composition.

Hung 18. Wu-lin men. See KC 3, KC 26, and Hung 14.

Pei hsin kuan 北新關, outside Wu-lin Gate. A Ming creation.

The term *li-chang* 里長, page 217, refers to the Ming system of local government. See KC 3, 26.

Ch'u-t'ang 褚堂, page 224, evidently the Ch'u-t'ang shih or Ch'u-t'ang Market which is mentioned in the Wan-li *Hang-chou fu chih*, *chüan* 34.16a, but not in earlier local histories.[11] The place-name Ch'u-chia t'ang 褚家塘 (*sic*) is found in Sung descriptions of Hang-chow as the name of an embankment.[12] As Ch'u-chia t'ang 褚家堂 in KC 26, page 392, as well as in other stories, it is the name of a locality within the city wall.

The expression *chin Hang-chou* 今杭州 (present-day Hangchow), page 213, appended as an explanation to the Yüan name for the city.

Hsiung A. (Main story only.)

Hsing-hua fu 興化府, page 12, a Ming creation.

Ch'u-chia t'ang 褚家堂, page 9, is a slight indication of Ming composition. See Hung 18.

Hsiung D. This story is set in the Hung-chih (1488–1505) reign-period of the Ming. It also contains distinctively Ming place-names, for example, Hu shih 湖市, page 64. Compare KC 3.

Tu Li-niang chi. This story contains a distinctively Ming place-name, mentioned several times. (Nan-hsiung fu 南雄府.) It also mentions the fifteenth century Classical tale *Chung-ch'ing li chi* 鍾情麗集.[13]

The above twelve stories form the pilot group. Apart from them, several

---

11 The earliest work I know of which lists it as a market is the *Hsi-hu yu-lan chih*, *chüan* 1.1, which was first published in 1541.

12 E.g., the [*Hsien-shun*] *Lin-an chih* 咸淳臨安志 of 1268, comp. Ch'ien Shuo-yu 潛說友 (Hangchow, 1830 ed.), *chüan* 38, lists it merely as an embankment. The 1549 *Jen-ho hsien chih* 仁和縣志, comp. Shen Ch'ao-hsüan 沈朝宣, *Wu-lin chang-ku ts'ung-pien* ed., *chüan* 2.41a, says that the river had long since dried up but that the name persisted.

13 See Sun K'ai-ti, *Jih-pen Tung-ching so-chien Chung-kuo hsiao-shuo shu-mu*, p. 165, on the date of the tale's composition.

other stories contain Ming place-names but are not, for one reason or another, admitted to the pilot group.

TY 8M and Hung 16 both contain the short-lived (1368–1372) place-name T'an-chou fu 潭州府, but both refer to it also as plain T'an-chou. It is possible that modern editors are mistaken in taking T'an-chou fu as a place-name and that the reference is really to the *fu* (administrative offices) of T'an-chou.[14] However that may be, the reference is not convincing enough for us to put these stories into the pilot group.

TY 28 contains two references to Su-chou fu 蘇州府, a Ming creation, but also refers to Su-chou. This would not be enough to qualify it as a middle story, even if there were no reason for believing that it has been adapted by a late editor.[15]

P'ei Hsiu-niang contains two Ming place-names, Yen-chou fu 兗州府 and Kuang-hsin fu 廣信府.[16] It is not placed in the pilot group because of the claim that it is listed in the *Tsui-weng t'an-lu*.[17]

TY 13 refers to Yen-chou fu once, on page 169. It is also claimed that TY 13 is listed in the *Tsui-weng t'an-lu*.

HY 21 refers to Huang-chou fu 黃州府, a Ming creation, once on page 464, as well as to plain Huang-chou, page 458. We noticed in Chapter III the severe adaptation which earlier stories suffered at the hands of the HY editor.

Hung 12, page 129, has Nan-hsiung fu 南雄府 once, but it also has plain Nan-hsiung frequently elsewhere.

The Ming place-names in two other stories can be explained as the result of adaptation. The place-name Jao-chou fu 饒州府 in HY 12 occurs in the introduction which, as was shown in Chapter III, is by a late editor. The *Kuo-se t'ien-hsiang* version of *Chang Yü-hu* contains a reference to Su-chou fu, but it was shown to be an abridgement of the *Yen-chü pi-chi* version, which in some forms has Su-chou instead of Su-chou fu.[18]

---

14 In TY 8, p. 97, the context is *ching lai Hunan T'an-chou fu, hsia-le kung-wen* 徑來湖南潭州府，下了公文, which could be translated as "he went directly to the administrative office of T'an-chou in Hunan and deposited the document." The context in Hung 16, p. 200, is *tsai T'an-chou fu-li tso t'i-k'ung* 在潭州府裡做提空, which could be translated as "he was a *t'i-k'ung* in the T'an-chou administrative office." No doubt the usual explanation, particularly in the former case, is the better, but the fact that the alternative possibility exists should make us hesitate to ascribe these stories to the Ming.

15 It was shown above, in Chapter III, to contain two newer criteria.

16 It also contains the place-name Ch'u-chia-t'ang. See under Hung 18.

17 For a discussion of these supposed identifications, see Hanan, "Sung and Yüan Vernacular Fiction," p. 170.

18 The Lin and Yü versions of the *Yen-chü pi-chi* have Su-chou, the Ho version, Su-chou fu. The *Wan-chin* version has Su-chou. The *Pai-chia kung-an* story *P'an Li Chung-li mou fu chan ch'i* is also excluded from the pilot group despite its late-Yüan place-name. (See Chapter III, n. 85.) It was only tentatively placed among the older stories.

Hung 7 refers to an item of dress which came into vogue only at the beginning of the Ming dynasty. Although the point seems too slight to place Hung 7 in the pilot group, it must be considered in determining that story's date. See the section "The Remaining Stories" below.

The Pilot Group of Early Stories

There is, of course, no short story which can safely be assumed to be of pre-Ming composition. Lo Yeh's *Tsui-weng t'an-lu* has been used in various attempts to identify Sung stories, but, as has been shown, it is too ambiguous to serve as primary evidence. As an illustration of this point, some of the stories supposedly referred to in the *T'an-lu* turned out to contain distinctively Ming place-names.[19] KC 36M is the only story for which we can conceivably claim Yüan authorship, but its identification is still questionable, and it would be dangerous to take it as the exemplar (the sole exemplar, mind!) of the pre-Ming story. If we are to have a pilot group at all, it must be drawn initially from texts which can be reliably dated, even if we need to go outside the genre of the short story to find them.

Our only recourse is to the group of six historical chronicles known as the *p'ing-hua*:

> *Wu Wang fa Chou p'ing-hua* 武王伐紂平話 (known hereafter as *Wu Wang*)
> *Ch'i kuo ch'un-ch'iu p'ing-hua* 七國春秋平話 (*Ch'i kuo*)
> *Ch'in ping liu kuo p'ing-hua* 秦併六國平話 (*Ch'in ping*)
> *Ch'ien Han shu p'ing-hua* 前漢書平話 (*Ch'ien Han*)
> *San kuo chih p'ing-hua* 三國志平話 (*San kuo*)
> *Wu Tai shih p'ing-hua* 五代史平話 (*Wu Tai*)

The first five works were published together in the same format in an edition dated *Chih-chih* 至治 (1321–1323) in Chien-an in Fukien. The sixth story, *Wu Tai*, has no date of publication, but it is probably a Yüan work.[20]

A seventh work, the *Ta Sung Hsüan-ho i-shih* 大宋宣和遺事 (*Hsüan-ho*), can be added to this list. It is post-Sung, since it accurately prophesies the end of the Sung dynasty. It is not precisely datable, but in its general characteristics, its rhetoric and its language, and its mode of composition (combining folklore material in the vernacular with quotations from historical works in Classical Chinese), it belongs to the *p'ing-hua* group. The only

---

19 E.g., *P'ei Hsiu-niang* has two or three Ming place-names.
20 See "Sung and Yüan Vernacular Fiction," pp. 162–163, for a discussion of the date of this and other similar works. These are the short titles of modern editions. For the full titles, see Sun K'ai-ti, *Chung-kuo t'ung-su hsiao-shuo shu-mu*, pp. 1–2.

other *p'ing-hua* is the *Hsüeh Jen-kuei cheng Liao shih-lüeh* 薛仁貴征遼事略 (*Hsüeh*), which also shares many of the characteristics of the others. It survives in an early Ming copy, in the *Yung-lo ta-tien*.[21]

Another narrative work which does not belong to the *p'ing-hua* genre but which is unquestionably early is the *Ta T'ang San-tsang ch'ü ching shih-hua* 大唐三藏取經詩話 (*Shih-hua*). It exists in two editions, both of which are claimed to be Southern Sung.[22]

The first eight works can be considered as a subgenre. They all contain a loose, chronological arrangement of two kinds of material, folklore and text drawn from quasi-historical works. They have stylistic similarities, and even language similarities, which seem to indicate that they have been influenced by the same dialect.[23] (Few Chinese vernacular works are "in" a spoken or speakable dialect; at the most they show traces of this or that dialect.) Their style conforms in general to the pre-1575 criteria of Chapter III.[24]

The portions of the *p'ing-hua* we shall use as a sample comprise the first section of each, usually about thirty pages in the modern editions. In *Hsüan-ho* and *Wu Tai,* I have selected instead what seemed to me the more vernacular sections. Since *Wu Tai* is much the largest work, I have selected rather more text from it than from the others. The samples are as follows: *Wu Wang*, pages 1–30, *Ch'i kuo*, pages 1–26, *Ch'in ping*, pages 1–40, *Ch'ien Han*, pages 1–23, *San kuo*, page 1–45, *Wu Tai*, pages 1–35, 159–176, 181–215, *Hsüan-ho*, pages 36–77, *Hsüeh*, pages 1–30, *Shih-hua*, entire.

Since the language and forms of the *p'ing-hua* tend toward those of Classical narrative, an examination of the prespeech position does not yield significant results. But the other positions we designated in Chapter II, that is, the positions immediately before a set piece, a couplet, and a poem, do provide a useful contrast with the practice of the pilot group of middle stories.

21 There is a modern edition edited by Chao Wan-li 趙萬里, Shanghai, 1957.

22 One edition is entitled *Ta T'ang San-tsang Fa-shih ch'ü ching chi*. For a survey of the evidence regarding the date of these editions, see Glen Dudbridge, *The Hsi-yu chi, A Study of Antecedents to the Sixteenth-Century Chinese Novel* (Cambridge, Cambridge University Press, 1970), pp. 26–29.

23 Shōji Kakuichi 莊司格一, "Heiwa ni okeru gohō—ninshō daimeishi o chūshin to shite"「平話」における語法——人稱代名詞を中心として, *Shūkan Tōyōgaku* 11 (1964), pp. 46–58, demonstrates the common usage among the *p'ing-hua* with regard to pronouns, which serve admirably to set the *p'ing-hua* off from the short stories.

24 The only significant anomaly that has appeared so far is that late criterion *i, cheng tsai* plus predicate, occurs in several of the *p'ing-hua*. The latter constitute a distinct genre, with their own linguistic and stylistic peculiarities, both of which differ somewhat from the practice of the short stories. However, there seems to be enough conformity between the two genres for us to use the *p'ing-hua* as a guide.

If we compare these positions exhaustively in both the *p'ing-hua* group and the middle group, we find that the following formulae peculiar to the *p'ing-hua* are the three most frequent in occurrence:[25]

> *Tan chien* 但見, followed by a set piece. Found in four works (*Ch'i kuo, Ch'in ping,* five instances, *Wu Tai,* three instances, *Hsüan-ho*).[26]
>
> *Tao-shih* 道是, followed by a poem. Found in three works (*Ch'in ping,* one instance, *Wu Tai,* four instances, *Hsüan-ho,* two instances).[27]
>
> *Tao* 道, followed by a poem, but preceded by a word for "poem," for example, *tz'u tao.* Found in two works (*Wu Tai,* seven instances, *Hsüan-ho,* three instances).[28]

Of the formulae peculiar to the middle group, none is as common as these. *Yu fen chiao* 有分教[29] and *tuan-ti shih* 端的是[30] each occur in two stories as the introduction to a couplet.

If we now examine this position in KC 36M, we find that it conforms closely to the patterns of the *p'ing-hua* group as distinct from the middle group. It has two instances of *tan chien* followed by a set piece, one of *tao-shih* followed by a poem, and one of *tao* followed by a poem. Given the initial likelihood, we may conclude that KC 36M is indeed an early story, quite possibly the Yüan story of which we have record.

But KC 36M on its own cannot serve as a sample of the early story. If we test the other older stories against these criteria, we find that four show results as decisive as KC 36:

> KC 24, four instances of *tan chien,* one of *tao-shih,* two of *tao.*
>
> KC 33M, five instances of *tan chien,* one of *tao-shih,* one of *tao.*
>
> TY 37, one instance of *tan chien,* one of *tao-shih,* one of *tao.*
>
> Hung 15, two instances of *tan chien,* one of *tao-shih,* one of *tao.*

These stories thus have some claim to be regarded as early rather than middle. But that is not their only claim. All of them, KC 36M and these four, represent the subject matter of oral stories listed in the *Tsui-weng t'an-lu.* In addition, it is possible to devise a simple test which will show

---

25 There are others that occur in two of the *p'ing-hua,* but not as frequently as the third criterion.

26 *Ch'i kuo,* p. 5; *Ch'in ping,* pp. 18, 20, 22, 25, 31; *Wu Tai,* pp. 13, 30, 169; *Hsüan-ho,* p. 48.

27 *Ch'in ping,* p. 3; *Wu Tai,* pp. 4, 9, 11, 170; *Hsüan-ho,* pp. 47, 72. The formula in *Hsüan-ho,* p. 47, is followed, tautologically, by *shih yüeh* 詩曰 "the poem runs as follows." This is a feature peculiar to the *Hsüan-ho;* on p. 69 it has a *shih yün* followed by a *shih yüeh,* although both are of the same meaning. Two instances of *tao,* those on pp. 41 and 44, are also followed by *shih yüeh.*

28 *Wu Tai,* pp. 5, 10, 11, 14, 15, 16, 215; *Hsüan-ho,* pp. 41, 44, 75.

29 KC 3, Hung 18.

30 KC 29, 38.

that some of the same broad, natural distinctions exist between these five stories and the middle group as exist between the *p'ing-hua* and the middle group. The pre-1575 criteria of Chapter III were established for a different purpose; they have the advantage for us here of being random and hence objective. If the two groups are distinct, we might expect the difference to show up in the incidence of those seventeen criteria.

In fact, three of the criteria serve to distinguish the groups quite clearly:[31]

3. *nai yen* in the prespeech position is not found in the five stories at all, but occurs seven times in all in three of the middle stories (KC 29, TY 7, Hung 18).

5. *ch'ang je,* and so on, in the prespeech position is not found at all in the twelve middle stories, but occurs seven times in all in four of the five other stories (KC 24, 36M, TY 37, Hung 15).

17. *t'ien-ti* is not found at all in the twelve middle stories, but occurs eight times in all in three of the five other stories (KC 33, TY 37, Hung 15).

The same distinction is found in the *p'ing-hua* group. Criterion 5 is found in *Ch'in ping, San kuo,* and *Hsüeh,* criterion 17 in *Hsüan-ho,* but criterion 3, not at all.

I have thus used the *p'ing-hua* as a temporary pilot group, a means by which to select five stories to represent the early period. However, the *p'ing-hua* will not be entirely abandoned; in establishing the criteria between the early and middle groups, I shall still use the presence (or absence) of the criterion in the *p'ing-hua* sample as supporting evidence.

The Criteria

The criteria will be drawn from the stylistic features of the "vernacular fiction style," that is to say, excluding dialogue and the various special styles such as verse and parallel prose. Since they are features that must occur frequently, most of them will necessarily be concerned with the basic operations of narrative, that is, causal and chronological relationships and shifts of style, and so forth. The new criteria, those additional to the ones we have just introduced, are arbitrarily selected with the aim of showing as starkly as possible the difference between the two pilot groups. They are not intended to test whether two groups can be simply and naturally differentiated; that fact has already been established.

To serve as criteria, stylistic elements must occur at least four times in at least three middle stories, or in at least three early stories. (Although

---

31 For the definition of these criteria, see Chapters II and III.

there are twelve middle stories, some are close to the Classical narrative style and exhibit few significant features.) An element can serve as an early criterion if it occurs in only two stories, provided it also appears in at least one of the *p'ing-hua* works. Criteria must be mutually exclusive in their incidence, and middle criteria cannot occur in *p'ing-hua* works, except in cases of extraordinary numerical preponderance.

The *middle* criteria are:

Prespeech, prethought position:

M1. *nai yen,* criterion 3 of Chapter II, defined as before.

KC 29, two instances, TY 7, Hung 18, four instances.

Three stories, seven instances. No instance in early group or in *p'ing-hua.*

M2. *ta-tao* 答道 "replied as follows."

KC 26, 38, two instances, TY 7, Hung 18.

Four stories, five instances. No instance in early group or in *p'ing-hua.*

The passing of time, the setting of time, and so on:

M3. *chiang-chi* 將及 before time expressions, "when it came to . . ." or "when . . . has passed."

KC 3M, Hung 14M, two instances, 18, A (M).

Four stories, five instances.[32] No instance in early group or in *p'ing-hua.*

M4. *kuang-yin ssu chien* 光陰似箭 "time (flew) like an arrow." The criterion has to be exactly in this form, since a number of roughly similar expressions occur among the early stories.

KC 26, 29, TY 7, Hung 18, D.

Five stories, five instances. No instance in early group or in *p'ing-hua.*

M5. *cheng chih* 正值 "it chanced to be just the time when . . ."

KC 3M, 38, Hung 14M, 18, D, two instances, *Tu Li-niang chi.*

Six stories, seven instances. No instance in early group or *p'ing-hua.*

M6. . . . . *p'ai shih-fen* 牌時分 "the hour of . . . ," where the word before *p'ai* is one of the "twelve branches."

KC 3M, 26, two instances, 29, 38, five instances, Hung 18,[33] D.

Six stories, eleven instances. No instance in early group, one instance in *p'ing-hua, Ch'in ping,* page 13.

M7. *cheng yao* 正要 "was just about to . . . (when) . . ."

KC 3M, two instances, 26, two instances, 38, two instances, Hung 14M,[34] A (M).

---

32 KC 29, p. 429, has *chiang-chi* before a clause meaning "by the time that . . .", which is a roughly similar usage.

33 Hung 18 has an obvious omission on p. 216. See the T'an Cheng-pi edition, p. 231, n. 75.

34 Hung 14M, p. 166, has *cheng yao . . . chien* 間, which appears to be a combination of two constructions of similar meaning. A(M), p. 7, has *cheng erh yao* 正爾要.

Five stories, eight instances. No instance in early group or in *p'ing-hua*.

M8. *chiu-pien* 就便 "then," a compound adverb.

KC 3M, Hung 14M, three instances, A (M).

Three stories, five instances. No instance in early group or in *p'ing-hua*.

Narrator's comment on action:

M9. *yu fen chiao* 有分教, lit. "there was a fate that caused . . ." that is, "it would befall that . . ." The formula is used to introduce the prophecy of some dire consequence that will result from a character's action.

KC 3M, two instances, 26,[35] 38, two instances, Hung 17, three instances, 18, five instances.

Five stories, thirteen instances. No instance in early group or in *p'ing-hua*.

M10. *chih chiao* 直教 "directly causing," used in a similar fashion to M9 above, and often in conjunction with it.

KC 26, Hung 18, two instances, A (M).

Three stories, four instances. No instance in early group or in *p'ing-hua*.

M11. . . . *pu-t'i* 不題 "and there we leave the matter."

This differs from *pu-t'i* at the head of a sentence ("let us drop the subject of . . ."), which seems to be a late criterion.

KC 26, two instances, 38, two instances, Hung 14M, two instances.

Three stories, six instances. No instance in early group or in *p'ing-hua*.

M12. *k'uang* 況 "moreover." A commonplace in Classical Chinese, it functions as a criterion only in a vernacular context. It is to be distinguished from *k'uang-chien* 況兼 and *k'uang-ch'ieh* 況且, which are not criteria.

KC 3M, 26, Hung 14M, four instances, A (M), four instances.

Four stories, ten instances. No instance in early group and only one instance in *p'ing-hua* (*Hsüeh*, page 20) despite their closeness to Classical narrative.

The *early* criteria are:

Prespeech, prethought position:

E1. *ch'ang je tao*, and so on. Criterion 5 of Chapter II, defined as before.

KC 24, TY 36M, two instances, TY 37, Hung 15, three instances.

Four stories, seven instances. Instances in *Ch'in ping, San kuo, Hsüeh*. No instance in middle group.

---

35 KC 26, p. 399, has *yu fen chih chiao*, a combination of M9 and M10 below.

E2. *tu-li tao* 肚裡道 or *tu-li ssu-liang tao* 肚裡思量道, "thought to himself." *Tu-nei* 肚內 and *tu-chung* 肚中 accepted in place of *tu-li*.

KC 33M, 36M, two instances, TY 37, Hung 15.

Four stories, five instances. No instance in *p'ing-hua* or middle group.

Position introducing verse:

E3. *tao-shih* 道是 "which runs as follows."[36]

All five stories of the early group.

Five instances. Instances in *Ch'in ping, Wu Tai, Hsüan-ho*. No instance in middle group.

E4. *tao* 道, preceded by some word for poem. Meaning as in E3 above. Equivalent to the more common *yün* or *yüeh*.

All five stories in the early group, two instances in KC 24.

Six instances. Instances in *Wu Tai, Hsüan-ho*. None in the middle group.

Position introducing couplet or poem or set piece:

E5. *k'an shih* 看時 "when he looked . . . ," or *k'an . . . shih* "when he looked at . . ." A short phrase, such as *chih chien* 只見 "what he saw was . . ." or *sheng-te* 生得 "in appearance he was" may intervene between *k'an shih* and the couplet, and so on.

All five stories of the early group, two instances in KC 24.

Six instances. No instance in the *p'ing-hua*. None in the middle group.

Position before a set piece:

E6. *tan chien* 但見 "(all) he saw was . . ." Although a very common element in late fiction, this formula is not found in the middle group. All five stories of the early group, four instances in KC 24, five in KC 33M, two in KC 36M, TY 37, two in Hung 15.

Fourteen instances. Instances in *Ch'i kuo, Ch'in ping, Wu Tai, Hsüan-ho*. No instance in middle group.[37]

The passing of time, the setting of time, and so on:

E7. *tao-te* 到得, before a timeword or time phrase, "when . . . arrived." It is found before a clause only in late stories.

KC 36M, TY 37, Hung 15.

Three stories, three instances.

Instances in *Ch'i kuo, Wu Tai*. No instance in middle group.

---

36 Like several of the early criteria, particularly E6 and E10 below, this one is found quite commonly among *late* stories. It serves as a criterion only as between early and middle. Note that *tao-shih* is sometimes used to introduce speech, as in Hung 15; these cases are not counted here. The instance in Hung 15, p. 178, does introduce a poem, however, and is counted.

37 *Tu Li-niang chi* has *tan chien* once, but not before set piece, the sine qua non of which is parallelism.

E8. *pu to shih* 不多時, "before long." This criterion must come before the relevant verb, not after it, in the meaning of "for a short while."

KC 24, 36M, three instances, TY 37, Hung 15.

Four stories, six instances.

Instances in *San kuo, Wu Tai, Hsüan-ho*. No instance in middle group.

E9. *ch'ien hou* 前後, "or thereabouts," after a time expression.

KC 24, 36M, four instances, TY 37, two instances.

Three stories, seven instances. One instance in *Ch'i kuo*. Two instances in *San kuo, preceding* the time expression.[38] No instance in middle group.

E10. *ch'ing-k'o* 頃刻 or *ch'ing-k'o chien* 頃刻間 or *ch'ing-k'o chih chien* 頃刻之間, "in a moment." A commonplace in Classical Chinese, this expression functions as a criterion in a vernacular context.

KC 36M, TY 37.

Two stories, two instances.

Instances in *Wu Wang, San kuo, Wu Tai*.

No instance in middle group.

E11. *ch'üeh-tai* 却待 or *ch'ia-tai* 恰待,[39] "was just about to . . . (when) . . ."

KC 36M, three instances, TY 37, Hung 15.

Three stories, five instances. One instance in *Hsüan-ho*. No instance in middle group.

E12. *shuo yu wei liao* 說猶未了, "before he had finished speaking."

KC 24, Hung 15.

Two stories, two instances. Instances in *Shih-hua*.

No instance in middle group.

Other expressions:

E13. *t'ien-ti*, criterion 17 of Chapter III, defined as before.

KC 33M, two instances, TY 37, three instances, Hung 15, three instances.

Three stories, eight instances.

One instance in *Hsüan-ho*. No instance in middle group.

E14. *i-ssu* 一似, "just like." At any point or position, not merely introducing a couplet.[40]

KC 33M, two instances, KC 36M, two instances, TY 37.

Three stories, five instances. Instances in *Wu Wang, Hsüan-ho*. No instance in middle group.

---

38 See p. 43.

39 The two forms often occur in the same story and are apparently interchangeable. Note that *ch'üeh-tai yao* 却待要, which occurs once in KC 26, is not accepted.

40 But not, of course, in dialogue or the various special styles.

E15. *ta i k'an shih* 打一看時 or *ta i k'an,* "when he took a look," and closely similar expressions such as *ta i kuan k'an* 打一觀看 and *ta i wang* 打一望.

All five stories of the early group, two instances in KC 24. Six instances. One instance in *Hsüan-ho.*

No instance in middle group.

Tables 9 and 10 show the incidence of separate criteria occurring in the

TABLE 9.   Incidence of Separate Criteria in the Pilot Group of Middle Stories.

Story	Early criteria	Middle criteria	Total	
			Early to middle	
KC 3M		M9, 7, 8, 5, 6, 12, 3	0	7
KC 26		M7, 12, 6, 11, 4, 2, 9, 10	0	8
KC 29 (part)		M6, 1, 4	0	3
KC 38		M5, 2, 11, 6, 7, 9	0	6
TY 7		M2, 4, 1	0	3
Hung 9			0	0
Hung 14M		M12, 3, 5, 11, 8, 7	0	6
Hung 17		M9	0	1
Hung 18		M9, 1, 4, 10, 6, 2, 3, 5	0	8
A(M)		M12, 8, 7, 10, 3	0	5
D		M5, 4, 6	0	3
Tu Li-niang chi		M5	0	1

TABLE 10.   Incidence of Separate Criteria in the Pilot Group of Early Stories.

Story	Early criteria	Middle criteria	Total	
			Early to middle	
KC 24	E4, 6, 5, 15, 8, 12, 1, 9, 3		9	0
KC 33M	E13, 6, 5, 14, 15, 4, 2, 3		8	0
KC 36M	E9, 5, 7, 4, 6, 15, 8, 2, 14, 10, 1, 11, 3		13	0
TY 37	E13, 4, 1, 10, 6, 5, 11, 9, 3, 2, 7, 8, 14, 15		14	0
Hung 15	E6, 7, 12, 4, 11, 2, 1, 3, 8, 5, 13, 15		12	0

middle and early stories, respectively. The number of instances of a particular criterion in a particular story is not given.

Application of the Criteria

In the classification of stories in Chapter III, we set three separate criteria as the minimum, provided there was no incidence of the opposing criteria. If there was any incidence of the opposing criteria, it must be outweighed in at least a four-to-one ratio. I shall use the same conditions here for the stories classified as middle (Table 11), but in view of the high numbers of criteria in our early group, I shall set two different standards for the stories classified as early, the regular one and a more stringent one, in which the minimum figure will be five and the minimum ratio six to one. Obviously, one can accept the stories classified according to the more stringent standard with a great deal more confidence.

The story *P'ei Hsiu-niang*, which because of the claim that it is referred to in the *Tsui-weng t'an-lu* has been thought of as a Sung story, is clearly middle period. As we remarked above, it contains two distinctively Ming place-names as well as a reference to Ch'u-chia t'ang, a probable indication of Ming composition. Note that Hung 12 also contains a distinctively Ming place-name. The *Pai-chia kung-an* story, *P'an Li Chung-li mou fu chan ch'i*, which is possibly an "older" story, has three middle criteria (M5, 11, 4) to one early (E6).[41]

TABLE 11.   Stories Classified as Middle.

Story	Early criteria	Middle criteria	Total Early to middle	
Hung 4		M9, 4, 5, 1	0	4
Hung 12	E1	M9, 2, 10, 4, 1	1	5
Hung 20		M12, 4, 10, 6, 7	0	5
P'ei Hsiu-niang		M6, 5, 1	0	3

41 See Chapter III. Whether middle or late, it is certainly a Ming story, containing a late-Yüan place-name.

TABLE 12.   Stories Classified as Early by the Regular Standard.

Story	Early criteria	Middle criteria	Total	
			Early	to middle
KC 15M	E10, 6, 5, 2, 1, 9, 11, 8	M10, 9	8	2
TY 6M	E15, 1, 11, 3, 7	M7	5	1
TY 8M	E5, 14, 1		3	0
TY 36P	E6, 15, 4		3	0
TY 36M	E4, 13, 8, 5	M5	4	1
TY 39	E 2, 15, 11, 12		4	0
HY 14	E 14, 9, 1, 8	M2	4	1
HY 21	E1, 4, 2		3	0
Hung 2P	E3, 7, 4, 13		4	0
Hung 2M	E5, 3, 1, 11		4	0
Hung 3M	E12, 2, 15, 1		4	0
Hung 13	E15, 14, 8, 4	M4	4	1

TABLE 13.   Stories Classified as Early by the More Stringent Standard.

Story	Early criteria	Middle criteria	Total	
			Early	to middle
TY 14M	E12, 5, 2, 8, 14, 11, 1		7	0
TY 19	E5, 11, 14, 15, 10, 2, 1		7	0
TY 20	E11, 7, 2, 14, 1, 6	M9	6	1
TY 30M	E4, 6, 1, 10, 14		5	0
HY 12 (part)[a]	E8, 15, 4, 6, 14		5	0
HY 31 (part)[b]	E6, 11, 14, 1, 10, 8, 9, 15		8	0
Hung 8M	E4, 6, 13, 5, 14, 8, 12, 9, 7		9	0

[a] The beginning of this story has been shown to have been either heavily adapted or else newly supplied by a late editor. The part of HY 12 under consideration here consists of page 235 to the end.

[b] The end of this story has been shown to have been either heavily adapted or else newly supplied by a late editor. The part of the story under consideration here runs from the beginning through page 667.

Reassessment of the Criteria

In Table 14, the effectiveness of the middle criteria is assessed as in Chapter III. Column 1 lists the middle criteria; column 2 gives the number of stories from the middle pilot group in which the criterion appears; column 3 gives the number of stories from those newly classified as middle in which the criterion appears; column 4 is the sum of columns 2 and 3; column 5 gives the titles of the early stories, from a total of twenty-four, in which the criterion appears; and column 6 juxtaposes the figures of columns 4 and 5.

The least adequate criterion is clearly M9, especially since it is a rare feature of the late stories and hence unlikely to have been added by a late editor. Note that no story has yet been classified as middle solely with the aid of criterion M9.

Table 15 is a corresponding table for the early criteria, substituting early for middle and vice versa.

It is clear that the early criteria are more reliable than the middle. Moreover, it is much easier to find additional early criteria than to find additional middle criteria. For example, the onomatopeic phrase *p'i-jan tao-ti* 匹然倒地 "fell down with a crash," which occurs in eight early stories (TY 8M, 14M, 20, 30M, 37, HY 14, 31, Hung 15) but in no middle stories, is representative

TABLE 14.   Comparative Effectiveness of the Middle Criteria.

Criterion	Pilot group	Just classified	Total middle stories	Early stories	Total	
					Middle	to early
M1	3	3	6		6	0
M2	4	1	5	HY 14	5	1
M3	4	0	4		4	0
M4	5	3	8	Hung 13	8	1
M5	6	2	8	TY 36M	8	1
M6	6	2	8		8	0
M7	5	1	6	TY 6M	6	1
M8	3	0	3		3	0
M9	5	2	7	KC 15M, TY 20	7	2
M10	3	2	5	KC 15M	5	1
M11	3	0	3		3	0
M12	4	1	5		5	0
Size of groups	12	4	16	24	16	24

of a number of four-character expressions which distinguish the early story.[42] Similarly, *li-pu-te*, criterion 15 of Chapter III, which occurs in nine early stories (KC 15M, 36M, TY 8M, 14M, 20, 30M, 37, HY 14, 31) and in only one middle story (TY 7), is typical of several narrator's comments that are confined, or practically confined, to the early story. It is not that the middle story does not have expressive phrases and narrator's comments; it is merely that the early story has more of them. Nor is it that the early stories we possess happen to be a particularly homogeneous group and that therefore it is easy to find criteria they have in common, for the standardized expressions are often repeated within the same story. In Chapter VIII, we shall consider whether this stylistic feature is determined by the early story's relationship to oral literature.

Early and middle stories are also sharply distinguished by their use of thematic material, as will be shown in the next chapter. To take an obvious instance, the tavern and the teahouse are focal points for the plot of the early story, but insignificant in the private, domestic world of the middle story.

TABLE 15.   Comparative Effectiveness of the Early Criteria.

Criterion	Pilot group	Just classified	Total early stories	Middle stories	Total	
					Early	to middle
E1	4	12	16	Hung 12	16	1
E2	4	7	11		11	0
E3	5	3	8		8	0
E4	5	8	13		13	0
E5	5	7	12		12	0
E6	5	7	12		12	0
E7	3	4	7		7	0
E8	4	8	12		12	0
E9	3	4	7		7	0
E10	2	4	6		6	0
E11	3	8	11		11	0
E12	2	4	6		6	0
E13	3	3	6		6	0
E14	3	10	13		13	0
E15	5	8	13		13	0
Size of groups	5	19	24	16	24	16

42 TY 30M has *p'ieh* 劈 for *p'i*. It is quite commonly written 劈.

Unfortunately, there are no other works with which we can check the effectiveness of our criteria.[43] The vernacular novels which are thought to be early, the *Shui-hu chuan* and the *P'ing-yao chuan,* exist only in late editions, and the data of this chapter throw more light on them than they are capable of throwing on the short story.

The obvious test would be a comparison of the official titles and institutional terms used by each group. A cruder but simpler method is to compare the degree of detail in the time reference of the early and middle groups. Although we cannot claim that because a story merely mentions a reign-period and gives no other precise indication of time it is necessarily a product of that dynasty, we can say that, in general, such stories are likely to be closer to that dynasty than other stories which give full detail of their time setting. Of the twenty-four early stories, fourteen are set in the Sung; of the sixteen middle stories, ten are set in the Sung. (The time setting of a few early and middle stories cannot be determined.) The three stories which refer to their time setting solely by mention of a reign-period are all early (KC 24, TY 8M, 14M), and the three stories which, though clearly set in the Sung, make no explicit mention of it, are also all early (KC 36M, HY 31, Hung 15). On the other hand, three of the four stories that refer to the dynasty as Nan Sung are middle. (KC 38, *Tu Li-niang chi, P'ei Hsiu-niang;* the early story is TY 6M.) This helps to confirm that our grouping does relate effectively to dating.

The Prologues

The prologues to the pilot groups and to the stories just classified are here treated in the same way as the prologues were treated in Chapter III.

Three stories in the middle pilot group have prologues, KC 3, Hung 14, and A. None of the prologues has any criteria, early or middle. KC 3P consists of a series of famous stories from earlier Chinese history told in anecdotal form. Hung 14P is an abridgement and slight adaptation of a T'ang dynasty Classical tale;[44] and A (P) is a severe abridgement and adaptation of a Classical tale found in the *Tsui-weng t'an-lu.*[45] There is thus

43 Some confirmation is given by the *Ch'ien-t'ang hu yin Chi Tien Ch'an-shih yü-lu,* a semi-Classical narrative published in Hangchow in 1569. It has two middle criteria, M5 and M7, and no early.

44 See Chapter VI, n. 27.

45 This is the *Hung-hsiao mi yüeh Chang Sheng fu Li Shih niang* 紅綃密約張生負李氏娘, Lo Yeh's *T'an-lu,* pp. 96–103. The prologue presents only the first part of the story, the elopement, and contrives a happy ending by omitting the young man's eventual betrayal of his wife. Note that the *T'an-lu's* reference to the *T'ai-p'ing kuang-chi* is clearly in error. The gist of the first part of the story is given in another work. (See *T'an-lu,* appendix, pp. 131–132.) There is also a possible reference to an oral story on this subject, under the title of *Yüan-yang teng* 鴛鴦燈. See p. 4.

a broad similarity about the composition of these prologues; they are all old stories, to some degree abridged and adapted to serve as prologues.[46] In their adapted form, they are clearly middle period, like their main stories.

Two stories of the early pilot group have prologues, KC 33 and KC 36. KC 33P has no criteria; KC 36P has one early criterion, E8, and no middle. The former is a prologue of the poem-chain kind which will be shown to be characteristic of the earliest stories. Both prologues must be classified early.

None of the stories just classified as middle has a prologue.

Six of the stories just classified as early have prologues, as follows:

KC 15P, one early criterion, E4, and no middle.

TY 8P, as above.

TY 14P, as above.

TY 30P, one early criterion, E10, and no middle.

Hung 3P, one early criterion, E6, and no middle.

Hung 8P, no criteria.

It is significant that five of these six stories (all but TY 30) have prologues of the poem-chain variety. It appears that the poem-chain is the most common kind of prologue among early stories. All six prologues must be classified early.

The Historical Stories in Classical Chinese

Another category of stories of which the date cannot be determined by stylistic criteria alone consists of eight stories in Classical Chinese, all of them on well-known historical subjects. They are as follows:

KC 25, no criteria.

Hung 21, one early criterion, E4, one middle, M5.

Hung 22, one middle criterion, M2.

Hung 23, no criteria.

Hung 24, no criteria.

Hung 25, one early criterion, E1.

Hung 26, one middle criterion, M3.

Hung 27, one middle criterion, M6.

These stories form a distinct group in several respects. Their themes are those of well-known historical or pseudohistorical figures or incidents, especially early figures; this in itself is enough to set them off from most other early and middle stories. Their language is Classical Chinese, with

---

46 There is also a remarkable similarity about the way the prologues are attached to the main stories of KC 3 and Hung 14.

very little concession to the vernacular; in this respect, they are matched only by some of the virtuoso stories. They do not begin immediately on their main stories, but have very short preambles or else prologue stories.[47] Furthermore, there are distinct similarities among the formulae with which these prologues and stories are ushered in. For example, four of the stories refer to their introductory poems as "words," using the term yen-yü 言語, and five stories begin the main story with chin-jih shuo "today we shall tell of." The combination of these two features is not found anywhere else among the early or middle stories.[48] Since seven of them appear together in the I-chen chi 欹枕集 section of the Hung stories, there is every reason to believe that these eight works are of the same approximate date and by the same author.

KC 25 is closely akin to the other seven stories in terms of its historical subject, its language, and even its stylistic features (both yen-yü and chin-jih shuo). The I-chen chi originally contained ten stories, and KC 25 is presumably one of the three missing works. If this is true, it means that Feng Meng-lung, in copying stories from the I-chen chi, worked his way in order through the four stories he found suitable:

Hung 21 (the first story in the I-chen chi)	—KC 7
Hung 22 (second)	—KC 16
KC 25 (third, fourth, or fifth)	—KC 25
Hung 27 (tenth)	—KC 34

There is other evidence that these stories were by a single author and that they were published for the first time in the I-chen chi. The I-chen chi is the only section of the surviving Hung stories in which consecutive titles are matched in pairs; Hung 21 and 22, 23 and 24, 25 and 26 form rough couplets. Furthermore, in contrast to the titles of the other Hung stories, theirs are long (at least seven characters), lack a concluding chi 記 or chuan 傳, and generally take the form of a transitive sentence, like the typical chapter headings of the Chinese novel. Since it is clear that the Pao-wen-t'ang catalogue lists Hung editions—its titles of stories are frequently identical, and always close, as compared with those of other editions—we can make certain deductions about the rest of the I-chen chi. Although the

---

47 Hung 25 is the sole exception. The first part of Hung 25 is also a little closer to the vernacular than the rest of the stories. On the other hand, it has a passage explaining the geographical names of the district which bears a marked similarity to a passage at the beginning of Hung 26. On the basis of this similarity, Inada Osamu 稲田尹, "Sōgen wahon ruikeikō" 宋元話本類型考, part iii, Kagoshima daigaku bunka hōkoku 鹿兒島大學文科報告 9 (1960), 126, actually suggested that Hung 25 and Hung 26 might be by the same author.

48 Indeed, reference to the opening poem as yen-yü is not found elsewhere among the early and middle stories. I am using the complete versions of Hung 21 and 22 in KC.

catalogue does not list the *I-chen chi* stories in order, it does roughly group them. Thus, the title of Hung 27 appears at the end of page 116, the titles of Hung 21, 22, and 26 on page 117, and those of Hung 23, 24, and KC 25 on page 118. It is possible that the other two missing stories are also listed on page 118; *Ch'u Wang yün meng yü jen lu* 楚王雲夢遇仁鹿 and *Ou-yang Hsüeh-shih shang hai-t'ang* 歐陽學士賞海棠[49] would form a roughly balanced couplet. These two stories, or others like them, would then have been the third and fourth stories in the complete *I-chen chi,* while KC 25, which has too long a catalogue title (nine characters) to match any other, would be the fifth story.

Another five or six titles of the same type can be discerned in the catalogue.[50] Possibly the same author was responsible for another half-section of five stories which have not survived.

These arguments raise the difficult question of how the Hung stories were first issued. Were the stories published individually and later collected, or was the collection (or its sections) issued first? The Pao-wen-t'ang catalogue lists the stories individually, but it also groups them roughly, as we have seen. It is surely significant that the five extant Hung stories which are not listed by the catalogue are a whole half-section.[51] Furthermore, the title of one of the sections, with the added note "ten titles," is also included in the catalogue.[52] What we know of the two other pre-*San yen* collections provides two slightly different patterns. To the best of our knowledge, the four stories issued by Hsiung Lung-feng in the Wan-li period, although in the same format, did not appear under a single title. The *Hsiao-shuo ch'uan-ch'i,* another Wan-li publication, brings together four disparate short stories under a colorless title. It may be a mistake, in considering commercial publishing, to suppose that there must have been a single orthodox way of issuing stories, but if we seek an explanation that will satisfy the facts we possess, we must assume that stories were issued in sets of loose, essentially individual, works, and the sets could be either kept together or broken up. This would also explain why the last pages of Hung 20 were lost, and also the first and last pages of several stories in the *I-chen chi.*[53]

49 Accepting the editor's emendation, p. 118.
50 See pp. 117, 123 of the *Pao-wen-t'ang shu-mu.*
51 The five not listed are Hung 16 through Hung 20, the entire first half of the *Yü-ch'uang chi* 雨窗集.
52 The *Sui-hang chi* 隨航集, p. 128. It is the third of the six section headings of the *Liu-shih chia hsiao-shuo* as listed in one edition of the *Hui-k'e shu-mu ch'u-pien* 彙刻書目初編. See Lévy, "Etudes," p. 99.
53 One reason why so many early and middle stories have altered endings or beginnings may be that the stories were published individually and the outer pages suffered. Note that several Classical tales were published in individual editions in the Ming.

It is thus most likely that the *I-chen chi* was issued as a set in the first instance, and that its ten stories were by a single author. We may infer that he was a contemporary of Hung P'ien.

A Textual Note on Hung 21 and 22

The text at the beginning of three Hung stories, 21, 22, and 23, is missing. In the cases of Hung 21 and 22, we have a complete text in KC 7 and KC 16, respectively, from which to deduce what the original must have been. Since the rest of Hung 21 and 22 has been copied fairly faithfully into the KC versions, one would expect the same to be true of the beginning section. When one comes to fit the KC text of the missing section into a whole number of double pages, however, one gets an anomalous result.

In the case of Hung 21, the extra KC text amounts to three double pages and about eleven and a half columns. Since the main change made by Feng Meng-lung is the addition of poems, one would immediately suspect that the *tz'u* and the set piece are his contribution. This leaves five and a half columns unaccounted for. The likeliest explanation is that the KC prologue has been added or expanded. (It comes to about eight columns.) This is the more likely in that the word *yen-yü* describing a poem, one of the common traits of these historical stories, comes about halfway through the prologue. Therefore, the missing text of Hung 21 probably consisted of three double pages of text roughly identical with that in the corresponding part of KC 7 when the first part of the prologue, the *tz'u,* and the set piece have been excluded.

Hung 22 is a simpler problem. The KC 16 version of the missing text comes to three double pages plus about four columns. Most of this is to be accounted for by assuming that the four-line poem and its introduction, three columns in all, have been added by Feng Meng-lung. The introductory formula, *yu shih wei cheng* "there is a poem in evidence," is not found in any of the Hung group of historical stories. The missing text of Hung 22 therefore probably also consisted of three double pages, roughly identical with the corresponding text of KC 16 when the poem and its formula have been omitted.

The Adapted Stories

In Chapter III, we showed that five HY stories, HY 12, 13, 14, 31, and 33, had been severely adapted by a late editor. Reviewing these stories now according to our present criteria, we see a striking confirmation of the original judgement.

Three of the stories have so far been shown to be early: HY 12, 14, and 31. The suspect opening of HY 12 has no early or middle criteria, nor has HY 14 any middle criteria. HY 31, however, has eight early criteria in the story before the last section and two middle criteria (M11, 4) in the last section. This confirms the judgement made in Chapter III that the last section of HY 31 has been added.[54]

The two other stories are a mixture of early and middle criteria:

HY 13	E6, 12, 7	M3, 2, 11, 5
HY 33P	E10	M2, 11
HY 33M	E11, 13	M11, 5, 2

The middle and early criteria are not spatially separated in as clear a fashion as in HY 31, but the last two middle criteria in HY 33M occur after the early criteria.[55] This reinforces the tentative view of Chapter III that the end of HY 33M was the place which suffered the most adaptation or addition of text.

It is likely that HY 13 and perhaps also HY 33M (the prologue is another matter) were originally early stories. In each, it is possible to find examples of the standardized expressions which characterize the early stories only. For instance, HY 33M has a case of *ch'a shou pu li fang-ts'un* 叉手不離方寸 "crossed his hands right over his heart (and said)" in the prespeech position.[56] And both HY 33M and HY 13 have *tao-pu-te ko* 道不得個 "surely, indeed" introducing a couplet.[57]

What is noteworthy is the repetition of middle criteria in these stories and in HY 31. Criterion M11 appears in all four (including 33P), M2 in

54 To summarize Chapter III's results, the last pre-1575 criterion occurred on p. 668 and the first late criterion on p. 670. There were two instances of late criteria on p. 670, two more plus a probable late criterion on p. 671, and one more on the last page, 672. According to our present criteria, the last early criterion occurs on p. 667 and the first middle criterion on p. 668. There is one instance of a middle criterion on p. 668, one on p. 669, and one on p. 670. The two sets of criteria tally so well that one is inclined to believe that the HY editor's exemplar lacked the last pages and that the ending is entirely his work. The break must have come on p. 668.

55 From the last column on p. 702 to the end of the story on p. 706, HY 33M has only middle and late criteria. P. 702 has one late criterion, p. 703 a late and a middle, and p. 705 a middle.

56 HY 33, p. 698. It is found also in KC 36M, TY 37, Hung 2M.

57 HY 33, p. 702, HY 13, p. 247. It is found also in KC 33M, TY 8, TY 19, TY 20. On the other hand, Ch'u-chia-t'ang is mentioned on p. 698, a place-name which has been taken as some indication of Ming composition. Note that HY 33 and TY 28 are the only stories with a Hangchow bridge called Chien-ch'iao 箭橋, presumably a mistake for the 薦橋 of the local histories. See the 1579 *Hang-chou fu chih, chüan* 45.1b.

three, and M5 in three. (HY 14 also has an instance of M2.) These function as criteria when distinguishing middle stories from early stories, but they do not function as criteria when distinguishing middle stories from late; they are, in fact, commonplace in the late story. Obviously, though they appear here as "middle criteria," they are merely further evidence of the adaptation of these stories by a late editor.

There is no evidence that HY 33P was originally an early story. Just as no pre-1575 criteria were discovered in it in Chapter III, so no early criteria—criterion E10 is common enough in late stories—have been discovered here. It seems that this prologue story was either written by the late editor, or, just as possibly, that it was enlarged and severely adapted by him. If the latter case is true, we have no means of knowing the original date of the story.

There is one other story, TY 28, which showed a mixture of criteria in Chapter III and which also shows a mixture now. Quite possibly it is a case analogous to the stories we have just dealt with. In classifying it as pre-1575, we noted that it had two late criteria. Now, in testing it against the early and middle criteria, we find that it has six early (E8, 7, 2, 1, 14, 9) and four middle (M9, 2, 5, 4). Three of the middle criteria (M2, 5, 4) occurred in the adaptation of the HY stories by a late editor, and we have shown that M9 is the weakest of the middle criteria. It is likely, therefore, that TY 28 was originally an early story which was adapted by a late editor, and that its "middle" and "late" criteria both reflect this fact. Its incidence of a distinctively Ming place-name ought also perhaps to be viewed in this light.

The Virtuoso Stories

"Virtuoso" or "precious" is a name I have given to the species of short story in which the plot is secondary to the elegantly expressed sentiments and poetic virtuosity of the main characters. Such stories are full of poems "composed" by the characters, and their language is generally fairly close to Classical Chinese.

These stories are difficult to classify on the basis of stylistic features alone. I treat them together here, not because they can be classified en bloc like the historical stories, but merely for convenience.

Among the stories already classified, there are four middle-period virtuoso stories, Hung 9, *Tu Li-niang chi, P'ei Hsiu-niang,* and A (P). The only virtuoso stories classified as early are some of those with poem-chain prologues.

Some of the stories can be tentatively classified. As Table 16 shows, Hung 5 and *Chang Yü-hu* are more likely to be early than middle. TY 10, with four instances of criterion E6, and TY 29, with two instances, are also likely to be early, since that criterion is the most common among early stories yet almost nonexistent among middle. Hung 6 is almost identical with the adapted version of a T'ang Classical tale that is contained in the *Tsui-weng t'an-lu*;[58] it merely adds a few poems and an opening paragraph to convert a tale into the semblance of a short story. In its present form, it can only be considered as middle period. (Compare Hung 14P and A (P), both of which were adapted from Classical tales.)[59] Hung 10 is an extended dialogue in verse, very similar to its neighbor, the middle story Hung 9. From A Ying's description of it, Hung 29 seems to be a Ming virtuoso tale.[60] *Ch'ien-t'ang meng* has an apparent poem-chain prologue on the subject of Hangchow, rather like Hung 3P. Another part of its description of Hangchow is duplicated in the twenty-chapter *P'ing-yao chuan*.[61] Moreover, it

TABLE 16.   Incidence of Criteria among Virtuoso Stories.

Story	Early criteria	Middle criteria	Total Early to middle	
KC 11	E4	M3, 2	1	2
TY 10	E6		1	0
TY 29	E6		1	0
Hung 1			0	0
Hung 5	E6, 10		2	0
Hung 6			0	0
Hung 10			0	0
Hung 28	E6		1	0
Hung 29	—	—	—	
B		M12	0	1
Chang Yü-hu	E1, 11, 6	M2	3	1
Ch'ien-t'ang meng			0	0

58 *P'ei Hang yü Yün-ying yü Lan-ch'iao* 裴航遇雲英于藍橋, pp. 88–90. It is derived from P'ei Hsing's 裴鉶 *Ch'uan-ch'i* 傳奇, which is quoted in the *T'ai-p'ing kuang-chi, chüan* 50.

59 The rough adaptation referred to here is very different from the adaptation practiced by Feng Meng-lung and X. These stories change little of the original language and show few of the features of the short story.

60 *Hsiao-shuo hsien-hua*, p. 42. The story is apparently set in the last reign-period of the Yüan.

61 See the opening of chap. 1, a description of Kaifeng, not Hangchow.

exists in an earlier edition than any other story, and for these various reasons can be considered early. The other stories, KC 11, Hung 1, 28, and B cannot be classified, not even in the highly tentative manner above.

The *Tsui-weng t'an-lu* list, however it is interpreted, tallies fairly well with these tentative results. It contains apparent references to TY 10, 29, Hung 5, and *Ch'ien-t'ang meng,* which we have suggested are early, and to B,[62] which we have not attempted to date.

One other story may be considered here, the *Cheng Yüan-ho p'iao-yü Li Ya-hsien chi* which is found in the Lin and Yü versions of the *Yen-chü pi-chi.* It could not be classified with any reasonable likelihood in Chapter III. Our present criteria are of little use; it has one middle criterion, M5. However, on general grounds, it is likely to be early or middle, since all of the other short stories contained in the miscellanies proved to be so. It is a rough adaptation of a well-known Classical tale and can be grouped with Hung 6, Hung 14P, and so on, and is therefore most likely a middle story.[63]

The Remaining Stories

Eight stories, including prologues, have not been discussed so far. They are shown in Table 17.

TABLE 17.   Incidence of Criteria in the Unclassified Stories.

Story	Early criteria	Middle criteria	Total	
			Early to middle	
TY 13P	E6		1	0
TY 13M	E6, 3, 9	M2	3	1
TY 16	E6, 11	M12	2	1
TY 23P		M1	0	1
Hung 7	E8	M7	1	1
Hung 11	E6		1	0
Hung 16	E12, 15	M4	2	1
Hung 19		M1, 2	0	2

62 It is by no means certain that the *T'an-lu* is even referring to the stuff-material of B. See Hanan, "Sung and Yüan Vernacular Fiction," p. 170.
63 A second story of undetermined date was HY 40. Its opening section was certainly by a late writer, quite possibly X himself. On the whole, it seems most likely that the story is by a late author, although there is no firm evidence to preclude its being a much revised early story.

Some of them can be classified tentatively. TY 13M, page 175, has an instance of *p'i-jan tao-ti,* which as we have seen is confined to early stories, as well as other standardized expressions. It can be taken as early, and its prologue with it. Hung 11, a very short piece, has four instances of criterion E6, and also a *li-pu-te,*[64] an adequate early criterion; it can also be regarded as early. TY 16 is a more difficult case, but it has a number of the characteristic standardized expressions, including *tao-pu-te,*[65] and is probably early.

Hung 19 is almost certainly middle; it has four instances of M1 and two of M2. The other three stories cannot be classified, even tentatively, by these means. It is noteworthy that Hung 7, a *chantefable,* refers to the *wang-chin* 網巾, a cap of silk net which came into vogue only at the beginning of the Ming dynasty.[66] On this evidence, it may be classed as a middle story. Hung 7 and Hung 16 are in some respects the same kind of story—a young girl who flouts her parents' wishes and displays a gift for, in Hung 7, rhymed tirades, and in Hung 16, religious riddles. But this is not enough to classify the latter story.

The Relationship between the Hung and Hsiung Stories

We have examined the connection between the *San yen* stories and the Hung and Hsiung stories, but not the connection between the latter two. They have one story in common, Hsiung C being the same as Hung 9. André Lévy has pointed out that two double pages of this story are missing in our extant copy of Hung 9 and that the corresponding text is also missing in the *Kuo-se t'ien-hsiang* reprint.[67] But of course this need not mean that the Hsiung text is primary, since it could derive from an earlier and more careful printing of the Hung story.

The Hung and Hsiung stories have several other things in common, most of them superficial. Almost all of the Hung stories preface the introductory poem with the word *ju-hua* "introduction," as do all four Hsiung stories. The concluding formula, *hua-pen shuo-ch'e, ch'üan tso san ch'ang* 話本說徹, 權作散場 "the story is over, so please disperse for now" is found

---

64 P. 115.

65 P. 227. The expressions include *wang chih so ts'o,* a Classical gobbet which was used in Chapter III as a probable older criterion, *hsiang tz'u* 相次 "next," and *fang-ts'ai* 方才 "no sooner than," followed by *chih chien* 只見.

66 The point was made by Yeh Te-chün 葉德均, *Sung-Yüan-Ming chiang-ch'ang wen-hsüeh* 宋元明講唱文學 (Shanghai, 1957), p. 58. See Wang Ch'i 王圻, *San ts'ai t'u hui* 三才圖會, Taipei, 1970 facsimile of 1607 ed., clothing section *chüan* 1, p. 1513.

67 "Etudes," pp. 107–110.

only in the Hung and Hsiung stories, in Hung 2, 4, 12 and Hsiung A.[68]
Another concluding or penultimate couplet "right up to the present, in
wind and moon, on river and lake, from time immemorial the tale has been
told by fishermen and woodcutters" is found only in Hsiung B, Hung 1,
and 18. Both groups of stories tolerate a variety of words, *yüeh*, *yün*, and *tao*,
in the immediate prespeech position of the same story, a confusion which
the *San yen* editors spasmodically attempt to sort out. In these and other
respects, the connection between the Hung and Hsiung stories is a close
one. The most likely explanation, unprovable though it is, is that the Hsiung
stories are reprints of some of the stories from the Hung collections and
that their distinction is that they are better printed and have illustrations.

However this may be, it is true that we are dependent to an extraordinary
degree on Hung P'ien for our knowledge of the early and middle story.
Did he change the original texts that he reprinted? We must ask the question, even though there is no way of answering it adequately. Obviously,
some of the superficial uniformity of the texts must be owing to him, the
ju-hua and so forth. Two adjacent stories, Hung 12 and 13, end with similar
formulae not found elsewhere. One could compare the Hung early stories
with the non-Hung early stories to see if there is any systematic difference,
but if there were no substantial differences it would not prove anything,
because even the non-Hung stories may have come from the missing Hung
collections. For what it is worth, the incidence of the early criteria does not
show any systematic differences.

Another inescapable question concerns the relationship between the
Hung collections and the Pao-wen-t'ang library, of which we have the
catalogue. The fact that the five Hung stories not mentioned in the catalogue
comprise the entire first section of the *Yü-ch'uang chi* 雨窗集 may lead us
to suppose that the Pao-wen-t'ang library was dependent on the Hung
collections, that is, that all of the stories mentioned in the catalogue may
have been published by Hung P'ien. In that case, practically all of our
extant early and middle stories must have been subjected to his editing.
What evidence there is suggests that this was not so.[69] The proportion of
middle to early in the extant Hung stories is weighted heavily in favor of

---

68 Hung 2 has *ch'ieh* 且 for *ch'üan*. This concluding formula has sometimes been taken
as an indication that the text is a storyteller's "prompt-book." It occurs in only one early
story, Hung 2, and in three middle stories, Hsiung A, Hung 4, and Hung 12. It will be
suggested in the next chapter that Hung 4 and Hung 12 may have been derived from plays.
Clearly, the formula originated in the storyteller's rhetoric, but was later used for other
purposes. It may even have been added by the Hung editors.

69 It is possible to guess which of the Pao-wen-t'ang titles are likely to be those of short
stories. On the whole, they are listed later in the catalogue than the bulk of the Classical
tales, and it is fairly easy to tell their titles from those of *pi-chi* and other collections. Even
by a conservative count, there are well over sixty titles, the number of Hung P'ien's
collections.

the middle stories, as many as eighteen middle to eight early stories. (A few are undatable.) On the other hand, the stories referred to in the catalogue but not contained in the extant Hung collections are in the opposite proportion, fourteen early stories to eight middle. It seems, then, that the library was not entirely dependent on the Hung publications, important though they may have been. One would expect a commercial publisher to emphasize the more up-to-date kind of story, as the Hung collections do. But the Pao-wen-t'ang was a private library, and it also gave some weight, as libraries do, to what is old and rare.

We can get some confirmation of this by looking at the early and middle stories reprinted by Feng Meng-lung which are neither in the Hung collections nor in the library catalogue. There are twelve or thirteen, all but one of which are early. It seems that Feng Meng-lung may have had access to stories outside of those in the Hung collections and outside of those available to the Pao-wen-t'ang collectors. (It is not that he deliberately chose the early over the middle period, for his first anthology, KC, shows a preponderance of middle stories, eleven to six.) It is likely, from what we know of his practice, that he was using different anthologies at different times. In KC he used the *I-chen chi* collection plus other Hung stories, and all of the other early and middle stories he used were among those that were available to the Pao-wen-t'ang collectors. In TY, there is a remarkable difference. Two stories (33, 38) are reprinted from the Hung collections, and four or five others are among those mentioned in the catalogue, but the great majority, ten or eleven, is outside of both of these groups.[70] As many as four stories are referred to in editorial comments as "Sung stories," "old editions," and the like. It is possible that behind TY we can dimly discern the presence of some collection or collections different from anything used by Hung P'ien or available to the Pao-wen-t'ang. Whether close examination would show some common characteristics among these TY stories is doubtful. (The superficial characteristics that mark the Hung stories have been entirely obscured in their *San yen* versions.) But it does appear that the early stories were handed down by more than one different agency.

The Meaning of "Middle" and "Early"

Twenty-nine[71] stories have been described as middle-period, and thirty-two stories as early; six stories have not been dated. Our starting definition

---

70 TY 6M, 7, 10, 13, 14, possibly 16, 19, 28, 30, 36, 39. In comparison, HY has only six pre-1575 stories, all of them early. Four are listed in the catalogue.

71 Thirty, if one counts the *Cheng Yüan-ho* story, thirty-one if one also counts the *P'an Li Chung-li mou fu chan ch'i*. The twenty-nine are made up of the twelve pilot stories, the four newly classified stories, the eight "historical" stories, Hung 6, 7, 10, 19, and 29.

of "middle" was simply "Ming dynasty, but not late." The term "early" was left vague; it was just assumed that early stories would, in general, prove to be earlier than middle.

All of the middle stories except TY 7 and *P'ei Hsiu-niang* are either preserved in the Hung collections or mentioned in the Pao-wen-t'ang catalogue. For all except these two, the *terminus ante quem* is therefore circa 1550. For these two stories, it is conceivably a little later. The *terminus post quem* for all of the middle stories is, of course, the beginning of the Ming dynasty, 1368. Since it is unlikely that distinctively Ming place-names will be used in the very early Ming in stories about other dynasties, I shall set the date somewhat later, at circa 1400. However, some of the middle stories are certainly later than this. Hsiung D is set in the Hung-chih reign-period, which ended in 1505, and we may suppose that the story was written after this date, that is, between 1505 and 1550. (T'ien Ju-ch'eng describes its subject as a favorite of the Hangchow storytellers in his *Chih-yü*, published in 1541.) Lang Ying's 郎瑛 *Ch'i-hsiu lei-kao* 七修類稿, *chüan* 45. 653–654,[72] tells of an event which took place in the T'ien-shun period (1457–1464), an event which we can identify as the plot of KC 26. (A Hangchow man like T'ien Ju-ch'eng, Lang says that the anecdote was still current in Hangchow. His *Lei-kao* was published in the Chia-ching period [1522–1566].) It thus seems likely that KC 26 was written at the close of the fifteenth century or in the first half of the sixteenth. I shall argue in the next chapter that the author of KC 26 also wrote KC 38, and possibly KC 3 as well; if that is true, these stories too would be mid-Ming. It will also be shown that KC 29 is the result of a long process of development; it is likely to have been composed late in the middle period. About the other stories we cannot be more precise, though it is possible that they too are mid-Ming rather than early-Ming.

The early stories, if our hypothesis is correct, will in general be earlier than the middle stories, but it does not follow that they will necessarily be pre-Ming. Supposing that the early pilot group is of Yüan composition and that the middle pilot group was composed in the mid-Ming, we cannot insist that the dividing line between them should be 1368. There must also be borderline stories, although the tendency when using a method like ours is to polarize. A fairly conservative estimate for *terminus ante quem* is obviously needed, say circa 1450. Even this may be rather early for some of the barely classifiable stories.

72 See the Peking, 1959 edition.

VI The Middle-Period Stories: Their Authorship, Origins, and Types

Now that we have isolated some twenty-nine or more stories of the middle period, we can deduce a good deal about them—about their authorship, their mode of composition, and the literary qualities which distinguish them as a group from both the early and the late stories. We do not, of course, know the names of any middle-period authors, but it is still useful to delineate a group of stories which may be the work of a single author. Their mode of composition is one of the middle stories' most interesting aspects: their relationship to the oral narrative and the drama proves to be different from the accepted notion. Finally, the middle story as we know it, that is, as a result of the accidents of survival, is predominantly, perhaps entirely, a Hangchow creation. Many of the stories are concerned with Hangchow itself, and a significant number of them mine a very narrow vein in the social history of Hangchow—the wealthy class of merchants and businessmen, especially of the silk-weaving industry. It was in such stories that the writers of the middle period perfected the special kind of approach and technique which is here called "Hangchow realism."

The Common Authorship of KC 26, KC 38, and Perhaps KC 3

There is some circumstantial evidence that these three stories, and particularly the first two, were by a single author. They share a number of rhetorical features which distinguish them from the other middle stories,[1]

---

1 E.g., *shui hsiang* 誰想 "who would ever have thought that . . ." and *shih yu ts'ou-ch'iao, wu yu ou-jan* 事有湊巧, 物有偶然 "coincidence is a fact of life."

and KC 26 and KC 38 are the only stories with a particular variation of criterion M11.[2] In terms of the middle criteria, the three stories are more closely connected than any other combination of three from the middle pilot group, and KC 26 and KC 38 are more closely connected than any other pair of middle stories. In terms of poems and set pieces, KC 26 and KC 38 are also much closer than any other pair; they share both a short set piece and a four-line poem.[3] In geography, too, there is some similarity; the term *Hu shu* is found only in KC 3 and KC 26, and the *Hsin-ch'iao shih* of the former may be the *Pei Hsin-ch'iao* of the latter.[4] All three stories are listed in the Pao-wen-t'ang catalogue, but none is found in the extant Hung collections. Their proportions of older to newer criteria were closely similar.[5]

All three stories are set in Hangchow, and all three deal with crimes. In fact, all are quintessential "crime and consequences" stories, a predominant type in the middle period. KC 3 and KC 26 are concerned with the silk-weaving industry, KC 26 and KC 38 with the herb trade. In each case, the merchant families have a single son—he is not a significant character in KC 38—and in two of them, KC 3 and KC 26, he suffers from a congenital illness. The three stories are also the most finished of the middle stories, although this may, of course, be partly due to the fact that they survive only in Feng Meng-lung's edition. If they are indeed by the same author—the evidence given here can do no more than indicate the probability—then he must have lived fairly late in the middle period, for the event on which KC 26 is based is said to have occurred in the T'ien-shun period (1457–1464).

Other Authors

We have already suggested that the seven "historical" stories of the *I-chen chi,* together with KC 25 (which may have come from the same collection), are by a single author. We noted a number of stylistic features held in common and the use of a language which tended toward Classical Chinese. Since the seven stories survive in a single Hung collection, it was suggested that the author may have been associated with Hung P'ien.

---

2 *Chü pu t'i le* 具不題了 "and of all this we shall say no more."

3 For the poem, see KC 26, p. 395, and KC 38, p. 575. For the set piece, see KC 26, p. 399, and KC 38, p. 578. Most other pairs of stories are connected, if at all, only by a couplet, although Hung 4 and KC 38 share a four-line poem.

4 See KC 3, p. 63, and KC 26, pp. 391, 399.

5 KC 3, 26, and 38 had four older criteria to none, two and one, respectively.

They stand apart from other middle and early stories, not so much because they are about historical personages, as because they are about Confucian morality in public life. They contain the classic predicaments and *exempla*, such as studies in heroic magnanimity (Hung 21 and 22). In kind, their themes are those of Chinese traditional historiography in its moral dimension, and it was evidently this aspect which appealed to Feng Menglung, leading him to include three or four of them in his first collection and to write others of the same kind (KC 6, 8, 9, and so on). In their concern for public life and public morality, they contrast sharply with the characteristic middle story's concern for private life and "prudential morality."

The eight stories appear to be an attempt at popularization—witness the frequent geographical explanations—combined with an obvious exemplary intent. The popularization is not on a high level, since the style is not distinguished nor the geographical information always correct.[6] The stories indicate a remarkable vogue for the short story, in that something so alien to it, from the viewpoint of its origins, should have been embodied in the short-story form.

There is only one other discernible group of stories which can be attributed to a single author. It is argued below that a number of stories have been adapted from the drama—another testimony to the vogue for the short story in the middle period. Some of the adaptations are relatively crude and insipid, and it is possible that they are the work of the same man.

Stories Adapted from the Drama

The drama is the most unexpected origin of the middle-period story. In the late period, as we saw, it was almost always the drama which had been derived from the short story. Here the opposite process has occurred; I do not know of any play in the middle period which is clearly based on a middle-period story, whereas there are several short stories which must have been based on plays.

I have suggested elsewhere that Hung 4 may have been based on a play, though not necessarily on the extant Yüan *tsa-chü* play on the same theme.[7] The play and the story have virtually no text in common, and the grounds for believing the play (or a related play) to be the source were, first, that the time breaks in the story correspond to the act-divisions in the play, and

6 See Inada, "Sōgen wahon ruikeikō," part iii, p. 126, for the cases of Hung 25 and 27.
7 See Hanan, "The Early Chinese Short Story," pp. 191–192, n. 47.

second, that a characteristically dramatic technique of switching the focus of the narration from one character to another is used in both play and story at a corresponding stage in each. Several other points might have been added. The geographical location of both story and play is the same, and it is incorrect—a combination of geographical units which never occurred.[8] No other potential source is known for the story. Moreover, the story contains little visual description, an element that is obviously less appropriate in the drama than in narrative.

Although some of the same arguments can be applied to the other stories, in most cases no plays survive, and we cannot compare story and play in detail. What we can do is compare the short story's technique with typical narrative and dramatic technique, especially with regard to the focus of narration and the presence or absence of visual description.[9]

This needs a word of explanation. In narrative the focus of narration (simply, the character whose actions the narrator is following) changes, but it changes rarely. When the character is in contact with others, the narrator can focus on all of them, but he rarely moves briefly and rapidly from one character in one place to another character elsewhere. Such is the technique of the drama. The episode we referred to in Hung 4 is essentially dramatic, not narrative. The boy sets off to his native place, and in that instant the focus switches to the boy's uncle in that place, and then to his aunt, who wonders what has become of the boy. Just then, he raps on the door. This is, in fact, what happens in the extant play.[10] Unfortunately, most switches of narrative focus are not as clearly dramatic as this, and the argument cannot be made without ambiguity.

Even though we cannot be sure that Hung 4 is derived from the extant play, we can at least say that its dramatic exemplar is likely to have been a *tsa-chü* rather than a *hsi-wen,* partly because the time breaks of the story match the act-divisions of the extant *tsa-chü,* but chiefly because its structure seems closer to that of the *tsa-chü* rather than to that of the characteristically diffuse *hsi-wen.* In all likelihood, the nature of the exemplars, *tsa-chü* or *hsi-wen,* has determined to some degree the structure of the middle stories based upon them.

---

8 See Inada, "Sōgen wahon ruikeikō," part iii, p. 126, on Hung 4.

9 Visual description does, of course, appear in the drama, often among the lyrics. A feature of some of the early *ch'uan-ch'i* plays is the use of long passages of spoken description which are identical in form with the set pieces of narrative fiction.

10 This is the beginning of Act 3 in the play, *Pao Tai-chih chih chuan ho-t'ung wen-tzu* 包待制智賺合同文字 , of which two editions survive.

Hung 17 and KC 38 are other middle stories which may be based on plays.[11] Both are *kung-an* themes on which *tsa-chü* plays were written in the Yüan or early Ming, though none of the plays survive. Hung 17 has virtually no description. It explains the whole problem neatly in the first paragraph, as a play explains it in the first speech. (Generally, in the short story, the problem is only gradually broached; people are merely introduced in the first paragraph.) There are four obvious breaks in it, which could correspond to four acts and one induction of a *tsa-chü*. There are frequent switches of narrative focus, the first of which is typically dramatic. The hero, faced with the question of whether to marry the prostitute he is in love with, goes off to consult his aunt. The focus then switches to the aunt. She is briefly characterized, as she might describe herself in her opening speech in the drama, and then she sees her nephew arriving. It is significant that, excluding one or two Hung stories clearly derived from Classical tales, Hung 4 and Hung 17 are shorter than all other stories except Hung 1. And Hung 1, as argued below, is almost certainly derived from a *tsa-chü*. This fact suggests a somewhat hasty and crude adaptation, a judgement which is borne out by the stories themselves; despite exciting themes, they lack the suspense and interest of the typical short story.

Although KC 38 is much more carefully worked out, it, too, may be derived from a play. It has an inspirational ending of a kind not uncommon in the *tsa-chü*. It has some switching of focus, but more significant is its amount of thinking and planning—the narrative equivalent of the dramatic soliloquy—as the hero tries to make up his mind, consulting the temple gods, his father, and his sister.

Hung 12 and Hung 19 may also be derived from plays.[12] Although potentially exciting stories, full of ogres and immortals, they have virtually

11 There were no less than three *tsa-chü* on the subject matter of Hung 17, all of which are lost. See Fu Hsi-hua 傅惜華, *Yüan-tai tsa-chü ch'üan-mu* 元代雜劇全目 (Peking, 1957), pp. 105, 116, 158. There was also a *hsi-wen*, from which a few songs survive in anthologies. See Ch'ien Nan-yang 錢南揚 ed., *Sung-Yüan hsi-wen chi-i* 宋元戲文輯佚 (Shanghai, 1956), pp. 159–160. One of the *tsa-chü*, see *Ch'üan-mu*, p. 158, apparently existed in the earliest form of the *Lu kuei pu* 錄鬼簿, which has a preface dated 1330. See the *Chung-kuo ku-tien hsi-ch'ü lun-chu chi-ch'eng* 中國古典戲曲論著集成, vol. II (Peking, 1959), p. 176, n. 364. If the identification with the short title in the *Lu kuei pu* is correct, the time setting must have been changed, for Hung 17 is set in the Chih-cheng period (1341–1368). The *tsa-chü* on the topic of KC 38 is also lost. See *Ch'üan-mu*, p. 347.

12 For the surviving songs from the *hsi-wen* that correspond to Hung 12 and Hung 19, see Ch'ien Nan-yang, *Sung-Yüan hsi-wen chi-i*, pp. 173–180 and 192–193, respectively. Wu Hsiao-ling, in his review of a *Ku-chin hsiao-shuo* edition in *Han-hiue*, p. 450, says the story *Shen-yang-tung chi* 申陽洞記 in Ch'ü Yu's 瞿佑 *Chien-teng hsin-hua* 剪燈新話 is a translation of Hung 12 into Classical Chinese. This is incorrect; the stories have a few general resemblances only. For a close study of both stories, see Dudbridge, *The Hsi-yu chi*, pp. 118–126.

no passages of description. Both state the crux neatly in the first paragraph, and both have rapid switches of narrative focus. For example, in Hung 19, when the boy sets off to borrow money from the rich man, the focus suddenly switches to the latter. There is also much thinking and planning, as in KC 38. Hung 12 can be divided into a number of different scenes. There is a rapid switch of focus from the hero to his supernatural protector, then to the assistant delegated to accompany the hero on his dangerous journey. The assistant plans to play the fool a little to allay suspicion and, although the comedy is not exploited in the short story, his intention suggests the comic use made of supernatural figures in the drama. In addition, there are several other switches of focus, to the rebel leader, to the ogre, to the hero's captured wife, and so on.

There were *hsi-wen* on the same themes as both Hung 12 and Hung 19, and the stories' rambling plot structure may reflect derivation from a *hsi-wen* rather than from the tightly structured *tsa-chü*.[13]

Hung 1, which could not be classified as between the early and middle periods, is also probably based on a play. One of the poems it contains is actually a song from a *tsa-chü* with the same theme.[14]

It was suggested above that TY 7 is connected with an early-Ming *tsa-chü*. It is impossible to guess the precise nature of the connection. The stuff-material differs widely, and although TY 7 could have been derived directly from the play, in which case the author showed more originality than most other middle-period authors, it seems more likely to have been based on some intermediary.

The authentic part of KC 29, that is, excluding the last part added by Feng Meng-lung, has grown out of a Yüan play but is not itself based upon it. It is argued below that it is a development in oral narrative.

In sum, at least six stories appear to have been derived from plays: Hung 1, 4, 12, 17, 19, and KC 38. For all of these stories, *tsa-chü* or *hsi-wen* versions exist or existed from before the date of the stories' composition and in most cases the stuff-material is found in no other narrative genre before that date.[15] It is likely that they were derived directly from the dramatic versions

---

13 Formally, Hung 19 can almost be classed as a "linked" story. See Hanan, "Early Chinese Short Story," p. 185.

14 There were at least two *tsa-chü* and a *hsi-wen* on this theme. See Fu Hsi-hua, *Yüan-tai tsa-chü ch'üan-mu*, p. 200, his *Ming-tai tsa-chü ch'üan-mu* 明代雜劇全目 (Peking, 1958), p. 19, and Ch'ien Nan-yang, *Sung-Yüan hsi-wen chi-i*, pp. 96–102. T'an Cheng-pi, in his edition of *Ch'ing-p'ing-shan-t'ang hua-pen*, p. 5, n. 1, noted that the *tz'u* at the end of the story has been adapted from one of the surviving songs of the Yüan *tsa-chü* by Tai Shan-fu 戴善夫. Fragments of this play survive in sixteenth century songbooks.

15 The only exception is Hung 19, the story of Tung Yung, of which there are several prior versions.

and not through the medium of oral narrative, for otherwise they would not have retained their essentially dramatic features.

Some of these stories, not including KC 38, may be by a single author. There are stylistic features which unite some of them, especially Hung 4 and Hung 12,[16] but the main reason is a judgement of the stories' quality. Unlike most of the other middle-period stories, they are clumsy and insipid, and they do not exploit their fictional opportunities. We can only suppose that their attraction for the reading public was that they retold inherently exciting plots which could not entirely lose their point even in the most indifferent hands. The stories were adapted by a hack writer, most of them possibly by the same hack writer.

Stories Adapted from Oral Fiction

There is an obvious connection between some of the extant middle stories and professional oral fiction, but any attempt to explore the nature of the connection raises more questions than it can answer.

The sources of our knowledge of professional oral fiction are even sparser for the early Ming than for the Sung and Yüan.[17] The most detailed is the passage in T'ien Ju-ch'eng's *Hsi-hu yu-lan chih-yü* in which he describes the blind storytellers of his native city of Hangchow.[18] The genre they performed was the *t'ao-chen* 陶眞, a form of which nothing survives except a few lines quoted in other works.[19] It appears to have been a species of *chante-fable* with alternating verse and prose passages, the verse being of uniform line length. T'ien lists five topics as the most popular with the storytellers, and the remarkable thing about his list is that all of the topics are represented in some form in the extant fiction of the early and middle periods: two

16 Hung 4 and Hung 12 both begin with the formula *ch'ü che Tung-ching Pien-liang-ch'eng* 去這東京汴梁城. The *ch'ü che*, meaning apparently "at this," is shared with Hung 19 and a few other stories. (Hung 12 has an obvious misprint for *ch'ü*, and Hung 19 for *che*.) Hung 4 and Hung 12 are among the four stories which close with the *hua-pen shuo-ch'e*, etc., formula. They also have three middle criteria in common (M1, 4, 9) and make considerable use of *yün* in the prespeech position.

17 The chief sources are interpreted in Ch'en Ju-heng 陳汝衡, *Shuo-shu shih-hua* 說書史話 (Peking, 1958), pp. 95–129, and Yeh Te-chün, *Sung-Yüan-Ming chiang-ch'ang wen-hsüeh*.

18 *Chüan* 20.368.

19 See *Sung-Yüan-Ming chiang-ch'ang wen-hsüeh*, pp. 30–36, *Shuo-shu shih-hua*, pp. 115–118. The supposed anthology of Ming *t'ao-chen*, the *Yüeh-fu hung-shan* 樂府紅珊, is actually an anthology of play excerpts. See P. D. Hanan, "The Nature and Contents of the *Yüeh-fu hung-shan*," *Bulletin of the School of Oriental and African Studies* 26.2 (1963), 341–361. The *Yüeh-fu hung-shan* was compiled by Chi Chen-lun 紀振倫. See the 1800 edition in the British Museum.

early stories (Hung 13[20] and TY 28), two middle stories (Hsiung D and KC 29), and a longer piece, the *Ch'ien-t'ang hu yin Chi Tien Ch'an-shih yü-lu*.

It is by no means impossible that the stories have been adapted from the *chantefable* form.[21] One late story, HY 38, was based directly upon a written *chantefable*, the *Yün-men chuan*, and another, KC 28, has probably been influenced by a lost *chantefable*.[22] But if so, were our stories drawn from the oral or written forms of the *chantefables*? It may be that the written short story, mainly in prose, no longer corresponded closely to any oral genre in the middle period, but had become instead a mainly *literary* form, useful for the adaptation of the various genres of oral narrative. But we cannot confirm the point. We do not even know what the nearest oral equivalent to the written short story may have been.

KC 26's relationship to professional oral fiction is less certain than that of Hsiung D and KC 29. (KC 29 is dealt with separately below.) As has been noted above, the event on which KC 26 is based is supposed to have taken place in the T'ien-shun period (1457–1464), according to Lang Ying's *Ch'i-hsiu lei-kao*.[23] Lang Ying goes on to say that "Shen the Bird-fancier" became a household word in Hangchow for a "source of trouble." The *Ch'i-hsiu lei-kao* was written during the Chia-ching period (1522–1566); by that time the KC 26 stuff-material was alive in oral literature, at least in casual storytelling.

Several middle-period and undated stories resemble *chantefables* in form. In the case of Hung 10 and 12, both of which devote much of their space to dialogue in verse, the resemblance may be merely fortuitous. But two stories, Hung 7 and 14, must genuinely represent Ming dynasty *chantefables*.

Hung 7 is the tale of the rambunctious shrew Li Ts'ui-lien and of her short-lived and tumultuous marriage. The verse sections perform a natural function in the narrative, consisting mainly of her tirades at parents, brother, neighbors, in-laws, and so forth. There are thirty-one verse sections attributed to her, and they dominate the story. It is not certain precisely what genre Hung 7 exemplifies, for very few Ming *chantefables* survive, especially from the first half of the dynasty, and the terminology used by Ming writers is vague at best. It may be loosely described as a form of *tz'u-hua* 詞話,

---

20 The reference to the stuff-material of Hung 13 is questionable. The girl in KC 29 goes by both names in successive incarnations, and both could refer to her. This is the view held by Chang Ch'üan-kung; see n. 29 below. Most scholars assume that the two stories are being referred to. There is no evidence with which to settle the issue.

21 See Yeh Te-chün, *Sung-Yüan-Ming chiang-ch'ang wen-hsüeh*, p. 35.

22 See Chapter IV.

23 *Chüan* 45.653–654.

an early genre in which the verse sections are made up of a basic line of regular length. Despite their chaotic appearance on the printed page, the verse sections are in lines of three or seven syllables, with occasional hypermetrical syllables. The seven-syllable line divides into units of two, two and three. This is the staple kind of verse in Chinese *chantefables*. A single rhyme runs through most of the verse sections, but occasionally it changes in mid-section, the likely sign of a popular work. Unlike most *chantefable* forms which use a line of regular length, Hung 7 does not confine its rhyming words to the level tone. However, once established, the tone is consistent throughout the section. Hung 7 is a *tour de force* of popular literature, a brilliant match of subject and form. With due reservations, it would appear to represent a genuine specimen of oral literature. Presumably the fact that it is a *tour de force*, and that its interest would dissolve without the verse sections, has kept its *chantefable* form intact. A *chantefable* of similar poetic virtuosity which will be discussed in Chapter VIII, TY 19, may have preserved its form for the same reason.

Hung 14 is a prose narrative interspersed with ten songs, all to a single tune, which describe, resume, and comment. Each song has an introductory formula addressed to an accompanist. There is a striking similarity, in terms both of its general form and the wording of the formula, between Hung 14 and a *chantefable* genre known as the narrative *ku-tzu tz'u* 鼓子詞, of which one specimen survives from the Sung dynasty.[24] If Hung 14 is indeed a *ku-tzu tz'u,* the genre must have lasted into the Ming, even though there is no record of its existence after the Sung. The possibility that it is merely a literary man's revival of a defunct form can be ruled out; its subject is too lurid and its language too racy.

Near the end of the story there is an extraordinary passage addressed to the audience, asking them, if they want the full details, to "listen to Ch'iu-shan's 秋山 *Wen-ching yüan-yang hui* 刎頸鴛鴦會." *Wen-ching yüan-yang hui* is the main title of Hung 14. (There are two alternative titles.) Ch'iu-shan is usually thought to be the composer, or performer, or both, of Hung 14.[25] But the import of the passage is still a puzzle.[26] If Hung 14 is a storyteller's

24 See Yeh Te-chün, *Sung-Yüan-Ming chiang-ch'ang wen-hsüeh,* pp. 9–11, Ch'en Ju-heng, *Shuo-shu shih-hua,* pp. 37–41.

25 See Yeh Te-chün, p. 11.

26 Some of the Hung text is garbled at this point. The sentence immediately after is the introductory formula for the final *tz'u* of the story—it has been displaced by several columns. The whole passage runs: "Audience assembled here (在座看官), [if] you want the full details, please look at the narrative outline (敍大略) and at your pleasure listen to Ch'iu-shan's *Wen-ching yüan-yang hui.*" The meaning "narrative outline" is a guess. One is tempted to speculate that the passage, if it is not corrupt, may reflect a practice of issuing or showing some written outline or guide to the audience.

script, as scholars have assumed, the passage makes little sense; why does the story wait until the end to advertise itself? The only parallel is found in the short version of KC 29; at the end of the story, the reader is asked to look at such-and-such a work, if he wants to know all the facts. The cases are different, of course, for Hung 14 has reached its gory dénouement while KC 29 has left much untold, but we must surely suppose that Ch'iu-shan's work, whatever its nature, was not identical with Hung 14. One must have been oral, the other written; or the two must have belonged to different genres of the same literature. Most of the key words are ambiguous; "look at" and even "listen to" have extended their meanings from oral to written literature, and are by no means a sure guide. But if we are forced to speculate, we might guess that Hung 14 as it stands is intended for a reading public and that it refers its readers back to the performer whose work, after some fashion, it represents.

The precise way in which oral literature gets into written form is tantalizingly obscure. Questions remain, no matter what our interpretation is of the passage in Hung 14. We cannot be sure of the relationship between the story and any script which Ch'iu-shan may have possessed. The fact that the prologue story, thinly adapted from a T'ang tale,[27] is in Classical Chinese and could not be recited comprehensibly as it stands, suggests that some alterations were made in the storyteller's script, if such a script existed.

Besides their simple language, the songs of Hung 14 are marked by an insistent use of parallelism, a characteristic of verse occurring in oral-related literature. Except for the last two lines in each song, they are composed entirely of parallel couplets. Another story, Hsiung A(M), contains a long, parallelistic passage, spasmodically rhymed, entitled T'iao-kuang ching 調光經, "The Classic of Seduction." The story makes a remarkable use of patterned auditory effects, and may have some connection with oral literature. Several others, for example, Hung 18, Hung 20, KC 3M, TY 7, and P'ei Hsiu-niang, have no known sources yet share some of the features which are typical of, though not peculiar to, oral fiction.[28] But there is no way of determining their origins.

KC 29, a Paradigm of Oral Development

There is a recognized connection between KC 29 and Hung 13, although

---

27 The tale is known as Pu Fei-yen chuan 步非烟傳 or as Fei-yen chuan. There is a Shuo fu (1646) edition, chüan 112.

28 TY 7 has four tz'u to a single pattern. They exploit the opportunities for parallelism that the basic pu-sa-man form, with its couplets, provides.

its nature has not been finally settled.[29] In each story a girl named Hung-lien seduces or unwittingly tempts an upright monk, causing him to end his life. Each story continues into the next life, according to the prescription of *karma*. In KC 29, the wife of Hung-lien's patron gives birth to a daughter, Liu Ts'ui 柳翠, who, as a punishment for her father's evil deed—he arranged the seduction—is reduced to prostitution. Eventually, she is spiritually saved by another priest who recognizes in her the dead monk's reincarnation. In Hung 13, the errant priest is reborn as the poet Su Shih and his brother priest as Fo-yin.

Similarly, there is a clear connection between KC 29 and an extant *tsa-chü* play which may date from the Yüan dynasty. In his study of Yüan drama, Yen Tun-i 嚴敦易 could not settle the nature of the relationship, but one possibility that he mentions, that KC 29 might be a Sung or Yüan story, was disposed of in Chapter V.

The thesis I shall put forward is that KC 29 is derived from both Hung 13 and the play and not merely from them but from at least three other short stories as well. The derivation is in terms of plot and incident, and there is no textual borrowing as such, except for important personal names and place-names. (Key terms such as names can be carried in an oral tradition, as many literatures demonstrate.) The derivation is quite different from the literary derivation which we saw in operation among the late stories and which was characterized by heavy textual borrowing; this kind is typical of descent through the oral medium. The case of KC 29's derivation is particularly important; perhaps because it is relatively late, many of its oral sourceworks are reflected in surviving texts. It is therefore of great value as an example of the development of stuff-material in oral narrative, an example that will throw light on the development of other, longer works such as the *Shui-hu chuan* and the *P'ing-yao chuan,* and that is why it is discussed here in special detail.

First, KC 29 is derived in part, directly or indirectly, from the Yüan play. It makes little use of the play's plot; indeed, it reduces that plot to a mere epilogue. The play's function has been to suggest another plot, the previous incarnation, as the main plot of the short story. KC 29 is thus the reverse of a sequel: it stands as a prologue to the other work. Of course, a work can as easily "retroject" a prologue as it can project a sequel. (Shakespeare could have gone on to write a play on the boyhood of Falstaff instead of

29 The most detailed study of the relationship between these two stories is Chang Ch'üan-kung's 張全恭 "Hung-lien Liu Ts'ui ku-shih ti chuan-pien" 紅蓮柳翠故事的轉變, *Ling-nan hsüeh-pao* 嶺南學報 5.2 (1936), 54–74. See also Yen Tun-i 嚴敦易, *Yüan-chü chen-i* 元劇斟疑 (Peking, 1960), pp. 622–631. Note that by KC 29 I mean only the older part of the story, up to the end of p. 435.

the *Merrie Wives of Windsor*.) This claim cannot be positively proved, but it is surely significant that the Yüan play contains no hint of the earlier incarnation.[30] If true, it would throw light on the development of the great early Chinese novels, most of which seem to have developed by retrojection rather than projection. For example, the historical incident which is the nucleus of the *P'ing-yao chuan* cycle occupies only the last third of the twenty-chapter edition; the first two thirds are devoted to the childhood and youth of the principal demons. The *Shui-hu chuan* gives the individual sagas of the heroes before it touches on the facts of the historical rebellion. And the sections of the *Wu Tai shih p'ing-hua* which owe the least to written history, and which are written in the most vernacular language, are those that tell of the infancy and youth of the upstart warlords.

Second, KC 29 is derived in part, presumably by some oral medium, from a story represented by TY 7. The connection, which has not been pointed out, is based on the following points. In each story, someone comes from Wen-chou fu to Hangchow, where the action takes place. The local prefect, as patron of the temple, admires the young monk's talent in the one story, but is offended by the old priest's arrogance in the other. Each describes in detail the ritual burning of the dead monk's body, with much similar incident, and with the abbot's invocation given in full. (The corresponding episode in Hung 13 is glossed over.) The details of the dream, the pregnancy, and the reincarnation are also very close.

Now if, as I believe, the TY 7 story is derived in part from the early-Ming *tsa-chü* play *Hsiao Shu-lan ch'ing chi p'u-sa-man* 蕭淑蘭情寄菩薩蠻 by Chia Chung-ming 賈仲明,[31] it must precede the KC 29 story. Evidence for the connection between the play and TY 7 is as follows. Both plots center on a series of *tz'u* poems written to the *p'u-sa-man* tune. In the play, the patron's protégée writes the young man a series of *p'u-sa-man* as messages of love; in TY 7, the young monk writes a series of *p'u-sa-man*, some as messages and some at his patron's behest, one of which is mistaken as a love letter. Both young man and young monk come from Wen-chou fu to Hangchow and there receive the patronage of the local official. In each

---

30 Yen Tun-i, *Yüan-chü chen-i*, pp. 622–631, speculates that the incarnation may have been suppressed from the Yüan play and cites a passage which seems to him to read awkwardly. I find this unconvincing. The reasons for believing that the Hung-lien and Liu Ts'ui stories were not combined until the Ming dynasty are set forth plausibly by Chang, p. 73. The account of the Liu Ts'ui story by the dramatist Chu Yu-tun 朱有燉 (1377–1452), which contains no mention of Hung-lien, is important in showing that the two stories had not yet merged. Chu even refers us to a *tz'u* on the theme by K'ang Yü-chih 康與之. See Chang Ch'üan-kung, "Hung-lien Liu Ts'ui ku-shih ti chuan-pien," p. 66.

31 See Chapter V.

case, there is a triangular relationship of patron, protégé, and daughter (or protégée), and in each case the protégé writes poems for his patron.[32] In both play and story, the girl takes the initiative. In the story, to explain the pregnancy resulting from her affair with one of her patron's retinue, she falsely charges the young monk with being her lover; in the play, she lays direct siege to the young man, conduct that is certainly more forward than that of most Chinese heroines. Thus there is little doubt about the connection between the two, while of the two the play must be primary since its author wrote at the very beginning of the Ming dynasty.

Third, KC 29 is derived in part, presumably by some oral medium, from a story represented by Hung 13. The connection is well established and is indeed quite obvious. (Hangchow, the monk's temptation by a girl called Hung-lien, his fornication, disgrace, death, and reincarnation.)[33] Hung 13 is evidently a version of a much older type of folktale theme[34] and cannot be derived from KC 29.

Fourth, KC 29 is derived in part, presumably by some oral medium, from a story represented by Hung 1 or by one of the plays on that theme. This connection, which has not been pointed out before, depends on the following evidence. In each story, the prefect of Hangchow, surnamed Liu 柳,[35] sends someone to dishonor (in one case to rape, in the other to seduce) a person who resists his authority. As we have seen, Hung 1 derives from a Yüan tsa-chü on the same subject. It is likely that Hung 1 has influenced KC 29, rather than vice versa.

Fifth, KC 29 is derived in part, presumably by some oral medium, from the early story HY 12. HY 12, whose relationship to KC 29 has not been pointed out before, has connections with all of the short stories we have mentioned, with Hung 13, TY 7, and Hung 1, as well as with KC 29. Like Hung 13, it is a story of Su Shih and Fo-yin. Again, a priest's seduction is in question, only this time it is Su Shih who gets a girl to tempt Fo-yin to break his vows. (In Hung 13, it was the priest reincarnated as Su Shih who succumbed.) Like TY 7, the priest's song is misinterpreted as a love song by the official (deliberately, in Su Shih's case). Like Hung 1, the official is a celebrated tz'u poet (Liu Yung). Like KC 29, the girl, a singing-girl, is

---

32 In each case, the girl has a duenna called a kuan-chia p'o 管家婆.

33 The relationship even includes shared text. When the respective priests give shelter to the girls—one is a baby at the time—who prove to be their undoing, they utter the same proverb. And the last two lines of the prefect's mocking poem in KC 29, p. 432, are the same as the last two lines of the set piece of erotic description in Hung 13, p. 141.

34 See Chang Ch'üan-kung's article (n. 29 above) for Sung references to it.

35 This may be an example of a stimulus to the associative process, presumably unconscious, by which one story is combined with another.

threatened by the official and told to seduce the priest and bring back tangible evidence of the seduction. I am not concerned here with the complex network of relationships among these stories,[36] only with the likelihood that KC 29 has been influenced by the HY 12 story.

The relationships of the four short stories with KC 29 are roughly indicated in Table 18. (The Yüan play, which has a different kind of connection with KC 29, is not included.)

KC 29 is thus related to middle stories (TY 7, Hung 1) and early stories (Hung 13, HY 12), as well as to a play. However, it differs in one or two formal respects from the others. Where all of the other stories include the poems or songs of the participants—some of them can even be regarded as virtuoso stories—KC 29 has none. It even differs from the other Hangchow religious stories: TY 7, Hung 13, Hung 16. (Hung 16, which we have not mentioned, shares some points of plot with KC 29; the young heroine ends her life—to avoid marriage, hence also for a sexual reason—with a poem called a "last testament," as do the priests of KC 29, TY 6, and Hung 13.) This discrepancy may be explained by the assumption that KC 29 developed at a later stage than the other stories.

TABLE 18. Common Elements in KC 29 and Related Stories.

Element	KC 29	TY 7	Hung 13	Hung 1	HY 12
Wen-chou fu	X	X			
Prefect Liu	X			X	
Prefect of Hangchow	X	X		X	
Action in Hangchow	X	X	X	X	
Official sends agent to dishonor another	X			X	X
Patron figure	X	X		X	
Poems by priest		X	X		X
Priest's fornication (actual or proposed)	X	X	X		X
Priest ends life, is cremated, etc.	X	X	X		

36 Other stories outside of the vernacular literature could also be mentioned, for example, the story of how Su Shih disciplined a lecherous priest at the time he (Su) was prefect of Hangchow. See Lü-ch'uang hsin-hua 綠窗新話 (Shanghai, 1957), pp. 62–63, and Lo Yeh's Tsui-weng t'an-lu, p. 79. This discussion has been restricted to fiction and drama, but obviously, if one considers the associative process by which much oral and popular literature grows, the actual derivation of KC 29 may have been infinitely more complex.

We have also assumed that the development of the stuff-material of KC 29 was mainly through the medium of oral narrative. There is a good deal of indirect evidence for the assumption. We know that the KC 29 story was part of the repertoire of the Hangchow performers of *t'ao-chen* in the first part of the fifteenth century. T'ien shrewdly noted that the stories, though they dealt with Sung dynasty material, may have been "later imitations." The correspondences with other stories have none of the textual borrowing we noted in the late stories based on written sources. The only specific correspondences (such as Wen-chou fu, the surname Liu, the personal name Hung-lien) are the kind of inessential points which can be carried in an oral tradition but which a written tradition can easily change. Indeed, it is the lack of conscious purpose that often distinguishes borrowing through the oral medium, as may be seen in the well-documented oral literature of Europe, the *matière de Bretaigne,* for example. Finally, because such borrowing is not the conscious act of a single author, it is much more intricate than conscious borrowing from literary sources is likely to be. And the extent of the borrowing was undoubtedly much wider than the five works mentioned here. Thus, regardless of the genres concerned, the development of the stuff-material of KC 29 was probably in the medium of oral fiction, borrowing from the memory of other oral stories or plays. It evidently took place in Hangchow, and the development was complete by the early part of the sixteenth century. KC 29 is a written version of that oral story.

Here we can only glance at the complex relations among the other stories. One of them, Hung 1, seems to have been derived from a play, but most of the others must be related through the oral medium. Their correspondences are nontextual, yet intricate, often pointlessly so. Their relationship is like that of different tales belonging to the same general folktale type. This matter will be explored in Chapter VIII, where we shall be dealing with the larger number of oral-derived early stories.

The implication of this argument for our research in early vernacular literature is that we should look first at comparable oral literature for the sources of a saga's development, rather than at historical conditions. Oral narrative grows, above all, by absorbing other oral narrative.

Written Stories ab Initio

The largest group of stories, though not the most interesting, are those based on written sources or on no obvious sources at all. They include the four stories which have been adapted from Classical tales (Hung 6, Hung 14P,[37] Hsiung A[P], *Cheng Yüan-ho*); the four stories which are essentially Ming dynasty Classical tales tricked out with a few short-story formulae (Hung 9, Hung 10, Hung 29, *Tu Li-niang*), and most of the eight "historical" stories. With the exception of *Cheng Yüan-ho*, all of the stories in this group are of the "historical" or virtuoso types.

The Hangchow Origin of the Middle Stories

A large proportion of the middle stories is actually set in the city of Hangchow: KC 3, KC 26, KC 38, TY 7, TY 23P (possibly middle), Hung 1 (probably middle), Hung 9, Hung 14M, Hung 18, Hsiung A (M), Hsiung D, *P'ei Hsiu-niang*, twelve in all. By contrast, only one middle story, Hung 7, is set in Kaifeng, the favorite setting of the early stories.

The middle stories with a Hangchow setting include all five of the stories which we know to be related to oral literature, as well as four out of the five stories which we have guessed may be so related (KC 3M, TY 7, Hung 18, *P'ei Hsiu-niang*). They also include one written story *ab initio* (Hung 9), two stories probably derived from plays (Hung 1, KC 38), and TY 23P, which could have been derived from oral literature.[38] The stories *not* set in Hangchow prove to be strikingly different in origin. They include all but one of the written stories *ab initio* and only one story which we have guessed may be related to oral literature (Hung 20). The difference indicates that most, if not all, of the middle stories were actually written in Hangchow. We know that some of the stories grew out of Hangchow oral literature and hence were not set in Hangchow merely because that city was the conventional setting for middle-period fiction. Further, the stories not set in Hangchow, predominantly written stories *ab initio*, were dependent on sources such as Classical tales and plays which dictated their own settings; hence they, too, *may* have been written in Hangchow. This conclusion fits the fact that Hung P'ien, to whom we owe so much of our knowledge of the middle-period story, was a native of Hangchow and a member of an old Hangchow family, and it also fits the suggestion that the author of the eight "historical" stories may have been associated with Hung. Thus, to the best of our knowledge, and we must remember that it is

37 The process of vulgarization by which the tragic T'ang tale *Fei-yen chuan* is turned into the moralistic prologue to Hung 14 is most significant for an understanding of the temper of the middle-period story.

38 TY 23P consists of what is apparently folklore material about Ch'ien Liu 錢鏐, the founder of Hangchow.

limited by the accidents of survival, Hangchow was the virtually exclusive center of middle-period fiction.

Some corroboration is provided by the *Ch'ien-t'ang hu yin Chi Tien Ch'an-shih yü-lu*, which reflects the subject matter of one of the *t'ao-chen* current in Hangchow in the first half of the sixteenth century, as noted by T'ien Ju-ch'eng. It is set in Hangchow, and it exists in an edition of 1569 which states that it is narrated or expounded (*hsü-shu* 敘述) by a certain Shen Meng-pan 沈孟柈 of Jen-ho 仁和, that is, Hangchow. Thus it tallies precisely with the claims I have just made about the short stories. It is a vernacular work by an obscure Hangchow author which is based on Hangchow oral literature of the middle period.

I will discuss in the next section some of the characteristic types of short story in the middle period, but there are certain broad features of this fiction, especially of the stories derived from oral literature and the drama, that can be mentioned briefly here.

Several of the stories are concerned with wealthy merchants, especially those in the silk business. The hero of KC 3M runs a shop which sells silk thread to the weavers inside the city wall. The murdered boy's father, in KC 26, is a prosperous weaver from the same locality, outside the Wu-lin Gate. The hero of KC 38 is the manager of a herbalist's shop. In Hung 18, the hero is a travelling merchant in silk and other goods. The young lovers of Hung 20 and Hsiung D are both sons of wealthy merchants. The father of the boy in *P'ei Hsiu-niang* is the owner of a Hangchow weaving factory, a point that reminds one of Hsü I-k'uei's 徐一夔 brilliant description of a Hangchow weaving factory with "a dozen or more workers" in the late-Yüan–early-Ming period.[39] The merchants are not treated with disdain or shown as stingy, hectoring bullies as they are in some of the early heroic stories.[40] And their wealth gives them a good deal of social status; in *P'ei Hsiu-niang*, for example, the high official and his wife, pressed, it is true, by the knowledge that their daughter is sick with love for the textile merchant's son, decide that the match is acceptable.

These stories are domestic, concerned with the family, its stability and its continuation. Unlike the early heroic or adventurous stories, they do not deal with the outlaw life, or even with travelling, life on the open road. (The Chinese says life "on the rivers and lakes.") They never include scenes of—indeed, they barely mention—inns and teahouses, those centers around

39 Quoted by Fu I-ling 傅衣凌, *Ming-tai Chiang-nan shih-min ching-chi shih-t'an* 明代江南市民經濟試探 (Shanghai, 1957), pp. 79–80. It is from Hsü's *Shih feng kao* 始豐稿, *chüan* 3.
40 E.g., KC 36, TY 37.

which many of the early stories revolve. They are concerned with life in the family, and with occasional outings, often en famille, to the conventional scenic places on the conventional holidays.

In terms of these stories, family stability is threatened above all by sexual desire. Sex is the one wild card in the orderly game of life. There are clandestine love affairs, as in Hung 20 and *P'ei Hsiu-niang*; entanglements with prostitutes, as in KC 3M and Hung 17; or with licentious women, as in KC 38, Hung 14M, and Hung 18.[41] In KC 26, the dangerous quality is not sexual desire but idleness and wastefulness, an affront to the virtues of thrift and hard work. The lessons which the narrator draws are those of practical morality—what Professor C. T. Hsia calls prudential morality[42]— which emphasize that certain kinds of conduct will bring ruin to an individual and to his family.[43]

We have also noticed a few formal features which distinguish the middle story from the early story. It has fewer set pieces of description, and it has no poem-chain prologues. Its prologues, such as they are, are usually adapted from Classical originals.

Two Distinctive Story-Types Produced in Hangchow

In an earlier study, in the course of attempting a typology of the "early" stories (what I would now call early and middle), I described a distinctive type of story which was "plot-centered" and which used prediction by the narrator instead of revelation.[44] These stories were loosely called "folly and consequences" stories, or "crime and consequences" stories, because they generally dealt with the disastrous effects of some initial act of folly or crime.

Ten stories were so described, KC 3, 26, 38, TY 20, HY 16, 33, Hung 14, 17, 18, and 20. HY 16 was regarded as an "early" story solely because of the apparent reference to it in the Pao-wen-t'ang catalogue, and despite serious reservations.[45] It proved, as was shown in Chapter III, to be a late story by X. Of the other nine stories, two are early (in our present terms), TY 20

41 Note some similarities. Death follows sexual intercourse in Hung 14M and Hung 20, and almost follows in KC 3. In Hung 14M and KC 38, parents marry off a promiscuous daughter to avoid scandal.
42 "Society and Self in the Chinese Short Story," appended to *The Classic Chinese Novel*, pp. 299–301.
43 Shame is a potent motive for many actions. The over-riding desire is to protect the family's reputation.
44 See Hanan, "Early Chinese Short Story," pp. 192–193.
45 *Ibid.*, p. 181, n. 28.

and HY 33 (the main story only), and the rest are middle. None of the stories newly classified as early or middle in Chapter III are of this type.

The remarkable feature of this list is that the two early stories and most of the middle stories are set in Hangchow. We have already argued that the middle stories were written in Hangchow. Like several of the middle stories, the early stories, TY 20 and HY 33M, are about merchants. The head of the family in TY 20 is a lowly official who runs a wineshop in his house with a single worker, as in Hung 18. (Another similarity is that in both stories the daughter is seduced by someone within the household.) The victim in HY 33M is an unsuccessful small businessman, whose father-in-law is about to set him up with a family store. The youth who is un-justly executed has come into Hangchow from the country with silk screens to sell and is on his way to Ch'u-chia t'ang. It seems likely that this kind of story, with its distinctive subject matter, treatment, and narrator's rhetoric, was characteristic of Hangchow in both the middle and early periods[46] and that we can fairly speak of "Hangchow realism."

The other distinctive type associated with Hangchow was the religious story. The religion is Buddhism, and the stories are about priests and also generally about reincarnation. What unites the stories is similarity of theme rather than of genre characteristics. We have already noted the family re-lationship among four of these stories: KC 29, TY 7, HY 12M, and Hung 13.[47] With them can be grouped Hung 16, a story we could not date as between middle and early, and the *Ch'ien-t'ang hu yin Chi Tien Ch'an-shih yü-lu*. All six stories are set in Hangchow, and two or three of them at least reflect the subject matter of Hangchow oral literature. The *Yü-lu* was the work of a Hangchow author, Shen Meng-pan. It seems likely that all six stories were written in Hangchow and that the religious story, like the folly and consequences story, was a distinctive Hangchow type in both the early and middle periods.

46 A few late stories, such as HY 34, consciously continue the "crime and consequences" tradition. Several *kung-an* stories also provide a fairly close parallel.
47 Hung 13 and HY 12M both have some features of the virtuoso story.

VII   An Attempt to Distinguish the Earliest Stories

The method of using stylistic criteria to determine approximate date has been taken as far as it can properly go. Each time stories have been divided on either side of a time barrier, we have had to make assumptions, particularly about the uniform development of the vernacular fiction style, and, on the second occasion, there was no adequate means of checking our assumptions. Such an accumulation of them, each new one weakening the argument as a whole, seems to rule out all possibility of further subdivision.

Can we now return to the old, rejected arguments based on internal evidence?[1] After all, the dating of stories has now been pushed back almost two hundred years, well beyond the time at which, to the best of our knowledge, literati like Feng Meng-lung became interested in the writing of vernacular fiction. At least we shall be spared the hazard of mistaking late stories, such as KC 22, KC 39, or TY 4, for products of the Sung dynasty.[2] If it is true, as I shall argue below, that the earliest possible date for the first stories *as a group* is circa 1250, the gap has been narrowed to a maximum of two hundred years, a time in which imitation may not have been at a premium. Alas, the hope is largely unjustified. There is some evidence that Feng Meng-lung tried to imitate the form of certain types of early story, but the main reason that KC 22 and KC 39 were mistaken by scholars for Sung or Yüan works was that Feng's sources were themselves derived from authentic Sung works of history or biography. Some of the original expressions showed through, enough to produce the impression that the vernacular stories were themselves of Sung origin. Now a number of the early stories are derived from written works of the Sung dynasty and, in cases where we cannot find a source, we have no right to

---

1 See Hanan, "Sung and Yüan Vernacular Fiction," for a critique of these methods.
2 See Hanan, "Authorship," p. 199. These stories were generally taken as Sung or Yüan.

suppose that none existed. Thus any "Sung expressions" we find may still have originated with the author of the source, not with the vernacular author. The other dangers in the use of internal evidence to set a later limit have the same force as when we described them before.

Bibliographical evidence is no more helpful. The *Tsui-weng t'an-lu* is as tantalizing as ever, but unjustifiable as primary evidence. The *Lu kuei pu* reference may be to KC 36M,[3] but the point cannot finally be proved, and even if we were to accept it, one story could hardly serve as a sample.

Nevertheless, if we are going to proceed, we shall have to make use of these kinds of evidence, inadequate though they are in themselves. The only possibility of earlier dating seems to be to combine as many kinds of secondary evidence as possible, and see how far they corroborate each other.

An Experimental Grouping Based on "Historical" Criteria

We are forced to rely on internal evidence for a purpose that is not proper to it, that is, the establishment of a *terminus ante quem*. It will be used to establish not a date but, instead, an order in time, a relative dating among the stories as yet unfixed to a time scale. The criteria include one of those used before, the comparative closeness of stories to the Yüan dynasty *p'ing-hua* as measured by their preponderance of early criteria over middle. They also include one of those used by Nagasawa Kikuya 長澤規矩也 in his pioneer essay,[4] and others of a similar kind, some of which have been used before. Their common characteristic is that they present a prima facie claim of closeness to the Sung dynasty. The claim can rarely, if ever, be verified empirically. All of the criteria are open, in varying degrees, to the objections to the use of supposedly historical evidence for dating (other than for establishing an earlier limit); that is to say, that the evidence may have been carried in a tradition, oral or written, far beyond the date of the historical context in which it belongs: that it may derive from a source, and not be the contribution of the author of the story (this can be viewed as a special case of the above); and that, in any event, the evidence is often imprecise in terms of dating. If, however, our results in terms of six unrelated criteria tend to reinforce each other, we may perhaps conclude that they have some bearing on date of composition.

---

3 In an edition of the *Lu kuei pu* which reflects, after some fashion, a post-1345 revision of that work, a story (*hua-pen*) on the stuff-material of KC 36M is ascribed to Lu Hsien-chih 陸顯之, a dramatist who died at some time before 1330. On the question of identification, see "Sung and Yüan Vernacular Fiction," pp. 164–165.

4 "Keihon tsūzoku shōsetsu to Seiheisandō wahon" 京本通俗小說と清平山堂話本, *Tōyō gakuhō* 東洋學報 17.2 (1928), 111–139.

First, the results of Chapter V tested, in some degree, proximity to the narrative style of the Yüan dynasty *p'ing-hua*. We list here the ten[5] stories which had the greatest preponderance of early criteria over middle: KC 15M, KC 24, KC 33M, KC 36M, TY 14M, TY 19, TY 37, HY 31, Hung 8M, Hung 15.

Second, we remarked in Chapter V on how our results corresponded to the ways early and middle stories set in the Sung referred to that dynasty.[6] The argument here is that stories which, though set in the Sung, do not refer to the dynasty by name, are likely to be among the earliest. There are ten such stories, and they have a striking degree of correspondence to the list of stories above. They are: KC 24, KC 36M, TY 8M, TY 14M, TY 16, HY 31, Hung 2M, Hung 8M, Hung 15. All of the stories in the first list that are set in the Sung dynasty are present in this group. Three additional stories are listed here (TY 8M, TY 16, Hung 2M).

Third, the Southern Sung capital of Lin-an fu was known as *hsing-tsai* 行在, "the auxiliary seat (of government)." Supposedly the Quinsai of Marco Polo,[7] it seems a fair prima facie criterion of proximity to the Sung dynasty.[8] Of the nine stories set in Southern Sung Hangchow, three use the term: TY 8M, TY 14M, TY 20. TY 8M and TY 14M have appeared in one or both of the above lists.

Fourth, titles of officials and institutions that did not survive the Sung are found frequently in later literature. To offset the effects of tradition, I have excluded from consideration all titles which are found in the middle group of stories and made certain other restrictions.[9] The pertinent titles are as follows:

---

5 Ten is an arbitrary figure. The following are next in order: TY 20, TY 30M, HY 12. Note that TY 20 and TY 30M prove to be close to the group of earliest stories which we are delineating.

6 In the past this criterion has been taken as a sign of Sung composition. Here it is taken merely as a sign of early composition.

7 See A. C. Moule, *Quinsai with Other Notes on Marco Polo* (Cambridge: Cambridge University Press, 1957), pp. 1–11.

8 This has been used by a number of scholars as a criterion of Southern Sung composition.

9 A title must occur at least twice among early stories. Titles that follow proper names are not counted, on the assumption that they would be more easily carried by tradition. The list is meant to include all distinctively Sung titles, subject to the conditions mentioned. It has also been checked against the annotations in modern editions which specify a title as Sung. A few of these were not included, either because they were not distinctive enough, or because they could not be substantiated as Sung titles, for example, *ju-jen* 孺人, honorific term for the wife of a certain grade of official, which appears in KC 24 and Hung 2M; *so-yu* 所由, a kind of gendarmerie, claimed to be distinctively Sung in TY 20, p. 288, n. 27, which appears in TY 20 (as *yu-so*) and in Hung 2M; *yü-chia yüan-tzu* 獄家院子, claimed to be distinctively Sung in KC 36, p. 549, n. 9, which appears in KC 36M and TY 14M; *chi-pu shih-ch'en* 緝捕使臣, a police commandant, claimed to be distinctively Sung in TY 8, p. 104, n. 38, which appears in TY 8, TY 28, and HY 13.

ssu-li yüan 司理院[10]   : KC 15M, TY 37, Hung 2M.

chieh-chi 節級[11]   : HY 31, Hung 15.

tso-pan tien-chih 左班殿直[12]: Hung 2M, Hung 15.

pu-shu 部署[13]   : KC 15M, Hung 15.

ya-ssu 押司[14]   : TY 13, TY 28M.

Only the last two stories have failed to appear on one or more of the three previous lists.

Fifth, it is a common practice among early stories to refer to a place by two names which are not in the usual hierarchical relationship but which are historically consecutive. Superficially, it seems likely that combinations which reflect a change during the Sung dynasty will indicate proximity to the Sung. Ting-chou 定州 became Chung-shan fu 中山府 in 1113,[15] and the combination Ting-chou Chung-shan fu is found in two stories, KC 36M and TY 19. Sheng-chou 昇州 became Chien-k'ang fu 建康府 in 1129, and the combination is found in TY 8M. Yen-chou 延州 became Yen-an fu 延安府 in 1089, and the combination is once more found in TY 8M. Yüeh-chou 越州 became Shao-hsing fu 紹興府 in 1131, and the combination is found in KC 15P. Hangchow became Lin-an fu 臨安府 in 1129, and the combination is found in TY 28M. Soochow became P'ing-chiang fu 平江府 in 1113, and the combination is found in KC 36M.[16] All of these stories have appeared in previous lists.

Finally, several stories contain casual quotations of Sung poems.[17] (A casual quotation must be distinguished from a poem by the poet as fictional hero, which is more likely to come from a written source.) Again, it seems superficially likely that these stories will be among the earliest. They are: KC 15P, KC 24, KC 33P, KC 33M, TY 8P, TY 8M, TY 14P, TY 16, TY 30M, TY 37, Hung 2P, Hung 3P, Hung 8P, Hung 15, and the *Ch'ien-t'ang meng*.[18] Most of the stories have appeared in previous lists.

10 See Chang Fu-jui, *Les Fonctionnaires des Song, Index des titres* (Paris, Mouton, 1962), no. 1770.

11 *Ibid.*, no. 2926.

12 *Ibid.*, no. 3018.

13 *Ibid.*, no. 1532.

14 *Ibid.*, nos. 3257–3258.

15 For these dates, see Hope Wright, *Geographical Names in Sung China, An Alphabetical List* (Paris, Ecole Pratique des Hautes Etudes, 1956).

16 Note that Hsiung A(P) has "Soochow P'ing-chiang."

17 For the most part, the poems carry clear attributions. Two anonymous poems in Hung 2P and Hung 15, respectively, are identified as by Sung poets in Iriya Yoshitaka's 入矢義高 translation of the Hung stories into Japanese. See *Chūgoku koten bungaku zenshū* 中國古典文學全集, vol. VII (Tokyo, 1958), pp. 152, 215.

18 The *tz'u* in TY 37 is said to be by Chien-k'ang fu Shen Erh-kuan-jen 建康府申二官人. I assume that this is a reference to Shen Erh-kuan 申二官 who is credited with the authorship of a set of *tz'u* to a Chien-k'ang fu singing-girl. See T'ang Kuei-chang 唐圭璋, *Ch'üan Sung tz'u* 全宋詞, rev. ed. (Peking, 1965), vol. V, p. 3851. The same poem is attributed to the hero in KC 11. See p. 168.

These tests, inadequate as they are, are the only ones which suggest themselves. The results show a striking degree of concentration, as these figures make clear. (Prologues are omitted from consideration.)

Four criteria :   TY 8M, Hung 15.
Three criteria: KC 24, KC 36M, TY 14M, TY 37, HY 31.
Two criteria :   KC 15M, KC 33M, TY 16, TY 19, TY 28M, Hung 2M, Hung 8M.
One criterion: TY 13, TY 20, TY 30M, *Ch'ien-t'ang meng.*

Sixteen early stories have no criterion at all.

The fourteen stories with two or more criteria will form a trial group, and we shall endeavor to see whether they have stylistic and linguistic features which set them off from the rest of the stories. If they prove to have such features, we shall be in a position to establish this group, amended or supplemented as necessary, as the earliest stories we possess.

Some Linguistic and Stylistic Features of the Trial Group

LINGUISTIC FEATURES. Style, by our definition, is language considered within the contexts relevant to its use. It is thus at a higher level, analytically speaking, than language which is not so considered. We have already argued that to use linguistic criteria regardless of the appropriate contexts, that is to say, regardless of their stylistic aspects, is a crude method of trying to determine authorship or period. Such "raw" criteria are likely to be misleading. Unfortunately, this argument places much of the dialogue of the stories beyond the scholar's reach, because its contexts are not easy to fix precisely. Even when the contexts can be established, one only rarely finds utterances within the short space of the stories which are directly comparable. The pity is that it is precisely in the dialogue that one expects to find the most individual use of language, and hence the greatest differentiation from story to story. Accordingly, I shall make a tentative use of such criteria here, on the assumption that, crude though they may be, they may still tend, in general, to distinguish one group from another. Of course, not all of the contexts relevant to the proper study of style will be ignored, since direct speech, grammar, and broad meaning are among them. But other, finer considerations *will* be ignored, and we shall have to assume that the criteria will still work when put to such clumsy use.

It is far beyond the scope of this chapter, and indeed of the writer's competence, to give an account of the grammar of the early short story. However, in order to avoid the dangers of arbitrary choice, it is necessary either to explore the whole of some category oneself or to find some random method of selection. Studies of the language of the stories are few, and for the most part not suitable for my present purpose. Ōta Tatsuo's 太田辰夫 *Chūgokugo rekishi bumpō* 中國語歴史文法[19] is, as its English title says, *A Historical Grammar of Modern Chinese*, that is, it is concerned with the origin and history of key features of Modern Chinese; it is not concerned with those features of Early Modern Chinese which failed to survive into the present day. Yet it is precisely these features which, because they were limited in their use, are most likely to differentiate one story from another within the short time span in which we are working. Among a number of articles which deal with points of grammar of the early vernacular, the only one which explicitly contrasts the language of the short story with that of the Yüan *tsa-chü* and the Yüan *p'ing-hua* is Hu Chu-an's 胡竹安 "Sung Yüan pai-hua tso-p'in-chung ti yü-ch'i chu-tz'u" 宋元白話作品中的語氣助詞.[20] Of course, its choice of "Sung and Yüan" stories is impressionistic and includes a late story or two among a few middle and a good many early, but it is still usable as a basis for study. In any case, I am here not concerned with the quality of his analysis, only with his article as a purportedly complete exploration of a grammatical category. The category is the small one of what are called modal particles, that is, final particles used to express questions or commands or suggestions or certain other states of mind and feeling. The table at the end of the article contrasts the use of the twenty-five particles considered in the light of their frequency, in the three categories of literature, *tsa-chü* drama of the Yüan dynasty, the Yüan dynasty *p'ing-hua* narratives, and "fiction outside of the *p'ing-hua*." (The last proves to be the *Shui-hu chuan* and the short stories, the latter arbitrarily chosen.) Ten final particles are found frequently in the last category, and two of these, *tse-ko* 則個 and *hsiu* 休, are said to occur only rarely in the other two categories of literature.

Most of the ten do not differentiate our stories adequately. They either occur so frequently in all, like *tse-ko*, or so infrequently, that they are of no use as criteria. However, one criterion, *hsiu*, corresponds strikingly with our trial group.

As a final particle, *hsiu* has a range of meanings, but most commonly it is an abrupt suggestion or a command. The particle with which it corresponds most closely in Modern Chinese is probably *pa* 罷, although *pa* is also found among the early stories. The meaning of *hsiu* is discussed by Hu Chu-an on page 273, and, in much greater detail, by Chang Hsiang 張相 in his *Shih tz'u ch'ü yü-tz'u hui-shih* 詩詞曲語辭匯釋.[21] Chang's examples are drawn entirely from poetry, mainly of the Southern Sung. By its nature,

19 Tokyo, 1957.
20 *Chung-kuo yü-wen* 中國語文 (June 1958), pp. 270–274.
21 Peking, 1957 ed., pp. 315–316.

hsiu tends to take the last position in the line, but it is noticeable that, in most of the examples quoted, it is also a rhyming word. Hu Chu-an quotes examples from the short story, exclusively from dialogue, and also one example from the *Wu Tai shih p'ing-hua*. According to his tables it occurs rarely in Yüan *tsa-chü*, but, despite some random searching, I have not encountered any instances. It occurs quite frequently in the *Shui-hu chuan*, especially in the early and middle chapters, always in dialogue and always in a very restricted collocation. It does not occur at all in the middle or late stories we have considered, unless the common phrase *pu ju ssu hsiu* 不如死休, "the only course is to take my life," contains a fossilized use of it. It is possible that *hsiu* is not a particle in this phrase, but that *ssu hsiu* means to die and "make an end." In any case, it can be ignored as a cliché. *Hsiu* is thus, for practical purposes, a particle of extremely limited use, confined to the short stories and the *Shui-hu chuan*.[22]

The distribution of *hsiu* among the early stories is as follows: KC 15M, KC 36M, TY 14M, TY 19, TY 37, HY 14, HY 31, Hung 8M, Hung 15. Eight of these nine stories belong to the trial group. The exception is HY 14.

This result confirms the notion of the trial group as distinguishable by linguistic means. Of course, the mere presence of *hsiu* is not a guarantee that that story is among the earliest, and, much more important, the absence of *hsiu* is not a guarantee of the converse.

It is not difficult to pick items arbitrarily which will reinforce this grouping. For example, the combination *hsieh-ko* 些個 occurring before nouns, as in Modern Chinese, or after stative verbs, like *i-tien* 一點 in Modern Chinese, is largely confined to the trial group among early stories. The alternatives are plain *hsieh* 些 or *hsieh-tzu* 些子 or *hsieh-erh* 些兒, all of which are common in other Sung and Yüan literature.[23] The distribution of *hsieh-ko* among all early stories is as follows: KC 15M, KC 33M, KC 36M, TY 14M, TY 19, TY 20, TY 37, HY 14, Hung 11. The nine stories include six from the trial group. *Hsieh-ko* occurs not at all among middle stories and only rarely among late stories we have considered. Other linguistic criteria could also be adduced.[24]

22 It occurs in the *Shui-hu ch'üan chuan* ed. (Peking, 1954), pp. 233, 451, 580, 694, 697, 712, 714, 724, and 846, i.e., from chaps. 16 through 51, always immediately after *ch'ü* 去. It occurs once in *Wu Tai* (p. 82) and once in the twenty-chapter *P'ing-yao chuan* (chap. 2).

23 *Hsieh-ko* appears occasionally in *Chu Tzu yü-lei* 朱子語類, see the 1876 ed., *chüan* 65.2a, but the usual word is *hsieh-tzu*. It is found a few times in the twenty-chapter *P'ing-yao chuan*.

24 An effective criterion would be the adverb *ssu* before verbs, although one would have to specify the verb. *Ssu chiao* 廝叫, e.g., "to greet, hail," is confined to KC 33M, KC 36M, TY 13M, TY 37, HY 31, and Hung 15.

STYLISTIC FEATURES AMONG ESTABLISHED CRITERIA. We found in Chapter V that the older criteria in one or two cases also served to distinguish early stories from middle stories and pointed out that the use of these criteria, established for another purpose, avoided some of the dangers of arbitrary choice. We can therefore expect that among the early criteria of Chapter V there may be some which will differentiate the trial group from the rest of the stories. In fact, criterion E5, *k'an shih* 看時 or *k'an . . . shih* before a couplet, poem, or set piece, does so. Its distribution is: KC 15M, KC 24, KC 33M, KC 36M, TY 8M, TY 14M, TY 19, TY 36M, TY 37, Hung 2M, Hung 8M, Hung 15. Eleven of these twelve stories are among the fourteen of our trial group. The exception is TY 36M.

Although none of the other criteria works in this clear fashion, both of the probable criteria mentioned in Chapter V tend to do so. *P'i-jan tao ti* is found in eight stories, TY 8M, TY 13M, TY 14M, TY 20, TY 37, HY 14, HY 31, and Hung 15, most of which are in the trial group.[25] *Li-pu-te*, criterion 15 of Chapter III and the other probable criterion of Chapter V, occurs in these nine stories: KC 15M, KC 36M, TY 8M, TY 14M, TY 20, TY 37, HY 14, HY 31, Hung 11, six of which appear in the trial group.

OTHER STYLISTIC FEATURES. Other stylistic features which will serve as criteria are not too difficult to find. Among them are several formulae which occupy the position immediately before, or a little before, a couplet, poem, or set piece.

The demonstrative *che* 這 before a noun which is then followed by a couplet and so on is confined to KC 33M, TY 37, and Hung 15, all of which are in the trial group.

The expression *chih chien* 只見, common in the *p'ing-hua* and in the late stories, is confined to KC 15M, KC 24, TY 8M, TY 10, HY 13, HY 31, and Hung 8M. All but TY 10 and HY 13 are in the trial group.

The same expression, not directly before the couplet but with a phrase or clause intervening, is confined to KC 36M, TY 14M, TY 19, HY 31, and Hung 8M, all of which are in the trial group.

Another feature is the quantity of set pieces. It is possible that there is a correlation between type of story and number of set pieces, since it seems that it is the "linked" stories, all of which are in the trial group, and the "demon" stories, most of which are in the trial group, which tend to have large numbers of set pieces. If true, this would limit the value of this feature as a criterion. The stories which contain five or more set pieces are: KC 15M, KC 24, KC 33M, KC 36M, TY 14M, TY 16, TY 19, TY 37, HY 31,

25 Cf. *P'ing-yao chuan*, ch.1.10a. TY 30M has an aberrant form.

Hung 2M, Hung 3M, Hung 8M, Hung 15.[26] Twelve of these thirteen stories belong to the trial group. The exception is Hung 3M. The following contain four set pieces: TY 10, TY 30M, Hung 11, none of which is in the trial group.

A few other criteria: *hsiang tz'u* 相次 "next, thereupon" is confined to KC 33M, TY 19, TY 20, TY 37; the time formula *cheng* 正 plus verb plus *li* 哩(or 裡) "while just in the act of . . . ing" is confined to KC 15M, KC 36M, HY 14, Hung 15;[27] and the expression *cheng-jen* (*ti*) 正恁(的) plus verb, which has a similar meaning, is confined to TY 14M, TY 19, TY 37, HY 14, and Hung 2M.[28]

Though a strong claim can be made for the formulae which introduce a couplet and so forth, these last criteria are arbitrary and therefore weak. They have the virtue, however, of showing which stories tend to be associated with the trial group when one is seeking criteria to isolate it as far as possible. Since we have shown how a group constituted on the grounds of "historical" criteria also has its own distinctive linguistic and stylistic features, it is likely that the stories regularly associated with the group deserve to be admitted to membership. In the same way, original members of the group which have regularly failed to show any of the group's characteristics probably do not belong to it.

REASSESSMENT. With the exception of TY 16 and TY 28M, the stories thus also constitute a broad grouping by virtue of stylistic and other criteria. The same criteria work to associate two additional stories with the group, HY 14 and, to a smaller degree, TY 20. The nearest stories to the trial group, apart from TY 20 and HY 14, are TY 13M, TY 16, TY 30M, and Hung 11.

Twelve stories of the trial group thus clearly constitute an "earliest" group of stories, since the stylistic and linguistic features they possess reinforce the distinctions established by the historical criteria. The two others, TY 16 and TY 28M, though they shared the historical criteria, do not, on the whole, share the other features, TY 28M not at all, TY 16 in only one case. Since the historical criteria are admittedly weak, and were adopted on a trial basis only, we must assume that they are misleading with regard to these two, and indeed the evidence does seem flimsy in the case of TY

---

26 TY 19 has four ordinary set pieces, plus a number of rhymed and parallelistic compositions to a uniform pattern.

27 Cf. the incidence in the *Shui-hu ch'üan chuan*, pp. 26, 66, 73, 87, 315, 568, 606, 660, 741, 798, 1230.

28 Twice in TY 19 in the form of *cheng tsen-ti* 正怎的. *Tsen-ti* is used occasionally for *jen-ti*; see Hung 2M, p. 13, which the KC 35 version has changed to *jen*.

28.[29] They must therefore be excluded from the group of "earliest" stories. For the same reasons, TY 20 and HY 14 should be added to it.

Any attempt to classify stories always overemphasizes the differences between the groups. In fact, it is clear that some of the stories outside the "earliest" group are much closer to that group than to, say, the middle stories, or to other vernacular literature. Obviously, though there are real differences that can support this kind of division, they are such that the stories shade into one another. Of course, we cannot say in all cases that stories not in the "earliest" group are necessarily later, though that is assumed to be generally true. As far as the stories written in a language close to Classical Chinese are concerned, however, not even that assumption should be made. Thus TY 10, TY 29, and Hung 5, having few of the characteristics of the rest of the stories, cannot really be judged by these criteria. In fact, TY 10, by possessing some of the stylistic criteria, does seem quite close to the group.

Finally, we must ask whether any other, unsuspected factors have affected these results. In particular, have we identified a period style with the style of one type of story? There is some evidence that the "linked" story and the "demon" story have distinctive features of their own, and this may have affected the result of one of the "other stylistic" tests. This distortion would not be enough to change the composition of the group. Indeed, two "demon" stories, TY 30M and Hung 3M, were not included in the "earliest" group. The fact that all five "linked" stories turn up in the "earliest" group seems merely to reflect an obvious reality: they were among the earliest of all.

Fitting the Earliest Stories to a Time Scale

We have delineated a group of the "earliest" stories without attaching dates to the word "earliest."

If KC 36M really was written by Lu Hsien-chih, the problem is partly solved, for we may suppose that that story was composed circa 1300. Since KC 36M is, to the best of our knowledge, as early as any story, we could conclude that the earliest group dates from about this time and certainly not much earlier. And since this group of stories must be earlier, in general, than the rest of the early stories, which in turn are supposed to have been

---

29 TY 28 qualified because it possessed the title ya-ssu "clerk in magistrate's office," but ya-ssu is one Sung title which has been kept alive in the Shui-hu tradition—Sung Chiang is a ya-ssu. It is also frequently used in Yüan tsa-chü, though, oddly enough, not of Sung Chiang.

written before about 1450, we would probably be justified in dating the rest of the "earliest" group to the beginning and middle decades of the fourteenth century. Our tentative anterior and posterior dates might, in fact, span the Yüan dynasty, 1280 to 1368.

But this is to invest a great deal in what, after all, is a mere probability, Lu Hsien-chih's authorship. Suppose Lu was not the author of KC 36M, could we then assume, as many scholars insist, that we are in possession of numbers of Sung stories? I do not think so. Lu's work must have been celebrated; it is the only short story mentioned in Yüan or early-Ming literature. In the baffling problems of identification that plague the study of the Yüan *tsa-chü*, the mistakes have arisen from attributing some later play to an earlier playwright whose own play on the same theme has been lost.[30] And if there was another written story about Chao Cheng before the time of Lu's work, it is probable that the latter would have superseded it. It is therefore reasonable to believe that, if KC 36M is not by Lu Hsien-chih, it is by some later person and must date from 1300 or after. In that case, the earlier limit for the stories as a group will remain the same, though there will be much less evidence for the later limit.

KC 24 uses a source that must have been written after 1229. I shall discuss the composition of this story in more detail in the next chapter. Let us just note here that the author of KC 24 used an item in the *Kuei Tung* 鬼董 to amplify the ending of his main source, a story from the *I-chien chih*.[31] The two stories are, in fact, partial analogues, and the fact is recognized by the author of the *Kuei Tung* who points out in an editorial note that his story supplements the *I-chien chih* item. The conclusion must be that the author of KC 24 took this hint and combined both analogues into his own story, together with material from other sources as well. Thus the earliest conceivable date for KC 24 will be 1230.

Moreover, certain other stories refer to the Sung dynasty in ways that do not sound like the usage of Sung writers. KC 15P, for example, refers to it as *Sung ch'ao* 宋朝 "the Sung dynasty," and we have already seen that there is some evidence to believe that this prologue is as early as its main story. HY 14 uses the same manner of reference. TY 20 uses the term *Ta Sung* 大宋 "the Great Sung," which is found in a sprinkling of other early stories outside this group, as well as in some middle stories. HY 31 refers to the capital of the Northern Sung as Pien-liang ch'eng 汴梁城, a term which is also found in Hung 4, a middle story. Pien-liang seems, so far as

---

30 See Yen Tun-i, *Yüan-chü chen-i, passim.*
31 See also Hanan, "Sung and Yüan Vernacular Fiction," pp. 182–183.

our knowledge goes, to have come into general use for Kaifeng only in the Yüan dynasty. It is the usual word in the Yüan *tsa-chü* plays, and it is commonly found among middle stories, for example, KC 26, Hsiung A(M), Hung 12, 23, and 27. Of course, none of these points amounts to certain evidence; Sung writers *could* have referred to the dynasty explicitly, and some of the terms, though hardly all, could be the result of editorial emendation.

Thus among the earliest group of fourteen, we have good reason to believe that KC 36M was written no earlier than about 1300, and that KC 24 was written at some time after 1229, and we have some slight reason for thinking that four other stories may have been written after the beginning of the Yüan. A large proportion of the group conforms to the tentative earlier limit of about 1280, and it seems justifiable to set this limit for the group as a whole. In the extreme case, one might concede that a story or two could have been written a couple of decades earlier.

It is worth noting that, even if we were to reject these arguments, the stories as a group could still not have been very much earlier. The place-names mentioned in the stories were those that came into force in the first part of the twelfth century. KC 24 takes its source from the *I-chien chih*, which was written in installments during the latter part of the twelfth century.[32] KC 15P, which also refers to the *I-chien chih*, mentions a building which was only constructed in the Chia-ting 嘉定 period (1208–1224).[33] The Chinese short story as we know it could not have antedated the thirteenth century, and the likelihood is that it did not much antedate the Yüan dynasty.

Establishing a later limit is, as always, a much more delicate problem. We have not *proven*, only estimated, that the earliest stories must have been written during the Yüan. The conclusion arises from our previous dating of the middle stories—a lame argument. The earliest stories contain a number of archaisms which we find elsewhere only in the medley and in some of the *tsa-chü*, but the fact is not easy to present comparatively, and it would have only a vague significance at best. We shall have to let the estimate remain as it is.

32 See the Commercial Press edition, Shanghai, 1927. The preface to the section in which the item appears, *Ting chih* 丁志, is incomplete, lacking a date, and may well not belong to this section. The preface to the second section is dated 1166, the third 1171. The second refers to a gap of five years since the publication of the first section. It seems that at this stage Hung Mai was publishing installments at five-year intervals. *Ting chih* may then have appeared in 1176 or thereabouts. *Chüan* 16 carries a date of 1175 in one item.

33 See *Ku-chin hsiao-shuo*, p. 234, n. 8.

The Prologues of the Earliest Stories

A related question concerns the origin of the prologues attached to seven of the stories: KC 15, KC 33, KC 36, TY 8, TY 14, Hung 2, and Hung 8. Five of the seven have poem-chain prologues (all but KC 36 and Hung 2). We have already noticed "historical" criteria in both KC 15P and TY 8P (geographical combinations, see above), and all five stories make use of the work of Sung poets. Wherever we are able to check with a good text of the poem, we find that the writers of the prologues have taken the same course—they have copied a popular version much changed from the original, and they have frequently attributed the poem to the wrong poet. All these points show that the reader's initial suspicion that the prologues may have been attached by some "literary" editor—the suspicion is due to their incongruity, in one or two cases, when compared with the main story—is almost certainly baseless. The poem-chain prologues were evidently written along with the main story according to the prescriptions of a bizarre early form. And the writer was far from "literary-minded," or he would have taken some care with his quotation and his attributions. It is interesting, but of little value as evidence, to note that Feng Meng-lung thought that the poem-chain prologue was characteristic of the "Sung story," and that he appears to have marvelled at it as much as we do.[34]

The two prologue stories are a different problem. We have no evidence to date KC 36P and Hung 2P among the earliest stories, but both are short and written, in contrast to their main stories, in a language that is close to Classical. Another version of the Hung 2P story that includes the poem central to it is found in two Yüan publications, one of them Lo Yeh's *Tsui-weng t'an-lu*;[35] it may very well have been written by the author of Hung 2M. Much greater suspicion attaches to the prologue story of KC 36. It is listed, assuming the identification is correct, as a separate story in the Ming dynasty Pao-wen-t'ang catalogue, and it survives as a separate story in some of the late-Ming miscellanies. We know of stories being attached by editors as prologues to other stories—the prologue story to TY 6, perhaps[36]—but we do not know of a prologue story being separated from its main story and given an independent existence.

---

34 See the facsimile editions, KC 33.2b and TY 8.2a.

35 See p. 23. The other work is the *Shih-hua chüan-yung* 詩話雋永 of Yü Cheng-chi 喻正己 (*chi* is also found as *ssu* 巳). It is included in the *Shuo fu* (1646), *chüan* 84.

36 We do not know for certain that the two had separate origins. A clear example is Hung 11, used as prologue in *P'ai-an ching-ch'i* 21.

Attempting to Date the Rest of the Stories

Besides asserting that the fourteen stories are earlier as a group, we can also draw some conclusions about the other stories.

HY 21 has a reference to the length of the Sung dynasty[37] and also contains a distinctively Ming place-name, a point which we judged inconclusive before. Since it has no close affinity to the fourteen stories, we may assume it to be an early-Ming story. *Chang Yü-hu*, in one of the best editions of it we have,[38] also contains a Ming place-name; although as a virtuoso story its language is rather Classical and less directly comparable to that of the fourteen, we may also regard it as early Ming.

Other Ming place-names do not inspire the same confidence. Since neither TY 13M nor TY 28M is in Group A, we may choose to give some weight to the Ming place-names they contain. On the other hand, it has been suggested above that the supposedly Ming place-names in TY 8M and Hung 16 may not be Ming at all.

A number of stories can only be put in the category of "Yüan or early-Ming." These are: KC 11, TY 6M, TY 13M, TY 16, TY 28M, TY 30M, TY 36M, TY 39, HY 12, HY 13, HY 33M, Hung 3M, Hung 13, Hung 16, *Ch'ien-t'ang meng*. The likelihood, however, is that most of these stories are, in fact, early-Ming rather than Yüan. (The most probable exceptions are TY 13, TY 16, and TY 30M, which seemed to have the closest affinity with the fourteen stories.) In particular, KC 11 and Hung 16 were undetermined as between early and middle in Chapter V; it seems most likely that they are in fact "early-Ming or middle." TY 6M and HY 33M both refer to the dynasty as *Nan Sung* "Southern Sung," a term which, on prima facie grounds, seems to place them at some distance from the Sung. (Of course, HY 33M shows signs of alteration by a late editor, and the term may not have belonged in the original story.) Hung 3M and Hung 13, like KC 11 and Hung 16, show little affinity with the fourteen stories.

Some of the stories contain indications of Yüan or later composition. The poem beginning *Jen tung feng lao ch'ü* 任東風老去 "let the east wind blow as it will" in HY 13 reproduces the greater part of a *tz'u* from a Classical tale of the Yüan dynasty. The tale, the *Ch'un-meng lu* 春夢錄, is by one Cheng Hsi 鄭禧,[39] and it has an author's preface dated 1318. The text

---

37 See p. 454.

38 The Ho version of the *Yen-chü pi-chi*. The Lin and Yü versions and the *Wan-chin ch'ing-lin* have a nondistinctive form of the same place-name.

39 There are editions in the *Lü-ch'uang nü-shih* 綠窗女史 and in the *Shuo fu* (1646). The *tz'u* is also included, with the same attribution, in the *Hua-ts'ao ts'ui-pien, chüan* 11.18ab.

of the poem is identical as far as it goes, and the general (nontextual) context is much the same, a woman physically sick for lack of love. TY 6M contains a *tz'u* apparently written by a Yüan poet.[40] It is probably significant that some of the remaining stories contain ingredients of the earliest stories; KC 11, for example, attributes to its hero, Chao Hsü 趙旭, *tz'u* that appear in TY 37 and Hung 2P,[41] while Hung 3M has an extraordinarily close, though undetermined, relationship to Hung 8M.[42] There are other indications which need not be detailed here. Even if the reader disagrees with my interpretation of the other data in this chapter, he cannot conceivably put most of these stories in the Sung dynasty.

Hung 11 has shown some of the features of the earliest group, but is difficult to judge because it is so short. Similarly difficult are those stories written in a more or less Classical language, but there are slight indications that TY 10, TY 29, and Hung 5 may be among the earliest.

On the basis of this chapter's experimental ordering of stories, it seems possible to make three tentative subdivisions. Group A consists of the fourteen earliest stories. Group B consists of the stories closest to them, such as TY 13, TY 16, and TY 30, and of the stories which are, for reasons of length or language, difficult to judge: TY 10, TY 29, Hung 5, and Hung 11.[43] The remainder of the stories comprise Group C. According to the inadequate information we have, we may assume that most of Group A were written toward the end of the thirteenth century or during the fourteenth, and that most of Group C were written toward the end of the fourteenth century or during the fifteenth. Of the Group B stories, there is little to be said, except that most of them incline to Group A.

The Hua-ts'ao ts'ui-pien's Versions of Early Stories

The *Hua-ts'ao ts'ui-pien* is an anthology of early *tz'u* compiled at some time before 1583, quite possibly before 1559. Wu Ch'eng-en, putative author of the *Hsi-yu chi*, had a hand in its compilation.[44] It is remarkable among anthologies for its inclusion of *tz'u* from vernacular fiction. These *tz'u* can be considered as fragments of earlier editions than those we possess. We can recognize them because the *Ts'ui-pien* gives the name of the story;

---

40 See *Ch'üan Sung tz'u*, vol. V, p. 3894.

41 See TY 37, pp. 557–558, and KC 11, p. 168; Hung 2, p. 7 and KC 11, p. 166.

42 See Chapter VIII.

43 These are reinforced by a consideration of sourceworks. Use of *I-chien chih* and *Kuei Tung* is confined to Groups A and B.

44 See Liu Ts'un-yan, "Wu Ch'eng-en: His Life and Career," *T'oung Pao* 53.1–3 (1967), 43–52.

or because it simply uses the word *hsiao-shuo*, meaning vernacular fiction in this context; or because it attributes the authorship of the *tz'u* to fictional characters.

In the first category, there is a *tz'u* in *chüan* 5.55b of which the source is given as *hsiao-shuo Shan-t'ing-erh* 小說山亭兒 "the vernacular story *Shan-t'ing-erh*." *Shan-t'ing-erh* is part of the title of TY 37 and is the title of the same story in the Pao-wen-t'ang collection; the identical poem is found in it, on page 562. In the same way, the poem in *chüan* 6.31b derived from *Chang Lao hsiao-shuo* 張老小說 "the vernacular story of Chang Lao" is found in KC 33, page 495; its text is practically the same. There is also a *tz'u* from the *Shui-hu chuan*[45] and one from the *Hsüan-ho i-shih*.[46]

Three poems are simply described as from *hsiao-shuo*, without titles. Two of them cannot be identified as from any extant stories,[47] but the third is attributed to Chao Hsü, the hero of KC 11.[48] It is not found in KC 11, nor does the *Hua-ts'ao ts'ui-pien* contain any of the seven *tz'u* that belong to that story. It is possible, of course, that the *Ts'ui-pien* chose to print the very *tz'u* which a later editor chose to delete, but it is perhaps more likely that two vernacular versions once existed of the same stuff-material.

A number of *tz'u* found in KC 24 appear in the *Ts'ui-pien* attributed to their fictional authors; there are two by Cheng I-niang 鄭義娘, one by Han Ssu-hou 韓思厚, and one by the nun.[49] Their text is practically identical in the two works. The *Ts'ui-pien* and KC 24 share two other *tz'u*, but here there is no question of a direct relationship.[50] Surprisingly, the *Ts'ui-pien* contains one other *tz'u* attributed to Cheng I-niang which does not appear in KC 24.[51] It belongs clearly enough to the plot of KC 24—it should be spoken by I-niang's ghost after her husband has broken his promise. Why is it not in KC 24? We have the same choice of explanations as in the case

45 See Hanan, "Sung and Yüan Vernacular Fiction," p. 184, n. 121.

46 See *chüan* 9.5ab. The original source is given as the *Ch'ing yeh lu* 清夜錄.

47 *Chüan* 4.43a and 8.34a.

48 *Chüan* 5.28a. The word *hsiao-shuo* is, in effect, used of the source of this poem. See the table of contents of *chüan* 5, where this pattern title is identified as from *hsiao-shuo*. The Chao Hsü poem is the only specimen.

49 See *chüan* 3.40a, 5.32b, 8.33a, and 4.26b, respectively. The characters' names are somewhere between the forms found in the *I-chien chih* and those of KC 24. The heroine is given as Cheng I-niang 鄭意娘 as against the Wang I-niang 王意娘 of the *I-chien chih* and the Cheng I-niang 鄭義娘 of KC 24. The hero is given as Han Shih-hou 韓師厚, as in the *I-chien chih*; KC 24 has Ssu-hou 思厚. When the stuff-material is referred to by other short stories, there is a similar variation; the opening poem of TY 30P has Shih-hou, the opening poem of Hsiung A(P) has Ssu-hou. Note that KC 24 is not entirely consistent; it also contains the form 意娘.

50 The introductory poem appears in the *Ts'ao-t'ang shih-yü* 草堂詩餘 (Shanghai, 1958 ed.), p. 63, one of the two prime sources of the *Ts'ui-pien*. (The other is the *Hua-chien chi*; the *Ts'ui-pien*'s title reflects its dependence on the two works.) The emperor's poem of KC 24 appears in *chüan* 6.49b of the *Ts'ui-pien* in an inferior version.

51 *Chüan* 12.93b–94a.

of KC 11, but this time it is more likely that the poem has been excised.[52] Note that a late editor may not necessarily be to blame, for the Pao-wen-t'ang catalogue listed two works on this subject with slightly differing titles.

Several other stories may have been used by the *Ts'ui-pien* compiler. The most likely seems to have been TY 14P, which has several *tz'u* that are textually close to their counterparts in the anthology.[53]

There is one title, *Ch'ing-hu san t'a chi* 清湖三塔記, from which four *tz'u* are printed, which seems to parallel the title of an existing story, Hung 3. However, there is no clear connection between the two works.[54]

The *Ts'ui-pien* was intended as an anthology of early *tz'u*, T'ang, Five Dynasties, and Sung, plus an occasional specimen from the Yüan.[55] It is noteworthy that the stories we know it to have used, KC 24, KC 33, and TY 37, are all early stories and all in Group A.

Lost Stories Described by Ch'ien Hsi-yen and Ch'ien Tseng

There are other stories, now lost, which were ascribed to the Sung period by Ch'ien Hsi-yen 錢希言 of the late Ming and by Ch'ien Tseng of the Ch'ing. While the claim cannot be taken literally, we may still be able to deduce something about the stories' nature from the accompanying details. From Ch'ien Hsi-yen's description, we can tell that *Teng-hua p'o-p'o* 燈花婆婆 "Mother Lampwick" had a poem-chain prologue, consisted of more than one chapter, and was based on a combination of two T'ang tales.[56]

---

52 This is Sun K'ai-ti's opinion. See "Hsiao-shuo p'ang-cheng ssu-tse" 小說旁證四則, *Wen-hsüeh p'ing-lun* 文學評論 (1961, no. 5), p. 124.

53 E.g., the *tz'u* beginning *Yin-ch'ing* 陰晴 is found in *chüan* 3.59a, and these are the only two anthologies in which it survives. (See *Ch'üan Sung tz'u*, vol. I, p. 537.) The *tz'u* beginning *Ho shih* 何事 is closer to the version in *chüan* 6.46a than to any other. (*Ibid.*, vol. I, p. 470.) The *tz'u* beginning *Wu li* 無力 has the same attribution as that in *chüan* 2.29a. (*Ibid.*, vol. I, p. 201 and vol. V, pp. 3853–3854.) There is no direct connection between other poems shared by the two works, or between *tz'u* in other short stories and their *Ts'ui-pien* counterparts. The introductory poem in HY 13 appears in *chüan* 4.51a with a different attribution, and the *tz'u* in TY 39, p. 584, is in a different version from that in *chüan* 4.73b.

54 See *chüan* 2.25a (two poems), 2.41b, and 9.47b. Liu Tsun-yan, "Wu Ch'eng-en," points to the correspondence between two consecutive phrases, six characters in all, found in one of the Hung 3 poems and in one of these *tz'u*. This does not seem strong enough evidence for us to assume a direct connection.

55 See the 1583 preface.

56 See Sun K'ai-ti, "Hsiao-shuo p'ang-cheng" 小說旁證, *Kuo-li Pei-p'ing t'u-shu-kuan kuan-k'an* 國立北平圖書館館刊 9.1 (1935), 13–14. Sun quotes from *chüan* 1 and 3 of *T'ung hsin* 桐薪, a work by Ch'ien that has not been accessible to me. Part of the *Teng-hua p'o-p'o* story survives, in barely recognizable shape, at the beginning of Feng Meng-lung's adapted *P'ing-yao chuan*. It was once incorporated into the *Shui-hu chuan*, according to Yang Ting-chien's 楊定見 introduction to Li Chih's 李贄 supposed edition of the novel. See R. G. Irwin, *The Evolution of a Chinese Novel: Shui-hu chuan* (Cambridge, Mass., Harvard University Press, 1953), p. 47.

Since all of the stories with poem-chain prologues have proven to be early
—two are in Group C, the rest in Group A—it is highly likely that *Teng-hua
p'o-p'o* was also an early story. To judge from the sourceworks, it cannot
have been closely akin to any existing story, though it may have resembled
to some extent such stories of demons and exorcism as TY 30M. Ch'ien
Hsi-yen also tells us that *Tzu-lo kai t'ou* 紫羅蓋頭 was on the subject of the
god Erh-lang 二郎, but one's natural suspicion that it may have been identical with HY 13, in which a magician impersonates Erh-lang, turns out to
be unjustified; it was a different story, which embodied a related legend
of the god, or of someone impersonating him.[57]

Apart from these two titles, Ch'ien Tseng's catalogue lists several others
which have not been identified as extant stories.[58] In only one case, however, is there a clue as to the story's type; *Feng Yü-mei t'uan-yüan* 馮玉梅團圓
must have been a story of lovers forced to part but eventually reunited.
It is an unusual theme for the early and middle periods, even in stories of
the virtuoso type.[59]

57 See Ch'ien's *K'uai yüan* 獪園, 1774 ed., *chüan* 12, 15b–16a.
58 We are now in a position to see how the classifications made in Ch'ien Tseng's
catalogues compare with our results. Ten titles listed by Ch'ien are commonly identified
with extant stories. Six of these prove to be Group A (KC 33, TY 8, TY 14, TY 19, TY 37,
Hung 2M), two prove to be Group C (HY 33M, Hung 3), and two are middle stories (Hung
1 and Hung 4). Obviously Ch'ien Tseng used the term "Sung" fairly tolerantly. By way
of comparison, all four of the stories described by the *San yen* editors as Sung are early.
Three are in Group A (TY 8, TY 14, TY 19) and one is in Group C (HY 33).
59 Its original title is given in the catalogue as *Shuang ching ch'ung yüan* 雙鏡重圓. (The
catalogue is the MS. *Shu-ku-t'ang shu-mu* in Sun's possession.) It must have been at least a
middle-period story, since the title *Feng Yü-mei chi*, like *Teng-hua p'o-p'o* and *Tzu-lo kai
t'ou*, appears in the Pao-wen-t'ang catalogue.

VIII The Early Stories: Their Nature and Composition

More scholarly ink has been spilt over the historical origins of the early short story than over all the other questions relating to the whole genre. Nonetheless, most of the basic questions remain unanswered. What is the relationship of the extant short stories to oral literature? Were they derived from oral literature and intended for presentation to a reading public? Were they written for presentation to a listening public? What kind of author wrote them? How does their observable typology compare with the traditional typology of professional oral fiction? No doubt these questions are framed too simply—one of the dangers is to ask simple questions about possibly complex issues—but even if they are qualified in dozens of ways, they cannot be answered without new evidence or a new approach.

The establishment of a reliable group of early stories does provide us with a little new evidence, because past attempts to analyze the stories as a group have always been thwarted by the confusion of middle and late stories with early. One question at least, the question about typology, can now be attacked directly. And some light can be thrown on the other questions by a comparison of the stories themselves, their sources, and their analogues.

The Early Stories and the Traditional Typology of Oral Fiction

There are two main accounts of the traditional typology, the *Tu-ch'eng chi-sheng* 都城紀勝,[1] with an author's preface of 1235, and Lo Yeh's *Tsui-weng t'an-lu*, probably compiled in the Yüan dynasty. The *Tu-ch'eng chi-sheng* is a record of life in the capital of the Southern Sung, modern Hang-

---

1 *Tung-ching meng-hua lu wai ssu chung* 東京夢華錄外四種 ed. (Shanghai, 1958), p. 98.

chow, and its account of the typology of oral fiction is repeated, with minor divergences only, in the most famous description of Sung dynasty Hang-chow, the *Meng liang lu* 夢梁錄.[2]

There are some ambiguities in the *Chi-sheng*, but under the heading of *hsiao-shuo* 小說 five main classes[3] appear to be listed: *yen-fen* 煙粉, *ling-kuai* 靈怪, *ch'uan-ch'i* 傳奇, *kung-an* 公案, and *t'ieh-chi-erh* 鐵騎兒. The two last classes appear to be subdivided, the *kung-an* into the three subclasses of *p'u-tao* 搏刀, *kan-pang* 趕棒, and *fa-chi pien-t'ai* 發跡變泰. It is clear that these are classes of subject matter or plot rather than genre or form, because four of the terms, *yen-fen*, *ling-kuai*, *t'ieh-chi*, and *kung-an*, are also used by the *Chi-sheng* in classifying puppet plays.[4]

The *T'an-lu* gives eight classes of *hsiao-shuo* and, most valuable of all in defining the classes, it gives numerous story titles within each class. The eight are: *ling-kuai*, *yen-fen*, *ch'uan-ch'i*, *kung-an*, *p'u-tao*, *kan-pang*, *shen-hsien* 神仙, and *yao-shu* 妖術.[5] The *t'ieh-chi-erh* and the *fa-chi pien-t'ai* of the *Chi-sheng* have been omitted in favor of the last two classes.[6]

Testing the early stories against this typology, one finds both uncanny correspondences and equally striking discrepancies. As an example of the correspondences, the *T'an-lu* class of *p'u-tao* lists as titles the names of two heroes who appear in TY 37,[7] and in that story they prove to be experts in the weapon known as *p'u-tao*. Under *kan-pang* in the *T'an-lu*, we find the title of an oral story with the same subject matter as Hung 15[8] and, sure enough, the hero of Hung 15 proves to be an expert with the quarter staff. *Fa-chi pien-t'ai*, one of the *Chi-sheng's* classes, fits two stories admirably, KC 15M and HY 31. Both stories actually use the term *fa-chi pien-t'ai*, which may be translated as "stories of upstart heroes," and the openings of both stories contain similar visions of their heroes' future greatness.[9] (The *T'an-lu* does not contain this class, and it apparently allocates the oral story with the subject matter of HY 31 to the class of *ling-kuai*.)[10] A rough

---

2 *Ibid.*, pp. 312–313.

3 See J. L. Bishop, *The Colloquial Short Story in China* (Cambridge, Mass., Harvard University Press, 1956), pp. 8–10, for a translation and discussion of these passages. *Yin-tzu-erh* 銀字兒 may be an alternative term for *hsiao-shuo*.

4 See *Tu-ch'eng chi-sheng*, p. 97.

5 It first lists the classes with *yao-shu* before *shen-hsien*, then reverses the order in giving examples. Some of the characters differ from those used in *Chi-sheng*; *p'u-tao* is written 朴刀, the correct form.

6 But the poem in *T'an-lu*, p. 5, mentions *t'ieh-chi*.

7 See T'an Cheng-pi, *Hua-pen yü ku-chü*, pp. 29–30.

8 *Ibid.*, p. 32.

9 See Jaroslav Průšek, *The Origins and the Authors of the Hua-pen* (Prague, Academia, 1967), pp. 109–110.

10 T'an Cheng-pi, *Hua-pen yü ku-chü*, p. 15. The *T'an-lu* may be referring to a different, though related, version of the same basic stuff-material.

rationale can also be deduced for the classes of *ling-kuai*, *yen-fen*, *ch'uan-ch'i*, and *kung-an*[11] which makes sense in terms of some of the extant stories. Indeed the stuff-material of several of them is evidently referred to in the *T'an-lu*'s list of titles.

The main discrepancy concerns the demon stories, a group of six which defines itself more sharply than any other in the early period. Their stuff-material is not referred to in the *T'an-lu*.[12] The class of *yao-shu* "sorcery" would seem to fit them, but the titles in it, insofar as they are familiar to us, turn out to refer to stories of a different kind.[13] In all, counting other types as well, we find that about half the surviving early stories are hard to fit within the classification.

The division into stories which either fit or do not fit the scheme accords strikingly with a distinction of time and place. The stories which do fit it are set in the Northern Sung or earlier and in cities other than Hangchow; the stories which do not fit it are set, a surprising number of them, in Hangchow during the Southern Sung.

Of the stories with stuff-material referred to in the *T'an-lu*, only one, the *Ch'ien-t'ang meng*, is set in Hangchow. But this is an old story, of which an elaborate version is found at least as far back as the *Yün-chai kuang-lu* 雲齋廣錄 of the Northern Sung,[14] and it concerns a well-known poet, Ssu-ma Yu 司馬槱; the setting of the story is thus prescribed by tradition. As to time setting, KC 24 would probably be the latest story, if its stuff-material

---

11 In the early and middle periods, there are just three "real" detective stories, in the sense that the criminal's identity is hidden from the reader until the dénouement, and all of them are early, TY 13, HY 13, and Hung 2M. Oral stories with the stuff-material of TY 13 and HY 13 are possibly referred to in the *T'an-lu* list under *kung-an*; see T'an Cheng-pi, *Hua-pen yü ku-chü*, pp. 27–29. The Hung edition of Hung 2M carries the words *kung-an ch'uan-ch'i* beneath the story's title. The three stories form a natural subdivision within the *kung-an* class. Note, however, that the word *kung-an* in the *T'an-lu* covers a much wider variety of plot. And if we trust the common interpretation of the *Tu-ch'eng chi-sheng* passage and assume the text is not corrupt, the definition of the term *kung-an* in Sung times was even wider. What we are doing here is using the Ming dynasty meaning of *kung-an* about a section of the stories which were classified under *kung-an* in the Sung and in the Yüan. In fact, our meaning is even more restrictive, since it applies to "true" detective stories only.

12 The claim that the title *Ai-ai tz'u* 愛愛詞 refers to TY 30M cannot be sustained. See Hanan, "Sung and Yüan Vernacular Fiction," pp. 169–170.

13 The titles in this class refer to some indubitable demons, e.g., Wang Tse 王則 of Pei-chou 貝州, the rebel leader of the *P'ing-yao chuan*, but they are not demon stories within our restrictive use of the term. After its list, the *T'an-lu* mentions storytellers who "tell tales of ghosts and spirits at which even the hearts of the Taoist masters are chilled and trembling with horror." (Průšek's translation, *Origins*, p. 74.) But this is too general a description to refer specifically to the demon stories.

14 By Li Hsien-min 李獻民, preface dated 1111. For the tale on this subject, see the Shanghai, 1936 edition, *chüan* 7.

is indeed referred to in the *T'an-lu*;[15] it is set in the years just after the fall of Kaifeng. Other stories, not referred to in the *T'an-lu* but easily accommodated into its classes, are all set in the Northern Sung or earlier, and in cities other than Hangchow: Hung 2M (*kung-an*), TY 39 (*shen-hsien*), and KC 15M (*fa-chi pien-t'ai*).[16]

The stories difficult to classify—the early stories only, not those of undetermined date—include KC 36P, TY 6M, TY 8, TY 14, TY 16, TY 19, TY 20, TY 28, TY 30M, TY 36, HY 12, HY 14, HY 33M, Hung 3, Hung 8, Hung 11, and Hung 13. Eight of these are set in Hangchow during the Southern Sung. (All of the stories set in the Southern Sung seem to take place in Hangchow.) The eight are TY 6M, TY 8M, TY 14, TY 20, TY 28, HY 33M, Hung 3, and Hung 13. Of the remaining nine, two deal with well-known material which prescribes the setting (KC 36P and HY 12), and two have been derived from Classical versions (TY 30M and Hung 11). There is, of course, a subjective element in all such classification, and it may be that other scholars would classify these stories more readily than I, but when all the necessary reservations are made, there is still an anomaly to be explained: among the stories which the *T'an-lu* does not appear to refer to, there are a number which are distinct in both type and time setting from the stories of the *T'an-lu* list.

One possible explanation is that the *Chi-sheng* and the *T'an-lu* are describing oral fiction of an earlier period, earlier, that is, than the oral fiction corresponding to the "Hangchow" stories. Two periods of oral fiction would thus be reflected in our group of early stories, one set in the Northern Sung or before and described in the *Chi-sheng* and the *T'an-lu*, the other set in Hangchow during the Southern Sung. In the early periods of vernacular literature, there was always a distance between the story's setting and its composition—the Sung dynasty continued to be the favorite setting for the short story right up until Feng Meng-lung[17]—and we need not be surprised if, during most of the Southern Sung, oral fiction of the *hsiao-shuo* variety was preoccupied with the Northern Sung, the Five Dynasties, and the T'ang.[18]

---

15 The identification was suggested by Prušek; see *Origins*, pp. 79–80. For a discussion of the identification, see below. After its classified stories, the *T'an-lu* goes on to mention some "recent narratives" about the twelfth century generals.

16 In addition, *Chang Yü-hu*, which would fit the class of *ch'uan-ch'i*, is set in the early Southern Sung; Chang Hsiao-hsiang lived from 1132 to 1169. HY 21 would fit the class of *shen-hsien*, but it is not clear in what period it is set. It mentions the extent of the Sung dynasty and hence would appear to be set in the Yüan, but it refers to Loyang as the Western Capital, a term appropriate to the Northern Sung.

17 Very few Yüan *tsa-chü* are set in the Southern Sung, and those few are mostly about the generals of the early part of the period.

18 It is an accepted convention of the vernacular fiction that it is retelling traditional subject matter.

We do not know when the second hypothetical period might have begun, because we cannot date precisely the storytelling sections of the *T'an-lu*. But since the *Chi-sheng* was completed in 1235, and the *T'an-lu* list is likely to be later, the second period can hardly have begun before the last decades of the Southern Sung. It may be significant that Lo Yeh mentions, among some of the "new" historical tales, stories about the patriotic generals of the early Southern Sung, and that he broadens the *hsiao-shuo* classification to include sorcery.[19]

Even if the suggestion about two periods of storytelling is correct—it depends on a number of assumptions, among them that the *T'an-lu* account is relevant to the situation in Hangchow—we should not necessarily expect to find the fact reflected in the dates of composition of our extant stories, for the composition of a written version need not be close in time to the composition of the oral version. The earliest group of written stories, as established by admittedly inadequate methods in Chapter VII, contained works reflecting the oral fiction of both kinds, "Hangchow" stories like TY 8, TY 14, and TY 20, plus non-Hangchow demon stories like TY 19 and Hung 8, alongside *yen-fen, kung-an, fa-chi pien-t'ai*, and other stories set in the Northern Sung and earlier. Similarly, there are stories that reflect both periods of oral fiction among Groups B and C.

If we exclude just the "Hangchow" and demon stories from consideration, the remainder of Groups A and B match the traditional typology fairly well, a sign of the close relationship between oral literature and our earliest texts. Presumably, the typology first arose as a descriptive scheme, then acquired the force of tradition and became to some degree prescriptive; this may account for its effectiveness. Unsatisfactory as it is for the modern critic, who balks at describing literary classes in terms of their subject matter, it is still indispensable for work on the early stories.

Composition Based on Classical Chinese Narrative

Several early stories are adaptations of Classical Chinese narratives into the vernacular form. The narratives (the word is left deliberately vague) are earlier than the stories, and the derivation of one from the other is shown by the amount of text they have in common. In order to guarantee that the derivation is an immediate one, we have to specify the nature of the textual relationship. The shared text must be extensive, in both senses

---

19 It may also be significant that the *T'an-lu* omits the *Chi-sheng* class of *fa-chi pien-t'ai*. Note that the *Meng liang lu*, written probably in the early Yüan, garbles the term, evidently misunderstanding it.

of the word; it must be significant in quantity, that is, more than a mere handful of names, and it must not be local, confined to a single passage.

By this definition, five early stories can be seen as based on Classical narrative: KC 24, TY 29, TY 30P, TY 30M, and Hung 11. KC 24 is in Group A, the others in Group B. Several stories which are generally described as based on Classical sources do not qualify. Some have only the outline of the plot in common with their supposed source, others have a handful of personal and place names as well, while yet others have a local textual relationship. Even if we assume a direct *line* of derivation between narrative and story, it is still possible that the story's exemplar was some intermediary, for example a piece of oral fiction or drama. I shall consider these other possible relationships below, after a discussion of the five stories.

The main source of KC 24 is the item *T'ai-yüan I-niang* 太原意娘 "I-niang of T'ai-yüan" in Hung Mai's *I-chien chih*.[20] The relationship is indisputable; indeed, on one point the vernacular story actually appeals to the authority of its source by name. The story follows the line of the narrative fairly closely and retains a good deal of text from it. As we have found in considering the late stories, the heaviest debt is usually in terms of dialogue. What is dialogue in the one is usually retained as dialogue in the other, and the content and even the text of the dialogue are remarkably similar. This is paradoxical, because one would expect to find, in adapting a Classical narrative into a vernacular form, that dialogue was the least transferable element. While it is true that dialogue is often the most striking part of Classical fiction, the strongest reason is probably that dialogue is more closely focused than other elements in the narrative and thus needs less expansion to fit the vastly more detailed vernacular form. The story makes a great number of other changes in the course of adapting its source, but since these have been the subject of an article by Jaroslav Průšek,[21] there is no need to discuss them here.

Although it is chiefly dependent on the *I-chien chih*, KC 24 uses a number of other sources as well. The prologue, on the subject of the celebration of the *yüan-hsiao* festival in Hui-tsung's time, repeats a good deal of text from the *Tung-ching meng-hua lu* 東京夢華錄,[22] the famous description of the Northern Sung capital. The opening poem, a *tz'u* said to be by Hu Hao-jan 胡浩然, is almost identical with the *tz'u* attributed to him in the *Ts'ao-*

---

20 Shanghai, 1927 edition, *Ting chih* 丁志, *chüan* 9.1a–2a.
21 "The Creative Methods of the Chinese Medieval Story-tellers," reprinted in *Chinese History and Literature: Collections of Studies* (Dordrecht, Reidel, 1970), pp. 366–384. The article was first published in 1956.
22 *Tung-ching meng-hua lu wai ssu chung* edition, pp. 35–36.

t'ang shih-yü 草堂詩餘, the most popular Sung anthology of mainly Sung *tz'u*; it may have been copied from the anthology, for it is elsewhere attributed to another poet.[23] And the emperor's own poem is unlikely to have originated with the author of the story, since it is found in another anthology, in a somewhat different version.[24] All of these sources are used in a prologue which takes up only about a page and a half in modern editions.

The end of the story shows another kind of conflation. The author amplified the summary ending of the *I-chien chih* source with the aid of an analogue, an item from the *Kuei Tung*, as mentioned in Chapter VII. The textual relationship is not significant, a surname and a phrase only. But the author of the *Kuei Tung* points out in a note his story's connection with the *I-chien chih* item—he includes it in order to "supplement" the *I-chien chih*— and this appears to guarantee a close connection with KC 24. The author of KC 24 must have seen this note, recognized the unseemly brevity of the *I-chien chih* ending, a brevity not tolerable in the short-story form, and conflated the sources. In addition, it is likely that he used another source for one of the *tz'u* in this part of the story, that written by Han Ssu-hou 韓思厚 to the nun who becomes his second wife. Essentially the same poem is found in the *Chang Yü-hu* story (Group C) and also in a *tsa-chü* play on the same theme, the *Chang Yü-hu wu su nü chen kuan* 張于湖誤宿女眞觀, written by an anonymous author of Yüan or early-Ming time.[25] There would be little significance in this were it not that the poems' contexts are identical; in each case, the poem is written by the hero when he discovers an outspoken *tz'u* by an amorous nun in a Taoist nunnery left lying under the writing instruments on her desk. One kind of work must have borrowed both poem and context from the other. There is no way of determining their order in time, for the Chang Yü-hu stuff-material goes back beyond the existing play, but on general grounds it is likely that KC 24 borrowed the *tz'u* and its context from some form of the Chang Yü-hu story. It is central to the latter, merely peripheral to KC 24. Moreover, it is not foreshadowed in the *Kuei Tung* item, which has been changed by KC 24 to accommodate it.[26]

I have assumed that this complex use of sources is the work of a single

23 See T'ang Kuei-chang, *Ch'üan Sung tz'u*, vols. V, p. 3537, and II, p. 654.

24 *Hua-ts'ao ts'ui-pien*, *chüan* 6.49b.

25 See Fu Hsi-hua, *Yüan-tai tsa-chü ch'üan-mu*, p. 330. The poem is in Act 2. There was a lost play by Kuan Han-ch'ing on the same subject, *ibid.*, p. 50. The editor of KC noticed the use of this theme; see his note on p. 17b of the facsimile edition. For details of the sources of KC 24, see Hanan, "Sung and Yüan Vernacular Fiction," pp. 181–182.

26 In the *Kuei Tung*, the second wife is merely a widow. In KC 24, she is a widow who has become a nun.

author. Sun K'ai-ti, however, who was the first to notice the use of the *Kuei Tung* source, speculated that a second vernacular author might have rewritten the end of the story, using the *Kuei Tung* as the basis of his revision.[27] He points to the ending's weakness as the main grounds for his belief. If the criticism means that he is objecting to the drastic punishment meted out to Han Ssu-hou, we must reject it; this kind of ending is implicit in the *I-chien chih*, in accordance with a recognizable type of folktale. But presumably Sun was referring to the level of fictional skill shown in the last pages, and in that case one can only agree with him; the ending occasionally verges on unintended comedy. Even so, without other evidence, I think one must reject his suggestion. The copious use of sources at the end is consistent with that at the beginning. If Sun had been aware of the use of the *Tung-ching meng-hua lu* in the prologue, he might have been disposed to accept a conflation of sources at the end.[28]

From this description of the process of composition, one can see how complex KC 24's use of sources has been, probably more complex than any of the late stories we have so far considered. KC 24 helps to destroy the stereotype of the simple and crude early story (also naïve, fresh, and delightful) progressing to the sophisticated late story (also bookish and remote from life).[29]

TY 29 is based on a Classical tale of the virtuoso variety, the romance of a talented young man and his equally talented lover.[30] A version of the tale, entitled *Chang Hao* 張浩 and subtitled *Hua-hsia yü Li Shih chieh hun* 花下與李氏結婚, is contained in the *Ch'ing-so kao-i pieh-chi* 青瑣高議別集,[31] which is conjecturally attributed to the Northern Sung author Liu Fu 劉斧. A textually related version, entitled *Chang Hao ssu t'ung Li Ying-ying* 張浩私通李鶯鶯, is found in the Southern Sung collection *Lü-ch'uang hsin-hua* 綠窗新話.[32] TY 29, though closely related to both versions in terms of plot and text, is actually derived from neither. It shares some text, including names, with one, and it shares other text, and some names, with the other. Obviously, we do not have the exemplar of TY 29, but we can gain a fairly clear idea of it from the two Classical versions.

27 "Hsiao-shuo p'ang-cheng ssu-tse," p. 124.

28 If there has been any emendation, it must have been by an early- or middle-period editor. The *tz'u* appears in the *Hua-ts'ao ts'ui-pien* attributed to the nun of KC 24. See Chapter VII, n. 49.

29 See, e.g., Cheng Chen-to 鄭振鐸, "Ming-Ch'ing erh-tai ti p'ing-hua chi" 明清二代的平話集, *Chung-kuo wen-hsüeh yen-chiu* 中國文學研究 (Peking, 1957), p. 364.

30 It is a common theme in early drama. See T'an Cheng-pi, *Hua-pen yü ku-chü*, p. 24.

31 *Ch'ing-so kao-i* (Shanghai, 1958 ed.), pp. 205–207. See the preface for the argument for attributing to Liu Fu the *Pieh-chi*.

32 By Huang-tu feng-yüeh chu-jen 皇都風月主人 (pseud.). Edited by Chou I, Shanghai, 1957, pp. 52–55.

TY 29 followed its exemplar much more closely than did any of the other stories under discussion. It makes few concessions to the short-story form, or, to put it another way, it realizes few of the short story's potentialities. Its language verges on Classical Chinese, and it has neither introductory nor concluding comments. It has enough genre characteristics to qualify as a short story, but is an example of the most economical adaptation possible. It has set pieces, but on at least two occasions they occur just where a sequence of descriptive phrases comes in the Classical, and some of the language is kept. Nothing is wasted.

This is not to say that nothing is changed. There are subtle differences of character and theme. For example, the hero's friend and confidant, a Confucian moralist, plays a much greater role in the short story, and a guilty dream which the short story inserts is clearly intended to show the hero's crisis of conscience as he wrestles with romantic longings and Confucian propriety. There is also a development in the girl's character; she becomes a more forceful person in the short story.

Some of the "natural" changes made when translating a Classical tale into a vernacular story have been described before. The mode of commentary, including the prologue, is a lens through which the whole work appears different; the descriptive mode is set off clearly, by prosodic means; and so forth. But there are differences also in the mode of presentation, quite apart from the story's tendency to particularize; the vernacular sometimes multiplies incidents that occur once in the Classical, and in dialogue the vernacular often builds up a climactic series of questions and answers which, though common enough in the drama, is rarely found in the Classical.

Each of the stories we have considered so far has treated its sources in a different way. KC 24 relied on a number of different sources, but it kept the outline of the main source, *I-chien chih*, even though that outline was not really consonant with the typical shape of the short story. It begins with an evocative scene and a character who shortly thereafter drops out of the story; all this is implicit in the source, and it is exploited magnificently in KC 24, but it is hardly characteristic of vernacular fiction.[33] TY 29 is a deft, economical adaptation of a Classical virtuoso tale; it makes the minimum changes needed to qualify as a vernacular story. TY 30 is different again. Both prologue and main story have their sources, single sources in each case, but both are brilliantly adapted, especially the latter, into the vernacular form.

33 Apart from the linked stories.

TY 30P is a version of the famous romance of Ts'ui Hu 崔護, which goes back at least to the *Pen-shih shih* of the T'ang dynasty.[34] A shorter version is found in the *Lü-ch'uang hsin-hua*, entitled *Ts'ui Hu mi shui feng nü-tzu* 崔護覓水逢女子.[35] The exemplar used by TY 30P was neither of these related versions, since the story sides textually with both at different times, but its nature can probably be inferred from them. The romance of Ts'ui Hu was one of the most popular subjects of Sung and Yüan times; two *yüan-pen* are recorded from the Sung dynasty, plus a Yüan *tsa-chü* and a *hsi-wen*.[36] It exemplifies the obvious principle that a prologue story should be well known, while the main story is comparatively new; by contrast with its prologue, the main story of TY 30 exists in only one other version, buried in the *I-chien chih*.

Prologue and main story are well matched in structural elements. Both concern young men on a spring outing beyond the city. Each meets a girl; in the one story, she gives him a cup of water; in the other, as a waitress in a wineshop, she serves him wine. Both young men return at the same time in the following year to find the place deserted and to be told by the girl's father that she has pined away as a result of the previous year's visit. Finally, in both stories the young men arouse their future wives from death or coma. Obviously, the prologue has been chosen with care to fit the main story.

Yet, curiously enough, the main story has also been adapted to fit the prologue. It is based squarely on the item *Wu Hsiao Yüan-wai* 吳小員外 "Master Wu" in the *I-chien chih*,[37] with names and a good deal of text in common, except that it makes an abrupt change in the ending. This is not like the case of KC 24, where the *Kuei Tung* was used merely to elaborate an ending which was already implicit in the main source. Here the whole direction of the story has been turned around. When the realization dawns that the waitress is really a demon and that the young man is literally bewitched by her, a Taoist master orders him to move away to a distant place to shake off the girl's thrall. This failing, the master gives him a magic sword with which to strike the girl down as she visits him that night. In the *I-chien chih* story, he succeeds in killing her, but in TY 30M, he kills instead an innocent servant who happens to come knocking on his door. He and his friends and the master are all held for murder. In prison, he is visited by the girl in a dream, and she tells him how to clear himself (the

34 *Ku-chin i-shih* 古今逸史 (Shanghai, 1937) ed., 8b–9b.
35 Pp. 44–45 of the Chou I edition.
36 See T'an Cheng-pi, *Hua-pen yü ku-chü*, p. 26.
37 *Chia chih* 甲志, *chüan* 4.1b–2b.

servant is found alive), and gives him a magic medicine which he uses to win the hand of a rich man's daughter, ill of a mysterious disease. The daughter happens to bear an uncanny resemblance to the demon-girl.

The author has converted a typical demon story, the culmination of which is the act of exorcism, into something between a romance and a fairy tale. As a result, it matches the prologue story quite well. If one looks closely, one can still see a measure of contradiction in the story. How is the demon-girl suddenly transformed into the divine being of the last part of the story? If she has been a fairy all along, why does she sap his health and vitality like the typical demon? Is the Taoist master really meant to be so incompetent? At the same time, these questions do not trouble one greatly in reading the story, and it is true that there have been some subtle changes. The horror of the demon story is frequently reduced to comedy, a some-what similar process to that in TY 28, although TY 28 remains a demon story in outline. The language of narration is light and lively as befits a romance.

There are similarities of style in prologue and main story. The prose is frequently rhythmical,[38] and there is an abundant use of clichés. This fact, taken together with the close matching of prologue and main story, proba-bly indicates that both are by the same hand. Because the changed ending contributes to the close matching, I think it, too, was by the same author. Without it, the stories would not really match very well; moreover, the ending is actually referred to in the passage of commentary that links the prologue with the main story. Although we found two late criteria in the last part of the main story, they were not supported by the presence of middle criteria, and I do not believe they are significant.

Hung 11 is a short and insipid moral tale. It is based on the item *Lin Chi yin-te* 林積陰德, which may be freely translated "Lin Chi's good deed," in the *I-chien chih*, the great sourcebook for early vernacular fiction.[39] (Three of the five stories draw on it.) The names are identical and there is a great deal of text in common. The story follows its source faithfully,[40] duly stopping to add a comment or paint a picture by means of a set piece, as prescribed by the short-story form. It translates the source so directly and naïvely into the new form that it serves as a good example of the process at its simplest.

38 See the description of the young man's reaction on seeing the girl in the prologue (p. 459) and the description of the girl's appearance in the main story (p. 462).

39 *Chia chih, chüan* 12.1ab. It was copied into another Southern Sung work, the *Hou te lu* 厚德錄 of Li Yüan-kang 李元綱. It is impossible to say which was the exemplar of Hung 11.

40 The only substantial change is that the *I-chien chih* has the finder of the money take it to the local prefect for adjudication.

The five stories were all written up from Classical narratives.[41] (If we wish to go back a stage further, beyond the Classical narrative, we may come to an anterior oral version, but that is another matter, which I shall deal with below.) This fact may seem to lend some support to a form of the "prompt-book theory" which holds that our early stories were written in the first instance as scripts for the storyteller.[42] Assuming for the moment that the *T'an-lu* really is a list of such scripts, we find that three of the five stories, KC 24, TY 29, and TY 30P, appear to be referred to in it, in the *yen-fen* and *ch'uan-ch'i* classes. The evidence is weak in the case of TY 29 and TY 30P, for both are famous stories which may have existed in numerous versions. (We possess at least two Classical versions of each, and a third must have existed, to provide their exemplars.) Moreover, TY 30P seems to be by the same hand that wrote the main story, and it is unlikely that the *T'an-lu* would refer to a story by the title of its prologue. Thus the only evidence worth mentioning is that provided by KC 24.

There are two questions to ponder. Regardless of whether the *T'an-lu's* referent was in written form, does *hui-ku hsia* 灰骨匣 (its supposed title in the *T'an-lu*) refer to the same stuff-material as we find in KC 24? Secondly, if the referent was in written form, was it the same version as KC 24? The answer to the first question must be a qualified yes. The *T'an-lu* title is in the right class, *yen-fen*, which may be defined functionally as encounters of men with female ghosts, and it is true that a casket of ashes plays an important part in KC 24. But there are two reservations: that the precise words *hui-ku hsia* are not used in KC 24, nor in the title of the Yüan play, nor in the titles of the two texts listed in the Pao-wen-t'ang catalogue and, secondly, that the reburial of a ghost's corpse is a very common folklore theme. However, the second question cannot be answered, even tentatively. It is a likely assumption that no two authors would choose independently to develop the same *I-chien chih* item, and we do know that the author of KC 24 worked directly from that source. But we still have to fit KC 24, the play (dating from about 1300), and the oral (and perhaps written) story referred to in the *T'an-lu* into a line or lines of derivation. Conceivably, the play could have been based on KC 24 and the oral story on the play. Or KC 24 could have been written for a reading public and the oral story

41 It is argued below that two of the five stories are among the handful of early stories which have any prominent ethical concerns.

42 Almost all scholars held this view until recently. The etymological explanation of *hua-pen* as meaning "prompt-book," one of the principal arguments for the theory, has been shown to be arbitrary; the word could simply mean "story." See Masuda Wataru 増田渉, "'Wahon' to iu koto ni tsuite" 「話本」ということについて, *Jimbun kenkyū* 人文研究 16.5 (1965), 22–33.

derived from it. The evidence provided by KC 24 does not lead us to a firm conclusion.

This does not mean that full-fledged stories, as distinct from mere notes, were never written initially for oral performance. It is quite probable that some stories were written like plays, or like another narrative form, the medley, primarily for performance. Of course, the line between writing for oral performance and writing for a reading public is frequently blurred. All written texts can be performed, merely by reading them aloud, and the purposes of composition, even when they are discoverable, may turn out to be quite complex. (The English broadside ballad, like many Chinese *chantefables*, was both read *and* performed.) This confusion is compounded by the fact that the short story is based on a corresponding oral form and shows a constant tendency to simulate the oral manner. But despite these qualifications there remains a real question—were some of our extant stories initially written as material for the oral storyteller?—which we may never be able to answer, for simple lack of evidence.

However, the *general* statement that our early stories were written primarily for oral performance seems highly questionable. If our tentative dating of the earliest group of stories is even roughly correct, they must have been composed during a period in which a reading public already existed for vernacular fiction and other popular material. Consider the two editions of the *Hsi-yu chi* story which survive from the Southern Sung, the five *p'ing-hua* published between 1321 and 1323, and the *Wu Tai shih p'ing-hua*, a probable Yüan edition. The five *p'ing-hua* texts are illustrated on each page, in precisely the same manner as the *Hsin-k'an ch'üan-hsiang Ch'eng-chai Hsiao Ching chih chieh* 新刊全相成齋孝經直解 "Ch'eng-chai's *Classic of Filial Piety* with simple commentary, in a new printing with full illustrations" by Kuan Yün-shih 貫雲石, of which the preface is dated 1308. His commentary is in the vernacular, and its text is one of the best sources for the spoken language in the Yüan dynasty. The scope of Sung and Yüan popular publishing can be appreciated if one compares it with early-Ming publishing; hardly any editions of vernacular fiction survive from the whole first half of the Ming dynasty. In general, it seems likely that most of the stories written in a period in which the publication of vernacular fiction was a thriving business would have been intended largely for a reading public.

An equally important question, but one which is usually slighted in favor of the prompt-book controversy, asks whether we can distinguish between stories based on written sources and stories based on oral fiction, regardless of the purposes for which they were composed. The only firm answers are in respect of the five stories discussed above, but no doubt there are other stories of which the Classical sources have been lost. It was suggested above that the *fa-chi pien-t'ai* stories, representing an older type which the *T'an-lu* did not include and which the *Meng liang lu* evidently did not understand, might be among those based on an oral tradition. (On the other hand, Feng Meng-lung, in working up KC 21 from literary material, managed to fabricate a perfectly respectable *fa-chi pien-t'ai*, presumably with KC 15M as a model.) In general, one would expect the linked stories, which exhibit a structure thought to be characteristic of a kind of oral narrative, to be among the oral-derived stories. The question will arise again below in considering other types of story.

Apart from the lost story *Teng-hua p'o-p'o* which was based on two T'ang tales,[43] no other early story can be shown to be based primarily on Classical narrative. The story which comes nearest to meeting the criteria is KC 33, which is very close to the *Chang Lao* 張老, a tale from the *Hsü Hsüan-kuai lu* 續玄怪錄 of the T'ang dynasty.[44] The stuff-material is the same, although there are minor differences, and the names are also the same. But there is no other textual similarity except for a short passage near the end when Wei I-fang 韋義方 is identified by the cap he has been given; the girl in the herbalist's shop uses much the same speech in both versions.[45] The main difference is at the beginning, where KC 33 has a fairy tale linked to its poem-chain prologue. The textual relationship here is very different from that of the five stories we have discussed. Since the Chang Lao stuff-material is well known, we cannot be sure that the T'ang tale is the exemplar of KC 33. It is quite possible that KC 33 derives from the tale through some intermediary.

A number of other stories, such as TY 10, *Ch'ien-t'ang meng*, and so on have celebrated themes of which Sung Classical versions exist, but there is no significant textual connection. Sharing a couple of famous poems with another text is no guarantee of direct derivation.

There is a group of stories which has a curiously close relationship in terms of plot to Classical narrative, but which has absolutely no textual correspondence, even with regard to names. The Classical narratives are described by modern scholars as "sources," which is either a vague or an

43 See Chapter VII. The two tales are from the *Yu-yang tsa-tsu* 酉陽雜俎; see items *Li Chi-chung* 李積中 and *Seng Chih-yüan* 僧智圓 in *T'ai-p'ing kuang-chi, chüan* 363 and 364, respectively.
44 It is reprinted in the *T'ai-p'ing kuang-chi, chüan* 16, with that attribution.
45 P. 500 of KC 33.

inaccurate use of that word. The stories are TY 8, TY 14, HY 14, and Hung 2M. They are all Group A stories, and TY 8 and TY 14 are set in the Southern Sung. The Classical parallel to TY 8 is an item in a Yüan dynasty work, the *I-wen tsung-lu* 異聞總錄,[46] whose hero is a silversmith named Kuo rather than a jadeworker named Ts'ui. He flees to T'an-chou 潭州 with the girl, as in TY 8, and at her suggestion. However, the import of the two stories is quite different; in the Classical narrative, the girl does not come from a noble household, and she is a ghost from the beginning. The parallel to TY 14 is an item in the *Kuei Tung*,[47] which also served as source for the ending of KC 24; I shall deal with this parallel in the next section. There are two Classical parallels to HY 14, the item *E-chou Nan-shih nü* 鄂州 南市女 in the *I-chien chih*,[48] and an item in another Sung work, the *Ch'ing-tsun lu* 清尊錄;[49] the two are not textually related to each other. The Hung 2M parallel is another item in the *I-chien chih*, *Wang Wu-kung ch'i* 王武功妻 "Wang Wu-kung's wife."[50] As in TY 8, the family's status is raised in the vernacular story. Some of the details are extremely close; both men, for example, are described as residing in such-and-such a lane in the capital, although there is no call for either story to give a precise address. There is also some inconclusive evidence that the Hung story may have come originally from the *I-chien chih* because it incorporates a motif, the man who is in love with a married woman and who sits in the teashop across the road from her house, that does not appear in "Wang Wu-kung's wife" but is found in the very next item.[51]

How are these relationships to be explained? If the Classical parallels were indeed the exemplars of the short stories, the process of composition must have been radically different from anything we have seen so far among either early or late stories. It is not easy to understand how a story could remain so close to its source in terms of plot, while avoiding all textual echoes. If the writer worked with the text in front of him, it would surely take a conscious effort to avoid all imitation. There was, needless to say, no premium on originality; one or two stories even mention with pride— in one case, falsely[52]—the sources on which they are based. It is possible that an author might have created a story from his memory of a source, a

46 *Ts'ung-shu chi-ch'eng* ed., *chüan* 1.12.
47 *Kuei Tung Hu* ed., *chüan* 4.3b–5b.
48 *Chih keng* 支庚, *chüan* 1.1ab.
49 *Ku-chin shuo-hai* 古今說海 ed., *Shuo-lüeh* 說略, *chi* 己.
50 *Chih-ching* 支景, *chüan* 3.4b–5a.
51 The item entitled *Hsi-hu an ni* 西湖庵尼.
52 See the cliché with which Hung 13 ends. In fact, the story has nothing to do with the *T'ai-p'ing kuang-chi*.

memory which retained the details of the plot but obliterated all the words, but this hardly seems likely in all four cases.

If the stories and their parallels are not immediately related, are they in a direct line of derivation? That is to say, is the story derived from the parallel through one or more intermediaries? (The alternative would be a lateral relationship, not a lineal one.) It is probable that at least some of them are in a direct line. It has been suggested that Hung 2M perhaps combines two adjacent items in the *I-chien chih*. More important, Lo Yeh specifies the *I-chien chih* as one of the main sourcebooks for oral fiction. The intermediary could hardly have been a Classical narrative; if so, we should expect some of the text to be retained. (This is what happened with TY 29 and TY 30P, whose exemplars can be inferred from other versions.) The obvious intermediaries are oral fiction and the drama.

Hung 2M is one of the most popular themes in Sung and Yüan drama; titles of a Sung play, a Chin play, and of a Sung or Yüan *hsi-wen* are recorded.[53] The title of the last is *Hung Ho-shang ts'o hsia shu* 洪和尚錯下書, which resembles one of the alternative titles of the short story, *Ts'o hsia shu*. From the titles alone, we can see that Hung 2M and the plays were closer to each other than any one of them was to the *I-chien chih* item. We can never know the details of the derivation, but it is a reasonable assumption that the stuff-material developed from the *I-chien chih* through the medium of either oral fiction or the drama.

No other versions are recorded of the three remaining stories, and one can only speculate that they developed through oral fiction. It may be significant that TY 8 and TY 14 are among the small number of stories with poem-chain prologues, one of which, KC 15, may have been derived in part from oral fiction.[54]

The connection of the earliest extant texts with Classical narrative is remarkable. Of the five stories with Classical exemplars, one is in Group A and four are in Group B. All four stories with Classical parallels are in Group A. KC 33, which has either a Classical exemplar or a very close Classical parallel, is also in Group A. Although one could scarcely define the word "parallel" without including some other stories with celebrated themes like TY 10, KC 36P, and the *Ch'ien-t'ang meng*, the connection remains striking. From this evidence, it appears that the earliest stories were more closely related to Classical narrative than any other extant stories

---

53 T'an Cheng-pi, *Hua-pen yü ku-chü*, p. 40.
54 The germ of the Hung 13 plot also existed in the Southern Sung. See Index to the Extant Stories.

written before the seventeenth century, when Feng Meng-lung revived the genre with his wholesale adaptations.

Group A contains one story derived immediately from Classical narrative (KC 24) and four or five others which are derived through some intermediary, presumably oral fiction or the drama. The remaining eight stories, for which no parallels or sources[55] have been discovered, are KC 15, KC 36, TY 19, TY 20, TY 37, HY 31, Hung 8, and Hung 15. As many as five of the eight are linked stories, and I have argued that, if any stories have evolved in part through oral fiction, it is likely to be they. Thus, even in the earliest group, the oral-derived stories seem to be in the majority. If one combines Groups A and B, the statement is still true, though the proportion is different.

Finally, we cannot help noticing the importance of the influence, immediate and otherwise, of the *I-chien chih* on early fiction. There are five stories derived from it, in one form or another, in Groups A and B, but there are no stories derived from it to be found in Group C. In addition, KC 15P mentions the *I-chien chih* in connection with an anecdote about Hung Mai, thus helping to confirm its own early date. Since the *I-chien chih* has no discernible influence upon the short story again until the time of Feng Meng-lung,[56] its copious use in A and B helps to confirm the grouping made in Chapter VII.

The Short Story's Relationship to the Folktale

If we trace the derivation of a story back beyond its Classical exemplar or parallel, we may come to oral narrative. KC 24, TY 30M, and Hung 11, for example, are based on items in the *I-chien chih*, and the *I-chien chih* is based, for the most part, on stories which Hung Mai had heard; frequently he gives the informant's name at the end of an item. Many stories he must have garnered himself, but others were sent to him in written form. He remarks in one of his prefaces[57] that, after the success of the first installment, it was pirated in other parts of the country, even as far away as Szechuan, and that many people wrote to him contributing stories. Only on rare occasions does he include materials copied from published works. For the most part, then, what lies behind the *I-chien chih* is oral fiction.

The term "folktale," though it serves for the title of this section, will not

---

55 Within the definition given above.

56 E.g., TY 12P and TY 34P.

57 See his preface to the second book, *I-chih* 乙志, written in 1166. In the five years since the first book, enough stories had been sent in to make a second necessary.

do for the kind of oral fiction Hung Mai collected. Even when defined, the term does not discriminate among the genres of oral narrative, which is our concern here. The written short story is a recognizable genre which we believe to imitate, to some degree at least, a genre of oral fiction called the "oral short story." It is a matter of conjecture how far the form of the written short story actually resembled that of a transcribed oral story at different periods. Nor do we know how far it blurs or accentuates the divisions that must have existed between different forms of the oral short story. However, it is obvious that we can deduce a good deal about the oral story from an examination of our extant written stories, and we need a term which will distinguish the form or forms of the material Hung Mai collected from the form of the oral short story.

We do not know what the form of Hung Mai's material was. Its simplicity in the *I-chien chih* could be deceptive. No oral fiction is entirely devoid of conventions, not even so lowly a form as the barrack-room yarn. In transcribing their stories into a different medium and a different language, it seems unlikely that Hung Mai and his informants even tried to provide correlatives for the features of oral fiction. It is much more likely that they allowed the conventions of Classical fiction to take over and mold the oral material. We know that this kind of storytelling was an amateur activity, not professional work like the oral short story, and we assume it was not much different from the custom of casual storytelling which is still popular at many levels of Chinese society. But we do not know anything else about it,[58] and I therefore use the term "casual fiction" or "casual storytelling" to distinguish it from the known genres of professional oral fiction, such as the oral story (*hsiao-shuo*) and the medley (*chu-kung-tiao*).

We are concerned here with the effect of this great world of casual fiction upon the short story, in particular with the patterns in the casual fiction which we find transferred to the short story. Later we shall take up the subject of the influence of one story upon another within the small domain of the short-story genre.

A survey of all the motifs, themes (here meaning chains of motifs), and plots common to both Sung casual fiction and the short story would be a vast undertaking. Here I shall restrict myself to two or three plots or

---

58 One of its characteristics is that it is represented as being the "actual experience" of the narrator, or of an acquaintance, or of the acquaintance of an acquaintance. Of course, the reader is not expected to take the claim too seriously. What is interesting is the extent to which the claim of actual experience conditions the form of the fiction itself. It depreciates the value of structure and symmetry and places a premium on disjointed bits of information that have an authentic ring about them. Contrast the posture of the narrator of vernacular fiction, who claims to be retailing traditional material.

themes which are important from the viewpoint of the short story, beginning with the plot of what I have called the demon story.

The demon plot has not been recognized for the common type it is. It proves to be the most important, and certainly the most restrictive, type among the early stories, and it provides the best example of the influence of Sung casual fiction. Six stories can be classed as demon stories: TY 14, TY 19, TY 28, TY 30M, Hung 3, and Hung 8; three of them are in Group A (TY 14, TY 19, Hung 8), one is in Group B (TY 30M), and two are in Group C (TY 28, Hung 3). There is only one demon story, Hsiung D, among the middle stories, and there is none at all among the late stories, not even an attempt at one.[59] The demon story became associated with the West Lake of Hangchow—TY 14, TY 28, and Hung 3 are all set there— and one kind of demon story, the White Snake, developing from TY 28, later became enormously popular in dozens of different genres and versions.[60] Of the six early stories, TY 30M has a Classical exemplar in the *I-chien chih*, and TY 14 has a parallel in the *Kuei Tung*. There is a close family resemblance, even a textual connection, between Hung 3 and Hung 8, which will be discussed below.

There is a common structure to all of the demon stories which cannot fail to appear on even the most cursory examination. The structure can be abstracted as three universal actors and four universal actions. The actors, in the order of their appearance, are a young man, unmarried; a demon, that is, an animal spirit or the ghost of a dead person, in the guise of a young girl; and an exorcist, usually a Taoist master. The four actions may be labelled Meeting, Lovemaking, Intimation of Danger, and Intercession by the Exorcist. The young man goes out on a spring day to a resort on the outskirts of the city, meets a beautiful girl, and they make love. At length he realizes she is a threat to his life and calls in the help of a Taoist master, who makes the girl return to her real form as ghost or animal spirit and punishes her. In the more complex plots, actions may be repeated several times, particularly the action of Intimation. The "revelation" procedure is in regular use, in which the truth is only gradually revealed to the reader as it is to the hapless young man. The stories are intended to induce suspense.

---

59 The *Pai-chia kung-an* has some quasi demon stories, such as nos. 3 and 4, in which Judge Pao himself does the exorcising. The important difference is that the demon-girls are not maleficent. Apart from the *Pai-chia kung-an*, the closest thing to a demon story among late fiction would probably be TY 27.

60 For a collection of vernacular narrative on this theme, see Fu Hsi-hua, *Pai-she chuan chi* 白蛇傳集, Shanghai, 1955.

There are other common, but not universal, elements. For example, in some stories there are second and third demons, one of them posing as the girl's mother. And the day of the meeting is usually the Ch'ing-ming festival, a time of services for the souls of the dead.

The plot of "Master Wu," the source in the *I-chien chih* of TY 30M, can be abstracted as follows. Note that essential elements of the plot which are outside the four universal actions, are enclosed by brackets.

> *Meeting*. Master Wu, unmarried, the son of a wealthy family, goes to the Chin-ming Pond, a pleasure resort outside Kaifeng, on a spring day. There he meets a girl serving in a wineshop and is attracted to her. [But her parents return suddenly, and Wu and his companions depart.] *Second Meeting*. Next year, in spring, they return. Though her parents say the girl is dead, the young men meet her on the way back to the city, and she takes them to where she is living. *Lovemaking*. Wu and the girl become lovers. *Intimation*. Wu falls seriously ill. *Intercession*. A Taoist master is called, and he advises Wu to go away for a period to shake the girl off. When the period passes and she continues to bewitch him, the master gives Wu a sword and tells him to strike the girl dead when she visits him that evening. He kills her. [Wu and the master are put in jail for murder, but are released when the girl's parents say she has been dead all the while.]

This contains the four universal actions, plus one repetition and two individual elements.

The structural changes made in this plot by the author of TY 30M can be clearly seen in an abstract. All the elements are the same, the spring day becoming the Ch'ing-ming festival, up to a point near the end of the Intercession, from which the action runs:

> Wu strikes and kills, not the girl but a servant by mistake. [Wu and the priest are put in jail for murder. The girl appears to Wu in a dream, explains she is a fairy, and tells him to have the servant's grave searched. The servant is discovered alive. She also gives Wu a magic pill, with which he cures the ailing daughter of a rich man. The daughter, whom he marries, has an uncanny resemblance to the demon-fairy and even bears the same personal name.]

This is a neat conversion of a demon story into something different, a fairy story.

The plot of the TY 14 parallel, an item in the *Kuei Tung*, can be abstracted as follows:

> *Meeting*. Fan, a young single man whose father owns a pawnshop, goes out to the West Lake with a friend. He finds a girl's shoe with a note inside asking the finder to come courting her at Madam Wang's. Fan

eventually finds the place, a teahouse. A meeting is arranged with the girl at a wineshop. *Lovemaking*. They become lovers. *Intimation*. A servant sees demon figures attending on the girl, and the maid, when once he comes upon her unawares, is a skeleton. *Intercession*. Chang, an exorcist, is consulted. *Second Intimation*. A month later, Fan and his friend go outside the city wall. The friend gets into a quarrel and they have to return by a roundabout route, over the hills. There is a rain squall and they seek shelter, only to find that the person who gives them shelter is in league with the demons. After a number of narrow escapes, they are caught and beaten. *Second Intercession*. They are saved by the appearance of an official and his retinue. The ghosts are identified. [We are told that the event took place at the end of the Shao-hsing reign. The compiler "has only just come to hear of it."]

In comparison, the abstract of TY 14 runs:

Meeting. Wu Hung is single, a graduate. Matchmaker Wang visits him and proposes a match. Wu accompanies the matchmaker to a wineshop. *Mock Intimation, intended to mislead the reader*. When Wu peeps at the girl and her maid, and exclaims "But they're no mortal creatures!" the reader expects to learn that they are ghosts, but all Wu means is that they are "divinely" pretty. *Lovemaking*. *Intimation*. Wu sees the maid unawares—she is a corpse. He conceals his astonishment. *Second Intimation*. Wu goes out on the Ch'ing-ming festival, and meets a friend who is mischievously set on keeping him out all night and away from his bride's bed. They go drinking, then visit the graves of the friend's ancestors. There is a sudden rain squall. They take refuge in a cottage, but see a man leap out of his grave, and they flee. They are exhausted, their legs like "the beaten cock in a cockfight." They hide in a temple, from which they can hear people outside hunting for them. Just as Wu is abusing his friend for making them stay out late, they hear the voice of Wu's wife outside, scolding the friend in the same vein. They lie quiet, and eventually she goes away. After other adventures, they get back, only to find Wang's house is locked and bolted. They learn that Wang has been dead over five months. Wu's wife has vanished. *Intercession*. A Taoist master sees the miasma of bewitchment around Wu and, with the aid of a genie, catches the ghosts. They are the ghosts of suicides. [Wu leaves the earthly life and goes off to join the master, who appears to be an immortal.]

Note the higher level of artifice in the short story, the deliberate juxtaposition of Wu's comment, and the neat juxtaposition of his abuse and the wife's scolding.

No source or parallel has yet been discovered for TY 19. The exorcist, Lo Kung-yüan 羅公遠, is a celebrated T'ang Taoist master who is credited with many feats of magic at the court of Hsüan-tsung,[61] but I have found none which resembles this tale. Its elements, though conforming to the general demon formula, differ from those of the other stories[62]—it is a hunting story, with a magic falcon, exotic in terms of the usual demon story —and one would not be surprised to learn that it is a Chinese domestication of an international folktale. It begins with a description of the court of Hsüan-tsung, the relations between Yang Kuei-fei and An Lu-shan, and the gift of a white falcon to Minister Ts'ui. From that point on, it takes the shape of a demon story.

Meeting. His son, Ts'ui Ya, young and unmarried, goes out hunting in the spring, taking his father's white falcon. A series of adventures follows: the wineshop, the haunted mountain, the chase of the red hare, the forest, the skeleton which steals the falcon and is shot at by Ts'ui. Finally, they arrive at a manor, where a girl in a red dress welcomes Ts'ui. *Lovemaking.* She proposes marriage to him. Though afraid, he stays the night. *Intimation.* There is a sudden noise outside. Hearing somebody say the "general" has arrived, he peeps out and sees that the "general" is the skeleton he shot at, accompanied by the waiter in the mysterious wineshop. The general is swearing revenge on the man who shot him; when he manages to lay his hands on the man, he will "eat his heart and liver." Ts'ui's presence is betrayed, but the girl tries to intercede for him, saying theirs is a predestined marriage. Ts'ui escapes, then suddenly finds himself surrounded by twenty men. At the point of panic, he realizes they are his own retinue. [Ts'ui tells his adventures to his parents. His father disbelieves him, confines him to his study.] *Second Meeting.* Unable to bear the confinement, Ts'ui goes out walking and meets the girl in a carriage driven by the waiter. *Second Lovemaking.* He takes her home and hides her in his study. [A servant tells his father.] *Intercession.* Lo Kung-yüan is summoned, and with the aid of two assistants, captures the demons. The waiter is a tiger, the girl is the red hare, and the skeleton is the ghost of a general who died in battle there long ago.

Despite the exotic touches, this is a bona fide demon story. Although like TY 14 it involves a chase, it is closer to Hung 3 and Hung 8 in several features: the trinity of demons, the threat to eat his heart and liver, the shooting with bow and arrow, the girl's plea for his life.

Hung 3 and Hung 8 have an umbilical connection which will be discussed later. After a poem-chain introduction on the subject of the West Lake, Hung 3 runs:

---

61 He is the subject of stories in several *Tao tsang* works.
62 Its form also differs. It appears to be a kind of *chantefable*.

Meeting. Hsi is the only son of an official. He is married. (But note that nothing is ever said of his wife.) His uncle is a Taoist master. On a visit to the West Lake on the Ch'ing-ming festival, he meets a girl who says she is lost. He takes her home with him. [An old woman arrives to fetch the girl home. She takes Hsi back with her, so that the girl's mother can thank him.] *Intimation*. As they drink, the question is asked whether, now they have a "new one," they should serve up the old one. Hsi sees a young man brought out and killed and is offered the young man's heart and liver to eat. *Lovemaking*. The girl's mother demands that Hsi sleep with her. *Second Intimation*. Hsi falls ill. Another man is caught and now Hsi is the "old one." The girl first pleads for his life, and then when the old woman imprisons him beneath an iron cage, the girl saves him and brings him home. He is told to shut his eyes as she flies with him through the air, but he feels her throat—feathers! He has been away two weeks. [His mother makes him move to a place near the Chao-ch'ing ssu, a famous West Lake temple.] *Second Meeting*, *Third Intimation*. Next year, he again goes out on the Ch'ing-ming festival. He shoots a crow, which turns into the old woman, and he is captured again. The whole series is now repeated: he is about to be killed when the girl pleads for him, he is imprisoned again, she rescues him again, this time dropping him into a pond. *Intercession*. His uncle, the Taoist master, diagnoses the evil and with the aid of a genie catches the demons. The girl turns out to be a silky fowl, the old woman an otter, the mother a white snake. [Hsi goes off with his uncle to become a Taoist adept.]

Hsi is the only hero of a demon story who is married, but his marriage is of no importance in the story. The noteworthy point about this plot is its repetition of the whole of the Intimation action, the element which carries most of the demon story's suspense.

After a poem-chain prologue on the subjects of spring and the city of Loyang, Hung 8 runs:

Meeting. P'an Sung, described as "Master P'an" (cf. TY 30M) is single, the son of a goldsmith. He goes out on the Ch'ing-ming festival and meets an old woman with skin "like a plucked chicken" who says she is his aunt and invites him home. There he meets a girl, Wang Ch'un-ch'un, a next-door child who had died a few years before. *Intimation*. Warned by her of his danger, he flees through the garden, to a wineshop. *Intercession*. There he meets Hsü, a Taoist master. *Second Intimation, Second Meeting*. He sees some birds and runs over to catch one of them. Out of Hsü's sight, he is recaptured and imprisoned under a chicken coop. A woman in white comes out and prepares a feast. Then a man enters and makes a scene. *Lovemaking*. P'an and the woman in white are to sleep together. He is afraid, but stays with her the night. (Cf. TY 19.) *Third Intimation*. After seeing someone killed for his heart and liver, he is again rescued by Wang Ch'un-ch'un, but through a tunnel, not by air like the hero of Hung 3. In a temple he sees three divine figures, images of the demons he has escaped from. *Second Intercession.* Hsü invites him to stay in a Taoist temple. *Fourth Intimation.* While he is fishing one day, the old woman takes his hook. *Third Intercession.* Another Taoist master, Chiang, is brought into the case. *Fifth Intimation.* P'an is again accosted, this time in his study. *Fourth Intercession.* Chiang captures the demons with the aid of genie. The old woman is a white chicken, the threatening man is a mottled red snake, and the woman in white a cat.

Here the Intimation and Intercession actions have both been multiplied in order to heighten the suspense.

TY 28, the White Snake story, is too well known to need summarizing. Repetition is its dominant structural feature, not repetition of Intimation alone, but also of the other universal actions. (I count four of each.) Great play is made with the unsuccessful attempts of various experts to exorcise the demon. Here is an abstract of the first such attempt:

Hsü, the hero, visits a temple on a festive occasion and is noticed in the audience by a Taoist master. The master warns Hsü that he has been bewitched by his wife, and gives him charms to use against her. One is to be placed in his hair, the other to be burned at midnight. Before he can apply the charms, his wife wakes up and chides him with betraying her wifely affection. Next day she goes to the temple and routs the Taoist master with superior magic.

After the Taoist master and a snake-charmer have both failed to subdue her, she is finally captured by a Buddhist priest and changed back into a white snake. At the end of the story, Hsü joins the Buddhist order. It is interesting that this is the only strict demon story in which the successful magician is Buddhist and in which the Taoists are made to look foolish. This may be a sign of the comparatively late development of this story; in terms of our extant stories, Buddhist fiction is found once among the C stories (Hung 13), once among the undetermined stories (Hung 16), but becomes one of the most popular types in the middle period. Another individual feature of TY 28 is the demon-girl's nature. Unlike the other demon-girls, she is a sympathetic person, mischievous yet devoted to her husband. The dangers which her husband faces are comparatively mundane. As a character type, she suggests the girls in the quasi demon stories of the *Pai-chia kung-an*, in which Judge Pao plays the part of the exorcist; they are attractive figures, and there is no hint that their husbands are in mortal danger from them. Like TY 28, these stories represent a dilution of the strict demon-story formula.[63]

63 See nos. 3 and 4.

The only other demon story is Hsiung D, a middle-period work which we know to have existed in sixteenth century Hangchow oral fiction. Its abstract runs:

Meeting. Hsü Ching-ch'un, unmarried, an only son, goes out on the West Lake in spring and meets a girl who says she is lost. *Lovemaking.* He takes her home and they become lovers. *Intimation.* He is discovered by a neighbor, delirious and exhausted. [He recovers, marries someone else.] *Second Meeting, Second Lovemaking.* One night, returning home through Hangchow city, he meets the girl and they make love again. *Second Intimation.* He staggers home in a pitiful state. *Intercession.* A Taoist master is called to help. He sends two genie to catch the demons.

This is the standard demon plot, it is even set by the West Lake, but it has few individual elements. In its simplicity, it resembles some of the demon plots found in the *I-chien chih.* Its middle-period origins are shown in its emphasis on Hsü's activities as a merchant.

Besides the two already summarized, several other demon plots can be noticed in the *I-chien chih,* the *Kuei Tung,* and other Sung works. They include "The beautiful lady of Nan-ling," "Liu Tzu-ang" 劉子昂, "Ku Tuan-jen" 顧端仁,[64] and "The strange lady from the capital"[65] in the *I-chien chih;* the item about Chou Hao 周浩 from the *Kuei Tung;*[66] and "A spring visit to West Pond" in the *Ch'ing-so kao-i pieh-chi.*[67] They vary greatly in complexity; the *Kuei Tung* item, with four Intimations, is as complex as any vernacular story. This item and "Ku Tuan-jen" are both set at the West Lake,[68] while the *Kuei Tung* story also seems to have other links with Hung 3 and TY 28; it has two demon-girls, one a turtle-spirit from the West Lake, the other an otter-spirit from the Ch'ien-t'ang River. A number of seemingly individual elements in TY 28 are also found among the *I-chien chih* items: the scene in which the husband who is given two charms by a Taoist master is berated by his wife for his disloyalty;[69] the demon-girl who brings her lover stolen goods;[70] the man who spies on the demon-girl as she takes a bath, and sees a large white snake coiled up inside the room.[71]

---

64 *Chih-i* 支乙, *chüan* 8.3ab, *I-chih* 乙志, 5.2ab, and *Chih-i,* 1.3a–4a, respectively.

65 *Chia-chih, chüan* 8.2ab.

66 *Kuei Tung Hu* ed., *chüan* 2.1a–2b.

67 Pp. 185–192. The *Mu-tan teng chi* 牡丹燈記 in the *Lü-ch'uang nü-shih* 綠窗女史, where it is attributed to Ch'en Yin 陳愔 of the Yüan dynasty, is a partial demon story. The text mentions a *feng-liu hua-pen* 風流話本 "romantic story," the very words TY 28 uses in self-description.

68 TY 14, TY 28, and Hung 3 are all set at the West Lake.

69 See "The strange lady from the capital," "Liu Tzu-ang," etc.

70 "The beautiful lady of Nan-ling."

71 See "The wife of Magistrate Sun," *Chih-hsü* 支戌, *chüan* 2.2ab. Cf. TY 28, p. 437.

Judging by the *I-chien chih* and the *Kuei Tung*, it seems clear that the demon plot flourished in casual oral fiction during the latter half of the twelfth century and the first half of the thirteenth. We are concerned not with the date of its first appearance but with the period of its popularity, and it is significant that the great compendium of early fiction, the *T'ai-p'ing kuang-chi*, does not contain stories of the strict demon type.

Perhaps the demon plot was not thought suitable for dramatic presentation, but in any case, no play on a known demon theme is recorded before the time of the *Hsi-hu san-t'a chi* 西湖三塔記[72] (the same title as Hung 3) in the early decades of the Ming dynasty.

Our general conclusion must be that the demon plot, originating in casual oral fiction and reaching a peak of popularity in the Southern Sung, was then transferred, by one route or another, to the written short story. In the case of TY 30M, the route is quite clear; it runs from casual oral fiction through a Classical account in the *I-chien chih* to the written short story. TY 14 presents a much more difficult problem. The route could run from casual oral fiction to a Classical account in the *Kuei Tung* to an oral short story to the written short story. This was the suggestion made earlier. Alternatively, it could by-pass the *Kuei Tung* altogether. This seems likely to be the route taken by some of the other stories. However, it should be noted that not all can be traced back independently to casual oral fiction; some must have developed as variations of other oral short stories. Such an explanation is true of either Hung 3 or Hung 8, and quite possibly both, and it is certainly true, to some degree, of TY 28.

My concern here is merely to show that the ultimate origin of a pronounced type of early short story lay in the casual oral fiction of the Sung. I shall not attempt to deal with the social significance of the demon stereotype, nor with the ways in which the short stories treat the stereotype, but merely note that the extant demon stories range from fairly simple narrations like Hung 3 and Hung 8 to quite elaborate works like TY 28. Some stories have increased the suspense of the demon plot, by a variety of means; in one, TY 30M, the whole direction of the demon plot has been turned around; and in another, TY 28, the stereotype of the demon plot has been pervasively, if subtly, changed.

The demon plot is the outstanding example of the influence of casual oral fiction, but there are many others.[73] The simplest to describe is proba-

---

72 See Fu Hsi-hua, *Ming-tai tsa-chü ch'üan-mu*, p. 37. The play was by Chu Ching 邾經, fl. c. 1370.

73 One should remember that it was fashionable to collect ghost stories. Other kinds of casual oral fiction are no doubt underrepresented in written literature.

bly the case of KC 24, because, like TY 30M, it is based on the *I-chien chih*. The plot of the source can be shown to combine three themes (chains of motifs) found commonly in the *I-chien chih*. These are:

> Away from home, a man meets the wife of a relative and eventually realizes she is a ghost. (This theme is often associated with the fall of Kaifeng.)
> In his dream, a man is visited by a woman's ghost, who asks him to give her bones proper burial.
> On her deathbed, a wife makes her husband promise not to marry again. He breaks his promise, and she claims his life.

The best example of the first theme is the item "Yang San-niang-tzu" 楊三娘子.[74] It tells how Wei Kao moves south, after the collapse of the Northern Sung, and meets a girl, the maid of his cousin, surnamed Yang. He has not had news of the cousin or of her husband in a long while. The cousin invites him to her house, tells him her husband is dead, and he offers to take the message to her parents. She introduces her neighbors, an old man and an old woman. She asks Wei to marry her, and he does. A few days later, he meets the girl's brother in Hangchow. The brother is astonished, for she died some time before. They go to find the house, but it is just a graveyard. One of the graves is hers, and those on either side are the graves of her "neighbors" . . . There is no need to point out the several similarities between this plot and that of the source of KC 24, but it is noteworthy that the anomalous position of Yang in KC 24 is ultimately traceable to this kind of theme.[75] The second theme is so common, at many periods, as hardly to need illustration. There are stories, like "Hsieh San-niang" 解三娘 in the *I-chien chih*,[76] which are set during the collapse of the Northern Sung, but perhaps a closer parallel is the story "Tsang-ku chi" 葬骨記 in the *Ch'ing-so kao-i*;[77] it combines some of the first theme with the second. The third theme is equally common, in the *I-chien chih* and elsewhere.[78]

Thus the progression in the case of KC 24 is from a complex piece of oral fiction which unites three or more other themes to the Classical account in the *I-chien chih* to the written short story.

There are many other examples of the influence of casual fiction. The magic fish, which the fisherman either kills or releases, is one of the most popular Chinese themes; it appears in KC 36P, in TY 20, in both of which

---

74 Supplement, *chüan* 10.6a–7a.
75 Note the two relatives go together to look for the girl's house and find, in the one case a graveyard, in the other a ruin.
76 *Chia-chih*, *chüan* 17.2b–4a.
77 *Ch'ien-chi* 前集, *chüan* 1.9. The *Ch'ien-t'ang meng* is another example of this theme.
78 See *Chia-chih*, *chüan* 2.1ab, "Lady Chang."

it supplies causation for the events that follow, and in TY 39. The beginning of KC 36P, which is not the historical part, describes how Shih Ch'ung helps a river god by shooting his rival; this is an old story which appears in a different form—butterflies, not fish—in HY 31.[79] The list of similar examples is endless.

The Common Storehouse of Fictional Ideas and Conventions

The other context in which the short story must be examined is that of the early vernacular fiction itself. Taken as a group, the early short stories are remarkable for the number of thematic patterns and formulaic passages which they share, not only with each other but also with long vernacular fiction, especially the *Shui-hu chuan*. There seems to have been a common storehouse of convention from which the early vernacular fiction drew. To judge from its nature, this convention must have belonged initially to oral, not written, literature.

Before we discuss this common property of early fiction, there is one exclusive relationship which must be mentioned. Hung 3 and Hung 8 have been described as in an umbilical relationship; that is not overstating the case. Even from the bald accounts given, it must have been apparent how close the two plots are. Numerous points of correspondence can, in fact, be discovered, enough to set these two apart from all of the other stories we have dealt with. (They are probably closer together than Hung 1 and Feng Meng-lung's rewriting of it, KC 12.) We can only conclude that one story is derived from the other, or from some prototype of the other.

One would readily assume that this derivation took place in oral literature, were it not for the large amount of text which the two stories share. No less than six set pieces are common to both; this is about half the total in Hung 8 and more than half the total in Hung 3. In none of the set pieces is the language identical, but in five it is largely the same, while the sixth shares a rhyme, a rare feature in set pieces anywhere.[80] The contexts are approximately the same, and some of them are highly restrictive, for example, the description of the old woman with her "chicken skin."[81] Outside of the set pieces, there is only an incidental similarity of language, such

---

79 The earliest story of this type appears in the *Shui-ching chu* 水經注, in which the contending creatures are oxen. See Sun K'ai-ti, "Hsiao-shuo p'ang-cheng erh-tse" 小說旁證 二則, *Wen-hsüeh p'ing-lun* (1962.1), p. 115. A close parallel to the fish story of KC 36P is the *Meng lung chuan* 夢龍傳, in the *Ch'ing-so kao-i hou-chi* 後集, *chüan* 9.169–170.

80 See Hung 3, p. 31, and Hung 8, p. 75.

81 Hung 3, p. 26, Hung 8, p. 69.

as one might expect to find in any two stories so close to one another. No other pairs of stories share text to this degree, and what text they do share can be explained without postulating an exclusive relationship between the stories. TY 14, for example, shares a set piece with Hung 8, describing the magician's genie, and also a poem about the magic wind that swirls up as he vanishes,[82] but these can be seen as part of the common property of early oral fiction.

It seems impossible that one story could have been derived from the written text of the other. If so, there would surely be other verbal echoes besides the set pieces. Moreover, the minor plot differences are so pointless as to be inexplicable in terms of a literary revision or adaptation.

It is tempting to suppose that the derivation took place in oral literature and that the set pieces somehow survived it. A storyteller might have adapted his (or someone else's) oral story to a new locale and retained most of the set pieces. It is not unlikely that the set pieces should have been the most durable verbal element in the story; they are in a different language (Classical), a different prosodic form (parallel prose), and they may have counted as the highlights of the story. It would accord with the practice of some modern storytellers (who do not possess full-length scripts) of keeping a written version of the story's highlights, including its poetry.[83] If true, this supposition would throw a new light on the relationship of early fiction to oral literature. But it can be merely speculative.

This is not the place to begin a study of formulaic language in early fiction. Such a study might achieve its most significant results at the level of the simile or phrase, rather than at the level of the whole set piece or *tz'u*. There are other set pieces held in common: TY 16 with TY 29, KC 33M and TY 37; TY 37 with TY 14M; and TY 8M with Hung 15, in addition to those mentioned above. But the numbers are not impressive, and their main importance lies in showing that formulaic language was used by stories of different types, demon stories and *fa-chi pien-t'ai* stories, linked and unitary.

On the level of theme, with little or no textual correspondence, there is a great deal of duplication. Here are some examples of whole incidents: the scene in which the hero visits the *man-t'ou* 饅頭 shop and narrowly escapes becoming the filling in the *man-t'ou* is found twice in the *Shui-hu chuan*,[84] as well as in KC 36M; the daring robbery in which the guards

82 At the end of each story.
83 See Ssu Su 思蘇, "Shuo shu yu wu chüeh-pen" 說書有無脚本, *Ch'ü-i* 曲藝 52 (1962), 44–45.
84 See the *Shui-hu ch'üan-chuan* ed. (Peking, 1954), chaps. 27 and 17 (reported).

are drugged and watch paralyzed as the loot is carried off is also found in
the same two works;[85] the tournament at T'ai-shan is found in Hung 15
as well as the *Shui-hu chuan*;[86] the scene in which the two escorts attempt
to kill their prisoner but are foiled by the man trailing them is found twice
in the *Shui-hu chuan*,[87] as well as in the *P'ing-yao chuan*[88] and TY 36M;
TY 19 and KC 33 begin with men in charge of valuable creatures, a falcon
and a horse, respectively, which the Emperor has bestowed on them, and
in each case the creature escapes; TY 37 and KC 36M both begin with the
miserly shopkeeper exercising his meanness and unwittingly causing his
own downfall; KC 33M and TY 16 both have the scene in which an old
man summons two matchmakers and asks them to arrange a match with
a young girl; the hero of Hung 15 leaves Kaifeng for T'ai-shan because of
a prophecy of disaster, as does Lu Chün-i 盧俊義 in the *Shui-hu chuan*;[89]
HY 13, KC 36M and chapter 12 of the *P'ing-yao chuan* have the scene in
which a wily police sergeant solves a problem that has been baffling his
superiors; and so forth. We have already mentioned the supernatural vision
of the hero's future greatness which is found near the beginning of both
the *fa-chi pien-t'ai* stories, KC 15M and HY 31.

There are many other patterns. Both stories concerned with bandits,
TY 37 and Hung 15, are set in Shantung, like the *Shui-hu chuan*. They are
the only two early stories set in Shantung. As prefect of Kaifeng, three
stories have the imaginary Prefect T'eng 滕, KC 36M, HY 13, and Hung
2M, while only two have the famous Judge Pao, a historical figure.[90]

Thematic patterns are especially common among the linked stories,
including the *Shui-hu chuan*, but are not confined to them. Though the
stories set in Hangchow have their own patterns, including the various
themes that make up the demon story, they have few patterns in common
with the linked stories, perhaps because their subject matter is so different.
In terms of external literary form, however, there are features in common
between the two groups.

Some Characteristics of the Early Short Story

The most distinctive feature of the early short story, and the one which

---

85 Chap. 16.
86 Chap. 74.
87 Chaps. 8–9, 62. Note how often the *Shui-hu* complex repeats itself, borrowing from
its own store of ideas and conventions.
88 Twenty-chapter *P'ing-yao chuan*, chap. 8.
89 Chap. 61.
90 TY 13. He is mentioned briefly in KC 36M.

most surprised Feng Meng-lung,[91] was its poem-chain prologue. It is confined to the prologues of seven stories, KC 15, KC 33, TY 8, TY 14, Hung 3,
Hung 8, and the *Ch'ien-t'ang meng*, of which five are in Group A, and two,
Hung 3 and *Ch'ien-t'ang meng*, are in Group C. Both of the latter are lyrical
descriptions of the West Lake, and it is possible that the poem-chain prologue was a very early feature which later became restricted in its use. The
poem-chain is found attached to all types of stories, from KC 15, which is
a *fa-chi pien-t'ai* story of linked structure, to Hung 8, which is a demon
story of unitary structure; and it accompanies stuff-material of both of the
hypothetical periods of oral fiction. None of the stories with written exemplars has a poem-chain prologue, and it seems, for reasons which will
be given below, that it must have been a feature of the oral short story.

"Poem-chain" is a vague word. The manner in which the poems are
linked to each other, and the way in which the prologue as a whole is joined
to the main story, both differ from story to story. The prologue to TY 14,
which can serve as an example, begins by quoting a *tz'u* by Shen T'ang
沈唐 (style Kung-shu 公述, wrongly transcribed Wen-shu 文述 in TY) which
appears in an almost identical version in the popular Sung anthology *Ts'ao-
t'ang shih-yü*. The narrator then says that Shen's *tz'u* is the product of that
kind of synthetic composition known as *chi-chü* 集句, by which lines are
selected from other poems and fitted together. Thirteen lines are then
repeated, the original author identified, and the original poem given. It is
an impressive display of virtuosity, except that half the authorial attributions are wrong,[92] the text of the poems differs widely from that of the
"best" versions, and the identification of sources is far-fetched. (Indeed,
some of the poets cited lived after the time of Shen T'ang himself.) The
impressive display is actually a fraud, as it is in the case of most of the poem-
chain prologues. The prologue to TY 8 is arranged on another scheme; it
is a list of poems on spring, with each poet criticizing the last poem and
producing his own. The prologue to KC 15 sets the poems in narrative, a
celebration in which one of Hung Mai's guests points out that every line in
the master's poem has been taken from another work, and proceeds to
document his thesis. It also contains an elaborate palindrome. In the prologue to KC 33, the poems are linked by a gossamer thread of associative

---

91 See the original editorial notes to KC 33.1b and TY 8.2a (Shih-chieh shu-chü
fascimile editions).

92 At least five of the *tz'u* in the TY 14 prologue are wrongly attributed: see T'ang
Kuei-chang, *Ch'üan Sung tz'u*, vol. I, p. 584; vol. I, p. 537; vol. II, p. 934; vol. II, p. 630;
and vol. I, p. 161. The versions differ markedly from those in the best editions and anthologies; they are, in general, simplified and popularized.

thinking. There is an initial poem on snow, and the narrator remarks that there are three common images for snow, giving a poem to illustrate each. He then says that there are three deities that preside over snowfall—the association is solely one of number—and proceeds to describe their function. The other poem-chain prologues are lyrical descriptions of place (Hangchow, Loyang) and season.

The connection between prologue and main story is sometimes tenuous, an interesting parallel to certain kinds of modern *t'an-tz'u*. In the case of TY 14, for example, the explicit connection is nil; at the end of the poem-chain, the narrator says

Shen Wen-shu (the author of the initial poem) was a gentleman and today I am going to tell about a gentleman . . .

TY 8 has scarcely any connection at all. In KC 15, Hung Mai's poem is on the subject of the flute, and mention of the flute leads us to the subject of the flute-carver, and it is the flute-carver, at the beginning of the main story, who sees a vision of the hero's future. In KC 33, too, there is a labyrinthine connection to the main story; mention of the snow deities leads us to the subject of a snow-spirit, and it is this snow-spirit who is incarnated as the fabulous horse who . . . The prologues of the other three stories serve some function in evoking the place in which the story is to be set, though they give a standard description of the beauties and delights of Hangchow and Loyang without regard to the distinctive nature of the main story.[93]

Despite their dissimilarities, the common impulse behind the poem-chain prologues is virtuosity. Virtuosity it is, even if the poems are in bad versions and half the attributions are wrong. (One suspects that these were considered minor matters.)[94] And when it comes to the prologue's purpose, its relationship to the main story, the impulse becomes something more than virtuosity, a kind of playfulness, a wilful delight in sheer lack of function, in illogical progression. The real function of the prologue, one may guess, is that it gives the narrator a chance to assert his dominance over the story, and to display his wit, skill, and imagination.

Nevertheless, the literary quality of the prologues, the popular, simplified versions of poems and the frequent misattributions of author, to say nothing of their easygoing rhyming conventions, do give an important indication of the stories' level of composition. They could hardly have been composed,

93 Note that the lost story *Teng-hua p'o-p'o* began with a chain of *tz'u* on a single theme written by sixteen Sung poets. See Chapter VII, n. 56.

94 Poems quoted in other stories are also grossly inaccurate. See Po Chü-i's poems quoted in TY 10.

as distinct from recorded, by men of a good level of literary education.[95]

In their tenuous connection with the main story, the poem-chain prologues exemplify a general feature of the early short story—its oblique beginning. Where the middle and late stories usually begin with the hero, his lineage, his status, and his character, the early stories choose an indirect approach. TY 19 begins with a pseudo-historical background, a description of the court of the T'ang emperor Hsüan-tsung and an account of the relations between Yang Kuei-fei and An Lu-shan. We are then told that the emperor was presented with a white falcon which he, in turn, presented to Minister Ts'ui, and which Ts'ui took with him when he was rusticated. However, the story proper concerns only Ts'ui's son, who goes hunting with the falcon. Four of the linked stories begin not with the main hero or heroes, but with some secondary character, typically a rich shop-owner. KC 36M begins with the miserly owner of the pawnshop, TY 37 with the strict owner of the teashop, HY 31 with another owner of a pawnshop; KC 15M is the exception, beginning with the flute-carver. KC 33M, KC 36P and TY 20 all begin with the fairy tale cause of the main action. By contrast, the four stories which have been shown to be based on written exemplars begin with relative directness. TY 29, TY 30M, and Hung 11 begin simply and directly with the hero; KC 24 is more oblique, beginning with the *yüan-hsiao* celebrations at the court of Hui-tsung, but the prologue is magnificently functional in terms of the main story.

Prologue stories, as distinct from other types of prologue, also existed in the early period: they are found attached to the main stories of KC 36, TY 13, TY 30, TY 36, HY 33, and Hung 2. There is legitimate doubt as to whether KC 36P was originally attached to its main story, and there is a question about the date of HY 33P. Both prologue and main story of TY 30 are based on written exemplars and are probably by the same hand. The remainder are all very short, well-known stories in a rather Classical language.

Two other major characteristics of early fiction will merely be mentioned here. One is its lack of specific, individualizing detail in comparison with the middle and late fiction; the exceptions that come most readily to mind, such as HY 13 and TY 28, are Group C stories which may have been revised by a late editor. The second is the copious use of the set piece for descriptive purposes. The set piece is found in all types of story, from the demon to the *fa-chi pien-t'ai*, but the frequency of its use varies with the date of composition; Group A stories have large numbers, Group C stories few or none, and middle-period stories virtually none at all. This fact must

---

95 Considering the high standard of literary allusion in much of the Yüan drama, it is hard to believe that these works were written *ab initio* by respected playwrights.

reflect a change between the oral short story of, say, late-Sung and its nearest equivalent in mid-Ming. But it also raises the question of where the late-Ming habit of using set pieces came from. The set piece may have survived in long fiction and been transferred to short. It certainly existed in some Ming *ch'uan-ch'i* drama, for the purpose of verbal scene-painting.[96] But it is quite possible that it was revived by Feng Meng-lung and others on the model of the early short story.[97]

The structural division into linked and unitary stories is important in the early period. There are five or six linked stories: KC 15, KC 36, TY 37, HY 31, Hung 15, and possibly KC 33. All are Group A stories, and the first five are all heroic stories within a broad meaning of that term. None has a known written exemplar, with the possible exception of KC 33, and KC 15 even states that its material is a tale which "has been handed down by the old men[98] of the capital" and contrasts it with official history. The stuff-material of all of them belongs to the hypothetical first period of oral fiction and in five out of six cases it is actually listed in the *T'an-lu*, an extraordinary proportion. All have oblique beginnings, except Hung 15. Not only is their structure linked, but at least three of them, KC 15, KC 36, and TY 37, have a pair of heroes each.

Among the heroic stories, KC 15 and HY 31 belong to the class of *fa-chi pien-t'ai*. (This is a class which Lo Yeh does not mention, and which we have speculated may have belonged to an earlier period of oral fiction.) The *fa-chi pien-t'ai* is not found among the middle-period stories—indeed there is only one conceivable linked story of the middle period, Hung 19, a fairy tale of Taoist hagiography like KC 33—and does not reappear in short fiction until the time of the *San yen*. Feng Meng-lung may have written KC 21 on the model of KC 15; it has been shown that he took as exemplar a quasi-historical sixteenth century source. TY 21, a late story not by Feng, is the only other *fa-chi pien-t'ai* story; it may have been written in imitation of the same antique type.

The stuff-material of two of the other heroic stories, TY 37 and Hung 15, is placed by the *T'an-lu* within the classes of *p'u-tao* and *kan-pang*, respectively, and we have remarked how they fit those descriptions. It is significant that both classes also contain titles which seem to refer to stories now incorporated in the *Shui-hu chuan*,[99] because we have shown some-

---

96 See, e.g., Li K'ai-hsien's 李開先 *Pao-chien chi* 寶劍記, scene 3. (*Ku-pen hsi-ch'ü ts'ung-k'an* First Series ed.) It is a descriptive set piece, in the form of a monologue.

97 The *Chin P'ing Mei* took many of its set pieces from the *Shui-hu chuan*.

98 The term *lao-lang* 老郎 in this context is usually thought to mean storyteller. A similar phrase occurs at the end of HY 13 and in some late stories, such as KC 2.

99 The subjects tentatively identified as belonging to the *Shui-hu* complex are in the *kung-an*, *p'u-tao*, and *kan-pang* classes, especially the last two.

thing of the similarities of theme and convention between the heroic stories and that novel. Both stories come from the same realm of fiction that ultimately produced the *Shui-hu chuan* ; it is noteworthy that both are bandit stories and both are set in Shantung. The fifth heroic story, KC 36, although it is not classed by Lo Yeh, is even more closely related to the *Shui-hu chuan* stuff-material, with its moral approval of robbers who steal "ill-gotten wealth," its ingenious burglaries, its drugs, its *man-t'ou* shop. These early heroic stories are the best context in which to see the rise of the *Shui-hu chuan* cycle, even better than the *p'ing-hua*.

One of the stories of unitary structure, TY 19, has a radically different form from any of the other early stories. It is a *chantefable*, with alternating prose and verse sections. Most of the verse sections are to a single, intricate pattern, which is rigidly observed, with no hypermetrical syllables. The pattern takes the form of successive pairs of lines of gradually increasing length, from one syllable up to seven: one, one, two, two, three, three, four, four, five, five, six, six, seven, seven. The verse exploits the obvious opportunity for parallelism in a manner which we have observed to be characteristic of popular literature. Rhymes are not necessarily restricted to the level tone, and they occasionally change in mid-section. This pattern of verse is not found in other *chantefables*, to the best of my knowledge. The function of the verse sections is mainly that of description, like some of the songs in the middle-period story, Hung 14.

Two general characteristics, regardless of class or type, can be widely discerned in the early unitary story: its use of the "revelation" type of plot and its lack of interest in personal ethics. Both seem to follow from the exceptional value placed by the early short story on sheer narrative power, on suspense.

"Revelation" is to be contrasted with "prediction," in which the narrator knows all and tells all and is constantly warning of the dire results which will spring from each trivial action.[100] Prediction is particularly common among the "folly and consequences" stories of the middle period. Examples of revelation plots are the *kung-an* and demon types; all of the former, and all but one of the latter, are found in the early period, nine stories in all. But the revelation plot is also found in a number of other stories, such as TY 8, TY 16, and KC 24, all of which are early.

The lack of explicit or implicit moralizing is most marked in the fiction of the early period. The heroic stories have their own kind of popular heroic ethic; to take one example, a rich man's stinginess is castigated and

---

100 See Hanan, "Early Chinese Short Story," p. 193.

receives the most savage reprisal. But the unitary stories are largely devoid of ethical concerns. The demon stories do not lay the young men's peril seriously to any fault of character. The errant husband of KC 24 is not really blamed for breaking his promise. The tragic events of TY 8 or HY 14 are told for their own sake; they are not made the text of a sermon. Even the villain of a *kung-an* story like HY 13 is not explicitly damned by the narrator. With the exception of a handful of stories, KC 36P, HY 33, and Hung 11 in particular, the narrator of the early story is not concerned with the definition of ethical values. How great the contrast is with the middle-period stories! The whole class of "folly and consequences" is concerned with attributing each disaster to some individual's fault of character, to his sins of omission or commission, and the structure of the stories is determined, superficially at least, by that concern. And the second, distinctive class of middle-period stories is the Buddhist story, with its emphasis on the results of sin, through *karma*, in the next incarnation.

It seems that the degree of ethical concern, and the kind of ethical concern, differ widely from period to period. The stories of the late period were written, for the most part, by literati like Feng Meng-lung and X, and they exhibit a set of Confucian principles, in the least restrictive sense of that term, mixed on occasion with a simple heroic ethic of the kind derived from the histories. Even when arguing against some point of Confucian doctrine, for example, the role of women, they are seeking to broaden the ethical system rather than to eradicate it. At any rate, they are always aware of ethical implications. The stories of the middle period were evidently composed by men of a much humbler class in society, and they are either Buddhist in inspiration or else they reveal a down-to-earth morality that inexorably links deeds to punishments. The latter kind of story best deserves C. T. Hsia's term of "prudential morality."[101] One is tempted to associate this kind of morality with the harsh popular religion of the *shan shu* 善書 of the Sung dynasty and after,[102] with the exception that here the punishment takes place in life rather than in Hell. Why do the stories of the early period differ again? Is it because of their closer association with oral literature, or because they were associated with a different kind of oral literature?[103] The question cannot be answered yet.

---

101 *The Classic Chinese Novel*, appendix.

102 See Wolfram Eberhard, *Guilt and Sin in Traditional China*, Berkeley and Los Angeles: University of California Press, 1967.

103 Two of the exceptions to this rule are stories based on written exemplars, TY 29 and Hung 11. Perhaps a different kind of writer chose to develop stories directly from Classical narrative. Or perhaps the cause is to be found in the different process of composition—stories based on oral literature reflect more of the values of that literature.

The classes of unitary story which are distinctively early have been described before, the *kung-an* and the demon stories. There is a group of stories which involve female ghosts, KC 24, TY 8, TY 10, TY 16, HY 14, and the *Ch'ien-t'ang meng*, such as are not found in the middle or late periods. Some of them can be placed in the traditional class of *yen-fen*, but they are not likely to form a satisfactory grouping in the modern critic's estimation. There are three stories about Taoist immortals, KC 33, TY 39, and HY 21,[104] with the characteristic comedy of that genre.

The virtuoso story, in which the emphasis is on the poetic virtuosity of a *ts'ai tzu* 才子 or "man of talent" rather than on narrative interest, is found in the short stories of all three periods, as well as in the Classical tale from the Sung to Ming. The early virtuoso stories, TY 6M, TY 10, TY 29, HY 12, *Chang Yü-hu*, the *Ch'ien-t'ang meng* and perhaps Hung 5 and KC 11, are not a very distinguished group. None is in Group A, but this may be only because they are mostly written in a rather Classical language and make fairly small use of the vernacular fiction's style markers.

Finally, there is a handful of stories which seem to foreshadow popular types during the middle period. Hung 13 is related to the virtuoso story— it is a Buddhist tale about Su Shih and his friend Fo-yin—but it is also the first Hangchow religious story. The story itself is in Group C, but the germ of its stuff-material goes back at least to the Southern Sung. A story of undetermined date, Hung 16, is a full-fledged Hangchow religious story. The other distinctive type of middle-period story, the "folly and conse-quences" story, is foreshadowed by TY 20 and HY 33, both of which are set in Hangchow. TY 20 is in Group A, HY 33 in Group C. The difference is significant. Whereas HY 33 is a genuine folly and consequences story, attributing the chain of disasters to an initial failure of character, TY 20 locates the cause of the chain firmly in the supernatural, in the killing of a magic fish. The earlier story belongs to the class in terms of its form, but not in its spirit.

A Note on the Authorship of the Early Short Stories

As we have seen, the most inaccessible question of the early and middle story is that of authorship. True, we know the name of one Yüan author,

---

104 In HY 21, a Group C story written in the Ming, the Taoist immortal is humbled by a mere Buddhist priest. In TY 28, another Group C story, the Taoists fail to exorcise the demon, and it is left to a Buddhist priest to subdue her. The numbers are admittedly small, but in the context of the short story perhaps we can see a change from an emphasis on Taoists in the Group A stories to Buddhists in the middle stories.

Lu Hsien-chih, who is described by the *Lu kuei pu* as writing a story with the same stuff-material as KC 36M; indeed it is quite possible that KC 36M is actually the story that he wrote. But can we generalize from this one fact and conclude that other stories were written by men like the playwright Lu Hsien-chih? It is always conceivable that the *Lu kuei pu* mentioned his authorship precisely because it was atypical, because writing a story was an exceptional thing for a playwright to do. Lacking solid evidence, we can do little else than attempt to delineate questions such as this.

There is a small amount of evidence about authorship which we must assess, in addition to the incidental evidence about the process of composition which we have discussed already. In order of reliability, the evidence consists of: contemporary external evidence, confined to the *Lu kuei pu* and the *T'an-lu*; explicit references to authorship, found in three stories, KC 15M, TY 28, and HY 13; the comparative evidence of other genres of oral literature, and of the short story in other periods; and later external evidence. For our purposes here, the last two classes can be largely disregarded. Vernacular literature and the drama provide several different models of authorship, and it is impossible to know which is the most suitable; in terms of date, the closest genre is that of the Yüan dynasty *p'ing-hua*, of whose authorship, as distinct from mode of composition, we know practically nothing. And the later external evidence is so much later, beginning only in the seventeenth century with Feng Meng-lung's prefaces and notes, that it is of no value as primary evidence.

Lo Yeh's description of storytelling is anything but an objective assessment. Its language is cast in the form of a panegyric, and we cannot be sure how closely it fits the case of a typical storyteller. On the other hand, its statement about the use of the *I-chien chih* and other sourcebooks certainly rings true, even if the quotation of poetry is at a lower level than Lo Yeh implies. According to this account, the storyteller himself composed the oral story, searching out his material from literary sources and interlarding it with famous poems. Presumably, as a literate person, he made some kind of script for himself, but what form it took, and what use he made of it, we have no means of knowing. It is possible that some of our extant stories are ultimately derived from such a storyteller's notes or script. But there must also have been many stories which evolved in oral literature without a written source.

Of the stories which make explicit statements about their authorship, both KC 15M and HY 13 remark at the close that their stories have been handed down by "the old men of the capital." The former goes on to contrast the legend with official history, while the latter says that the story has now "for the first time been compiled into a historical romance." The "old men" are generally held to be storytellers. If this is so, the statement would fit the case of KC 15, which is a linked story, but it may be merely conventional, and it may even have been inserted by a late editor. (Several indubitably late stories are referred to in the same terms, including some which we know to have been based on written sources.) The statement in the other story, TY 28, is more significant. It tells how the events on which the story is based caused a furore in the district, and then it remarks that the *ts'ai-jen* 才人 turned the events into a *feng-liu hua-pen* 風流話本, a "romantic story."[105] *Ts'ai-jen*, "man of talent," is commonly used in the Yüan and early-Ming periods to mean "playwright." The remark may be a cliché—it is introduced by *yu fen chiao*, criterion M9, which often precedes stereotyped expressions—but it occurs in no other short story, and it must be given some weight.

Reference to *ts'ai-jen* raises the question of the *shu-hui* 書會, a shadowy term which has nevertheless dominated all modern accounts of the authorship of vernacular fiction. There is no point in retracing the researches of Sun K'ai-ti,[106] Feng Yüan-chün 馮沅君,[107] and others into the term's meaning. Its relevant uses can here be reduced to two: in the *Wu-lin chiu-shih*, which is an account of Southern Sung Hangchow, it appears in the section on entertainers as the name for the performers, and perhaps also composers, of various ballad and other genres;[108] in Yüan and early-Ming contexts, it stands for groups of writers engaged in the composition or adaptation of plays and perhaps other kinds of literature.[109] From this second use, we can see the significance of TY 28's mention of *ts'ai-jen*, "playwrights."

Though the suggestion that playwrights played a large part in the early vernacular fiction would receive support from the *Lu kuei pu* reference to Lu Hsien-chih, it is contradicted by the *T'an-lu*, which attributes composition to the storytellers themselves. It has been conjectured, perhaps to resolve the contradiction, that the *shu-hui* were organizations of storytellers rather than writers.[110] But again, Lo Yeh makes no mention of any such organization.

105 TY 28, p. 421.
106 "Yüan-ch'ü hsin-k'ao" 元曲新考, reprinted in *Ts'ang-chou chi* 滄州集 (Peking, 1965), vol. II, pp. 349–355.
107 *Ku-chü shuo-hui* 古劇說彙 (Peking, 1956), pp. 15–22, 57–73.
108 *Tung-ching meng-hua lu wai ssu chung* ed., *chüan* 6.454. The heading comes between the chessmasters and the tellers of historical narrative.
109 Circles of playwrights, known as *shu-hui*, played a part in the composition of Yüan drama, as the *Lu kuei pu* makes clear.
110 Ch'en Ju-heng, *Shuo-shu shih-hua*, pp. 89–94.

Use of the terms *ts'ai-jen* and *shu-hui* in the vernacular fiction itself is extremely rare. Apart from the instance of *ts'ai-jen* in TY 28, there is one in Hung 15 and one in the *Shui-hu chuan*.[111] *Shu-hui* or *shu-hui hsien-sheng* "gentleman of the *shu-hui*" occurs three times, twice in the *Shui-hu chuan* and once in Hung 2M.[112] One of the instances of this term in the *Shui-hu*, together with the instance in Hung 2M, refer to the authors of topical poetry. They suggest that attribution of a quoted poem to the *shu-hui* carried a certain prestige that made it worth claiming, and hence that the actual authorship may well have been on a lower level. But the other instance in the *Shui-hu* cannot be explained away. In a singular passage, the narrator apologizes for the diffuseness of his story, citing the difficulty of integrating the various narratives handed down by the *shu-hui*.[113] This must mean that there was a tradition, to put it no higher, that the *Shui-hu* narratives were first composed by *shu-hui*, but it still leaves open the question of what the *shu-hui* consisted of.

Attribution to the *shu-hui* has abetted, and in turn been abetted by, the hypothesis that our earliest texts were initially written as scripts for the oral performer, not as matter to be read. After all, if the *shu-hui* were playwrights who wrote plays for actors to perform, what is more likely than that they also wrote stories for storytellers to relate? But to say this is to impose an unnecessary dichotomy of our own making. We have seen that there was a reading public in the Yüan, and probably earlier, for popular fiction in the vernacular. As a possible parallel, we may note that there was a mass reading public during the Ch'ing dynasty and after even for such uncompromising *chantefable* forms as the *pao-chüan* 寶卷 and the *t'an-tz'u*. (The best evidence is the huge number of popular editions.) If the *shu-hui* were writers rather than performers, the purposes for which they wrote may still have been both varied and complex.

In sum, there is direct evidence that storytellers composed their own materials; there is other direct evidence that a Yüan playwright wrote a story; and there is some oblique evidence that the *shu-hui*, probably groups of writers who composed plays and the like, may also have written stories. Beyond this, all is conjecture.

But before we even conjecture, we should clarify what authorship consisted of. For example, it is perfectly conceivable that a playwright like Lu Hsien-chih might have written down an existing oral story in some fashion,

111 Hung 15, p. 173; *Shui-hu ch'üan-chuan*, chap. 114, p. 1717.
112 *Shui-hu ch'üan-chuan*, chap. 46, p. 760, chap. 114, p. 1710; Hung 2, p. 18.
113 Chap. 114, p. 1710.

but it is hardly credible that, if he were creating a story *de novo*, he would write anything like TY 14 or Hung 8. Even if we restrict the notion of authorship to *those who wrote our extant stories in approximately the form we have them*, we must still define authorship according to the mode of composition.

By this definition, there will be four principal kinds of author.

First, authors who create stories *de novo*. *De novo* is intended as a relative term; no one writes in a vacuum of fictional ideas. All it means is that the plot had not yet been worked out in detail in some previous work of fiction or drama. Not surprisingly, we have no evidence of any stories composed in this way. The form of the short story did not accommodate autobiography, and it was de rigueur to set the story back in time, the "age of fiction" being at least one, and preferably two, centuries before the time of writing. If *de novo* composition had taken place, we would not recognize it.

Second, authors who base their work on existing oral short stories. Needless to say, this does not mean recording. There was no tradition of accurate recording, nor was there any convenient means, and where the oral and written literatures are so far apart in prestige, there must inevitably have been a tendency to rework and "improve" the oral stories. Centuries later, Feng Meng-lung, aware of the value of the old vernacular literature, still allowed himself to commit various gross "improvements" on the text of the short stories and the *P'ing-yao chuan*. What scruples would a contemporary writer entertain, faced with an evanescent oral work?

This chapter has tended to show that this was the commonest process of composition in the early period. It seems particularly likely in the case of the heroic and demon stories; it is probably significant that the one demon story we know not to have been composed like this, TY 30M, is also the only mutated demon story. If we trust them, the statements on authorship which we find in the three stories would fit this explanation. In all likelihood, Lu Hsien-chih was this kind of author.

The process amounts to putting an oral form into a "corresponding" written form, one which retains at least some of the original features. It is possible that some of our stories correspond to variant forms of oral fiction, as was suggested in the case of TY 19.

Third, authors who base their work on existing Classical narrative. Five stories were shown to have been composed in this manner, and a number of other stories, especially some of the virtuoso stories, may have been similarly composed, making this the second most important process of composition. The sources may be full-fledged Classical tales, as in the case of TY 29, or merely casual oral fiction recorded in the form of Classical narrative. In general, these stories are rather more carefully written than the average and do not betray the solecisms of the demon stories.

Fourth, authors who base their work on existing pieces in other genres of fiction, including casual oral fiction, or on plays. We know no such stories for certain, but several of our stories appear to have been composed in this way.

To the best of our present knowledge, the second, third, and fourth processes are all important in the early period. They lead to different results, as we might expect; composition based on oral fiction leads to a less polished and integrated story than composition based on Classical narrative, which calls for a greater contribution from the author. This difference may explain the general disparity between the two kinds of story better than any difference of author. We have not, of course, answered the question of what kind of author might have been responsible. We can only guess that there may have been a range of authorship which, at one extreme, might have reached up to the more popular playwrights of the Yüan.

IX   A Summary of Conclusions

The arrangement of this study has been subordinated to the solution, or partial solution, of a set of problems, and the answers lie strewn throughout the book. The best summary of our results is the Index to the Extant Stories, which is a guide to all the significant findings for each individual story. This summary is a guide to general conclusions only.

One hundred and forty-nine extant and accessible short stories were written before 1628, excluding the *Pai-chia kung-an*. They have been divided among three major periods, an *early* period stretching from before the Yüan to circa 1450, a *middle* period from circa 1400 to circa 1575, and a *late* period from circa 1550 to the 1620's. Most stories can be dated more accurately than this; for example, almost all of the middle stories were in existence before 1550, and the great majority of late stories was actually written in the 1620's.

There are thirty-four early stories. (Five more are either early or middle, and one other may just conceivably be an early story heavily adapted by a late editor.) Most can be divided, very tentatively, into two groups, A and C. The fourteen stories of Group A were, in all likelihood, mostly written in the Yüan, and the twelve stories of Group C were mostly written in the early Ming. Eight other stories, comprising Group B, present no clear evidence.

The early stories are analyzed in Chapter VIII. They are compared with the traditional typology of professional oral fiction in the Sung dynasty; they match fairly well, with the exception of those stories set in the Southern Sung. The composition of four stories derived from Classical narrative is examined and also the composition of five stories related nontextually to Classical narrative. The latter are probably derived via some intermediary, such as oral fiction or the drama. The importance of the *I-chien chih* is stressed; six early stories are connected with it in some fashion, all of them in Groups A and B. The early story's relationship to casual oral fiction is explored, in particular through the "demon" type of folktale. The extraordinary homogeneity of motif and formula in the early story is described, and the close family relationship between two early stories, Hung 3 and Hung 8, is assessed. Some characteristics of the earliest stories are given: their poem-chain prologues, oblique beginnings, linked structure, "revelation" plots, and lack of interest in ethical values. The question of authorship is discussed briefly. To the best of our knowledge, the most common kinds of composition are those based on oral fiction and Classical narrative.

There are thirty-one middle stories. (Five more are either early or middle.)

They are analyzed in Chapter VI. The work of at least two anonymous authors can be discerned, both of whom may have been writing in the sixteenth century. A surprising number of middle stories have been derived from the drama, others from oral fiction, yet others from Classical narrative. The complex relationship of KC 29 to other stories and plays is studied in general outline. The extraordinary importance of the city of Hangchow is stressed. Two distinctive types were perfected in the middle period, the crime and consequences story and the religious story.

There are seventy-eight late stories. (One more is either a late story or an early story much rewritten.)

They are analyzed in Chapter IV. Most of the late stories were written by just two authors, an unknown author, here called X, who may also have written the late-Ming collection *Shih tien t'ou*, and Feng Meng-lung, editor of the *San yen* series. X wrote at least twenty-two stories, all of them in *Hsing-shih heng-yen*, which he may also have helped to edit. With varying degrees of probability, Feng may be said to have written twenty-one stories, all of them in *Ku-chin hsiao-shuo* and *Ching-shih t'ung-yen*. He may also have written another eleven stories in the same collections. Three other stories were in existence before the *San yen* were published, one of them by a known author, Teng Chih-mo. Five stories are so distinct in style as certainly to be of separate authorship from the rest; it is possible that two of them, KC 19 and KC 37, were written by the same man. The remaining sixteen stories cannot be ascribed even tentatively to an author, but since the sources of many of them were reprinted in Feng's anthologies, it is likely that some at least were by Feng or his associates. The relationship of the late stories to Feng's Classical anthologies, especially the *Ch'ing shih*, is explored. The methods of composition of the late stories are also examined; most are derived from the Classical tale, but some are based on the written *chantefable*, the vernacular short story and the *kung-an* story. Feng's and X's characteristics as writers are contrasted, and an estimate given of Feng Meng-lung's contribution to the short-story genre.

Works Cited

Works Cited

Where no location is given, the editions cited are preserved in the Harvard-Yenching Library. The abbreviation *TSCC* stands for *Ts'ung-shu chi-ch'eng ch'u-pien* 叢書集成初編. For editions of the individual vernacular stories, see Chapter I.

PRIMARY WORKS

Chang Yü-hu wu su nü chen kuan 張于湖誤宿女眞觀. Anon. In *Ku-pen hsi-ch'ü ts'ung-k'an*, Fourth Series.

Ch'ang ming lü 長命縷. By Mei Ting-tso 梅鼎祚 (1549–1615). In *Ku-pen hsi-ch'ü ts'ung-k'an*, First Series.

Ch'ao Shih Pao-wen-t'ang shu-mu 晁氏寶文堂書目. Comp. Ch'ao Li 晁瑮 (d. 1560). Published with another catalogue, Shanghai, 1957.

Che-ch'ing tsa-shuo 摭青雜說. By Wang Ming-ch'ing 王明清 (b. 1127). *TSCC*.

[*Hsin-k'an ch'üan-hsiang*] *Ch'eng-chai Hsiao Ching chih chieh* 新刊全相成齋孝經直解. By Kuan Yün-shih 貫雲石. Preface d. 1308. Fac. ed., Peking, 1938.

Chi-sheng. See under *Tu-ch'eng chi-sheng*.

Ch'i-hsiu lei-kao 七修類稿. By Lang Ying 郎瑛 (1487–1566 or after). Peking, 1959.

Ch'i kuo ch'un-ch'iu p'ing-hua 七國春秋平話. Shanghai, 1955 reprint.

Ch'i nan-tzu chuan 奇男子傳. Attributed to Hsü T'ang 許棠 (T'ang). Collated by Feng Meng-lung. In *Ho-k'e san-chih*.

Ch'i nü-tzu chuan 奇女子傳. Comp. Wu Chen-yüan 吳震元 (Ming). Late-Ming ed. (Naikaku Bunko).

Chiao Shih pi-ch'eng 焦氏筆乘. By Chiao Hung 焦竑 (1541–1620). *TSCC*.

Chien-teng hsin-hua 剪燈新話. By Ch'ü Yu 瞿佑 (1341–1427). In *Chien-teng hsin-hua wai erh chung*.

Chien-teng hsin-hua wai erh chung 剪燈新話外二種. Shanghai, 1957.

Ch'ien Han shu p'ing-hua 前漢書平話. Shanghai, 1955 reprint.

Ch'ien-t'ang hu yin Chi Tien Ch'an-shih yü-lu 錢塘湖隱濟顚禪師語錄. By Shen Meng-pan 沈孟柈. 1569 ed. (Naikaku Bunko). Reprinted in *Ming-Ch'ing p'ing-hua hsiao-shuo hsüan*.

Chih-nang 智囊. Comp. Feng Meng-lung 馮夢龍 (1574–1646). Edo period Japanese edition.

[*Hsin-tseng*] *Chih-nang pu* 新增智囊補. Comp. Feng Meng-lung. Late-Ming ed.

Chin P'ing Mei tz'u-hua 金瓶梅詞話. Fac. ed. of late Wan-li ed. Tokyo: Daian, 1963.

Ch'in ping liu kuo p'ing-hua 秦併六國平話. Shanghai, 1955 reprint.

Ching-lin hsü-chi 涇林續記. By Chou Hsüan-wei 周玄暐 (*chin-shih* 1586). *TSCC*.

Ching-pen t'ung-su hsiao-shuo 京本通俗小說. Represented, at the time of its "discovery," as an older collection than the *San yen*, but actually based upon the *San yen* (TY and HY). Shanghai, 1954 reprint.

Ching-shih t'ung-yen 警世通言. Comp. Feng Meng-lung. Fac. of first (1624) ed. Taipei: Shih-chieh shu-chü, 1958.

————Peking, 1957.

Ch'ing ni lien-hua chi 青泥蓮花記. Comp. Mei Ting-tso 梅鼎祚 (1549–1615). Compiler's preface d. 1600. Lithographic ed., Peking, 1910.

Ch'ing-p'ing-shan-t'ang hua-pen 清平山堂話本. Modern title under which the surviving vernacular stories published by Hung P'ien 洪楩 (fl. c. 1541) are collected and issued. Peking, 1955 reprint of 1934 fac. ed.

————Ed. T'an Cheng-pi 譚正璧. Shanghai, 1957.

Ch'ing shih. See *Ch'ing shih lei-lüeh.*

Ch'ing shih lei-lüeh 情史類略. Comp. Chan-chan wai-shih 詹詹外史 (pseud.) Preface by Feng Meng-lung. Ch'ing ed. by the Chieh-tzu yüan 芥子園.

———— Ch'ing ed. by the Li-pen-t'ang 立本堂. (Kubo Collection, National Taiwan University.)

Ch'ing-so kao-i 青瑣高議. Comprises *ch'ien-chi* 前集 (10 *chüan*), *hou-chi* 後集 (10) and *pieh-chi* 別集 (7). Attributed to Liu Fu 劉斧 (N. Sung). Shanghai, 1958. Includes the work of other writers besides Liu. The *Sung History*, bibliographical essay, ascribes a *ch'ien-chi* and a *hou-chi* to Liu Fu, but each in only 9 *chüan*. See the preface to the 1958 ed. for the arguments for attributing the *pieh-chi* to him.

Ch'ing tsun lu 清尊錄. By Lien Pu 廉布 (Sung). In *Ku-chin shuo-hai.*

Chiu-yüeh chi 九籥集. Comprises *Chiu-yüeh ch'ien-chi* (19 *chüan*) and *Chiu-yüeh chi* (14). By Sung Mao-ch'eng 宋楙澄 (fl. 1600). Preface d. 1612. (Naikaku Bunko.)

Cho keng lu 輟耕錄. By T'ao Tsung-i 陶宗儀 (c. 1330–1400). *TSCC.*

Chu Tzu yü-lei 朱子語類. Comp. Li Ching-te 黎靖德 (Sung). 1876 ed.

Ch'u-k'e P'ai-an ching-ch'i 初刻拍案驚奇. By Ling Meng-ch'u 凌濛初 (1580–1644). Ed. Wang Ku-lu 王古魯, Shanghai, 1957.

Ch'un meng lu 春夢錄. By Cheng Hsi 鄭禧 (Yüan). Preface d. 1318. In *Lü-ch'uang nü-shih.*

Chung-kuo ku-tien hsi-ch'ü lun-chu chi-ch'eng 中國古典戲曲論著集成. 10 vols. Peking, 1959.

Ch'ü-hai tsung-mu t'i-yao 曲海總目提要. Actually the *Yüeh-fu k'ao-lüeh* 樂府考略 (See *Ch'ü-hai tsung-mu pu-pien* 補編, Peking, 1959, introduction.) Peking, 1959.

Ch'üan-pu Pao Lung-t'u p'an pai-chia kung-an. See under *Pao Lung-t'u* . . .

Ch'üan Sung tz'u 全宋詞. Comp. T'ang Kuei-chang 唐圭璋. Rev. ed., 5 vols., Peking, 1965.

Erh-k'e P'ai-an ching-ch'i 二刻拍案驚奇. By Ling Meng-ch'u 凌濛初 (1580–1644). Ed. Wang Ku-lu 王古魯, Shanghai, 1957. First published 1632.

[*Hsin-k'e*] *Erh-t'an* 新刻耳譚. By Wang T'ung-kuei 王同軌 (Ming). 1602 ed. (Naikaku Bunko.)

Erh-t'an lei-tseng 耳譚類增. 54 *chüan*. By Wang T'ung-kuei. 1603 ed. (Peking National Library Rare Book Collection, Palace Museum, Taipei.)

Fei-yen chuan 非烟傳. By Huang-fu Mei 皇甫枚 (T'ang). *Shuo fu,* 112.

Fen-men ku-chin lei-shih 分門古今類事. Comp. Wei-hsin Tzu 委心子 (pseud.) Preface d. 1169. *TSCC.*

Fu-chai jih-chi 復齋日記. Comp. Hsü Hao 許浩 (fl. 1500). *TSCC.*

Hai Jui kung-an. See entry below.

[*Hsin-k'e ch'üan-hsiang*] *Hai Kang-feng hsien-sheng chü kuan kung-an chuan* 新刻全像海剛峯先生居官公案傳. By Li Ch'un-fang 李春芳. 1606 ed. (Peking Library).

[*Wan-li*] *Hang-chou fu chih* 萬曆杭州府志. Comp. Ch'en Shan 陳善 et al. First ed., 1579. Fac. ed. in *Ming-tai fang-chih hsüan* 明代方志選, Taipei, 1965.

Hang-chou fu chih 杭州府志. Comp. Shao Chin-han 邵晉涵 et al. 1784 ed.

Ho-k'e san-chih 合刻三志. Comp. Ping-hua chü-shih 冰華居士 (pseud.). Late-Ming ed. (Naikaku Bunko).

Hou te lu 厚德錄. Comp. Li Yüan-kang 李元綱 (Sung). *TSCC.*

Hsi-hu chia-hua 西湖佳話. By Mo-lang Tzu 墨浪子 (pseud.) Shanghai, 1956 reprint of early-Ch'ing ed.

Hsi-hu erh-chi 西湖二集. By Chou Chi 周楫 (late Ming). Shanghai, 1936.

Hsi-hu yu-lan chih 西湖遊覽志. By T'ien Ju-ch'eng 田汝成 (*chin-shih* 1526). Peking, 1958.

Hsi-hu yu-lan chih-yü 西湖遊覽志餘. By T'ien Ju-ch'eng, see entry above. Peking, 1958.

Hsiao-p'in chi 效顰集. By Chao Pi 趙弼 (fl. c. 1475). Peking, 1957.

Hsiao Shu-lan ch'ing chi p'u-sa-man 蕭淑蘭情寄菩薩蠻. By Chia Chung-ming 賈仲明 (1343–1422). In *Yüan-ch'ü hsüan.*

Hsin Lieh-kuo chih 新列國志. By Feng Meng-lung. Late-Ming ed.

Hsin-min kung-an 新民公案. Japanese MS of edition with 1605 preface. (National Taiwan University.)

Hsing-shih heng-yen 醒世恆言. Comp. Feng Meng-lung. Fac. of first (1627) ed. Taipei: Shih-chieh shu-chü, 1959.

———Ed. Ku Hsüeh-chieh 顧學頡. Peking, 1956.

Hsiu-ku ch'un-jung 繡谷春容. Comp. by Ch'i-pei chai 起北齋 (pseud.) Wan-li ed. (Tōyō Bunka Kenkyūjo.)

Hsiung Lung-feng ssu-chung hsiao-shuo 熊龍峯四種小說. Modern title given to four stories published by Hsiung Lung-feng c. 1590. Ed. Wang Ku-lu 王古魯. Shanghai, 1958.

Hsü Wen-hsien t'ung-k'ao 續文獻通考. 1887 ed.

Hsü Yen-i pien 續豔異編. 19 *chüan.* Printed with the *Yen-i pien* (40 *chüan*). Late-Ming ed. (National Central Library, Taipei.)

[*Hsin-k'an Ta Sung*] *Hsüan-ho i-shih* 新刊大宋宣和遺事. Shanghai, 1954 reprint.

Hsüeh Jen-kuei cheng Liao shih-lüeh 薛仁貴征遼事略. Preserved in *Yung-lo ta-tien* 永樂大典. Ed. Chao Wan-li 趙萬里. Shanghai, 1957.

Hu-hai hsin-wen I-chien hsü-chih ch'ien-chi 湖海新聞夷堅續志前集. Comp. by the Ssu-shan t'ang 思善堂 (Yüan). Ming MS. (Peking National Library Rare Book Collection, Palace Museum, Taipei.)

Hua-ts'ao ts'ui-pien 花草粹編. Comp. Ch'en Yao-wen 陳耀文 from a draft by Wu Ch'eng-en 吳承恩. Ch'en's preface d. 1583. Fac. ed., Peking, 1933.

Hua-ying chi 花影集. By T'ao Fu 陶輔. T'ao's preface d. 1523. Korean ed., colophon d. 1586. (British Museum.)

[*Ch'üan-hsiang lei-pien*] *Huang-Ming chu-ssu kung-an chuan* 全像類編皇明諸司公案傳. 6 *chüan.* Comp. Yü Hsiang-tou 余象斗. Ming ed. (Ueno Library.)

[*Hsin-k'an*] *Huang-Ming chu-ssu lien-ming ch'i-p'an kung-an chuan* 新刊皇明諸司廉明奇判公案傳. Comp. Yü Hsiang-tou 余象斗. Edo period MS of 1598 ed. (Naikaku Bunko.) Note that a 2-*chüan* edition of this work is also extant (Naikaku, Hōsa Bunko). The 6-*chüan* work of similar title (see entry above) is evidently a sequel to this work.

Huang-shan mi 黃山謎. Comp. Feng Meng-lung. Shanghai, 1935 reprint.

[*Liu Shih*] *Hung shu* 劉氏鴻書. By Liu Chung-ta 劉仲達. 1611 ed.

I-chen chi 欹枕集. Collection of stories published by Hung P'ien, a section of his *Liu-shih chia hsiao-shuo.* Incomplete. Reprinted in *Ch'ing-p'ing-shan-t'ang hua-pen.*

I-chien chih 夷堅志. By Hung Mai 洪邁 (1123–1202). Shanghai, 1927.

I chien shang-hsin pien 一見賞心編. Comp. Lo-yüan Tzu 洛源子 (pseud.) Late-Ming ed. (Naikaku Bunko.)

I-hsieh chi 易鞋記. By Tung Ying-han 董應翰 (Ming). In *Ku-pen hsi-ch'ü ts'ung-k'an*, First Series.

I-hu chuan 義虎傳. By Chu Yün-ming 祝允明 (1460–1526). *Shuo fu hsü*, 43.

I lin 異林. By Hsü Chen-ch'ing 徐禎卿 (Ming). *Shuo fu hsü*, 46.

I-wen tsung-lu 異聞總錄. Anon. *TSCC.*

Jen-ho hsien chih 仁和縣志. By Shen Ch'ao-hsüan 沈朝宣. Preface d. 1549. In *Wu-lin chang-ku ts'ung-pien.*

Ku-chin hsiao-shuo 古今小說. Comp. Feng Meng-lung. Fac. ed. of first edition. Taipei: Shih-chieh shu-chü, 1958.

———Ed. Hsü Cheng-yang 許正揚, Peking, 1958.

Ku-chin i-shih 古今逸史. Comp. Wu Kuan 吳琯 (*chin-shih* 1571). Shanghai, 1937.

[*Ch'üan-hsiang*] *Ku-chin Lieh-nü chuan* 全像古今列女傳. The *Lieh-nü chuan* supplemented by Mao K'un 茅坤 (1512–1601). 1591 ed.

Ku-chin Lieh-nü chuan yen-i 古今列女傳演義. Anon. Late-Ming ed. by the San-to chai 三多齋. (National Central Library, Taipei.)

Ku-chin ming-yüan shih-kuei 古今名媛詩歸. Comp. Chung Hsing 鍾惺 (1574–1624). Late-Ming ed.

Ku-chin shuo-hai 古今說海. Comp. Lu Chi 陸楫. First ed., 1544. Shanghai, 1909 ed.

Ku-chin t'an-kai 古今譚概. By Feng Meng-lung. Fac. ed. of first ed., Peking, 1955.

Ku-pen hsi-ch'ü ts'ung-k'an 古本戲曲叢刊. Shanghai and Peking. First Series 1954, Second Series 1955, Third Series 1957 . . . Facsimile reprint series of Yüan, Ming, and Ch'ing plays.

K'uai yüan 獪園. By Ch'ien Hsi-yen 錢希言. Preface d. 1613. 1774 ed. (Naikaku Bunko.)

Kuang-i chi 廣異記. By Tai Fu 戴孚 (Sung). *TSCC.*

Kuei Tung 鬼董. Colophon dated 1326, but clearly by a Sung author. In *Chih-pu-tsu-chai ts'ung-shu* 知不足齋叢書.

Kuei Tung Hu 鬼董狐. Almost identical version of entry above. Shanghai, 1916 ed. by the Han-fen-lou 涵芬樓.

Kuo-se t'ien-hsiang 國色天香. Comp. Wu Ching-so 吳敬所. 1587 ed. (Naikaku Bunko.)

Li-tai hsiao-shih 歷代小史. Comp. Li Shih 李栻 (*chin-shih* 1565). Shanghai, 1940 ed.

Liang Kung chiu chien 梁公九諫. n.d. In *Shih-li-chü ts'ung-shu.*

[*Yu-hsiang*] *Lieh hsien ch'üan chuan* 有象列仙全傳. Comp. Li P'an-lung 李攀龍 (1514–1570). Rev. Wang Shih-chen 王世貞. Ming ed.

[*Hsien-shun*] *Lin-an chih* 咸淳臨安志. By Ch'ien Shuo-yu 潛說友. Hangchow, 1830 reprint of 1268 ed.

Liu hung chi 流紅記. By Chang Shih 張實. In *Ch'ing-so kao-i ch'ien-chi.*

Lu kuei pu 錄鬼簿. Original work, and some revisions, by Chung Ssu-ch'eng 鍾嗣成. Preface d. 1330. Collated ed. of extant versions in *Chung-kuo ku-tien hsi-ch'ü lun-chu chi-ch'eng*, vol. II.

Lu kuei pu hsü-pien 錄鬼簿續編. Probably by Chia Chung-ming 賈仲明 (1343–1422). Edition as above.

Lung-t'u kung-an 龍圖公案, 10 *chüan*. 1821 ed. by the Kuei-wen t'ang 貴文堂.

Lü-ch'uang hsin-hua 綠窗新話. Comp. Huang-tu feng-yüeh chu-jen 皇都風月主人 (pseud.). Ed. Chou I 周夷, Shanghai, 1957. Presumably a Southern Sung work, since it is mentioned in Lo Yeh's *Tsui-weng t'an-lu.*

Lü-ch'uang nü-shih 綠窗女史. Late-Ming ed.

Lü-t'iao kung-an 律條公案. By Ch'en Yü-hsiu 陳玉秀. Late-Ming ed. (Naikaku Bunko.)

Meng liang lu 夢梁錄. By Wu Tzu-mu 吳自牧. Composed after 1275, and probably after 1280. In *Tung-ching meng hua lu wai ssu chung.*

Mi teng yin-hua 覓燈因話. By Shao Ching-chan 邵景詹. Preface d. 1592. In *Chien-teng hsin-hua wai erh chung.*

Ming-Ch'ing p'ing-hua hsiao-shuo hsüan 明清平話小說選. *Ti-i chi* 第一集. Comp. Lu Kung 路工. Shanghai, 1958.

Ming shan tsang 名山藏. Comp. Ho Ch'iao-yüan 何喬遠. 1640 ed.

Mu-tan teng chi 牡丹燈記. By Ch'en Yin 陳愔 (Yüan). In *Lü-ch'uang nü-shih.*

Pai-chia kung-an. See under *Pao Lung-t'u p'an pai-chia kung-an*.

Pai-she chuan chi 白蛇傳集. Comp. Fu Hsi-hua 傅惜華. Shanghai, 1955.

Pai-shih hui-pien 稗史彙編. Comp. Wang Ch'i 王圻. 1608 ed.

P'ai-an ching-ch'i. See under *Ch'u-k'e; Erh-k'e*.

Pak t'ongsa ŏnhae 朴通事諺解. In *Keishōkaku sōsho* 奎章閣叢書, Seoul, 1943.

Pao-chien chi 寶劍記. Attributed to Li K'ai-hsien 李開先 (1502–1568). In *Ku-pen hsi-ch'ü ts'ung-k'an*, First Series.

[*Ch'üan-pu*] *Pao Lung-t'u p'an pai-chia kung-an* 全補包龍圖判百家公案. Anon. 1594 ed. (Hōsa Bunko, Nagoya.)

Pao Tai-chih chih chuan ho-t'ung wen-tzu 包待制智賺合同文字. Anon. In *Yüan-ch'ü hsüan*.

Pao-wen-t'ang shu-mu. See under *Ch'ao Shih Pao-wen-t'ang shu-mu*.

Pen shih shih 本事詩. By Meng Ch'i 孟啓 (T'ang). In *Ku-chin i-shih*.

[*San Sui*] *P'ing-yao chuan* 三遂平妖傳. Twenty *hui*. Wan-li ed., part of which may be in a later reprint. (Tenri Central Library.)

P'ing-yao chuan 平妖傳. Forty *hui*. Expanded version of entry above, by Feng Meng-lung. First published 1620. Shanghai, 1956.

San-chiao ou-nien 三教偶拈. Comp. Feng Meng-lung. (Sōkōdō Bunko, Tōyō Bunka Kenkyūjo.)

San kuo chih p'ing-hua 三國志平話. Shanghai, 1955 reprint.

San kuo chih t'ung-su yen-i 三國志通俗演義. By Lo Kuan-chung 羅貫中 (fl. 1364). Fac. ed. of the so-called "Hung-chih edition," Shanghai, 1929.

San pao en 三報恩. By Pi Wei 畢魏. Preface by Feng Meng-lung dated 1642. In *Ku-pen hsi-ch'ü ts'ung-k'an*, Second Series.

San Sui P'ing-yao chuan. See under *P'ing-yao chuan*.

San ts'ai t'u hui 三才圖會. By Wang Ch'i 王圻. Facsimile of 1607 ed., Taipei, 1970.

San yüan chi 三元記. By Shen Shou-hsien 沈受先. In *Ku-pen hsi-ch'ü ts'ung-k'an*, First Series.

Shan-chü hsin-hua 山居新話. By Yang Yü 楊瑀 (1285–1361). In *Chih-pu-tsu-chai ts'ung-shu*.

Shih-erh hsiao ming lu shih-i 侍兒小名錄拾遺. By Chang Pang-chi 張邦幾 (Sung). *TSCC*.

Shih-erh lou 十二樓. By Li Yü 李漁 (1611–1680?). Shanghai, 1949.

Shih-hua chüan-yung 詩話雋永. By Yü Cheng-chi 喻正己 (Yüan). *Shuo fu*, 84.

Shih-li-chü ts'ung-shu 士禮居叢書. Comp. Huang P'ei-lieh 黃丕烈 (1763–1825). Shanghai, 1922.

Shih tien t'ou 石點頭. By T'ien-jan ch'ih sou 天然癡叟 (pseud.). Shanghai, 1935. First published in late Ming.

Shuang-huai sui-ch'ao 雙槐歲鈔. By Huang Yü 黃瑜 (Ming). *TSCC*.

Shuang-pei chi 雙盃記. Anon. Fac. of Wan-li ed. in *Ku-pen hsi-ch'ü ts'ung-k'an*, Second Series.

Shuang-yü chi 雙魚記. By Shen Ching 沈璟 (1553–1610). In *Ku-pen hsi-ch'ü ts'ung-k'an*, First Series.

Shui-hu ch'üan chuan 水滸全傳. Variorum ed. of the "full" texts of the novel. Peking, 1954. Reprinted Hong Kong, 1958.

Shuo fu 說郛. 1646 ed.

Shuo fu hsü 說郛續. 1646 ed.

Sung-pai lei-ch'ao 宋稗類鈔. Comp. P'an Yung-yin 潘永因. 1669 ed.

Sung-Yüan hsi-wen chi-i 宋元戲文輯佚. Comp. Ch'ien Nan-yang 錢南揚. Shanghai, 1956.

Ta Sung Hsüan-ho i-shih. See *Hsüan-ho i-shih*.

Ta T'ang Ch'in Wang tz'u-hua 大唐秦王詞話. By Chu Sheng-lin 諸聖鄰. Fac. ed. of Ming edition, Peking, 1956.

Ta T'ang San-tsang Fa-shih ch'ü ching chi 大唐三藏法師取經記. Fac. ed. of S. Sung (?) edition, attached to fac. ed. of *Ta T'ang San-tsang ch'ü ching shih-hua*, Peking, 1955.

Ta T'ang San-tsang ch'ü ching shih-hua 大唐三藏取經詩話. Version of entry above. Shanghai, 1954 reprint.

T'ai-hsia hsin-tsou 太霞新奏. Comp. Feng Meng-lung. Fac. ed. of late-Ming ed., n.d.

T'ai-p'ing kuang-chi 太平廣記. Comp. Li Fang 李昉 et al. (N. Sung). Peking, 1959.

T'ai-p'ing kuang-chi ch'ao 太平廣記鈔. Ed. Feng Meng-lung. Preface d. 1626. (Jigendō 慈眼堂 at Nikko.)

T'an-lu. See under *Tsui-weng t'an-lu*.

T'ang che yen 唐摭言. By Wang Ting-pao 王定保 (Five Dynasties). *TSCC*.

[*Hsü Hsien*] *T'ieh-shu chi* 許仙鐵樹記. By Teng Chih-mo 鄧志謨. Teng's preface d. 1603. (Naikaku Bunko.)

T'ien-hsiang-lou wai-shih chih-i 天香樓外史誌異. By Hsüeh Ch'ao 薛朝. Preface d. 1603. Lithographic ed. of Yüan Mei's 袁枚 rev. ed., 1900. (Hanan.)

T'ien Shu-ho wen-chi 田叔禾文集. Posthumous collection of T'ien Ju-ch'eng's 田汝成 writings. Ed. T'ien I-heng 田藝蘅. 1563 ed. (Hōsa Bunko, Nagoya.)

T'ing shih 桯史. By Yüeh K'e 岳珂 (1183–1234). *TSCC*.

Ts'ai chou chi 彩舟記. By Wang T'ing-na 汪廷訥 (fl. 1608). In *Ku-pen hsi-ch'ü ts'ung-k'an*, Second Series.

Ts'ao-t'ang shih-yü 草堂詩餘. Peking, 1958 ed. based on Hung-wu (1368–1398) ed.

Tsui hsing shih 醉醒石. By Tung-Lu Ku-k'uang Sheng 東魯古狂生 (pseud.). Shanghai, 1956 ed.

[*Hsin-pien*] *Tsui-weng t'an-lu* 新編醉翁談錄. By Lo Yeh 羅燁. Shanghai, 1957 reprint of Yüan (?) edition.

Ts'ui-pien. See under *Hua-ts'ao ts'ui-pien*.

Tu-ch'eng chi-sheng 都城紀勝. By Nai-te weng 耐得翁 (pseud.). Preface d. 1235. In *Tung-ching meng hua lu wai ssu chung*.

Tun-huang pien-wen chi 敦煌變文集. Comp. Wang Chung-min 王重民 et al. Peking, 1957.

Tung-ching meng-hua lu 東京夢華錄. By Meng Yüan-lao 孟元老. Preface d. 1147. See entry below.

Tung-ching meng-hua lu wai ssu chung 東京夢華錄外四種. Shanghai, 1958.

Tung-hsüan pi-lu 東軒筆錄. By Wei T'ai 魏泰 (Sung). *TSCC*.

Tung-p'o wen-ta lu 東坡問答錄. In *Pao-yen-t'ang pi-chi* 寶顔堂祕笈.

Wan-chin ch'ing-lin 萬錦情林. Comp. by Yü Hsiang-tou 余象斗. 1598 ed. (Chinese Literature Dept., Tokyo Univ.)

Wan-li yeh-huo pien 萬曆野獲編. By Shen Te-fu 沈德符 (1578–1642). Preface to rev. ed. d. 1619. Peking, 1959.

Wang-hu T'ing chi 望湖亭記. By Shen Tzu-chin 沈自晉 (1580–1660). In *Ku-pen hsi-ch'ü ts'ung-k'an*, Second Series.

Wu-ch'ao hsiao-shuo 五朝小說. Feng Meng-lung claimed as compiler. Late-Ming ed. (Hōsa Bunko, Nagoya.)

Wu-lin chang-ku ts'ung-pien 武林掌故叢編. 1882 ed.

Wu-lin chiu-shih 武林舊事. By Chou Mi 周密 (1232–1298). In *Tung-ching meng hua lu wai ssu chung*.

[*Hsin-pien*] *Wu Tai shih p'ing-hua* 新編五代史平話. Shanghai, 1954 reprint.

Wu Wang fa Chou p'ing-hua 武王伐紂平話. Shanghai, 1955 reprint.

Yeh chi 野記. By Chu Yün-ming 祝允明 (1461–1527). In *Li-tai hsiao-shih*.

Yen-chü pi-chi 燕居筆記. Ed. Lin Chin-yang 林近陽. Ming edition. (Naikaku Bunko.)

———Ed. Ho Ta-lun 何大掄. Early Ch'ing ed.

———Ed. Yü Kung-jen 余公仁. Early Ch'ing ed. (Zushoryō of the Kunaishō in Tokyo.)

Yen-i pien 艷異編. Compilation attributed to Wang Shih-chen 王世貞 (1526–1590) and annotation to T'ang Hsien-tsu 湯顯祖 (1550–1617). Shanghai, 1936 ed. of a late-Ming ed. in 40 *chüan*.

Yüan-ch'ü hsüan 元曲選. Comp. Tsang Mao-hsün 臧懋循. First published 1616. Rev. ed., Peking, 1958.

Yü-ch'uang chi 雨窗集. Collection of stories published by Hung P'ien, a section of his *Liu-*

shih chia hsiao-shuo. Incomplete. Reprinted in *Ch'ing-p'ing-shan-t'ang hua-pen.*

Yüan-shan-t'ang ch'ü-p'in 遠山堂曲品. By Ch'i Piao-chia 祁彪佳 (1602–1645). In *Chung-kuo ku-tien hsi-ch'ü lun-chu chi-ch'eng,* vol. VI.

Yüeh-fu hung-shan 樂府紅珊. Comp. Chi Chen-lun 紀振倫. Preface d. 1602. 1800 ed. (British Museum.)

Yün-chai kuang-lu 雲齋廣錄. By Li Hsien-min 李獻民. Preface d. 1111. Shanghai, 1936.

Yün-men chuan 雲門傳. Anon. Late-Ming ed. (Peking National Library Rare Book Collection, Palace Museum, Taipei.)

SECONDARY WORKS

A Ying 阿英 (pseud. of Ch'ien Hsing-ts'un 錢杏邨). *Hsiao-shuo erh-t'an* 小說二談. Shanghai, 1958.

———*Hsiao-shuo hsien-t'an* 小說閒談. Shanghai, 1936.

———"Yü-t'ang-ch'un ku-shih ti yen-pien" 玉堂春故事的演變, reprinted in A Ying, *Hsiao-shuo erh-t'an,* pp. 1–31.

Bishop, John Lyman. *The Colloquial Short Story in China.* Cambridge, Mass.: Harvard University Press, 1956.

Chang Ch'üan-kung 張全恭. "Hung-lien Liu Ts'ui ku-shih ti chuan-pien" 紅蓮柳翠故事的轉變, *Ling-nan hsüeh-pao* 嶺南學報 5.2 (1936), 57–74.

Chang Fu-jui. *Les Fonctionnaires des Song, Index des titres.* Paris: Mouton, 1962.

Chang Hsiang 張相. *Shih tz'u ch'ü yü-tz'u hui-shih* 詩詞曲語辭匯釋. Peking, 1953 reprint.

Chao Ching-shen 趙景深. "Ching-shih t'ung-yen ti lai-yüan ho ying-hsiang" 警世通言的來源和影響, *Hsiao-shuo hsi-ch'ü hsin-k'ao,* pp. 1–14.

———*Hsiao-shuo hsi-ch'ü hsin-k'ao* 小說戲曲新考. Shanghai, 1939.

———"Hsing-shih heng-yen ti lai-yüan ho ying-hsiang" 醒世恆言的來源和影響, *Hsiao-shuo hsi-ch'ü hsin-k'ao* (Shanghai, 1939), pp. 15–29.

———*T'an-tz'u k'ao-cheng* 彈詞考證. Shanghai, 1938.

———*Yin-tzu chi* 銀字集. Shanghai, 1946.

Ch'en Ju-heng 陳汝衡. *Shuo-shu shih-hua* 說書史話. Peking, 1958.

Cheng Chen-to 鄭振鐸. "Ming-Ch'ing erh-tai ti p'ing-hua chi" 明清二代的平話集, reprinted in Cheng Chen-to, *Chung-kuo wen-hsüeh yen-chiu* 中國文學研究, Peking, 1957, pp. 360–474.

Dudbridge, Glen. *The Hsi-yu chi, A Study of Antecedents to the Sixteenth-century Novel.* Cambridge: Cambridge University Press, 1970.

Eberhard, Wolfram. *Guilt and Sin in Traditional China.* Berkeley and Los Angeles: University of California Press, 1967.

Ellegård, Alvar. *A Statistical Method for Determining Authorship: The Junius Letters.* Gothenburg Studies in English, 13. Acta Universitatis Gothenburgensis. Gothenburg, 1962.

Enkvist, Nils Erik, John Spencer, and Michael J. Gregory. *Linguistics and Style.* Oxford: Oxford University Press, 1964.

Erdman, David V., and E. G. Fogel. *Evidence for Authorship.* Ithaca, N.Y.: Cornell University Press, 1966.

Feng Yüan-chün 馮沅君. *Ku-chü shuo-hui* 古劇說彙. Peking, 1956.

Fu Hsi-hua 傅惜華. *Ming-tai ch'uan-ch'i ch'üan-mu* 明代傳奇全目. Peking, 1959.

———*Ming-tai tsa-chü ch'üan-mu* 明代雜劇全目. Peking, 1958.

———*Yüan-tai tsa-chü ch'üan-mu* 元代雜劇全目. Peking, 1957.

Fu I-ling 傅衣凌. *Ming-tai Chiang-nan shih-min ching-chi shih-t'an* 明代江南市民經濟試探. Shanghai, 1957.

Hanan, Patrick D. "The Authorship of Some *Ku-chin hsiao-shuo* Stories," *Harvard Journal of Asiatic Studies* 29 (1969), 190–200.

———"The Composition of the *P'ing-yao chuan,*" *Ibid.,* 31 (1971), 201–219.

———"The Early Chinese Short Story: A Critical Theory in Outline," *Ibid.*, 27 (1967), 168–207.

———"The Nature and Contents of the *Yüeh-fu hung-shan*," *Bulletin of the School of Oriental and African Studies* 26.2 (1963), 346–361.

———"Sources of the *Chin P'ing Mei*," *Asia Major* NS 10.1 (1963), 23–67.

———"The Text of the *Chin P'ing Mei*," *Ibid.*, 9.1 (1962), 1–57.

———"Sung and Yüan Vernacular Fiction: A Critique of Modern Methods of Dating," *Harvard Journal of Asiatic Studies* 30 (1970), 159–184.

Harada Suekiyo 原田季清. "*Jōshi* ni tsuite" 情史に就て, *Taidai bungaku* 臺大文學 2.1 (1937), 53–60.

———*Wahon shōsetsu ron* 話本小說論. *Gengo to bungaku* 言語と文學, no. 2, Taihoku Imperial University, Taipei, 1938.

———"*Zōkō Chinō-ho* ni tsuite" 增廣智囊補に就て, *Taidai bungaku* 2.3 (1937), 48–53.

Ho Ping-ti. *Studies on the Population of China, 1368–1953*. Cambridge, Mass.: Harvard University Press, 1959.

Hsia, C. T. *The Classic Chinese Novel: A Critical Introduction*. New York: Columbia University Press, 1968.

Hu Chu-an 胡竹安. "Sung Yüan pai-hua tso-p'in-chung ti yü-ch'i chu-tz'u" 宋元白話作品中的語氣助詞, *Chung-kuo yü-wen* 中國語文 (June 1958), pp. 270–274.

Inada Osamu 稻田尹. "Sōgen wahon ruikeikō" 宋元話本類型考. Series of four articles. *Kagoshima daigaku bunka hōkoku* 鹿兒島大學文科報告 7 (1958), 73–94; 8 (1959), 131–160; 9 (1960), 97–133; 13 (1964), 1–32.

Iriya Yoshitaka 入矢義高. Translation of Hung stories into Japanese. In *Chūgoku koten bungaku zenshū* 中國古典文學全集 vol. VII, Tokyo, 1958.

Irwin, Richard Gregg. *The Evolution of a Chinese Novel: Shui-hu-chuan*. Cambridge, Mass.: Harvard University Press, 1953.

Karashima Takeshi 辛島驍. Translation of the *San yen* stories into Japanese in the incomplete series *Zenyaku Chūgoku bungaku daikei* 全譯中國文學大系, Tokyo, 1958–1959. Vol. VI contains translations, notes and commentaries (sources, influences, etc.) on the first twelve stories in TY. Vols. X–XIV treat all forty stories in HY.

Karlgren, Bernhard. "New Excursions in Chinese Grammar," *Bulletin of the Museum of Far Eastern Antiquities* 24 (1952), 51–80.

Lévy, André. "Deux Contes philosophiques Ming et leurs sources," *Bulletin de l'Ecole Française d'Extrême-Orient* 13.2 (1967), 537–550.

———Etudes sur trois recueils anciens de contes chinois," *T'oung Pao* 52.1–3 (1965), 97–148.

Li Tien-yi 李田意. "Jih-pen so-chien Chung-kuo tuan-p'ien hsiao-shuo lüeh-chi" 日本所見中國短篇小說略記, *Ch'ing-hua hsüeh-pao* 清華學報 NS 1.2 (1957), 63–81.

Liu Ts'un-yan. "Wu Ch'eng-en: His Life and Career," *T'oung Pao* 53.1–3 (1967), 1–97.

Liu Wen-ying 柳文英. "Ming-tai ti ch'uan-ch'i hsiao-shuo" 明代的傳奇小說, *Kuang-ming jih-pao* 光明日報, March 28, 1958.

Ma Yau-woon 馬幼垣. "Hsiung Lung-feng so-k'an tuan-p'ien hsiao-shuo ssu-chung k'ao-shih" 熊龍峯所刊短篇小說四種考釋, *Ch'ing-hua hsüeh-pao* 清華學報 NS 7.1 (1968), 257–278.

Masuda Wataru 增田涉. "'Wahon' to iu koto ni tsuite" 「話本」ということについて, *Jimbun kenkyū* 16.5 (1965), 22–33.

Ming-jen chuan-chi tzu-liao so-yin 明人傳記資料索引. 2 vols. National Central Library, Taipei, 1965.

Mosteller, Frederick, and D. L. Wallace. *Inference and Disputed Authorship: The Federalist*. Reading, Mass.: Addison-Wesley Publishing Co., 1964.

Moule, A.C. *Quinsai with Other Notes on Marco Polo*. Cambridge: Cambridge University Press, 1957.

Nagasawa Kikuya 長澤規矩也. "Genson Mindai shōsetsusho kankōsha-hyō shokō" 現存明代小說書刊行者表初稿, *Shoshigaku* 書誌學 3.3 (1934), 41–48; 3.4 (1934), 1–4.

———"*Keihon tsūzoku shōsetsu to Seiheisandō wahon*" 京本通俗小說と清平山堂話本, *Tōyō gakuhō* 東洋學報 17.2 (1928), 111–139.

———*Nikkōzan Jigendō shoko genson kanseki bunrui mokuroku* 日光山慈眼堂書庫現存漢籍分類目錄. Nikko, 1961.

———*Sōkōdō Bunko bunrui mokuroku* 雙紅堂文庫分類目錄. Tokyo, 1961.

Ōta Tatsuo 太田辰夫. *Chūgokugo rekishi bumpō* 中國語歷史文法. Tokyo, 1958.

Pritchett, V. S. "The Anti-Soporific Art," *New Statesman and Nation*, December 6, 1968, p. 793.

Prušek, Jaroslav. "The Creative Methods of the Chinese Medieval Story-tellers," reprinted in *Chinese History and Literature: Collections of Studies* (Dordrecht, Reidel, 1970), pp. 366–384. The article was first published in 1956.

———*The Origins and the Authors of the Hua-pen*. Prague: Academia, 1967.

Sawada Mizuho 澤田瑞穗. "Wahon shōsetsu no 'hasseki hentai' ni tsuite" 話本小說の「發跡變泰」について, *Tenri daigaku gakuhō* 天理大學學報 27 (1958), 41–56.

Shōji Kakuichi 莊司格一. "Heiwa ni okeru gohō—ninshō daimeishi o chūshin to shite" 「平話」における語法——人稱代名詞を中心として, *Shūkan Tōyōgaku* 集刊東洋學 11 (1964), 46–58.

Ssu Su 思蘇. "Shuo shu yu wu chüeh-pen" 說書有無脚本, *Ch'ü-i* 曲藝 52 (1962), 44–45.

Sun K'ai-ti 孫楷第. Introduction to *Chin-ku ch'i-kuan* 今古奇觀. Ya-tung, Shanghai, 1933.

———*Chung-kuo t'ung-su hsiao-shuo shu-mu* 中國通俗小說書目. Rev. ed., Peking, 1957.

———"Hsiao-shuo p'ang-cheng" 小說旁證, *Kuo-li Pei-p'ing t'u-shu-kuan kuan-k'an* 國立北平圖書館館刊 9.1 (1935), 11–20.

———"Hsiao-shuo p'ang-cheng erh-tse" 二則, *Wen-hsüeh p'ing-lun* 文學評論 (1961, no. 6), pp. 112–114.

———"Hsiao-shuo p'ang-cheng erh-tse," *Ibid.* (1962, no. 1), pp. 115–120.

———"Hsiao-shuo p'ang-cheng san-tse" 三則, *Ibid.* (1961, no. 4), pp. 113–117.

———"Hsiao-shuo p'ang-cheng ssu-tse" 四則, *Ibid.* (1961, no. 5), pp. 123–129.

———"Hsiao-shuo p'ang-cheng wu-tse" 五則, *Ibid.* (1962, no. 2), pp. 100–107.

———*Jih-pen Tung-ching so-chien Chung-kuo hsiao-shuo shu-mu* 日本東京所見中國小說書目. Shanghai, 1953 reprint.

———*Ts'ang-chou chi* 滄州集. 2 vols. Peking, 1965.

———"Yüan-ch'ü hsin-k'ao" 元曲新考, reprinted in *Ts'ang-chou chi*, II, 317–359.

T'an Cheng-pi 譚正璧. *Hua-pen yü ku-chü* 話本與古劇. Shanghai, 1956.

Tu Lien-che 杜聯喆. "Ming-jen hsiao-shuo chi tang-tai ch'i-wen pen-shih chü-li" 明人小說記當代奇聞本事舉例, *Ch'ing-hua hsüeh-pao* 清華學報 NS 7.2 (1969), 156–175.

Uchida Michio 內田道夫. "Kō U shin monogatari" 項羽神物語, *Tōhōgaku* 東方學 12 (1956), 25–39.

Wright, Hope. *Geographical Names in Sung China, An Alphabetical List*. Paris: Ecole Pratique des Hautes Etudes, 1956.

Wu Hsiao-ling 吳曉鈴. Review of KC edition. *Han-hiue* 2.4 (1949), 443–455.

Yeh Te-chün 葉德均. *Sung-Yüan-Ming chiang-ch'ang wen-hsüeh* 宋元明講唱文學. Shanghai, 1957.

Yen Tun-i 嚴敦易. *Yüan-chü chen-i* 元劇斟疑. Peking, 1960.

Yule, G. Udny. *The Statistical Study of Literary Vocabulary*. Cambridge: Cambridge University Press, 1944.

Reference List of Selected English Translations

For a comprehensive listing of *San yen* stories in English and other European languages, see Bishop, *Colloquial Short Story*, pp. 128–135. Two recent publications, in German and French respectively, should be added to his list. *Die Jadegöttin, Zwölf Geschichten aus dem mittelalterlichen China* (Berlin: Rütten und Loening, 1968), consists of stories translated by Liane Bettin and Marianne Liebermann, with an afterword by Jaroslav Prušek. The translated stories are, in order: KC 24, KC 15, TY 13, TY 28, HY 31, TY 7, TY 16, KC 39, TY 14, HY 13, TY 39 and TY 8. André Lévy, *Etudes sur le conte et le roman chinois*, Publications de l'Ecole Française d'Extrême-Orient, vol. 82 (Paris, 1971) includes translations of TY 20, Hung 10, and Hung 14.

The following five collections contain the most reliable English translations.

Harold Acton and Lee Yi-hsieh, *Four Cautionary Tales*, A. A. Wyn, New York, 1947. (A reprint of *Glue and Lacquer*, London: Golden Cockerel Press, 1941.)

> *Love in a Junk* translates HY 28, omitting the prologue story.
> *Brother or Bride?* translates HY 10. The prologue story is separated from the main story and printed in italics.
> *The Everlasting Couple* translates HY 9. The prologue story is separated from the main story and printed in italics.
> *The Mandarin-duck Girdle* translates HY 15, omitting the short prologue.

Cyril Birch, *Stories from a Ming Collection: Translations of Chinese Short Stories Published in the Seventeenth Century*, Bloomington and London: Indiana University Press, 1958. Paperback edition by Grove Press (Evergreen E473).

> *The Lady Who Was a Beggar* translates KC 27.
> *The Pearl-sewn Shirt* translates KC 1.
> *Wine and Dumplings* translates KC 5.
> *The Journey of the Corpse* translates KC 8. The Classical source of this story, from the *T'ai-p'ing kuang-chi*, is translated under the title of *The Story of Wu Pao-an*.
> *The Canary Murders* translates KC 26.
> *The Fairy's Rescue* translates KC 33.

John Lyman Bishop, *The Colloquial Short Story in China: A Study of the San-Yen Collections*, Harvard-Yenching Institute Series 14, Cambridge, Mass.: Harvard University Press, 1956.

> *Master Shen's Bird Destroys Seven Lives* translates KC 26.
> *Chin-nu Sells Love at Newbridge* translates KC 3.

Fan Chü-ch'ing's Eternal Friendship translates KC 16, which is a slight adaptation of
Hung 22.

Wang An-shih Thrice Corners Su Tung-p'o translates TY 3.

Chi-chen Wang, *Traditional Chinese Tales*, New York: Columbia University Press,
1944. Reprinted by Greenwood Press, New York, 1968. The last five stories are vernacular,
the rest Classical tales. The vernacular translations make slight abridgements in their
originals.

The Jade Kuanyin translates the *Ching-pen t'ung-su hsiao-shuo* version of TY 8,
omitting the poem-chain prologue.

The Judicial Murder of Tsui Ning translates the *Ching-pen* version of HY 33.

The Flower Lover and the Fairies translates HY 4.

The Oil Peddler and the Queen of Flowers translates HY 3.

The Three Brothers translates HY 2.

Yang Hsien-yi and Gladys Yang, *The Courtesan's Jewel Box: Chinese Stories of the Xth-
XVIIth Centuries*, Peking: Foreign Languages Press, 1957.

The Jade Worker translates the *Ching-pen* version of TY 8, omitting the poem-chain
prologue.

The Honest Clerk translates the *Ching-pen* version of TY 16.

Fifteen Strings of Cash translates the *Ching-pen* version of HY 33.

The Monk's Billet-doux translates KC 35, which is an adaptation of Hung 2.

The Foxes' Revenge translates HY 6.

The Hidden Will translates KC 10, omitting the introductory poem.

The Two Brothers translates HY 10, omitting the prologue story.

The Beggar Chief's Daughter translates KC 27, omitting the prologue.

A Just Man Avenged translates KC 40.

The Tattered Felt Hat translates TY 22.

The Courtesan's Jewel Box translates TY 32, omitting half a page of introduction.

The Oil Vendor and the Courtesan translates HY 3.

The Old Gardener translates HY 4.

Marriage by Proxy translates HY 7.

The Proud Scholar translates HY 29, omitting the introductory poem.

The remaining five stories are from the *P'ai-an ching-ch'i* collections, *Ch'u-k'e* 1, 3, 18
and 22, and *Erh-k'e* 39. Note that *Ch'u-k'e* 3 is based on a tale by Sung Mao-ch'eng. Cf.
KC 1, TY 32. André Lévy has translated twelve stories from the *P'ai-an ching-ch'i* collections
in *L'Amour de la renarde*, Paris: Gallimard, 1970.

Note on the *San yen* Texts

The modern typeset editions used in this study are based only indirectly upon the earliest *San yen* editions. The earliest edition of KC is the T'ien-hsü-chai 天許齋 edition, as preserved in the Naikaku Bunko in Tokyo. A typeset edition based on photostats was published by the Commercial Press in 1947 and then reissued by the Wen-hsüeh ku-chi k'an-hsing she 文學古籍刊行社 in 1955. The Peking, 1958 edition annotated by Hsü Cheng-yang was based upon the 1955 edition. The earliest edition of TY is the Chien-shan-t'ang 兼善堂 edition (preface dated 1624), as preserved in the Hōsa Bunko in Nagoya. From a manuscript copy of it, a typeset edition was published in installments during 1935 and 1936 in the *Shih-chieh wen-k'u* 世界文庫 edited by Cheng Chen-to. On this edition was based the Peking, 1956 edition annotated by Yen Tun-i which I have used; TY 37, missing in the *Shih-chieh wen-k'u*, was supplied from another Ming edition of TY, that by the San-kuei-t'ang 三桂堂. The earliest edition of HY is the Yeh Ching-ch'ih 葉敬池 edition (with a preface dated 1627), as preserved in the Naikaku Bunko. It was reprinted in a typeset edition in 1936 as an addition to the *Shih-chieh wen-k'u* series, with a postface by Cheng Chen-to. On it was based the Peking, 1956 edition annotated by Ku Hsüeh-chieh which I have used. (It omits the erotic story, HY 23, entirely.) All three modern editions state that they have made minor emendations on the basis of other *San yen* editions and other anthologies.

The 1947 KC edition and the *Shih-chieh wen-k'u* editions of TY and HY excised all passages of explicit sexual reference. The later editors made similar excisions, occasionally extending the amount of text excised, but, unlike their predecessors, they did not mark the points in the text at which excisions had been made. The stories principally concerned are: KC 1, 3, 4, 17, 23, 29, 30, 38, TY 35, HY 3, 8, 10, 15, 16, 28, and 39. Numerous as the excisions are, they do not affect the stylistic data given in this study. They are generally slight, and most of them consist mainly of set pieces and poems, rather than of the narrative prose which has been the chief object of investigation. The only criteria which occur in an excised passage, in HY 8, 15b–17b, reinforce the conclusion that HY 8 is a late story written by X.

The main drawback of the modern editions is their inaccuracy, an inaccuracy which is traceable in each case to their exemplars, particularly the 1936 edition of HY. The KC and TY editions, although certainly not free of mistakes and discrepancies, are at least adequate for the purposes of this study. (The sole point that concerns us is that the *Shen* 申 of TY 37.3b in the 1624 facsimile edition is found as *chung* 中 on page 557 of the 1956 edition; *Shen* is the better reading, see 155n18 of this study.) But the HY edition is quite another matter. Although the 1936 edition is professedly based upon Yeh Ching-ch'ih's edition, it differs so frequently from it that one is tempted to believe that a second edition must also have been in use. These differences are reflected in the Peking, 1956 edition I have used. On the average, perhaps two or three characters per page differ from Yeh Ching-ch'ih's edition, but in some stories this figure rises as high as five characters per page, a good 1 percent of the text. Fortunately, the differences do not affect the conclusions drawn about the HY stories, and only rarely do they affect the stylistic data. In particular, the instance of M2 on page 267 of HY 14 does not appear in the 1627 edition; HY 14's classification as an early story is thus all the clearer (see Table 12, page 117 above), but the evidence for adaptation as given on page 126 of this study is somewhat weakened. And in HY 31, the instance of M11 on page 669 and the *yü-so* on page 671 do not appear in the 1627 edition. But although the data on pages 59 and 125 of this study are affected, ample evidence remains that the last pages of HY 31 were rewritten or supplied by a late editor.

Index of Stylistic Features

This is an index to the definitions of stylistic criteria given in Chapters II through V, both the formal and the "probable" criteria. It includes the main features of X's style as indicated in Chapter IV, but not the relatively minor features characteristic of Feng Meng-lung and the other authors. Unless otherwise noted, the features listed here belong to the vernacular fiction style. The effectiveness of the older and newer criteria is assessed on pages 46–49, and that of the early and middle criteria on pages 118–120.

Index to the Extant Stories, with Notes on Their Dates of Composition, Texts, and Sources

This index lists all of the extant stories, except for the *Pai-chia kung-an*, in the same order as on pages 8–16, whence their full titles may be obtained. If a story exists in more than one pre-1628 edition, the "best text" is chosen for reference, as established on pages 54–58. The story's other texts are accompanied only by such information as applies peculiarly to them *as texts*; they are marked by a double dagger. The comments after each story's title have no independent authority; they should on no account be taken as a substitute for the qualified and often highly tentative arguments of this study. "Late" means after circa 1550; "middle" means between circa 1400 and circa 1575; "early" means before circa 1450. The terms "newer" and "older" were used in Chapters II and III; "newer" was then discarded in favor of "late," while the "older" stories were divided in Chapter V into "middle" and "early." The division of the "early" stories into Groups A, B, and C is the product of the speculative reasoning of Chapter VII, and the reader may wish to ignore it. The comments are followed by a list of significant references.

The only fresh information deals with sources. A source is a work which shares enough text with the vernacular story for us to infer that the story's author actually made use of it in his composition. This new material applies mainly to the late stories, since the sources of the early and middle stories have already been dealt with in the course of this study. When, as occasionally happens, it is impossible to determine a story's particular exemplar among a number of related Classical texts, the information is given in any case, because it is useful to know that the author used *some such work*. A few prologues contain potted accounts of famous stories; since it is impossible to find out whether the author used a text or simply relied upon his memory, I have ignored them. Almost all pre-Sung sources are found in the *T'ai-p'ing kuang-chi* (abbreviation *TPKC*), and, for simplicity's sake, only that reference is given. (The title of the original work can generally be obtained from the *TPKC*.)

The secondary works most commonly cited are abbreviated as follows:

Chao Ching-shen, *Hsiao-shuo hsi-ch'ü hsin-k'ao* (Shanghai, 1939), pp. 1–29, comprising "*Ching-shih t'ung-yen* ti lai-yüan ho ying-hsiang" and "*Hsing-shih heng-yen* ti lai-yüan ho ying-hsiang." Abbr. Chao.

Patrick Hanan, "The Authorship of Some *Ku-chin hsiao-shuo* Stories," *Harvard Journal of Asiatic Studies* 29 (1969), 190–200. Abbr. Hanan.

Karashima Takeshi, *Zenyaku Chūgoku bungaku daikei* (Tokyo, 1958–1959), appendices to vols. VI, X–XIV. Abbr. Karashima.

Sun K'ai-ti, *Chin-ku ch'i-kuan* (Ya-tung, Shanghai, 1933), introduction. Abbr. Sun (1933).

Sun K'ai-ti, "Hsiao-shuo p'ang-cheng," *Kuo-li Pei-p'ing t'u-shu-kuan kuan-k'an* 9.1 (1935), 11–20. Abbr. Sun (1935).

Sun K'ai-ti, a series of five articles, each entitled "Hsiao-shuo p'ang-cheng," which appeared in the *Wen-hsüeh p'ing-lun* in 1961 (nos. 4, 5, and 6) and in 1962 (nos. 1 and 2). Abbr. Sun (1961, no. 4), etc.

T'an Cheng-pi, *Hua-pen yü ku-chü* (Shanghai, 1956), pp. 13–60, comprising "*Tsui-weng t'an-lu* so-lu Sung-jen hua-pen ming-mu k'ao" and "*Pao-wen-t'ang shu-mu* so-lu Sung-Yüan-Ming jen hua-pen k'ao." Abbr. T'an.

Wu Hsiao-ling, review of *Ku-chin hsiao-shuo* edition, *Han-hiue* 2.4 (1949), 443–455. Abbr. Wu.

No attempt is made to provide a bibliography for each story; only such articles at touch on the question of sources are listed. Reference is also made to the reprinting of sources in Feng Meng-lung's anthologies of Classical fiction, especially the *Ch'ing shih*. The occasional mention of a story's stuff-material and analogues relates only to points made in this study; for copious material on these subjects, see the works listed above. Most of the stories in the Hung and Hsiung collections, as well as in the miscellanies, are treated by T'an Cheng-pi; the KC stories are treated by Wu Hsiao-ling; and the TY and HY stories by Chao Ching-shen and Karashima. Sun K'ai-ti's "Hsiao-shuo p'ang-cheng" articles reprint sources and analogues: the 1935 article deals with TY 8 and TY 14; 1961, no. 4, deals with TY 32, KC 7, and KC 40; 1961, no. 5, with KC 24, KC 33, KC 6, and KC 28; 1961, no. 6, with HY 40 and HY 14; 1962, no. 1, with HY 31 and HY 23; and 1962, no. 2, with KC 17, HY 11, and TY 3.

Chien-t'ang meng: early (Group C). 1498 edition, 3n3; other text, 8, 58; incidence of older criteria, 40; virtuoso type, 127, 206; early, 127–128; stuff-material referred to in *yen-fen* class of *Tsui-weng t'an-lu*, 128, 172; Group C, probably early Ming, 165–166; poem-chain prologue, 200–201; theme, 206

    The stuff-material is found in Classical narrative as early as the *Yün-chai kuang-lu* of 1111, but no textual source for the vernacular story has been discovered. The poems interchanged between hero and ghost are found in numerous works; see also T'an, 20

Hung 1: middle period. Other texts, 8, 56; incidence of older criteria, 40; virtuoso type, 127–128; apparently adapted from *tsa-chü*, hence middle period, 138; influenced development of KC 29, 145–147; Hangchow origin, 148

    Similar stories existed as early as the Sung, for example, *Liu Ch'i-ch'ing yin tz'u te chi* 柳耆卿因詞得妓 in *Lü-ch'uang hsin-hua*, 103, which is quoted from a still earlier work; see also T'an, 45

Hung 2: early (Group A). Other text, 8, 56; incidence of older criteria, 40; analogues in *Pai-chia kung-an*, 64n79; prologue and main story classified as early, 117; main story in trial group of earliest stories, 156; in earliest group, 160; prologue probably of similar date, 164; Group A, 166; main story in *kung-an* category of traditional typology, 172n11; manner of composition, 184–185; thematic conventions, 199; nature of prologue, 202; reference to *shu-hui*, 209

    See T'an, 40–41

Hung 3: early (Group C). Incidence of older criteria, 40; main story classified as early, 117; prologue early, 121; Group C, probably early Ming, 165–166; not object of *Hua-ts'ao ts'ui-pien* reference, 168; outside traditional typology, 173; demon type, 191–192, 195; early-Ming play with same stuff-material, 195; relationship to Hung 8, 197–198; poem-chain prologue, 200–201

Hung 4: middle period. Other text, 8, 56, 64; incidence of older criteria, 40; classified as middle period, 116; probably from *tsa-chü*, 135–136; possibly by same author as Hung 12, 139

Hung 5: early (Group B). Other text, 8, 56; incidence of older criteria, 40; virtuoso type, probably early, 127, 206; stuff-material possibly referred to in *ch'uan-ch'i* class of *Tsui-weng t'an-lu*, 128; cannot fairly be judged by criteria of earliest stories, 161; Group B, 166

    See T'an, 41

Hung 6: middle period. Incidence of older criteria, 40; virtuoso type, probably middle period, 127; composition, 148

    Source: *P'ei Hang* 裴航 in *TPKC* 50; see T'an, 42

Hung 7: middle period. Incidence of older criteria, 40; middle period, 128–129; *chantefable* form, 140–141

    Li Ts'ui-lien, in a related legend, is a common figure in Chinese folk literature; see T'an, 45

Hung 8: early (Group A). Other text, 8, 56, 64; incidence of older criteria, 40; main story classified as early, 117; prologue early, 121; main story in trial group of earliest stories, 156; in earliest group, 160; prologue also, 164; Group A, 166; outside traditional typology, 173; demon type, 192–193, 195; relationship to Hung 3, 197–198; poem-chain prologue, 200–201

Hung 9: middle period. Other texts, 8, 56, 129; incidence of older criteria, 40; middle pilot group, 105; incidence of middle criteria, 115; virtuoso type, 126; composition, Hangchow origin, 148

Hung 10: middle period. Incidence of older criteria, 40; virtuoso type, probably Ming, 127; composition, 148

    See T'an, 44

Hung 11: early (Group B). Adapted as prologue to *P'ai-an ching-ch'i* 21, 17; incidence of older criteria, 40; probably early, 128–129; Group B, 160, 166; outside traditional typology, 173; composed from Classical narrative, 180; direct opening, 202; ethical attitude, 205

incidence of older criteria, 41; prologue older, 50; Pao-wen-t'ang reference, 51; main story in middle pilot group, 105; incidence of middle criteria, 115; prologue middle, 120–121; prologue a virtuoso story, 126; composition of prologue, 120n45, 148; main story's possible relation to oral literature, 142; Hangchow origin, 148; item related to prologue is found in *Ch'ing shih*, 87n64

See T'an, 46–47; the prologue's stuff-material may be referred to in *ch'uan-ch'i* class of *Tsui-weng t'an-lu*

Hsiung B: early (Group C) or middle period. Pao-wen-t'ang reference, 52; virtuoso type, not distinctively early or middle, 127–128; question of *Tsui-weng t'an-lu* reference, 128

‡Hsiung C: see under Hung 9. Contains more of original text than Hung 9, 56, 129

Hsiung D: middle period, early sixteenth century. Classified as older, 43, 47; Pao-wen-t'ang reference, 52; middle pilot group, 105; incidence of middle criteria, 115; composed between 1505 and 1550, 132; stuff-material current in sixteenth-century Hangchow oral literature, 140; Hangchow origin, 148; merchant's son, 149; demon type, 194

Hsiao-shuo ch'uan-ch'i 1: inaccessible. Stories 1 and 2 are described by Lu Kung as "Sung or Yüan hua-pen," 4n12, 54

Hsiao-shuo ch'uan-ch'i 2: inaccessible. Stories 1 and 2 are described by Lu Kung as "Sung or Yüan hua-pen," 4n12, 54; possible Pao-wen-t'ang reference, 54

‡*Hsiao-shuo ch'uan-ch'i* 3: inaccessible. See under TY 1

‡*Hsiao-shuo ch'uan-ch'i* 4: inaccessible. See under HY 11

Chang Yü-hu su nü chen kuan: early (Group C). Other texts, 10; Lin and Ho *Yen-chü pi-chi* provide better version, 57–58; both versions classified as older, 43; Pao-wen-t'ang reference, 51; Ming placename, 106; virtuoso type, probably early, 127, 206; Group C, probably early Ming, 165–166; fits traditional typology, 173n16

Cheng Yüan-ho p'iao-yü Li Ya-hsien chi: middle period. Other texts, 10; question of Pao-wen-t'ang reference, 54; Lin *Yen-chü pi-chi* the better text, 58; differs from *Hsiao-shuo ch'uan-ch'i* 2, 54n32; virtuoso type, probably middle, 128; composition, 148

The stuff-material is referred to in *Tsui-weng t'an-lu*; see T'an, 26, 52

‡*Ch'ien-t'ang meng*: see under the same title, at the head of this index

‡*Hsiang-ssu chi*: see under Hung 9

‡*Hung-lien nü yin Yü-t'ung Ch'an-shih*: see under KC 29. KC 29 up to page 435 is best text, followed by Ho, 57

‡*Liu Ch'i-ch'ing Wan-chiang Lou chi*: see under Hung 1. Hung 1 is best text, followed by Ho, 56

‡*Lü-chu chui lou chi*: see under KC 36P. Pao-wen-t'ang reference, 51; KC 36P is best text, followed by Ho and Lin, 58

P'ei Hsiu-niang yeh yu Hsi-hu chi: middle period. Other text, 10; Lin is better text, though fragmentary, 58; classified as older, 43, 47; Ming place-name, 106; stuff-material possibly referred to in *Tsui-weng t'an-lu*, 106; classified as middle, 116; virtuoso type, 126; later limit, 132; Hangchow origin, 148; silk-merchant's son, 149; theme of clandestine affair, 150

Tu Li-niang mu se huan hun: middle period. Other text, 10; Ho the better text, the other in the form of a Classical tale, 57; Pao-wen-t'ang reference, 53; Ho version in middle pilot group, 105; incidence of middle criteria, 115; virtuoso type, 126; composition, 148

‡*Tung-p'o Fo-yin erh shih hsiang hui*: see under Hung 13

KC 1: late, probably by Feng Meng-lung. Classified as newer, 44; prologue by Feng, 85; main story probably by Feng, 85; reference in *Ch'ing shih*, 90; attitude toward women, 101; typifies late story, 96n101; grouped thematically with KC 2, 101n115

Source: *Chu shan* 珠衫 in *Chiu-yüeh ch'ien chi*, *chüan* 11, by Sung Mao-ch'eng (fl. 1600); reprinted with alterations in *Ch'ing shih* 16. See Patrick Hanan, "The Making of *The Pearl-sewn Shirt* and *The Courtesan's Jewel Box*," to appear in the *Harvard Journal of Asiatic Studies* 33 (1973)

KC 2: late, by Feng Meng-lung. Main story in pilot group of newer stories, 35; incidence of newer criteria, 42; prologue newer, 50; by Feng Meng-lung, 84; based on a late-Ming courtcase story, 94–95; attitude toward women, 101; statement of derivation untrustworthy, 93n90; grouped thematically with KC 1, 101n115

Source of prologue: *Nieh I-tao* 聶以道 in *Shan-chü hsin-hua* 山居新話 by Yang Yü 楊瑀 (1285–1361); reprinted in *Cho-keng lu* 11 and in Feng's *Ku-chin t'an-kai* 18.758. See Wu, 445. Source of

‡KC 20: see under Hung 12

KC 21: late, by Feng Meng-lung. Classified as newer, 44; by Feng, 84; perhaps patterned on the *fa-chi pien-t'ai* story, 203

    Source: *Hsi-hu yu-lan chih-yü*, 14.265, 1.3–6, 1.8, 1.10, 21.378; see Hanan, 192–193

KC 22: late, by Feng Meng-lung. Main story classified as newer, 44; prologue newer, 50; by Feng, 84

    Source of main story: *Hsi-hu yu-lan chih-yü*, 2.14, 20.364, 5.85–95, 12.219; see Hanan, 193

‡KC 23: see under Hsiung A

    KC 23 is based, not on Hsiung A, but on some common antecedent, a lost vernacular version; see Ma Yau-woon, "Hsiung Lung-feng," 260–263

KC 24: early (Group A). Pilot group of older stories, 35; incidence of older criteria, 41; Pao-wen-t'ang references, 51; early pilot group, 109–110; incidence of early criteria, 115; in trial group of earliest stories, 156; in earliest group, 160; uses post-1229 source, 162; *I-chien chih* source, 162; Group A, 166; poems in *Hua-ts'ao ts'ui-pien* include one not in KC 24, 167–168; stuff-material possibly referred to in *Tsui-weng t'an-lu* in *yen-fen* class, 172–173; opening poem perhaps from the *Ts'ao-t'ang shih-yü*, 167n50; composed from Classical narratives, 175–177; purpose and mode of composition, 181–182; relationship to folktale stereotypes, 196; oblique beginning, 202; plot type, 204; lack of ethical concern, 205; theme, 206

    On sources, see Hanan, "Sung and Yüan Vernacular Fiction," 179–182; Sun (1961, no. 5); Průšek, "Creative Methods"

KC 25: middle period. For *I-chen chi* references, see under Hung 21. Pao-wen-t'ang reference, 52; probably belonged to the *I-chen chi* and by same author who wrote Hung 21–27, 121–123, 134–135; composition, 148

KC 26; middle period, probably by same author as KC 38 and KC 3. Pao-wen-t'ang reference, 52; middle pilot group, 104; incidence of middle criteria, 115; written at close of fifteenth or beginning of sixteenth century, 132; by author of KC 38, who may also have written KC 3, 133–134; relationship to oral fiction, 140; Hangchow origin, 148; silk-weaving, 149; theme of idleness, 150; folly and consequences type, 150

KC 27: late, by Feng Meng-lung. Main story classified as newer, 44; prologue newer, 50; by Feng, 84; typifies the late story, 96n102

    Source of main story: *Hsi-hu yu-lan chih-yü* 23.415–416, reprinted in *Ch'ing shih* 2; see Hanan, 193

KC 28: late. Main story classified as newer, 44; prologue newer, 50; question of authorship, 85n57; mention of *chantefable*, 93

    Precise source not discovered among many textually related Classical versions, including items in Lin *Yen-chü pi-chi* 10, *Shuang-huai sui-ch'ao* 10, *Chiao Shih pi-ch'eng* 3, *Pai-shih hui-pien* 48, and *Chih-nang pu* 26. The last version differs from that in *Ch'ing shih* 2

KC 29: middle period. The ending (from page 11b in the facsimile edition, or from page 435 in the modern edition) has apparently been added by Feng Meng-lung. Other texts, 12; KC 29 the best text if Feng's ending is disregarded, 57; a late criterion in the added ending, 68n2; Pao-wen-t'ang reference, 29n26, 53; classified as older, 43, 47; middle pilot group, 104; incidence of middle criteria, 115; written late in middle period, 132; topic in sixteenth-century Hangchow oral literature, 140; development, probably from oral narrative, 142–147; religious story-type, 151

    Ending based on *Hsi-hu yu-lan chih* 11.177–178; see Hanan, 196

‡KC 30: see Hung 13. Prologue added and ending expanded by Feng Meng-lung. Adaptation, 28

    Feng's prologue based on *Hsi-hu yu-lan chih* 11.141–142; see Hanan, 195

KC 31: late, probably by Feng Meng-lung. Classified as newer, 44; probably by Feng, 85

    See Lévy, "Deux Contes," on analogues

KC 32: late, probably by Feng Meng-lung. Probably newer, 62; probably by Feng, 84

    Source of prologue: *Hsi-hu yu-lan chih-yü* 4.68–73; see Hanan, 194. Precise source of main story not discovered among several closely-related Classical versions, including the *Hsü Tung-ch'uang shih fan chuan* 續東窗事犯傳 in *Hsiao-p'in chi*, and versions apparently derived from it in Ho *Yen-chü pi-chi* 8, *Kuo-se t'ien-hsiang* 10, and *Ta Sung Chung-hsing t'ung-su yen-i* 大宋中興通俗演義 (1552 edition, Naikaku Bunko); see also Hanan, 194; Wu, 453

KC 33: early (Group A). Main story in pilot group of older stories, 35; incidence of older criteria, 41; prologue older, 50; Pao-wen-t'ang reference, 51; stuff-material referred to in *shen-hsien* class of *Tsui-weng t'an-lu*, 109, 171; main story in early pilot group, 109–110; incidence of early criteria, 115; prologue early, 121; main story in trial group of earliest stories, 156; in earliest group, 160; prologue of similar date, 164; Group A, 166; *Hua-ts'ao ts'ui-pien* reference, 167; question of relation-

Ch'ing shih. In identifying hero's father as from Nanking, not Honan, it is closer to TY than they, but it makes an obvious change of locale from Shansi to Chekiang late in story. Clearly, TY 24 is not based directly on any of these three versions. Nor is it based on the play; the play's characters, as mentioned in *Pai-shih hui-pien* and *Ch'ing shih*, have quite different names. Note that *Ch'ing shih* describes its source as the lost Ming work *Ching-lin tsa-chi* 涇林雜記 of Chang Fu-chün 張復俊 (fl. 1550). On the development of the stuff-material, see A Ying, "Yü-t'ang-ch'un ku-shih ti yen-pien" 玉堂春故事的演變, *Hsiao-shuo erh-t'an*, 1–31

TY 25: late. Classified as newer, 45; possibly by Feng Meng-lung, 85; forms cohesive group with four other stories, 85

    Source: *Kuei Ch'ien meng kan lu* 桂遷夢感錄 in *Mi teng yin-hua*, 317–322

TY 26: late. Classified as newer, 45; possibly by Feng Meng-lung, 85

    Source: *T'ang Yin* 唐寅 in *Ch'ing shih* 5 describes its source as the lost work *Ching-lin tsa-chi* (see under TY 24). On development of the stuff-material, see Chao Ching-shen's "San hsiao yin-yüan" 三笑姻緣, in his *T'an-tz'u k'ao-cheng*

TY 27: late. Probably newer, 62; not the work of Feng Meng-lung or X, 75; unfamiliar stuff-material, 97n104

TY 28: early (Group C). Rewritten as *Hsi-hu chia-hua* 15, 17, 55n34; classified as older, 43; Ming place-name, 106; early, but adapted by a late editor, 126; topic current in sixteenth-century Hangchow oral literature, 140; in trial group of earliest stories, 156; excluded from earliest group, 160–161; Yüan or early Ming date, probably the latter, Group C, 165–166; outside traditional typology, 173; demon type, 193, 195; parallels in Classical narrative, 194; circumstantial detail, 202; refers to its manner of composition, 207–208; relation to Buddhism, Taoism, 193, 206n104

    On development of the stuff-material, see, for example, Chao Ching-shen's "Pai-she chuan" 白蛇傳, in his *T'an-tz'u k'ao-cheng*

TY 29: early (Group B). In pilot group of older stories, 35; incidence of older criteria, 41; Pao-wen-t'ang reference, 51; virtuoso type, probably early, 127; stuff-material apparently referred to in *ch'uan-ch'i* class of *Tsui-weng t'an-lu*, 128, 181; cannot be judged by the earliest criteria, 161; Group B, 166; composed from Classical narrative, 177–178; verbal formulae, 198; direct opening, 202; ethical attitude, 205n103; virtuoso type, 206

TY 30: early (Group B). Main story older, ending perhaps rewritten, 62; main story classified as early, 117; prologue early, 121; in Group B, 160, 165–166; main story outside traditional typology, 173; prologue composed from Classical narrative, 178–179; main story composed from Classical narrative, 179–180; stuff-material of prologue referred to in *ch'uan-ch'i* class of *Tsui-weng t'an-lu*, 181; main story deviates from demon type, 189, 195, 210; direct opening, nature of prologue, 202

    The *I-chien chih* source of TY 30M is reprinted in *Ch'ing shih* 10

TY 31: late. Pilot group of newer stories, 35; incidence of newer criteria, 42; possibly by Feng Meng-lung, 85; forms cohesive group with four other stories, 85; *Chih-nang pu* 25 version appears in *Ch'ing shih* 4, but not found elsewhere, 91

TY 32: late. Trial group of newer stories, 23; incidence of newer criteria, 42; possibly by Feng Meng-lung, 85; composition, 93n89; attitude toward women, 101; typifies the late story, 96n102; thematic grouping with TY 33, 34, and 35, 101n115

    Source: *Fu-ch'ing-nung chuan* 負情儂傳 in *Chiu-yüeh wen-chi* 5 by Sung Mao-ch'eng; see Patrick Hanan, "The Making of *The Pearl-sewn Shirt* and *The Courtesan's Jewel Box*," to appear in the *Harvard Journal of Asiatic Studies* 33 (1973). Source reprinted in *Ch'ing shih* 14

‡TY 33: see under Hung 18. Adaptation, 28, 38n9, 98n105; relationship to TY 35, 94n92; thematic grouping with TY 32, TY 34, and 35, 101n115

TY 34: late. Main story classified as newer, 45; prologue newer, 50; question of authorship, 85n57; attitude toward women, 101; source and composition, 91; relationship to *Ch'ing shih*, 91; thematic grouping with TY 32, TY 33, and TY 35, 101n115

    Source of prologue: *Chang k'e ch'i yü* 張客奇遇 in *I-chien chih*, *Ting* 丁 15, reprinted in *Ch'ing shih* 16. Source of main story: The heroine's long poetic plaint is found in Chung Hsing's *Ku-chin ming-yüan shih-kuei*, *chüan* 27, 13a–17b, in even greater length than in TY 34. It is preceded by a summary of the story which is identical with the plot of TY 34M. It is likely that TY 34M was based on a Ming Classical tale which is now lost except for the poem in the *Ku-chin ming-yüan shih-kuei* and an abridged version in *Ch'ing shih* 16. (It contains even less of the poem than TY 34M.) The stuff-material is loosely related to a totally different kind of Ming Classical tale, the *Huai-ch'un ya-chi* 懷春雅集, which is found in the miscellanies; see Liu Wen-ying, "Ming-tai ti ch'uan-ch'i hsiao-shuo"

ying chi version is reprinted in Lin *Yen-chü pi-chi* 9. *Ch'ing shih* 2 has a related version. HY 10 is closer to Lin at the beginning, to the *Ch'ing shih* at the end, so neither appears to be its immediate source. There is a textually distinct version in *Erh-t'an lei-tseng* 8. The inaccessible *Ming shih cheng sheng* 明詩正聲 (preface d. 1606) also contains a version; see Karashima, 10:35-37

HY 11: late. Adapted version of *Hsiao-shuo ch'uan-ch'i* 4. Text, 15; main story in pilot group of newer stories, 35; incidence of newer criteria, 42; prologue newer, 50; severe adaptation, 75; classifiable as a virtuoso story, 98

> Source of main story: *Tung-p'o wen-ta lu* 東坡問答錄; see Sun (1933), 29-30; Sun (1962, no. 2)

HY 12: early (Group C). The introduction (up to page 4b in the facsimile edition, or page 234 in the modern edition) has been added by a late editor. Story older, introduction newer, 59; review of adaptation, 124-125; Ming place-name in introduction, 106; rest of story classified as early, 117; influenced development of KC 29, 145-147; rest of story of religious type, 151; probably early Ming, Group C, 165-166; outside traditional typology, 173; shares some features of virtuoso type, 151n47, 206

> Similar stories abound; cf. *Lü-ch'uang hsin-hua*, 157, 226

HY 13: early (Group C). Question of Pao-wen-t'ang reference, 52; older, but probably adapted by a late editor, 60-61; early, review of adaptation, 124-125; contains poem from 1318 tale, probably of early Ming composition, Group C, 165-166; stuff-material apparently referred to in *kung-an* class of *Tsui-weng t'an-lu*, 172n11; thematic conventions, 199; circumstantial detail, 202; lack of ethical concern, 205; refers to manner of own composition, 207-208

HY 14: early (Group A). Classified as older, 43; probably adapted by a late editor, 60; classified as early, 117; adaptation reviewed, 124-125 (see also "Note on the *San yen* Texts" above); in earliest group, 160-161; reference to Sung, 162; Group A, 166; outside traditional typology, 173; manner of composition, 184-185; lack of ethical concern, 205; theme, 206

> On the Sung parallels, see Sun (1961, no. 6)

HY 15: late, by X. Main story in pilot group of newer stories, 35; incidence of newer criteria, 42; prologue newer, 50; by X, 69; relationship to *Ch'ing shih* 18 version, 91

> Source of main story: Item in *Ch'ing shih* 18, quoted from the lost *Ching-lin tsa-chi* (see under TY 24)

HY 16: late, by X. Not accepted into pilot group of newer stories, 33n3; main story classified as newer, 45; prologue newer, 50; Pao-wen-t'ang reference refuted, 53-54; by X, 69; relationship to *Chih-nang pu* version, 92; example of naturalism, 101

> The main story appears to combine two sources, *Chang Chin* 張藎 from *Ch'ing shih* 18, where it is ascribed to the *Ching-lin hsü-chi*, and *Lin-hai nü-tzu* 臨海女子 from *Erh-t'an* 8, reprinted in *Erh-t'an lei-tseng* 6 and *Chih-nang pu* 10. See also Chao, 19-20; Karashima, 11:11-13. Source not found in the *Ching-lin hsü-chi*

HY 17: late, by X. In pilot group of newer stories, 35; incidence of newer criteria, 42; by X, 69

> Source: Item in *Hou te lu* 1; see Chao, 20-21; Karashima, 11:18-19

HY 18: late, by X. Main story in trial group of newer stories, 24; incidence of newer criteria, 42; prologue newer, 50; by X, 69; unfamiliar material, 97n104

> Source of prologue: Item under the category of *Chieh-ts'ao* 節操 in *T'ang che yen* 唐摭言 by Wang Ting-pao; see Chao, 21; Karashima, 11:19-20

HY 19: late. Pilot group of newer stories, 35; incidence of newer criteria, 42; question of authorship, 86; not dependent on plays, 95n94

> Precise source uncertain. *Ch'ü-hai tsung-mu t'i-yao* 7 quotes an item from the *Sung-pai lei-ch'ao* which is not to be found in that work. The item is very close to the version in *Ch'ing shih* 2, much closer than to the related account in the *Cho-keng lu*, and probably represents the immediate source of HY 19; see also Chao, 21

HY 20: late, by X. In trial group of newer stories, 24; incidence of newer criteria, 42; by X, 69

> The play *Shuang-pei chi* 雙盃記, surviving in a Wan-li edition, is earlier than HY 20, with which it has a close textual relationship

HY 21: early (Group C). Pilot group of older stories, 35; incidence of older criteria, 41; Ming place-name, 106; classified as early, 117; probably early Ming, 165; Group C, 166; fits traditional typology, 173n16; theme, 206; only early story in HY not adapted, 74n22; relation to Buddhism, Taoism, 206n104

HY 22: late, by X. Classified as newer, 45; by X, 69; unfamiliar stuff-material, 97n104

DATE DUE